Marilyn Solis

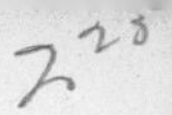

VICTORIANS ON *Literature* & *Art*

GOLDENTREE BOOKS

R. C. BALD, SAMUEL H. BEER & WILLIAM C. DEVANE
Series Editors

C. DAY LEWIS, Editor
English Lyric Poems, 1500–1900

DANIEL G. HOFFMAN and SAMUEL HYNES, Editors
English Literary Criticism (3 vols.): *The Renaissance; Restoration and 18th Century; Romantic and Victorian*

KATHERINE LEVER
The Novel and the Reader

MILTON MARX
The Enjoyment of Drama, 2nd Edition

HAROLD OREL, Editor
The World of Victorian Humor

ROBERT L. PETERS, Editor
Victorians on Literature & Art

EDWARD STONE, Editor
Henry James: Seven Stories and Studies

ROBERT L. PETERS
Wayne State University
EDITOR

VICTORIANS

ON

Literature

&

Art

New York
APPLETON-CENTURY-CROFTS, Inc.

671–2

LIBRARY OF CONGRESS CARD NUMBER: 61–7259

PRINTED IN THE UNITED STATES OF AMERICA

PREFACE

The Victorian Era was marked by a number of vivid contests, engaged in by highly energetic and articulate men; and most of these conflicts—the debates between churchmen and scientists, dissenters and traditionalists, social reformers and reactionaries—have received the attention which was their due: their histories have been well told, and their merits are still being analyzed and judged. The problem of the artist, his struggle to evolve a satisfying system of aesthetics and to define his role in society, has received less attention; yet it too, as any student of the age well knows, was one of the concerns of gifted men—of poets and painters, of aestheticians and social theorists; and the influence of their work pervades our culture today. Poets and painters shared this interest with essayists and social theorists; it was an effort which would have seemed almost concerted had it not taken place in an age of individualists.

Victorians on Literature & Art presents a series of prose documents helpful to our understanding of this dual effort. The first section reveals the artist working out a theory of art; the second, the artist working out his relationship to society. The selections included are all of the period, and though many of them are nearly forgotten, each in its time represented a significant voice. The list of writers represented is not meant to be exhaustive: some critics like John Morley, Frederic Harrison, and W. E. Henley, for example, are omitted in favor of their better-known contemporaries. An Appendix lists selected collateral items which the reader may wish to pursue. In the interests of space and readability, I have made free to excise passages which have no bearing upon the points at issue. Swinburne's "Under the Microscope," for example, is represented by its long final section, the only part to deal directly with Buchanan's "The Fleshly School" essay, while Whistler's "Ten O'Clock" lecture and his account of the Ruskin altercation, lively as they are, are redundant and scarcely harmed by cutting.

A note should be added on the William Morris tapestry, "The Passing of Venus," on the last page of the second group of illustrations. This tapestry, woven from the last cartoon Burne-Jones created for William Morris, was the largest and most important of all the tapestries undertaken by the Merton Abbey looms. It was seven years in the weaving (1901–1907), and was destroyed by fire in 1910 at an exposition in Brussels. In 1923 the work was recommissioned by George Booth for the Detroit Museum of Fine Arts. It was rewoven from the original Burne-Jones cartoon, and was completed in 1926.

ROBERT L. PETERS

Wayne State University

CONTENTS

Introductory Notes

IN THEIR ATTEMPTS to work out a theory of art, Victorian aestheticians, artists, and critics were of separate minds, and their approaches were mainly three. One group maintained that a "science" of criticism and art could be based on the methods of mathematics and literal observation. In this group were aestheticians like David Ramsay Hay, who wrote "geometries" of taste, and the Pre-Raphaelite painters and writers, Ford Madox Brown, William Holman Hunt, John Everett Millais, John Orchard, and William Sharp. The poets' vivid, often exaggerated word painting, and the artists' finicky accounting in brush, pen and language for the infinite hues and shapes of grass blades, flower structures, cloud formations, mottlings of insects, and fabrics of clothing, reflected an enthusiasm which they shared with geologists and evolutionists and which they attempted to make spiritually significant. For such literalists, the immense plethora of life bespoke the wondrous fertility of God. The aesthetic tone was apt therefore to become didactic: Brown and Hunt painted lavish sermons in oil even as Ruskin, who shared their literalist impulse and who lent his prestige to the Pre-Raphaelite Brotherhood, penned baroque verbal descriptions of heroic human beings, noble pictures, and prophetic natural forms.[1]

[1] It is interesting that Carlyle, although concerned with art only as one manifestation of a broad human experience, exerted a considerable influence upon this vogue for "natural supernaturalism." The phrase was his, and to explain it he declared that it was man's business to venerate the details of nature, to paint them or to capture their symbolic force in words, and eventually, with the aid of intuition, to find an ecstatic rapport with the transcendental unity behind all disparateness. It should also be observed that both Tennyson and Browning often shared the literalist impulse, though they were less doctrinaire than the majority of Pre-Raphaelites and seldom made literalism an end in itself. Tennyson seems to have been little interested in the visual arts and he kept aloof from controversy. Much of his early word painting was stimulated by his passion for Keats, although it is probable that his keen

Another segment of writers and painters attempted to counter this observant literalism by adopting a more intuitive and emotional approach. Pater, Whistler, Wilde, and Symons extolled the evanescent mood; the *virtue*—Pater's emphasized word—of personality; the subtle blurring of images and sounds; the vague, suggestive, partially articulated idea or form; the shimmery sensuous atmosphere. The artist, declared the voluble Whistler "is born to pick, and choose, and group" the elements of nature. "To say to the painter, that Nature is to be taken as she is, is to say to the player, that he may sit on the Piano." Private feeling and the unique worth of an individualistic, even eccentric experience give art its true character. *Intimité* was the name given by Pater to that "inward and peculiar" spirit of the creator's moods, and manner of apprehension." From such a point of view, a circumscribing literalism was sterile. What painter worthy of the name would employ his days recording wheat stalks, or would go on a pilgrimage to the Dead Sea, as Holman Hunt did, to pose a goat in the midst of an untracked margin of the shore—all for the sake of increased veracity? Better to cultivate a private aesthetics free of such distorted preconceptions.[2]

Finally, and these constituted a more considerable group, there were those men who fused elements from both points of view, sometimes in the same work of art or in the same piece of criticism. Ruskin, Rossetti, and Swinburne, among others, incorporated elements of both the literalists and the impressionists. Ruskin's "Pre-Raphaelitism" praises the virtues and warns against the excesses of an exaggerated fidelity to detail; and the early volumes of *Modern Painters* are filled with elaborate word pictures charged

assimilative mind caught too some of the Pre-Raphaelite enthusiasm. Browning was an inveterate gallery-goer, and knew painting and sculpture better than Tennyson did. Despite this knowledge, however, he was less concerned with theories of art as such than with the characters of the artists and the quality of their aspirations and achievements.

[2] There is in Hunt's "The Scapegoat" (See first group of illustrations) a force, in part symbolic, in part brooding, which transcends the literal effort of the artist—but Hunt was talented. For the immature artist there were dangers in the somewhat romanticized rejection of an art solidly based on nature: much of Victorian aestheticism with its several gossamer overtones was a retreat from the severe challenge of craft. The exquisite mood, a nervous, aberrant sensibility, the startling jewelled phrase—these came to excuse the absence of a traditional creative discipline. The best Pre-Raphaelites, in spite of their many shortcomings, were masters of technique.

with emotion. Rossetti loved finely-wrought detail: in poetry, seven stars adorn the damozel's hair, the woodspurge has "a cup of three," and "bashful-eyed" woodflowers shine through golden hair spread out along the grass; in painting, too, the jeweled accoutrements of costume and background absorbed his attention. At the same time, much of his art is personal and mystical; even his decorative impulse more often than not reflects a nervous, complex sensibility. Similar qualities are discernible everywhere in Swinburne's poetry, where esoteric fatigue and a personal lyric force exist side by side with elaborate, delicately wrought detail.

I

Swinburne, besides incorporating in his own work some of the main modes of Victorian art, was as conscious as any writer of the need for an individual aesthetic theory, and he sought to resolve the problem of the relation of the artist to his time. He is, therefore, a particularly useful figure to introduce our second theme: the proper relationship of the artist to society. Through an inverse didacticism—Swinburne liked to upset his public by "teaching" moral and religious values quite contrary to established ones, using on pagan subject matter a terminology borrowed from conventional religion and morality—he vigorously protested the hold over art exercised by a smug and narrow middle class. He assumed that the poet should not withdraw from the public arena; but he understood well the gigantic difficulties faced by the dedicated artists of his day.

The problem was entirely new to British artists; never before had they been challenged to provide aesthetic meaning for so broadly based a society. Earlier writers and painters (for example, Shakespeare, Milton, Hogarth, Swift, and Pope) had traditionally exposed human folly and excess, some of them braving royal and ecclesiastical wrath to do so; but they hardly felt compelled to improve public taste; art was the privilege of the wealthy, and the boundaries were clear. By the nineteenth century the noble patron who had encouraged the artist in return for a share of his fame was nearly extinct. Merchants, millowners, and other men of a hard-headed persuasion were in the ascendancy, impelled by the titanic forces of the Industrial Revolution, the great rationalist philosophies of the preceding century, and the French Revolutionary and

Napoleonic conflicts. The series of Reform victories also contributed to the dominance of the middle-class leaders who had worked hard to make them possible. These new men set not only the political and social tones, but the cultural as well, and their leadership was followed more often than not by remnants of the old aristocracy. In their fresh power and prosperity, they were voluble, smug, tenacious, narrow-minded, and suspicious of the arts which symbolized the privilege of the deposed class, and which could reflect no tangible utility.[3]

In such a climate, artists and philosophers found themselves more and more relegated to minor roles; that harmonic enjoining of poet and moment which was essential to Arnold's scheme of things could hardly transpire in a world so rigid and assertive.

Unfortunately, the cultural level of the royal family seemed but slightly above that of its subjects. One of Victoria's favorite poets was the banal but dedicated Martin Tupper, whose *Proverbial Philosophy*, partly as a result of her Majesty's approval, saw fifty editions and sold a million and a half copies in Britain and America. Victoria aroused the ire of native artists by requesting mediocre painters and sculptors from Germany and Italy to instruct herself and her family and to record their likenesses for posterity.

Prince Albert early displayed his eclectic fancy in a pavilion whose three rooms were each in a different style: the Pompeian, the Romantic, and the Raphaelesque. His skill as a deer stalker, his love for greyhounds,[4] and his general enthusiasm for an art derived from the animal world led to a rage for cast-iron stags and dogs, and for saccharine renditions in oil and stone of canines grieving by fresh graves or salivating in anticipation of the hunt. Albert's notorious centerpiece, designed for the Queen in 1849, further reveals his unusual aesthetic notions. At the base of this electroplated creation, likenesses of two of Victoria's favorite dogs gaze upon the body of a hare, while two others confront a live rat imprisoned in a trap. As a final irresistible bit of *nature*

[3] In Matthew Arnold's final lecture as Professor of Poetry at Oxford, significantly entitled "Culture and Its Enemies" (later published as "Sweetness and Light"), he voiced an eloquent complaint of bourgeois England's indifference to a humanized culture. He regretted that Newman's attempt to infuse British Hebraism with a cultural health based on the best that had been thought, said, and created in the world had proved unequal to the Philistine-Jacobin strength.

[4] See "A Greyhound, Eos," in second group of illustrations.

morte, another dead rodent lies beside a small sculptured footstool. Albert thoroughly enjoyed his position as President of Her Majesty's Fine Arts Commission, and his public pronouncements on art were well-meaning, flatulent efforts to reconcile the differences between the nation's scientific bias and its cultural pretensions. Through the royal patronage of the Academy painters, particularly of Landseer and Maclise, Albert was able to set a national standard of subject matter and execution. (Needless to say, the nonconformist painter was in for a bad time from the academicians.) He also lent his prestige to improving the artistic level of manufactured products and to stimulating the crafts movement which became so popular during the second half of the century. The Great Exhibition of 1851, his dearest project, was perhaps the greatest single conditioner of public taste.[5]

A number of Victorian artists, especially the early men, were able to adapt and compromise—but not before they had undergone some uncertain moments as they gazed out at their awesome, uncouth, vociferous public. Tennyson, for example, was lured by a Keatsian verse decoration and subject matter. "The Palace of Art" and "Maud" reflect his uneasiness; and "The Lotos-Eaters," whatever the possible symbolic interpretations, remains one of the finest poems of retreat in the language. Although the laureate did somewhat curtly evict his muse from her palace and send her to earth among the cottagers, we still carefully distinguish between Tennyson's public and private poetic utterances.

Carlyle also had his moments of quest. The frustrations of getting *Sartor Resartus* written and then published (nearly eight years elapsed before it appeared as a book in England) gave plenty of time for the young writer to think through the purposes of his art. On February 7, 1831, he observed in his *Journal* that his "Teufelsdröckh" was "not right—not *art;* yet perhaps a nearer approach to art than I have yet made. We ought to try," he said to himself; "I want to get it done. . . ." The year before he had asked his

[5] French artists were even less fortunate in their royalty. Louis-Philippe, the Citizen King, was said to be more bourgeois than the bourgeoisie and was caricatured in the radical journals, strolling past shops with his wife and children in the best middle-class fashion, his umbrella under his arm. Gauthier, Delacroix, Balzac, Courbet, Flaubert, Stendhal, and Baudelaire had all been repelled by popular and royal attitudes, and each in his separate way had decried bourgeois values and gloried in the contempt of the Philistines.

Journal whether aesthetics is really superior to religion, the beautiful to the good. Steeped as he was in German literature, he turned to Goethe and Schiller, who had set him to reflecting in the first place, and the answer, which in a less tentative form became one of the most stimulating ideas in *Sartor*, implied a view similar to that later proposed by Newman and Arnold: that although art contrasts good and evil, as Goethe also believed, it does so "*without* hostility," and "with peacefulness, like the difference of two poles which *cannot* coalesce yet do not quarrel—nay, should not quarrel, for both are essential to the whole." Then Carlyle permitted himself another question, also answered in *Sartor:* is Goethe's morality, with its aesthetic overtones, "*higher*" than any man has known before? Yes, he concluded. The poet-artist is the superior "priest," whose works of Beauty both include and transcend Truth. Rarely after *Sartor* was Carlyle again so devoted to aesthetics; once he had assumed a prophet's stance, his official robes grew increasingly leaden, scarcely allowing the speculative freedom of his apprentice years.

Browning also endured an early public indifference, followed by a discouraging reputation as a writer of esoterica; but once he had allayed public suspicion, he balanced his artistic role by writing two broad kinds of verse throughout a long career: one fulfilled his responsibilities to the public conscience; the other expressed more personal interests. With apparently equal facility he expressed bland religious affirmations, produced superb monologues inspired by an opulent Renaissance world, and wrote private lyrics of love, marriage, fate, and art. His resolution, on the whole, seemed less painfully arrived at than that of almost any other leading Victorian poet.[6] Even so, his Fra Lippi, struggling between artistic literalness and ideality, pleaded to have the question "settled forever one way."

Many later artists facing the Jacobin-Philistine, royal-public mountain of artistic authority were often severely repelled, and some of those who were unable to compromise dissipated much of their talent in assaults upon the mountain. Arthur Symons, for example, might possibly have become a more substantial poet had he spent more time at his craft and less in embellishing his anti-

[6] Arnold's abandonment of poetry for criticism is a special problem which scholars have not wholly resolved.

bourgeois attitudes. George Moore, whose uneven *Confessions of A Young Man* scathingly attacked public "Respectability," also expended valuable energy in this way.

Others sought their own themes and techniques in an attempt to carry art past the achievement of their elders. A number of them flaunted dandified and splenetic poses,[7] found highly rarefied exotic subject matters, spoke of art in religious terms, and experimented to see if they could merge the various genres into new hybrid forms. Their programs were ambitious, but beneath the surface lay considerable tentativeness and confusion. It is well known that Wilde, aestheticism's most advertised adherent, had his paradoxical side. For example, he rarely abandoned his peculiar but tenacious brand of socialism; and his most "aesthetic" works seem to have been written with one eye on the great beast. Even the exaggerated sense of sin he displayed after his debacle carried more than a little bourgeois tinge. Furthermore, when we recall the ease with which George Moore and Arthur Symons shifted their allegiance from aestheticism, and the anxiety which led Dowson, Thompson, and Beardsley to seek absolution through an orthodox religion, we can better appreciate the imprecise, immaturely formulated nature of a good part of the Victorian protest. By the mid-nineties, Victorian aesthetics would seem to have enmeshed itself in a hopeless tangle.

Yeats alone, of the important aesthetes, survived the muddle and moved with triumph into the twentieth century. As is well known, he purified his diction around 1895 (he published four volumes of poetry in the 1890's) and substituted an austere, denotative, lean idiom for a dreamy, vague, decorative one. His obsession with the image, an esoteric, almost physical manipulation of the traditional metaphor after the manner of the French Symbolist writers, began also about this time; and in a few years he was to abandon his efforts to mold an Irish culture, an effort which had never been wholly free from aesthetic inclinations. The significant fact in his resolution is that he preserves his sanity, increases his reputation as an artist, develops his own mythology, and becomes

[7] They found support for their attitudes in the work of the French writers, who had preceded them. By 1830 *l'art pour l'art* had been one of the main artistic trends in Paris. G. M. Young dates the influence of the French in England from the early fifties; by the eighties, Britain in art was "becoming a suburb of Paris."

more and more content to do without the inclusive public his predecessors had felt necessary. While his resolution is obviously neither the only possible one nor the final one, it developed inevitably from Victorian Pre-Raphaelitism and aestheticism. Few artists, indeed, have travelled so far to maturity.

Part 1

THE SHAPING OF ART

And I want you to think a little of the deep significance of this word "taste," for no statement of mine has been more earnestly or oftener controverted than that good taste is essentially a moral quality.

JOHN RUSKIN, "Traffic"

Art is an old language with a great many artificial affected styles, and sometimes the chief pleasure one gets out of knowing them is the mere sense of knowing.

GEORGE ELIOT, *Middlemarch*

Bad morality is not a necessary condition of good art; on the contrary, bad morality is necessarily bad art, for art is human, but immorality inhuman. The "art" of the present generation is in great part more immoral than any that has preceded it in England.

COVENTRY PATMORE, *Principle in Art, Etc.*

Thomas Carlyle

"THE AESTHETICS OF THE SYMBOL"

A NUMBER OF CRITICS, among them Arthur Symons, Northrup Frye, Harry Levin, and Frank Kermode, have acknowledged Carlyle's significance to modern literature, and to the development of modern symbolism in particular. There is a latent prophetism in "Symbols," but little of the hortatory which mars Carlyle's writing after the time of *Sartor* and *The French Revolution.* These he wrote before he was widely known and to please himself. As Emerson said approvingly in his first letter to the then struggling writer, *Sartor* was self-subsistent and bravely independent; readers should find no offense with an author "so catholic and jocund." Carlyle's "Symbol" conveys the greater of two meanings: the Intrinsic over the Extrinsic, the purely aesthetic-mystical over the pragmatic-didactic.

PROBABLY IT WILL elucidate the draft of these foregoing obscure utterances, if we here insert somewhat of our Professor's speculations on *Symbols.* To state his whole doctrine, indeed, were beyond our compass: nowhere is he more mysterious, impalpable, than in this of "Fantasy being the organ of the Godlike;" and how "Man thereby, though based, to all seeming, on the small Visible, does nevertheless extend down into the infinite deeps of the Invisible, of which Invisible, indeed, his Life is properly the bodying forth." Let us, omitting these high transcendental aspects of the matter, studying to glean (whether from the Paper-bags or the Printed Volume) what little seems logical and practical, and cunningly arrange it into such degree of coherence as it will assume. By way of proem, take the following not injudicious remarks:

"The benignant efficacies of Concealment," cries our Professor, "who shall speak or sing? SILENCE and SECRECY! Altars might still be raised to them (were this an altar-building time) for universal worship. Silence is the element in which great things fashion themselves together; that at length they may emerge, full-formed and

FROM *Sartor Resartus* (completed in 1831, but not published as a book until 1836 in Boston, the first British edition not appearing before 1838).

majestic, into the daylight of Life, which they are thenceforth to rule. Not William the Silent only, but all the considerable men I have known, and the most undiplomatic and unstrategic of these, forbore to babble of what they were creating and projecting. Nay, in thy own mean perplexities, do thou thyself but *hold thy tongue for one day:* on the morrow, how much clearer are thy purposes and duties; what wreck and rubbish have those mute workmen within thee swept away, when intrusive noises were shut out! Speech is too often not, as the Frenchmen defined it, the art of concealing Thought; but of quite stifling and suspending Thought, so that there is none to conceal. Speech too is great, but not the greatest. As the Swiss Inscription says: *Sprechen ist silbern, Schweigen ist golden* (Speech is silvern, Silence is golden); or as I might rather express it: Speech is of Time, Silence is of Eternity.

"Bees will not work except in darkness; Thought will not work except in Silence: neither will Virtue work except in Secrecy. Let not thy left hand know what thy right hand doeth! Neither shalt thou prate even to thy own heart of 'those secrets known to all.' Is not Shame (*Scham*) the soil of all Virtue, of all good manners and good morals? Like other plants, Virtue will not grow unless its root be hidden, buried from the eye of the sun. Let the sun shine on it, nay do but look at it privily thyself, the root withers, and no flowers will glad thee. O my Friends, when we view the fair clustering flowers that overwreathe, for example, the Marriage-bower, and encircle man's life with the fragrance and hues of heaven, what hand will not smite the foul plunderer that grubs up by the roots, and with grinning, grunting satisfaction, shows us the dung they flourish in! Men speak much of the Printing-Press with its Newspapers: *du Himmel!* what are these to Clothes and the Tailor's Goose?"

"Of kin to the so incalculable influences of Concealment, and connected with still greater things, is the wondrous agency of *Symbols.* In a Symbol there is concealment and yet revelation: here therefore, by Silence and by Speech acting together, comes a double significance. And if both the Speech be itself high, and the Silence fit and noble, how expressive will their union be! Thus in many a painted Device, or simple Seal-emblem, the commonest Truth stands out to us proclaimed with quite new emphasis.

"For it is here that Fantasy with her mystic wonderland plays into the small prose domain of Sense, and becomes incorporated therewith. In the Symbol proper, what we can call a Symbol, there is ever, more or less distinctly and directly, some embodiment and revelation of the Infinite; the Infinite is made to blend itself with the Finite, to stand visible, and as it were, attainable there. By Symbols, accordingly, is man guided and commanded, made happy, made wretched. He everywhere finds himself encompassed with Symbols, recognized as such or not recognized: the Universe is but one vast Symbol of God; nay if thou wilt have it, what is man himself but a Symbol of God; is not all that he does symbolical; a revelation to Sense of the mystic god-given force that is in him; a 'Gospel of Freedom,' which he, the 'Messias of Nature,' preaches, as he can, by act and word? Not a Hut he builds but is the visible embodiment of a Thought; but bears visible record of invisible things; but is, in the transcendental sense, symbolical as well as real."

"Man," says the Professor elsewhere, in quite antipodal contrast with these high-soaring delineations, which we have here cut-short on the verge of the inane, "Man is by birth somewhat of an owl. Perhaps, too, of all the owleries that ever possessed him, the most owlish, if we consider it, is that of your actually existing Motive-Millwrights.[1] Fantastic tricks enough man has played, in his time; has fancied himself to be most things, down even to an animated heap of Glass: but to fancy himself a dead iron-Balance for weighing Pains and Pleasures on, was reserved for this his latter era. There stands he, his Universe one huge Manger, filled with hay and thistles to be weighed against each other; and looks long-eared enough. Alas, poor devil! spectres are appointed to haunt him: one age he is hagridden, bewitched; the next, priestridden, befooled; in all ages, bedevilled. And now the Genius of Mechanism smothers him worse than any Nightmare did; till the Soul is nigh choked out of him, and only a kind of Digestive, Mechanic life remains. In Earth and in Heaven he can see nothing but Mechanism; has fear for nothing else, hope in nothing else: the world would indeed grind him to pieces; but cannot he fathom the Doctrine of Motives, and cunningly compute these, and mechanize them to grind the other way?

[1] Carlyle, by means of a characteristically satiric pun, attacks the Utilitarianism of James Mill and Jeremy Bentham.

"Were he not, as has been said, purblinded by enchantment, you had but to bid him open his eyes and look. In which country, in which time, was it hitherto that man's history, or the history of any man, went-on by calculated or calculable 'Motives'? What make ye of your Christianities and Chivalries, and Reformations, and Marseilles Hymns, and Reigns of Terror? Nay, has not perhaps the Motive-grinder himself been *in Love?* Did he never stand so much as a contested Election? Leave him to Time, and the medicating virtue of Nature."

"Yes, Friends," elsewhere observes the Profesor, "not our Logical, Mensurative faculty, but our Imaginative one is King over us; I might say, Priest and Prophet to lead us heavenward; or Magician and Wizard to lead us hellward. Nay, even for the basest Sensualist, what is Sense but the implement of Fantasy; the vessel it drinks out of? Even in the dullest existence there is a sheen either of Inspiration or of Madness (thou partly hast it in thy choice, which of the two), that gleams-in from the circumambient Eternity, and colors with its own hues our little islet of Time. The Understanding is indeed thy window, too clear thou canst not make it; but Fantasy is thy eye, with its color-giving retina, healthy or diseased. Have not I myself known five-hundred living soldiers sabred into crow's-meat for a piece of glazed cotton, which they called their Flag; which had you sold it at any market-cross, would not have brought above three groschen? Did not the whole Hungarian Nation rise, like some tumultuous moon-stirred Atlantic, when Kaiser Joseph pocketed their Iron Crown; an implement, as was sagaciously observed, in size and commercial value little differing from a horse-shoe? It is in and through *Symbols* that man, consciously or unconsciously, lives, works, and has his being: those ages, moreover, are accounted the noblest which can the best recognize symbolical worth, and prize it the highest. For is not a Symbol ever, to him who has eyes for it, some dimmer or clearer revelation of the Godlike?

"Of Symbols, however, I remark farther, that they have both an extrinsic and intrinsic value; oftenest the former only. What, for instance, was in that clouted Shoe, which the Peasants bore aloft with them as ensign in their *Bauernkrieg* (Peasants' War)? Or in the Wallet-and-staff round which the Netherland *Gueux*, glorying in that nickname of Beggars, heroically rallied and prevailed, though against King Philip himself? Intrinsic significance these had none: only extrinsic; as the accidental Standards of multitudes more or less sacredly uniting together; in which union itself, as above noted, there is ever something mystical and borrowing of the Godlike. Under a like category, too, stand, or stood, the stupidest heraldic Coats-of-arms; military Banners everywhere; and generally all national or other sectarian Costumes and Customs: they have no intrinsic, necessary divineness, or even worth; but have acquired an extrinsic one. Nevertheless through all these there glimmers something of a Divine Idea; as through military Banners themselves, the Divine Idea of Duty, of heroic Daring; in some instances of Freedom, of Right. Nay the Highest ensign that men ever met and embraced under, the Cross itself, had no meaning save an accidental extrinsic one.

"Another matter it is, however, when your Symbol has intrinsic meaning, and is of itself *fit* that men should unite round it. Let but the Godlike manifest itself to Sense; let but Eternity look, more or less visibly, through the Time-Figure (*Zeitbild*)! Then is it fit that men unite there; and worship together before such Symbol; and so from day to day, and from age to age, superadd to it new divineness.

"Of this latter sort are all true Works of art: in them (if thou know a Work of Art from a Daub of Artifice) wilt thou discern Eternity looking through Time; the Godlike rendered visible. Here too may an extrinsic value gradually superadd itself: thus certain *Iliads*, and the like, have, in three-thousand years, attained quite new significance. But nobler than all in this kind are the Lives of heroic god-inspired Men; for what other Work of Art is so divine? In Death too, in the Death of the Just, as the last perfection of a Work of Art, may we not discern symbolic meaning? In that divinely transfigured Sleep, as of Victory, resting over the beloved face which now knows thee no more, read (if thou canst for tears) the confluence of Time with Eternity, and some gleam of the latter peering through.

"Highest of all Symbols are those wherein the Artist or Poet has risen into Prophet, and all men can recognize a present God, and worship the same: I mean religious Symbols. Various enough have been such religious Symbols, what we call *Religions;* as men stood in this stage of culture or the other, and could worse or better body-forth the Godlike: some Symbols with a transient intrinsic worth; many with only an extrinsic. If thou ask to what height man has carried it in this manner, look on our divinest Symbol: on Jesus of Nazareth, and his Life, and his Biography, and what followed therefrom. Higher has the human Thought not yet reached: this is Christianity and Christendom; a Symbol of quite perennial, infinite character; whose significance will ever demand to be anew inquired into, and anew made manifest.

"But, on the whole, as Time adds much to the sacredness of Symbols, so likewise in his progress he at length defaces, or even desecrates them; and Symbols, like all terrestrial Garments, wax old. Homer's Epos, has not ceased to be true; yet it is no longer *our* Epos, but shines in the distance, if clearer and clearer, yet also smaller and smaller, like a receding Star. It needs a scientific telescope, it needs to be reinterpreted and artificially brought near us, before we can so much as know that it *was* a Sun. So likewise a day comes when the Runic Thor, with his Eddas, must withdraw into dimness; and many an African Mumbo-Jumbo and Indian Pawaw be utterly abolished. For all things, even Celestial Luminaries, much more atmospheric meteors, have their rise, their culmination, their decline."

"Small is this which thou tellest me, that the Royal Sceptre is but a piece of gilt-wood; that the Pyx has become a most foolish box, and truly, as Ancient Pistol thought, 'of little price.' A right Conjurer might I name thee, couldst thou conjure back into these wooden tools the divine virtue they once held."

"Of this thing, however, be certain: wouldst thou plant for Eternity, then plant into the deep infinite faculties of man, his Fantasy and Heart; wouldst thou plant for Year and Day, then plant into his shallow superficial faculties, his Self-love and Arithmetical Understanding, what will grow there. A Hierarch, therefore, and Pontiff of the World will we call him, the Poet and inspired Maker; who, Prometheus-like, can shape new Symbols, and bring new Fire from Heaven to fix it there. Such too will not always be wanting; neither perhaps now are. Meanwhile, as the average of matters goes we account him Legislator and wise who can so much as tell when a Symbol has grown old, and gently remove it.

"When, as the last English Coronation was preparing," concludes this wonderful Professor, "I read in their Newspapers that the 'Champion of England,' he who has to offer battle to the Universe for his new King, had brought it so far that he could now 'mount his horse with little assistance,' I said to myself: Here also we have a Symbol well-nigh superannuated. Alas, move whithersoever you may, are not the tatters and rags of superannuated worn-out Symbols (in this Ragfair of a World) dropping off everywhere, to hood-wink, to halter, to tether you; nay, if you shake them not aside, threatening to accumulate, and perhaps produce suffocation?"

Thomas Carlyle

"THE POET AND THE PROPHET"

THE CAREFUL READER of Carlyle's *Heroes and Hero-Worship* soon becomes aware of the work's many ambivalences. In "the Hero as Priest," for example, Carlyle speaks for an ideal society in which each citizen is his own "hero"—an engaging statement of a democratic ideal; later in the same essay he extols the virtues of the authoritarian great man. In "The Hero As Poet," one of the least repetitious and stylistically amorphous essays, Carlyle briefly distinguishes his prophetic impulse from his artistic and extols the beautiful over the good, the artist over the prophet. However, he does not prolong the distinction, and his venture into aesthetics soon merges with a hazy transcendentalism. The significant fact is that this swiftly glimpsed idea predicts one which in time becomes basic to Pater, Whistler, Wilde, and Yeats: Beauty as interpreted by the artist is not only distinct from morality but unreservedly superior to it. There is no evidence that Carlyle was disturbed by his separation of art and prophecy; he easily incorporated this special view into his broader doctrine.

THE HERO AS DIVINITY, the Hero as Prophet, are productions of old ages; not to be repeated in the new. They presuppose a certain rudeness of conception, which the progress of mere scientific knowledge puts an end to. There needs to be, as it were, a world vacant, or almost vacant of scientific forms, if men in their loving

FROM "The Hero as Poet," delivered as a lecture in 1840.

wonder are to fancy their fellow-man either a god or one speaking with the voice of a god. Divinity and Prophet are past. We are now to see our Hero in the less ambitious, but also less questionable, character of Poet; a character which does not pass. The Poet is a heroic figure belonging to all ages; whom all ages possess, when once he is produced, whom the newest age as the oldest may produce;—and will produce, always when Nature pleases. Let Nature send a Hero-soul; in no age is it other than possible that he may be shaped into a Poet.

Hero, Prophet, Poet,—many different names, in different times and places, do we give to Great Men; according to varieties we note in them, according to the sphere in which they have displayed themselves! We might give many more names, on this same principle. I will remark again, however, as a fact not unimportant to be understood, that the different *sphere* constitutes the grand origin of such distinction; that the Hero can be Poet, Prophet, King, Priest or what you will, according to the kind of world he finds himself born into. I confess, I have no notion of a truly great man that could not be *all* sorts of men. The Poet who could merely sit on a chair, and compose stanzas, would never make a stanza worth much. He could not sing the Heroic warrior, unless he himself were at least a Heroic warrior too. I fancy there is in him the Politician, the Thinker, Legislator, Philosopher;—in one or the other degree, he could have been, he is all these. So too I cannot understand how a Mirabeau, with that great glowing heart, with the fire that was in it, with the bursting tears that were in it, could not have written verses, tragedies, poems, and touched all hearts in that way, had his course of life and education led him thitherward. The grand fundamental character is that of Great Man; that the man be great. Napoleon has words in him which are like Austerlitz Battles. Louis Fourteenth's Marshals are a kind of poetical men withal; the things Turenne says are full of sagacity and geniality, like sayings of Samuel Johnson. The great heart, the clear deep-seeing eye: there it lies; no man whatever, in what province soever, can prosper at all without these. Petrarch and Boccaccio did diplomatic messages, it seems, quite well: one can easily believe it; they had done things a little harder than these! Burns, a gifted song-writer, might have made a still better Mirabeau. Shakespeare,—one knows not what *he* could not have made, in the supreme degree.

True, there are aptitudes of Nature too. Nature does not make all great men, more than all other men, in the self-same mould. Varieties of aptitude doubtless; but infinitely more of circumstance; and far oftenest it is the *latter* only that are looked to. But it is as with common men in the learning of trades. You take any man, as yet a vague capability of a man, who could be any kind of craftsman; and make him into a smith, a carpenter, a mason: he is then and thenceforth that and nothing else. And if, as Addison complains, you sometimes see a street-porter staggering under his load on spindle-shanks, and near at hand a tailor with the frame of a Samson handling a bit of cloth and small Whitechapel needle,—it cannot be considered that aptitude of Nature alone has been consulted here either!—The Great Man also, to what shall he be bound apprentice? Given your Hero, is he to become Conqueror, King, Philosopher, Poet? It is an inexplicably complex controversial-calculation between the world and him! He will read the world and its laws; the world with its laws will be there to be read. What the world, on *this* matter, shall permit and bid is, as we said, the most important fact about the world.—

Poet and Prophet differ greatly in our loose modern notions of them. In some old languages, again, the titles are synonymous; *Vates* means both Prophet and Poet: and indeed at all times, Prophet and Poet, well understood, have much kindred of meaning. Fundamentally indeed they are still the same; in this most important respect especially, That they have penetrated both of them into the sacred mystery of the Universe; what Goethe calls 'the open secret'. 'Which is the great secret?' asks one.—'The *open* secret,'—open to all, seen by almost none! That divine mystery, which lies everywhere in all Beings, 'the Divine Idea of the World, that which lies at the bottom of Appearance,' as Fichte styles it; of which all Appearance, from the starry sky to the grass of the field, but especially the Appearance of Man and his work, is but the *vesture,* the embodiment that renders it visible. This divine mystery *is* in all times and in all places; veritably is. In most times and places it is greatly overlooked; and the Universe, definable always in one or the other dialect, as the realized Thought of God, is considered a trivial, inert, commonplace matter,—as if, says the Satirist, it were a dead thing, which some upholsterer had put together! It could do no good, at present, to *speak* much about this; but it is a pity for every one of us if we do not know it, live ever in the knowledge of it. Really a most mournful pity;—a failure to live at all, if we live otherwise!

But now, I say, whoever may forget this divine mystery, the *Vates,* whether Prophet or Poet, has penetrated into it; is a man sent hither to make it more impressively known to us. That always is his message; he is to reveal that to us,—that sacred mystery which he more than others lives ever present with. While others forget it, he knows it;—I might say, he has been driven to know it; without consent asked of *him,* he finds himself living in it, bound to live in it. Once more, here is no Hearsay, but a direct Insight and Belief; this man too could not help being a sincere man! Whosoever may live in the shows of things, it is for him a necessity of nature to live in the very fact of things. A man, once more, in earnest with the Universe, though all others were but toying with it. He is a *Vates,* first of all, in virtue of being sincere. So far Poet and Prophet, participators in the 'open secret,' are one.

With respect to their distinction again: The *Vates* Prophet, we might say, has seized that sacred mystery rather on the moral side, as Good and Evil, Duty and Prohibition; the *Vates* Poet on what the Germans call the aesthetic side, as Beautiful, and the like. The one we may call a revealer of what we are to do, the other of what we are to love. But indeed these two provinces run into one another, and cannot be disjoined. The Prophet too has his eye on what we are to love: how else shall he know what it is we are to do? The highest Voice ever heard on this Earth said withal, 'Consider the lilies of the field; they toil not, neither do they spin: yet Solomon in all his glory was not arrayed like one of these.' A glance, that, into the deepest deep of Beauty. 'The lilies of the field,'—dressed finer than earthly princes, springing up there in the humble furrow-field; a beautiful *eye* looking out on you, from the great inner Sea of Beauty! How could the rude Earth make these, if her Essence, rugged as she looks and is, were not inwardly Beauty?—In this point of view, too, a saying of Goethe's, which has staggered several, may have meaning: 'The Beautiful', he intimates, 'is higher than the Good; the Beautiful includes in it the Good.' The *true* Beautiful; which however, I have said somewhere, 'differs from the *false,* as Heaven does from Vauxhall!' So much for the distinction and identity of Poet and Prophet.—

In ancient and also in modern periods, we find a few Poets who are accounted perfect; whom it were a kind of treason to find fault with. This is noteworthy; this is right: yet in strictness it is only an illusion. At bottom, clearly enough, there is no perfect Poet! A vein of Poetry exists in the hearts of all men; no man is made altogether of Poetry. We are all poets when we *read* a poem well. The 'imagination that shudders at the Hell of Dante,' is not that the same faculty, weaker in degree, as Dante's own? No one but Shakespeare can embody, out of Saxo Grammaticus, the story of *Hamlet* as Shakespeare did: but every one models some kind of story out of it; every one embodies it better or worse. We need not spend time in defining. Where there is no specific difference, as between round and square, all definition must be more or less arbitrary. A man that has *so* much more of the poetic element developed in him as to have become noticeable, will be called Poet by his neighbours. World-Poets too, those whom we are to take for perfect Poets, are settled by critics in the same way. One who rises *so* far above the general level of Poets will, to such and such critics, seem a Universal Poet; as he ought to do. And yet it is, and must be, an arbitrary distinction. All Poets, all men, have some touches of the Universal; no man is wholly made of that. Most Poets are very soon forgotten: but not the noblest Shakespeare or Homer of them can be remembered *for ever;*—a day comes when he too is not!

Nevertheless, you will say, there must be a difference between true Poetry and true Speech not Poetical: what is the difference? On this point many things have been written, especially by late German Critics, some of which are not very intelligible at first. They say, for example, that the Poet has an *infinitude* in him; communicates an *Unendlichkeit,* a certain character of 'infinitude,' to whatsoever he delineates. This, though not very precise, yet on so vague a matter is worth remembering: if well meditated, some meaning will gradually be found in it. For my own part, I find considerable meaning in the old vulgar distinction of Poetry being *metrical,* having music in it, being a Song. Truly, if pressed to give a definition, one might say this as soon as anything else: If your delineation be authentically *musical,* musical not in word only, but in heart and substance, in all the thoughts and utterances of it, in the whole conception of it, then it will be poetical; if not, not.—Musical: how much lies in that! A *musical* thought is one spoken by a mind that has penetrated into the inmost heart of the thing; detected the inmost mystery of it, namely the *melody* that lies hidden in it; the inward harmony of coherence which is its soul, whereby it exists, and has a right to be, here in this world. All inmost things, we may say, are melodious; naturally utter themselves in Song. The meaning of Song goes deep. Who is there that, in logical words, can express the effect music has on us? A kind of inarticulate unfathomable speech, which leads us to the edge of the Infinite, and lets us for moments gaze into that!

Nay all speech, even the commonest speech, has something of song in it: not a parish in the world but has its parish-accent;—the rhythm or *tune* to which the people there *sing* what they have to say! Accent is a kind of chanting; all men have accent of their own,—though they only *notice* that of others. Observe too how all passionate language does of itself become musical,—with a finer music than the mere accent; the speech of a man even in zealous anger becomes a chant, a song. All deep things are Song. It seems somehow the very central essence of us, Song; as if all the rest were but wrappages and hulls! The primal element of us; of us, and of all things. The Greeks fabled of Sphere-Harmonies: it was the feeling they had of the inner structure of Nature; that the soul of all her voices and utterances was perfect music. Poetry, therefore, we will call *musical Thought*. The Poet is he who *thinks* in that manner. At bottom, it turns still on power of intellect; it is a man's sincerity and depth of vision that makes him a Poet. See deep enough, and you see musically; the heart of Nature *being* everywhere music, if you can only reach it.

The *Vates* Poet, with his melodious Apocalypse of Nature, seems to hold a poor rank among us, in comparison with the *Vates* Prophet; his function, and our esteem of him for his function, alike slight. The Hero taken as Divinity; the Hero taken as Prophet; then next the Hero taken only as Poet: does it not look as if our estimate of the Great Man, epoch after epoch, were continually diminishing? We take him first for a god, then for one god-inspired; and now in the next stage of it, his most miraculous word gains from us only the recognition that he is a Poet, beautiful verse-maker, man of genius, or such-like!—It looks so; but I persuade myself that intrinsically it is not so. If we consider well, it will perhaps appear that in man still there is the *same* altogether peculiar admiration for the Heroic Gift, by what name soever called, that there at any time was.

I should say, if we do not now reckon a Great Man literally divine, it is that our notions of God, of the supreme unattainable Fountain of Splendour, Wisdom and Heroism, are ever rising *higher;* not altogether that our reverence for these qualities, as manifested in our like, is getting lower. This is worth taking thought of. Sceptical Dilettantism, the curse of these ages, a curse which will not last for ever, does indeed in this the highest province of human things, as in all provinces, make sad work; and our reverence for great men, all crippled, blinded, paralytic as it is, comes out in poor plight, hardly recognizable. Men worship the shows of great men; the most disbelieve that there is any reality of great men to worship. The dreariest, fatallest faith; believing which, one would literally despair of human things. Nevertheless look, for example, at Napoleon! A Corsican lieutenant of artillery; that is the show of *him* yet is he not obeyed, *worshipped* after his sort, as all the Tiaraed and Diademed of the world put together could not be? High Duchesses, and ostlers of inns, gather round the Scottish rustic, Burns;—a strange feeling dwelling in each that they never heard a man like this; that, on the whole, this is the man! In the secret heart of these people it still dimly reveals itself, though there is no accredited way of uttering it at present, that this rustic, with his black brows and flashing sun-eyes, and strange words moving laughter and tears, is of a dignity far beyond all others, incommensurable with all others. Do not we feel it so? But now, were Dilettantism, Scepticism, Triviality, and all that sorrowful brood, cast-out of us,—as, by God's blessing, they shall one day be; were faith in the shows of things entirely swept out, replaced by clear faith in the *things*, so that a man acted on the impulse of that only, and counted the other non-extant; what a new livelier feeling towards this Burns were it!

Nay, here in these ages, such as they are, have we not two mere Poets, if not deified, yet we may say beatified? Shakespeare and Dante are Saints of Poetry; really, if we will think of it, *canonized*, so that it is impiety to meddle with them. The unguided instinct of the world, working across all these perverse impediments, has arrived at such result. Dante and Shakespeare are a peculiar Two. They dwell apart, in a kind of royal solitude; none equal, none second to them: in the general feeling of the world, a certain transcendentalism, a glory as of complete perfection, invests these two. They *are* canonized, though no Pope or Cardinals took hand in doing it! Such, in spite of every perverting influence, in the most unheroic times, is still our indestructible reverence for heroism.—We will look a little at these Two, the Poet Dante and the Poet Shakespeare: what little it is permitted us to say here of the Hero as Poet will most fitly arrange itself in that fashion.

John Ruskin

PRE-RAPHAELITISM

The British Pre-Raphaelite artists early found inspiration in Ruskin's *Modern Painters;* and Ruskin was gratified to discover some of his chief aesthetic tenets—an unswerving fidelity to the facts of Nature, an enthusiasm for things medieval, and the importance of a pronounced Christian coloring—reflected in their meticulous work. Presently, when two leading Pre-Raphaelites, John Everett Millais and William Holman Hunt, were judged adversely by the art critic of *The Times,* their friend Coventry Patmore asked Ruskin to lend his considerable prestige to their cause by writing to the newspaper. Ruskin obliged with two mild letters, and when these received curt treatment he entered the foray with zest, composing the long essay which turned out to be as much an explanation of his beloved Turner as a defense of the painters. This essay, however, supplied the Brotherhood with renewed confidence, something they badly needed after the dismal failures of their magazine, *The Germ,* and of their painting exhibitions. He also extended a warning: The Pre-Raphaelites are "working too hard. They have wrought so long" that "their very sight has failed for weariness" and their hands have "refused any more to obey the heart." He advised them to seek the ideal selflessness of the great Turner, and thereby to preserve as much of their original spontaneity as possible.

From *Pre-Raphaelitism* (1851).

Courtesy of the Glasgow Art Gallery and Museum

THOMAS CARLYLE:
ARRANGEMENT IN GREY AND BLACK NO. 2

Painting by James McNeill Whistler, 1872

Courtesy of Sir William Acland, Bt.

JOHN RUSKIN

Painting by John Everett Millais, 1853

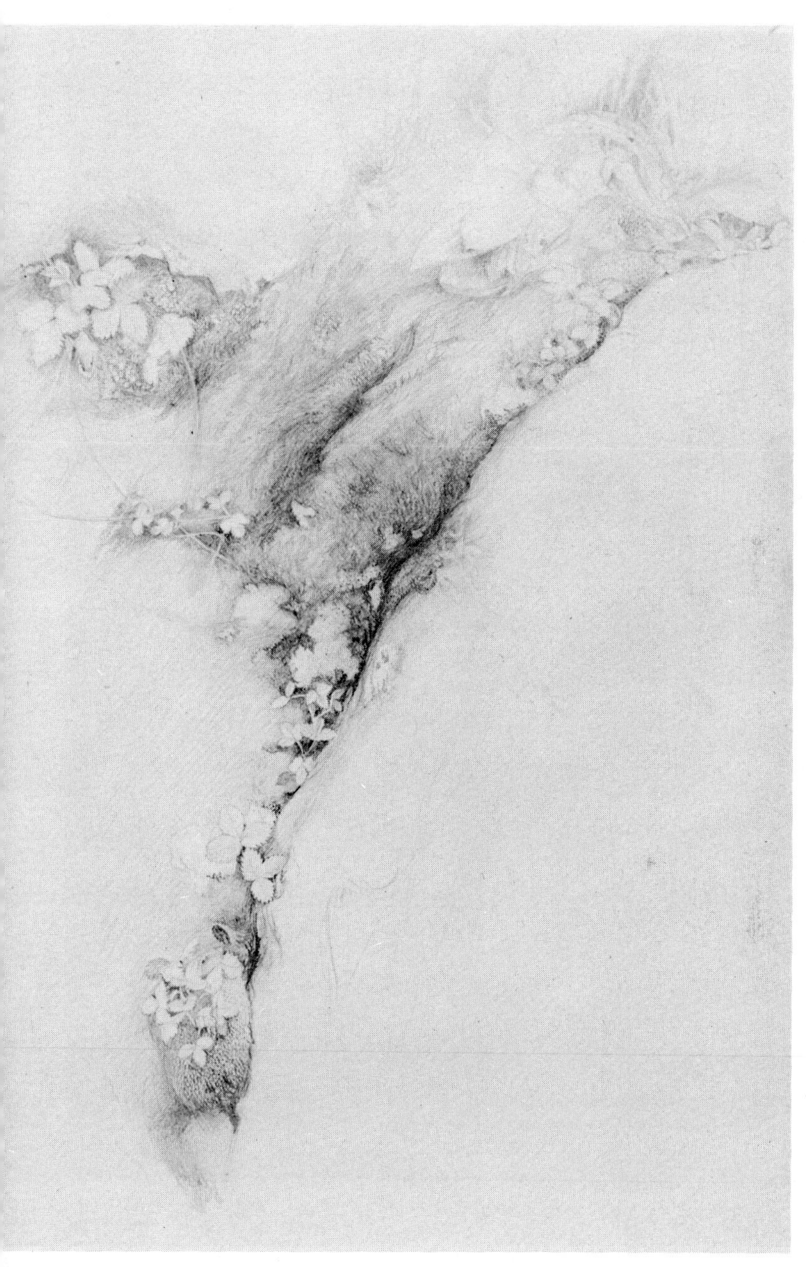

Courtesy of the Ashmolean Museum, Oxford

MOSS AND WILD STRAWBERRIES

Drawing by John Ruskin, c. 1880

ANTWERP: VAN GOYEN LOOKING OUT FOR A SUBJECT

Courtesy of the Trustees of the National Gallery, London

RAIN, STEAM, AND SPEED. *Painting by J. M. W. Turner, 1844*

Courtesy of the Trustees of The Lady Lever Art Gallery, Cheshire, England

THE SCAPEGOAT. *Painting by William Holman Hunt, 1854*

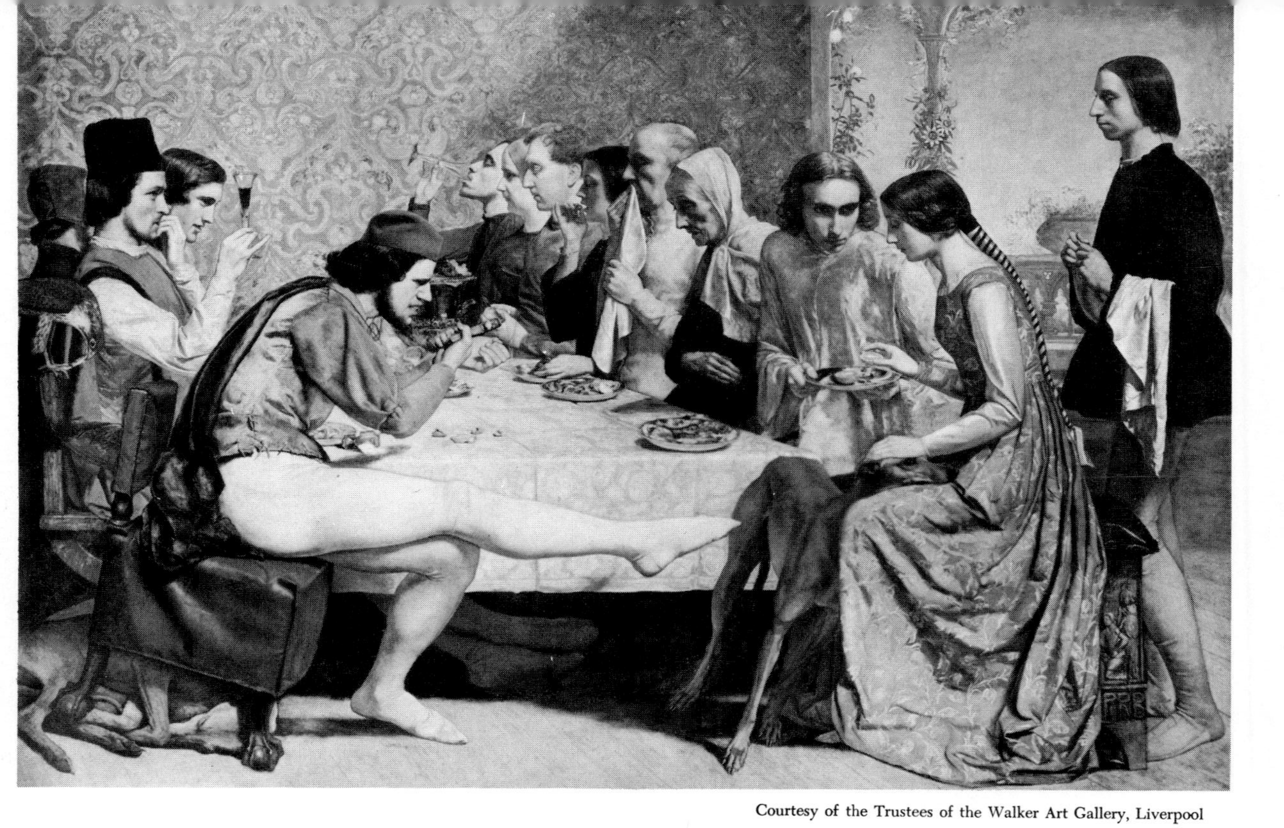

Courtesy of the Trustees of the Walker Art Gallery, Liverpool

LORENZO AND ISABELLA. *Painting by John Everett Millais, 1849*

Courtesy of the National Gallery of Ireland, Dublin

JANE BURDEN AS QUEEN GUENEVERE

Drawing by Dante Gabriel Rossetti, 1858

IN GENERAL, the men who are employed in the Arts have freely chosen their profession, and suppose themselves to have special faculty for it; yet, as a body, they are not happy men. For which this seems to me the reason, that they are expected, and themselves expect, to make their bread *by being clever*—not by steady or quiet work; and are, therefore, for the most part, trying to be clever, and so living in an utterly false state of mind and action.

This is the case, to the same extent, in no other profession or employment. A lawyer may indeed suspect that, unless he has more wit than those around him, he is not likely to advance in his profession; but he will not be always thinking how he is to display his wit. He will generally understand, early in his career, that wit must be left to take care of itself, and that it is hard knowledge of law and vigorous examination and collation of the facts of every case entrusted to him, which his clients will mainly demand; this it is which he has to be paid for; and this is healthy and measurable labor, payable by the hour. If he happen to have keen natural perception and quick wit, these will come into play in their due time and place, but he will not think of them as his chief power; and if he have them not, he may still hope that industry and conscientiousness may enable him to rise in his profession without them. Again in the case of clergymen: that they are sorely tempted to display their eloquence or wit, none who know their own hearts will deny, but then they *know* this to *be* a temptation: they never would suppose that cleverness was all that was to be expected from them, or would sit down deliberately to write a clever sermon: even the dullest or vainest of them would throw some veil over their vanity, and pretend to some profitableness of purpose in what they did. They would not openly ask of their hearers—Did you think my sermon ingenious, or my language poetical? They would early understand that they were not paid for being ingenious, nor called to be so, but to preach truth; that if they happened to possess wit, eloquence, or originality, these would appear and be of service in due time, but were not to be continually sought after or exhibited: and if it should happen that they had them not, they might still be serviceable pastors without them.

Not so with the unhappy artist. No one expects any honest or useful work of him; but every one expects him to be ingenious. Originality, dexterity, invention, imagination, every thing is asked of him except what alone is to be had for asking—honesty and sound work, and the due discharge of his function as a painter. What function? asks the reader in some surprise. He may well ask; for I suppose few painters have any idea what their function is, or even that they have any at all.

And yet surely it is not so difficult to discover. The faculties, which when a man finds in himself, he resolves to be a painter, are, I suppose, intenseness of observation and facility of imitation. The man is created an observer and an imitator; and his function is to convey knowledge to his fellow-men, of such things as cannot be taught otherwise than ocularly. For a long time this function remained a religious one: it was to impress upon the popular mind the reality of the objects of faith, and the truth of the histories of Scripture, by giving visible form to both. That function has now passed away, and none has as yet taken its place. The painter has no profession, no purpose. He is an idler on the earth, chasing the shadows of his own fancies.

But he was never meant to be this. The sudden and universal Naturalism, or inclination to copy ordinary natural objects, which manifested itself among the painters of Europe at the moment when the invention of printing superseded their legendary labors, was no false instinct. It was misunderstood and misapplied, but it came at the right time, and has maintained itself through all kinds of abuse; presenting in the recent schools of landscape, perhaps only the first fruits of its power. That instinct was urging every painter in Europe at the same moment to his true duty—*the faithful representation of all objects of historical interest, or of natural beauty existent at the period;* representations such as might at once aid the advance of the sciences, and keep faithful record of every monument of past ages which was likely to be swept away in the approaching eras of revolutionary change.

The instinct came, as I said, exactly at the right moment; and let the reader consider what amount and kind of general knowledge might by this time have been possessed by the nations of Europe, had their painters understood and obeyed it. Suppose that, after disciplining themselves so as to be able to draw, with unerring precision, each the particular kind of subject in which he most delighted, they had separated into two great armies of historians and naturalists;—that the first had painted with absolute faithfulness every edifice, every city, every battle-field, every scene of the slightest historical interest, precisely and completely rendering their aspect at the time; and that their companions, according to their several powers, had painted with like fidelity the plants and animals, the natural scenery, and the atmospheric phenomena of every country on the earth— suppose that a faithful and complete record were now in our museums of every building destroyed by war, or time, or innovation, during these last 200 years—suppose that each recess of every mountain chain of Europe had been penetrated, and its rocks drawn with such accuracy that the geologist's diagram was no longer necessary—suppose that every tree of the forest had been drawn in its noblest aspect, every beast of the field in its savage life—that all these gatherings were already in our national galleries, and that the painters of the present day were laboring, happily and earnestly, to multiply them, and put such means of knowledge more and more within reach of the common people—would not that be a more honorable life for them, than gaining precarious bread by "bright effects?" They think not, perhaps. They think it easy, and therefore contemptible, to be truthful; they have been taught so all their lives. But it is not so, whoever taught it them. It is most difficult, and worthy of the greatest men's greatest effort, to render, as it should be rendered, the simplest of the natural features of the earth; but also be it remembered, no man is confined to the simplest; each may look out work for himself where he chooses, and it will be strange if he cannot find something hard enough for him. The excuse is, however, one of the lips only; for every painter knows that when he draws back from the attempt to render nature as she is, it is oftener in cowardice than in disdain.

I must leave the reader to pursue this subject for himself; I have not space to suggest to him the tenth part of the advantages which would follow, both to the painter from such an understanding of his mission, and to the whole people, in the results of his labor. Consider how the man himself would be elevated: how content he would become, how earnest, how full of all accurate and noble knowledge, how free from envy—knowing creation to be infinite, feeling at once the value of what he did, and yet the nothingness. Consider the advantage to the people; the immeasurably larger interest given to art itself; the easy, pleasurable, and perfect knowledge conveyed by it, in every subject; the far greater number of men who might be healthily and profitably occupied with it as a means of livelihood; the useful direction of myriads of inferior talents, now left fading away in misery. Conceive all this, and then look around at our exhibitions, and behold the "cattle pieces," and "sea pieces," and "fruit pieces," and "family pieces"; the eternal brown cows in ditches, and white sails in squalls, and sliced lemons in saucers, and foolish faces in simpers;—and try to feel what we are, and what we might have been.

Take a single instance in one branch of archæology. Let those who are interested in the history of religion consider what a treasure we should now have possessed, if, instead of painting pots, and vegetables, and drunken peasantry, the most accurate painters of the seventeenth and eighteenth centuries had been set to copy, line for line, the religious and domestic sculpture on the German, Flemish, and French cathedrals and castles; and if every building destroyed in the French or in any other subsequent revolution, had thus been drawn in all its parts with the same precision with which Gerard Douw or Mieris [1] paint basreliefs of Cupids. Consider, even now, what incalculable treasure is still left in ancient basreliefs, full of every kind of legendary interest, of subtle expression, of priceless evidence as to the character, feelings, habits, histories, of past generations, in neglected and shattered churches and domestic buildings, rapidly disappearing over the whole of Europe—treasure which, once lost, the labor of all men living cannot bring back again; and then look at the myriads of men, with skill enough, if they had but the commonest schooling, to record all this faithfully, who are making their bread by drawing dances of naked women from academy models, or idealities of chivalry fitted out with Wardour Street armor, or eternal scenes from Gil Blas, Don Quixote, and the Vicar of Wakefield, or mountain scenes with young idiots of Londoners wearing Highland bonnets and brandishing rifles in the foregrounds. Do but think of these things in the breadth of their inexpressible imbecility, and then go and stand before that broken basrelief in the southern gate of Lincoln Cathedral, and see if there is no fibre of the heart in you that will break too.

[1] Douw (1613–1675) was a pupil of Rembrandt; Mieris (1635–1681), Dutch genre painter.

But is there to be no place left, it will be indignantly asked, for imagination and invention, for poetical power, or love of ideal beauty? Yes; the highest, the noblest place—that which these only can attain when they are all used in the cause, and with the aid of truth. Wherever imagination and sentiment are, they will either show themselves without forcing, or, if capable of artificial development, the kind of training which such a school of art would give them would be the best they could receive. The infinite absurdity and failure of our present training consists mainly in this, that we do not rank imagination and invention high enough, and suppose that they *can* be taught. Throughout every sentence that I ever have written, the reader will find the same rank attributed to these powers,—the rank of a purely divine gift, not to be attained, increased, or in any wise modified by teaching, only in various ways capable of being concealed or quenched. Understand this thoroughly; know once for all, that a poet on canvas is exactly the same species of creature as a poet in song, and nearly every error in our methods of teaching will be done away with. For who among us now thinks of bringing men up to be poets?—of producing poets by any kind of general recipe or method of cultivation? Suppose even that we see in youth that which we hope may, in its development, become a power of this kind, should we instantly, supposing that we wanted to make a poet of him, and nothing else, forbid him all quiet, steady, rational labor? Should we force him to perpetual spinning of new crudities out of his boyish brain, and set before him, as the only objects of his study, the laws of versification which criticism has supposed itself to discover in the works of previous writers? Whatever gifts the boy had, would much be likely to come of them so treated? unless, indeed they were so great as to break through all such snares of falsehood and vanity and build their own foundation in spite of us; whereas if, as in cases numbering millions against units, the natural gifts were too weak to do this, could any thing come of such training but utter inanity and spuriousness of the whole man? But if we had sense, should we not rather restrain and bridle the first flame of invention in early youth, heaping material on it as one would on the first sparks and tongues of a fire which we desired to feed into greatness? Should we not educate the whole intellect into general strength, and all the affections into warmth and honesty, and look to heaven for the rest? This, I say, we should have sense enough to do, in order to produce a poet in words: but, it being required to produce a poet on canvas, what is our way of setting to work? We begin, in all probability, by telling the youth of fifteen or sixteen, that Nature is full of faults, and that he is to improve her; but that Raphael is perfection, and that the more he copies Raphael the better; that after much copying of Raphael, he is to try what he can do himself in a Raphaelesque, but yet original, manner: that is to say, he is to try to do something very clever, all out of his own head, but yet this clever something is to be properly subjected to Raphaelesque rules, is to have a principal light occupying one-seventh of its space, and a principal shadow occupying one-third of the same; that no two people's heads in the picture are to be turned the same way, and that all the personages represented are to possess ideal beauty of the highest order, which ideal beauty consists partly in a Greek outline of nose, partly in proportions expressible in decimal fractions between the lips and chin; but partly also in that degree of improvement which the youth of sixteen is to bestow upon God's work in general. This I say is the kind of teaching which through various channels, Royal Academy lecturings, press criticisms, public enthusiasms, and not least by solid weight of gold, we give to our young men. And we wonder we have no painters!

But we do worse than this. Within the last few years some sense of the real tendency of such teaching has appeared in some of our younger painters. It only *could* appear in the younger ones, our older men having become familiarised with the false system, or else having passed through it and forgotten it, not well knowing the degree of harm they had sustained. This sense appeared, among our youths,—increased,—matured into resolute action. Necessarily, to exist at all, it needed the support both of strong instincts and of considerable self-confidence, otherwise it must at once have been borne down by the weight of general authority and received canon law. Strong instincts are apt to make men strange, and rude; self-confidence, however well founded, to give much of what they do or say the appearance of impertinence. Look at the self-confidence of Wordsworth, stiffening every other sentence of his prefaces into defiance; there is no more of it than was needed to enable him to do his work, yet it is not a little ungraceful here and there. Suppose this stubbornness and self-trust in a youth, laboring in an art of which the executive part is confessedly to be best learnt from masters, and we shall hardly wonder that much of his work has a certain awkwardness and stiffness in it, or that he should be regarded with disfavor by many, even the most temperate, of the judges trained in the system he was breaking through, and with utter contempt and reprobation by the envious and the dull. Consider, farther, that the particular system to be overthrown was, in the present case, one of which the main characteristic was the pursuit of beauty at the expense of manliness and truth; and it will seem likely, *à priori,* that the men intended successfully to resist the influence of such a system should be endowed with little natural sense of beauty, and thus rendered dead to the temptation it presented. Summing up these conditions, there is surely little cause for surprise that pictures painted, in a temper of resistance, by exceedingly young men, of stubborn instincts and positive self-trust, and with little natural perception of beauty, should not be calculated, at the first glance, to win us from works enriched by plagiarism, polished by convention, invested with all the attractiveness of artificial grace, and recommended to our respect by established authority.

We should, however, on the other hand, have anticipated, that in proportion to the strength of character required for the effort, and to the absence of distracting sentiments, whether respect for precedent, or affection for ideal beauty, would be the energy exhibited in the pursuit of the special objects which the youths proposed to themselves, and their success in attaining them.

All this has actually been the case, but in a degree which it would have been impossible to anticipate. That two youths of the respective ages of eighteen and twenty, should have conceived for themselves a totally independent and sincere method of study, and enthusiastically persevered in it against every kind of dissuasion and opposition, is strange enough; that in the third or fourth year of their efforts they should have produced works in many parts not inferior to the best of Albert Dürer,[2] this is perhaps not less strange. But the loudness and universality of the howl which the common critics of the press have raised against them, the utter absence of all generous help or encouragement from those who can both measure their toil and appreciate their success, and the shrill,

[2] Dürer (1471–1528), German painter and wood engraver.

shallow laughter of those who can do neither the one nor the other, —these are strangest of all—unimaginable unless they had been experienced.

And as if these were not enough, private malice is at work against them, in its own small, slimy way. The very day after I had written my second letter to the *Times* in the defence of the Pre-Raphaelites, I received an anonymous letter respecting one of them, from some person apparently hardly capable of spelling, and about as vile a specimen of petty malignity as ever blotted paper. I think it well that the public should know this, and so get some insight into the sources of the spirit which is at work against these men—how first roused it is difficult to say, for one would hardly have thought that mere eccentricity in young artists could have excited an hostility so determined and so cruel;—hostility which hesitated at no assertion, however impudent. That of the "absence of perspective" was one of the most curious pieces of the hue and cry which began with the *Times*, and died away in feeble maundering in the Art Union; I contradicted it in the *Times*—I here contradict it directly for the second time. There was not a single error in perspective in three out of the four pictures in question. But if otherwise, would it have been anything remarkable in them? I doubt if, with the exception of the pictures of David Roberts,[3] there were one architectural drawing in perspective on the walls of the Academy; I never met but with two men in my life who knew enough of perspective to draw a Gothic arch in a retiring plane, so that its lateral dimensions and curvatures might be calculated to scale from the drawing. Our architects certainly do not, and it was but the other day that, talking to one of the most distinguished among them, the author of several most valuable works, I found he actually did not know how to draw a circle in perspective. And in this state of general science our writers for the press take it upon them to tell us, that the forest trees in Mr. Hunt's *Sylvia*, and the bunches of lilies in Mr. Collins's *Convent Thoughts*, are out of perspective.

It might not, I think, in such circumstances, have been ungraceful or unwise in the Academicians themselves to have defended their young pupils, at least by the contradiction of statements

[3] Roberts (1796–1864) was a Scotch painter who loved to draw and paint architectural scenes.

directly false respecting them * and the direction of the mind and sight of the public to such real merit as they possess. If Sir Charles Eastlake, Mulready, Edwin and Charles Landseer, Cope, and Dyce would each of them simply state their own private opinion respecting their paintings, sign it, and publish it, I believe the act would be of more service to English art than any thing the Academy has done since it was founded. But as I cannot hope for this, I can only ask the public to give their pictures careful examination, and look at them at once with the indulgence and the respect which I have endeavored to show they deserve.

Yet let me not be misunderstood. I have adduced them only as examples of the kind of study which I would desire to see substituted for that of our modern schools, and of singular success in certain characters, finish of detail, and brilliancy of color. What

* These false statements may be reduced to three principal heads, and directly contradicted in succession.

The first, the current fallacy of society as well as the press, was, that the Pre-Raphaelites imitated the *errors* of early painters.

A falsehood of this kind could not have obtained credence anywhere but in England, few English people, comparatively, having ever seen a picture of early Italian Masters. If they had, they would have known that the Pre-Raphaelite pictures are just as superior to the early Italian in skill of manipulation, power of drawing, and knowledge of effect, as inferior to them in grace of design; and that in a word, there is not a shadow of resemblance between the two styles. The Pre-Raphaelites imitate no pictures: they paint from nature only. But they have opposed themselves as a body to that kind of teaching above described, which only began after Raphael's time: and, they have opposed themselves as sternly to the entire feeling of the Renaissance schools; a feeling compounded of indolence, infidelity, sensuality, and shallow pride. Therefore they have called themselves Pre-Raphaelites. If they adhere to their principles, and paint nature as it is around them, with the help of modern science, with the earnestness of the men of the thirteenth and fourteenth centuries, they will, as I said, found a new and noble school in England. If their sympathies with the early artists lead them into mediævalism or Romanism, they will of course come to nothing. But I believe there is no danger of this, at least for the strongest among them. There may be some weak ones, whom the Tractarian heresies may touch; but if so, they will drop off like decayed branches from a strong stem. I hope all things from the school.

The second falsehood was, that the Pre-Raphaelites did not draw well. This was asserted, and could have been asserted only by persons who had never looked at the pictures.

The third falsehood was, that they had no system of light and shade. To which it may be simply replied that their system of light and shade is exactly the same as the Sun's; which is, I believe, likely to outlast that of the Renaissance, however brilliant.

faculties, higher than imitative, may be in these men, I do not yet venture to say; but I do say, that if they exist, such faculties will manifest themselves in due time all the more forcibly because they have received training so severe.

For it is always to be remembered that no one mind is like another, either in its powers or perceptions; and while the main principles of training must be the same for all, the result in each will be as various as the kinds of truth which each will apprehend; therefore, also, the modes of effort, even in men whose inner principles and final aims are exactly the same. Suppose, for instance, two men, equally honest, equally industrious, equally impressed with a humble desire to render some part of what they saw in nature faithfully; and, otherwise, trained in convictions such as I have above endeavored to induce. But one of them is quiet in temperament, has a feeble memory, no invention, and excessively keen sight. The other is impatient in temperament, has a memory which nothing escapes, an invention which never rests, and is comparatively near sighted.

Set them both free in the same field in a mountain valley. One sees everything, small and large, with almost the same clearness; mountains and grasshoppers alike; the leaves on the branches, the veins in the pebbles, the bubbles in the stream: but he can remember nothing, and invent nothing. Patiently he sets himself to his mighty task; abandoning at once all thoughts of seizing transient effects, or giving general impressions of that which his eyes present to him in microscopical dissection, he chooses some small portion out of the infinite scene, and calculates with courage the number of weeks which must elapse before he can do justice to the intensity of his perceptions, or the fulness of matter in his subject.

Meantime, the other has been watching the change of the clouds, and the march of the light along the mountain sides; he beholds the entire scene in broad, soft masses of true gradation, and the very feebleness of his sight is in some sort an advantage to him, in making him more sensible of the aerial mystery of distance, and hiding from him the multitudes of circumstances which it would have been impossible for him to represent. But there is not one change in the casting of the jagged shadows along the hollows of the hills, but it is fixed on his mind for ever; not a flake of spray has broken from the sea of cloud about their bases, but he has watched it as it melts away, and could recall it to its lost place in heaven by the slightest effort of his thoughts. Not only so, but thousands and thousands of such images, of older scenes, remain congregated in his mind, each mingling in new associations with those now visibly passing before him, and these again confused with other images of his own ceaseless, sleepless imagination, flashing by in sudden troops. Fancy how his paper will be covered with stray symbols and blots, and undecipherable short-hand:—as for his sitting down to "draw from Nature," there was not one of the things which he wished to represent that stayed for so much as five seconds together: but none of them escaped, for all that: they are sealed up in that strange storehouse of his; he may take one of them out, perhaps, this day twenty years, and paint it in his dark room, far away. Now, observe, you may tell both of these men, when they are young, that they are to be honest, that they have an important function, and that they are not to care what Raphael did. This you may wholesomely impress on them both. But fancy the exquisite absurdity of expecting either of them to possess any of the qualities of the other.

I have supposed the feebleness of sight in the last, and of invention in the first painter, that the contrast between them might be more striking; but, with very slight modification, both the characters are real. Grant to the first considerable inventive power, with exquisite sense of color; and give to the second, in addition to all his other faculties, the eye of an eagle; and the first is John Everett Millais, the second Joseph Mallard William Turner.[4]

They are among the few men who have defied all false teaching, and have, therefore, in great measure, done justice to the gifts with which they were entrusted. They stand at opposite poles, marking culminating points of art in both directions; between them, or in various relations to them, we may class five or six more living artists who, in like manner, have done justice to their powers. I trust that I may be pardoned for naming them, in order that the reader may know how the strong innate genius in each has been invariably accompanied with the same humility, earnestness, and industry in study.

It is hardly necessary to point out the earnestness or humility in the works of William Hunt; but it may be so to suggest the high value they possess as records of English rural life, and *still* life. Who is there who for a moment could contend with him in the unaf-

[4] See examples of paintings of Millais and Turner in the illustrations.

fected, yet humorous truth with which he has painted our peasant children? Who is there who does not sympathize with him in the simple love with which he dwells on the brightness and bloom of our summer fruit and flowers? And yet there is something to be regretted concerning him: why should he be allowed continually to paint the same bunches of hot-house grapes, and supply to the Water Color Society a succession of pineapples with the regularity of a Covent Garden fruiterer? He has of late discovered that primrose banks are lovely; but there are other things grow wild besides primroses: what undreamt-of-loveliness might he not bring back to us, if he would lose himself for a summer in Highland foregrounds; if he would paint the heather as it grows, and the foxglove and the harebell as they nestle in the clefts of the rocks, and the mosses and bright lichens of the rocks themselves. And then, cross to the Jura, and bring back a piece of Jura pasture in spring; with the gentians in their earliest blue, and the soldanelle beside the fading snow! And return again, and paint a gray wall of Alpine crag, with budding roses crowning it like a wreath of rubies. That is what he was meant to do in this world; not to paint bouquets in china vases.[5]

I have in various other places expressed my sincere respect for the works of Samuel Prout: [6] his shortness of sight has necessarily prevented their possessing delicacy of finish or fulness of minor detail; but I think that those of no other living artist furnish an example so striking of innate and special instinct, sent to do a particular work at the exact and only period when it was possible. At the instant when peace had been established all over Europe, but when neither national character nor national architecture had as yet been seriously changed by promiscuous intercourse or modern "improvement"; when, however, nearly every ancient and beautiful building had been long left in a state of comparative neglect, so that its aspect of partial ruinousness, and of separation from recent active life, gave to every edifice a peculiar interest—half sorrowful, half sublime;—at that moment Prout was trained among the rough rocks and simple cottages of Cornwall, until his eye was accustomed to follow with delight the rents and breaks, and irregularities which, to another man, would have been offensive; and

[5] See Ruskin's own "Moss and Wild Strawberries" in first group of illustrations.

[6] Prout (1783–1851).

then, gifted with infinite readiness in composition, but also with infinite affection for the kind of subjects he had to portray, he was sent to preserve, in an almost innumerable series of drawings, *every one made on the spot,* the aspect borne, at the beginning of the nineteenth century, by cities which, in a few years more, rekindled wars, or unexpected prosperities, were to ravage, or renovate, into nothingness.

It seems strange to pass from Prout to John Lewis; [7] but there is this fellowship between them, that both seem to have been intended to appreciate the characters of foreign countries more than of their own—nay, to have been born in England chiefly that the excitement of strangeness might enhance to them the interest of the scenes they had to represent. I believe John Lewis to have done more entire justice to all his powers (and they are magnificent ones) than any other man amongst us. His mission was evidently to portray the comparatively animal life of the southern and eastern families of mankind. For this he was prepared in a somewhat singular way—by being led to study, and endowed with altogether peculiar apprehension of, the most sublime characters of animals themselves. Rubens, Rembrandt, Snyders, Tintoret, and Titian, have all, in various ways, drawn wild beasts magnificently; but they have in some sort humanized or demonized them, making them either ravenous fiends or educated beasts, that would draw cars, and had respect for hermits. The sullen isolation of the brutal nature; the dignity and quietness of the mighty limbs; the shaggy mountainous power, mingled with grace as of a flowing stream; the stealthy restraint of strength and wrath in every soundless motion of the gigantic frames; all this seems never to have been seen, much less drawn, until Lewis drew and himself engraved a series of animal subjects, now many years ago. Since then, he has devoted himself to the portraiture of those European and Asiatic races, among whom the refinements of civilization exist without its laws or its energies, and in whom the fierceness, indolence, and subtlety of animal nature are associated with brilliant imagination and strong affections. To this task he has brought not only intense perception of the kind of character, but powers of artistical composition like those of the great Venetians, displaying, at the same time, a refinement of drawing almost miraculous and appreciable

[7] John Frederick Lewis (1805–1876) was elected an associate of the Royal Academy in 1858, seven years after the appearance of Ruskin's essay.

only, as the minutiæ of nature itself are appreciable, by the help of the microscope. The value, therefore, of his works, as records of the aspect of the scenery and inhabitants of the south of Spain and of the East, in the earlier part of the nineteenth century, is quite above all estimate.

I hardly know how to speak of Mulready: [8] in delicacy and completion of drawing, and splendor of color, he takes place beside John Lewis and the pre-Raphaelites; but he has, throughout his career, displayed no definiteness in choice of subject. He must be named among the painters who have studied with industry, and have made themselves great by doing so; but having obtained a consummate method of execution, he has thrown it away on subjects either altogether uninteresting, or above his powers, or unfit for pictorial representation. "The Cherry Woman," exhibited in 1850, may be named as an example of the first kind; the "Burchell and Sophia" of the second (the character of Sir William Thornhill being utterly missed); the "Seven Ages" of the third; for this subject cannot be painted. In the written passage, the thoughts are progressive and connected; in the picture they must be co-existent, and yet separate; nor can all the characters of the ages be rendered in painting at all. One may represent the soldier at the cannon's mouth, but one cannot paint the "bubble reputation" which he seeks. Mulready, therefore, while he has always produced exquisite pieces of painting, has failed in doing anything which can be of true or extensive use. He has, indeed, understood how to discipline his genius, but never how to direct it.

Edwin Landseer is the last painter but one whom I shall name: I need not point out to any one acquainted with his earlier works, the labor, or watchfulness of nature which they involve, nor need I do more than allude to the peculiar faculties of his mind. It will at once be granted that the highest merits of his pictures are throughout found in those parts of them which are least like what had before been accomplished; and that it was not by the study of Raphael that he attained his eminent success, but by a healthy love of Scotch terriers.

None of these painters, however, it will be answered, afford examples of the rise of the highest imaginative power out of close

[8] William Mulready (1786–1863).
[9] See "Dignity and Impudence" in second group of illustrations.

study of matters of fact. Be it remembered, however, that the imaginative power, in its magnificence, is not to be found every day. Lewis has it in no mean degree; but we cannot hope to find it at its highest more than once in an age. We *have* had it once, and must be content.

Towards the close of the last century, among the various drawings executed, according to the quiet manner of the time, in greyish blue, with brown foregrounds, some began to be noticed as exhibiting rather more than ordinary diligence and delicacy, signed W. Turner. There was nothing, however, in them at all indicative of genius, or even of more than ordinary talent, unless in some of the subjects a large perception of space, and excessive clearness and decision in the arrangement of masses. Gradually and cautiously the blues became mingled with delicate green, and then with gold; the browns in the foreground became first more positive, and then were slightly mingled with other local colors; while the touch, which had at first been heavy and broken, like that of the ordinary drawing masters of the time, grew more and more refined and expressive, until it lost itself in a method of execution often too delicate for the eye to follow, rendering with a precision before unexampled, both the texture and the form of every object. The style may be considered as perfectly formed about the year 1800, and it remained unchanged for twenty years.

During that period the painter had attempted, and with more or less success had rendered, every order of landscape subject, but always on the same principle, subduing the colors of nature into a harmony of which the key-notes are greyish green and brown; pure blues and delicate golden yellows being admitted in small quantity, as the lowest and highest limits of shade and light: and bright local colors in extremely small quantity in figures or other minor accessories.

Pictures executed on such a system are not, properly speaking, works in *color* at all; they are studies of light and shade, in which both the shade and the distance are rendered in the general hue which best expresses their attributes of coolness and transparency; and the lights and the foreground are executed in that which best expresses their warmth and solidity. This advantage may just as well be taken as not, in studies of light and shadow to be executed with the hand: but the use of two, three, or four colors, always in the same relations and places, does not in the least constitute the work a study of color, any more than the brown engravings of the Liber Studiorum; nor would the idea of color be in general more present to the artist's mind, when he was at work on one of these drawings, than when he was using pure brown in the mezzotint engraving. But the idea of space, warmth, and freshness being not successfully expressible in a single tint, and perfectly expressible by the admission of three or four, he allows himself this advantage when it is possible, without in the least embarrassing himself with the actual color of the objects to be represented. A stone in the foreground might in nature have been cold grey, but it will be drawn nevertheless of a rich brown, because it is in the foreground; a hill in the distance might in nature be purple with heath, or golden with furze; but it will be drawn nevertheless of a cool grey, because it is in the distance.

This at least was the general theory,—carried out with great severity in many, both of the drawings and pictures executed by him during the period: in others more or less modified by the cautious introduction of color, as the painter felt his liberty increasing; for the system was evidently never considered as final, or as anything more than a means of progress: the conventional, easily manageable color, was visibly adopted, only that his mind might be at perfect liberty to address itself to the acquirement of the first and most necessary knowledge in all art—that of form. But as form, in landscape, implies vast bulk and space, the use of the tints which enabled him best to express them, was actually auxiliary to the mere drawing; and, therefore, not only permissible, but even necessary, while more brilliant or varied tints were never indulged in, except when they might be introduced without the slightest danger of diverting his mind for an instant from his principal object. And, therefore, it will be generally found in the works of this period, that exactly in proportion to the importance and general toil of the composition, is the severity of the tint; and that the play of color begins to show itself in slight and small drawings, where he felt that he could easily secure all that he wanted in form.

Thus the "Crossing the Brook," and such other elaborate and large compositions, are actually painted in nothing but grey, brown, and blue, with a point or two of severe local color in the figures; but in the minor drawings, tender passages of complicated color occur not unfrequently in easy places; and even before the year 1800 he begins to introduce it with evident joyfulness and longing in his rude and simple studies, just as a child, if it could be supposed to govern itself by a fully developed intellect, would cautiously, but with infinite pleasure, add now and then a tiny dish of fruit or other dangerous luxury to the simple order of its daily fare. Thus, in the foregrounds of his most severe drawings, we not unfrequently find him indulging in the luxury of a peacock; and it is impossible to express the joyfulness with which he seems to design its graceful form, and deepen with soft pencilling the bloom of its blue, after he has worked through the stern detail of his almost colorless drawing. A rainbow is another of his most frequently permitted indulgences; and we find him very early allowing the edges of his evening clouds to be touched with soft rose-color or gold; while, whenever the hues of nature in anywise fall into his system, and can be caught without a dangerous departure from it, he instantly throws his whole soul into the faithful rendering of them. Thus the usual brown tones of his foreground become warmed into sudden vigor, and are varied and enhanced with indescribable delight, when he finds himself by the shore of a moorland stream, where they truly express the stain of its golden rocks, and the darkness of its clear, Cairngorm-like pools, and the usual serenity of his aerial blue is enriched into the softness and depth of the sapphire, when it can deepen the distant slumber of some Highland lake, or temper the gloomy shadows of the evening upon its hills.

The system of his color being thus simplified, he could address all the strength of his mind to the accumulation of facts of form; his choice of subjects, and his methods of treatment, are therefore as various as his color is simple; and it is not a little difficult to give the reader who is unacquainted with his works, an idea either of their infinitude of aims, on the one hand, or of the kind of feeling which prevades them all, on the other. No subject was too low or too high for him; we find him one day hard at work on a cock and hen, with their family of chickens in a farm-yard; and bringing all the refinement of his execution into play to express the texture of the plumage; next day, he is drawing the Dragon of Colchis. One hour he is much interested in a gust of wind blowing away an old woman's cap; the next he is painting the fifth plague of Egypt. Every landscape painter before him had acquired distinction by confining his efforts to one class of subject. Hobbima painted oaks; Ruysdael, waterfalls and copses; Cuyp, river or meadow scenes in quiet afternoons; Salvator and Poussin, such kind of mountain scenery as people could conceive, who lived in towns in the seventeenth century. But I am well persuaded that if all the works of Turner, up to the year 1820, were divided into classes (as he has himself divided them in the Liber Studiorum), no preponderance could be assigned to one class over another. There is architecture, including a large number of formal "gentlemen's seats," I suppose drawings commissioned by the owners; then lowland pastoral scenery of every kind, including nearly all farming operations,—ploughing, harrowing, hedging and ditching, felling trees, sheep-washing, and I know not what else; then all kinds of town life—court-yards of inns, starting of mail coaches, interiors of shops, house-building, fairs, elections, &c.; then all kinds of inner domestic life—interiors of rooms, studies of costumes, of still life, and heraldry, including multitudes of symbolical vignettes; then marine scenery of every kind, full of local incident; every kind of boat and method of fishing for particular fish, being specifically drawn, round the whole coast of England;—pilchard fishing at St. Ives, whiting fishing at Margate, herring at Loch Fyne; and all kinds of shipping, including studies of every separate part of the vessels, and many marine battle-pieces, two in particular of Trafalgar, both of high importance,—one of the Victory after the battle, now in Greenwich Hospital; another of the Death of Nelson, in his own gallery; then all kinds of mountain scenery, some idealised into compositions, others of definite localities; together with classical compositions, Romes and Carthages and such others, by the myriad, with mythological, historical, or allegorical figures,—nymphs, monsters, and spectres; heroes and divinities.

What general feeling, it may be asked incredulously, can possibly pervade all this? This, the greatest of all feelings—an utter forgetfulness of self. Throughout the whole period with which we are at present concerned, Turner appears as a man of sympathy absolutely infinite—a sympathy so all-embracing, that I know nothing but that of Shakespeare comparable with it. A soldier's wife resting by the roadside is not beneath it; Rizpah, the daughter of Aiah, watching the dead bodies of her sons, not above it. Nothing can possibly be so mean as that it will not interest his whole mind, and carry away his whole heart; nothing so great or solemn but that he can raise himself into harmony with it; and it is impossible to prophesy of him at any moment, whether, the next, he will be in laughter or in tears.

This is the root of the man's greatness; and it follows as a matter of course that this sympathy must give him a subtle power of expression, even of the characters of mere material things, such as no other painter ever possessed. The man who can best feel the difference between rudeness and tenderness in humanity, perceives also more difference between the branches of an oak and a willow than any one else would; and, therefore, necessarily the most striking character of the drawings themselves is the speciality of whatever they represent—the thorough stiffness of what is stiff, and grace of what is graceful, and vastness of what is vast; but through and beyond all this, the condition of the mind of the painter himself is easily enough discoverable by comparison of a large number of the drawings. It is singularly serene and peaceful: in itself quite passionless, though entering with ease into the external passion which it contemplates. By the effort of its will it sympathises with tumult or distress, even in their extremes, but there is no tumult, no sorrow in itself, only a chastened and exquisitely peaceful cheerfulness, deeply meditative; touched without loss of its own perfect balance, by sadness on the one side, and stooping to playfulness upon the other. I shall never cease to regret the destruction, by fire, now several years ago, of a drawing which always seemed to me to be the perfect image of the painter's mind at this period,—the drawing of Brignal Church near Rokeby, of which a feeble idea may still be gathered from the engraving (in the Yorkshire series). The spectator stands on the "Brignal banks," looking down into the glen at twilight; the sky is still full of soft rays, though the sun is gone; and the Greta glances brightly in the valley, singing its evening-song; two white clouds, following each other, move without wind through the hollows of the ravine, and others lie couched on the far away moorlands; every leaf of the woods is still in the delicate air; a boy's kite, incapable of rising, has become entangled in their branches, he is climbing to recover it; and just behind it in the picture, almost indicated by it, the lowly church is seen in its secluded field between the rocks and the stream; and around it the low churchyard wall, and the few white stones which mark the resting places of those who can climb the rocks no more, nor hear the river sing as it passes.

There are many other existing drawings which indicate the same character of mind, though I think none so touching or so beautiful; yet they are not, as I said above, more numerous than those which express his sympathy with sublimer or more active scenes; but they are almost always marked by a tenderness of execution, and have a look of being beloved in every part of them, which shows them to be the truest expression of his own feelings.

One other characteristic of his mind at this period remains to be noticed—its reverence for talent in others. Not the reverence which acts upon the practices of men as if they were the laws of nature, but that which is ready to appreciate the power, and receive the assistance, of every mind which has been previously employed in the same direction, so far as its teaching seems to be consistent with the great text-book of nature itself. Turner thus studied almost every preceding landscape painter, chiefly Claude, Poussin, Vandevelde, Loutherbourg, and Wilson. It was probably by the Sir George Beaumonts and other feeble conventionalists of the period, that he was persuaded to devote his attention to the works of these men; and his having done so will be thought, a few scores of years hence, evidence of perhaps the greatest modesty ever shown by a man of original power. Modesty at once admirable and unfortunate, for the study of the works of Vandevelde and Claude was productive of unmixed mischief to him; he spoiled many of his marine pictures, as for instance Lord Ellesmere's, by imitation of the former; and from the latter learned a false ideal, which confirmed by the notions of Greek art prevalent in London in the beginning of this century, has manifested itself in many vulgarities in his composition pictures, vulgarities which may perhaps be best expressed by the general term "Twickenham Classicism," as consisting principally in conceptions of ancient or of rural life such as have influenced the erection of most of our suburban villas. From Nicolo Poussin and Loutherbourg he seems to have derived advantage; perhaps also from Wilson; and much in his subsequent travels from far higher men, especially Tintoret and Paul Veronese. I have myself heard him speaking with singular delight of the putting in of the beech leaves in the upper right-hand corner of Titian's Peter Martyr. I cannot in any of his works trace the slightest influence of Salvator; and I am not surprised at it, for though Salvator was a man of far higher powers than either Vandevelde or Claude, he was a wilful and gross caricaturist. Turner would condescend to be helped by feeble men, but could not be corrupted by false men. Besides, he had never himself seen classical life, and Claude was represented to him as competent authority for it. But he *had* seen mountains and torrents, and knew therefore that Salvator could not paint them.

One of the most characteristic drawings of this period fortunately bears a date, 1818, and brings us within two years of another dated drawing, no less characteristic of what I shall henceforward call Turner's Second period. It is in the possession of Mr. Hawkesworth Fawkes of Farnley, one of Turner's earliest and truest friends; and bears the inscription, unusually conspicuous, heaving itself up and down over the eminences of the foreground—"PASSAGE OF MONT CENIS. J. M. W. TURNER, January 15th, 1820."

The scene is on the summit of the pass close to the hospice, or what seems to have been a hospice at that time,—I do not remember such at present,—a small square-built house, built as if partly for a fortress, with a detached flight of stone steps in front of it, and a kind of drawbridge to the door. This building, about 400 or 500 yards off, is seen in a dim, ashy grey against the light, which by help of a violent blast of mountain wind has broken through the depth of clouds which hangs upon the crags. There is no sky, properly so called, nothing but this roof of drifting cloud; but neither is there any weight of darkness—the high air is too thin for it,—all savage, howling, and luminous with cold, the massy bases of the granite hills jutting out here and there grimly through the snow wreaths. There is a desolate-looking refuge on the left, with its number 16, marked on it in long ghastly figures, and the wind is drifting the snow off the roof and through its window in a frantic whirl; the near ground is all wan with half-thawed, half-trampled snow; a diligence in front, whose horses, unable to face the wind, have turned right round with fright, its passengers struggling to escape, jammed in the window; a little farther on is another carriage off the road, some figures pushing at its wheels, and its driver at the horses' heads, pulling and lashing with all his strength, his lifted arm stretched out against the light of the distance, though too far off for the whip to be seen.

Now I am perfectly certain that any one thoroughly accustomed to the earlier works of the painter; and shown this picture for the first time, would be struck by two altogether new characters in it.

The first, a seeming enjoyment of the excitement of the scene, totally different from the contemplative philosophy with which it would formerly have been regarded. Every incident of motion and of energy is seized upon with indescribable delight, and every line of the composition animated with a force and fury which are now no longer the mere expression of a contemplated external truth, but have origin in some inherent feeling in the painter's mind.

The second, that although the subject is one in itself almost incapable of color, and although, in order to increase the wildness of the impression, all brilliant local color has been refused even where it might easily have been introduced, as in the figures; yet in the low minor key which has been chosen, the melodies of color have been elaborated to the utmost possible pitch, so as to become a leading, instead of a subordinate, element in the composition; the subdued warm hues of the granite promontories, the dull stone color of the walls of the buildings, clearly opposed, even in shade, to the grey of the snow wreaths heaped against them, and the faint greens and ghastly blues of the glacier ice, being all expressed with delicacies of transition utterly unexampled in any previous drawings.

These, accordingly, are the chief characteristics of the works of Turner's second period, as distinguished from the first,—a new energy inherent in the mind of the painter, diminishing the repose and exalting the force and fire of his conceptions, and the presence of Color, as at least an essential, and often a principal, element of design.

Not that it is impossible, or even unusual, to find drawings of serene subject, and perfectly quiet feeling, among the compositions of this period; but the repose is in them, just as the energy and tumult were in the earlier period, an external quality, which the painter images by an effort of the will: it is no longer a character inherent in himself. The "Ulleswater," in the England series, is one of those which are in most perfect peace: in the "Cowes," the silence is only broken by the dash of the boat's oars, and in the "Alnwick" by a stag drinking; but in at least nine drawings out of ten, either sky, water, or figures are in rapid motion, and the grandest drawings are almost always those which have even violent action in one or other, or in all: e. g. high force of Tees, Coventry, Llanthony, Salisbury, Llanberis, and such others.

The color is, however, a more absolute distinction; and we must return to Mr. Fawkes's collection in order to see how the change in it was effected. That such a change would take place at one time or other was of course to be securely anticipated, the conventional system of the first period being, as above stated, merely a means of Study. But the immediate cause was the journey of the year 1820. As might be guessed from the legend on the drawing above described, "Passage of Mont Cenis, January 15th, 1820," that drawing represents what happened on the day in question to the painter himself. He passed the Alps then in the winter of 1820; and either in the previous or subsequent summer, but on the same journey, he made a series of sketches on the Rhine, in body color, now in Mr. Fawkes's collection. Every one of those sketches is the almost instantaneous record of an *effect* of color or atmosphere, taken strictly from nature, the drawing and the details of every subject being comparatively subordinate, and the color nearly as principal as the light and shade had been before,—certainly the leading feature, though the light and shade are always exquisitely harmonized with it. And naturally, as the color becomes the leading object, those times of day are chosen in which it is most lovely; and whereas before, at least five out of six of Turner's drawings represented ordinary daylight, we now find his attention directed constantly to the evening: and, for the first time, we have those rosy lights upon the hills, those gorgeous falls of sun through flaming heavens, those solemn twilights, with the blue moon rising as the western sky grows dim, which have ever since been the themes of his mightiest thoughts.

I have no doubt, that the *immediate* reason of this change was the impression made upon him by the colors of the continental skies. When he first travelled on the Continent (1800), he was comparatively a young student; not yet able to draw form as he wanted, he was forced to give all his thoughts and strength to this primary object. But now he was free to receive other impressions; the time was come for perfecting his art, and the first sunset which he saw on the Rhine taught him that all previous landscape art was vain and valueless, that in comparison with natural color, the things that had been called paintings were mere ink and charcoal, and that all precedent and all authority must be cast away at once, and trodden under foot. He cast them away: the memories of Vandevelde and Claude were at once weeded out of the great mind they had encumbered; they and all the rubbish of the schools together with them; the waves of the Rhine swept them away for ever; and a new dawn rose over the rocks of the Siebengebirge.

There was another motive at work, which rendered the change still more complete. His fellow artists were already conscious enough of his superior power in drawing, and their best hope was, that he might not be able to color. They had begun to express this hope loudly enough for it to reach his ears. The engraver of one of his most important marine pictures told me, not long ago, that one day about the period in question, Turner came into his room to examine the progress of the plate, not having seen his own picture for several months. It was one of his dark early pictures, but in the foreground was a little piece of luxury, a pearly fish wrought into hues like those of an opal. He stood before the picture for some moments; then laughed, and pointed joyously to the fish;—"They say that Turner can't color!" and turned away.

Under the force of these various impulses the change was total. *Every subject thenceforth was primarily conceived in color;* and no engraving ever gave the slightest idea of any drawing of this period.

The artists who had any perception of the truth were in despair; the Beaumontites, classicalists, and "owl species" in general, in as much indignation as their dulness was capable of. They had deliberately closed their eyes to all nature, and had gone on inquiring, "Where do you put your brown tree?" A vast revelation was made to them at once, enough to have dazzled any one; but to *them,* light unendurable as incomprehensible. They "did to the moon complain," in one vociferous, unanimous, continuous "Tu whoo." Shrieking rose from all dark places at the same instant, just the same kind of shrieking that is now raised against the Pre-Raphaelites. Those glorious old Arabian Nights, how true they are. Mocking and whispering, and abuse loud and low by turns, from all the black stones beside the road, when one living soul is toiling up the hill to get the golden water. Mocking and whispering, that he may look back, and become a black stone like themselves.

Turner looked not back, but he went on in such a temper as a strong man must be in, when he is forced to walk with his fingers in his ears. He retired into himself; he could look no longer for help, or counsel, or sympathy from any one; and the spirit of defiance in which he was forced to labor led him sometimes into violences, from which the slightest expression of sympathy would have saved him. The new energy that was upon him, and the utter isolation into which he was driven, were both alike dangerous, and many drawings of the time show the evil effects of both; some of them being hasty, wild, or experimental, and others little more than magnificent expressions of defiance of public opinion.

But all have this noble virtue—they are in everything his own: there are no more reminiscences of dead masters, no more trials of skill in the manner of Claude or Poussin; every faculty of his soul is fixed upon nature only, as he saw her, or as he remembered her.

I have spoken above of his gigantic memory: it is especially necessary to notice this, in order that we may understand the kind of grasp which a man of real imagination takes of all things that are once brought within his reach—grasp thenceforth not to be relaxed for ever. . . .

I am thus tedious in dwelling on Turner's powers of memory, because I wish it to be thoroughly seen how all his greatness, all his infinite luxuriance of invention, depends on his taking possession of everything that he sees,—on his grasping all, and losing hold of nothing,—on his forgetting himself, and forgetting nothing else. I wish it to be understood how every great man paints what he sees or did see, his greatness being indeed little else than his intense sense of fact. And thus Pre-Raphaelitism and Raphaelitism, and Turnerism, are all one and the same, so far as education can influence them. They are different in their choice, different in their faculties, but all the same in this, that Raphael himself, so far as he was great, and all who preceded or followed him who ever were great became so by painting the truths around them as they appeared to each man's own mind, not as he had been taught to see them, except by the God who made both him and them.

There is, however, one more characteristic of Turner's second period, on which I have still to dwell, especially with reference to what has been above advanced respecting the fallacy of overtoil; namely, the magnificent ease with which all is done when it is *successfully* done. For there are one or two drawings of this time which are *not* done easily. Turner had in these set himself to do a fine thing to exhibit his powers; in the common phrase, to excel himself; so sure as he does this, the work is a failure. The worst drawings that have ever come from his hands are some of this second period, on which he has spent much time and laborious thought; drawings filled with incident from one side to the other, with skies stippled into morbid blue, and warm lights set against them in violent contrast; one of Bamborough Castle, a large watercolor, may be named as an example. But the truly noble works are those in which, without effort, he has expressed his thoughts as they came, and forgotten himself; and in these the outpouring of invention is not less miraculous than the swiftness and obedience of the mighty hand that expresses it. Any one who examines the drawings may see the evidence of this facility, in the strange freshness and sharpness of every touch of color; but when the multitude of delicate touches, with which all the aerial tones are worked, is taken into consideration, it would still appear impossible that the drawing could have been completed with *ease*, unless we had direct evidence in the matter: fortunately, it is not wanting. There is a drawing in Mr. Fawkes's collection of a man-of-war taking in stores: it is of the usual size of those of the England series, about sixteen inches by eleven: it does not appear one of the most highly finished, but is still farther removed from slightness. The hull of a first-rate occupies nearly one-half of the picture on the right, her bows towards the spectator, seen in sharp perspective from stem to stern, with all her portholes, guns, anchors, and lower rigging elaborately detailed; there are two other ships of the line in the middle distance, drawn with equal precision; a noble breezy sea dancing against their broad bows, full of delicate drawing in its waves; a store-ship beneath the hull of the larger vessel, and several other boats, and a complicated cloudy sky. It might appear no small exertion of mind to draw the detail of all this shipping down to the smallest ropes, from memory, in the drawing-room of a mansion in the middle of Yorkshire, even if considerable time had been given for the effort. But Mr. Fawkes sat beside the painter from the first stroke to the last. Turner took a piece of blank paper one morning after breakfast, outlined his ships, finished the drawing in three hours, and went out to shoot.

Let this single fact be quietly meditated upon by our ordinary painters, and they will see the truth of what was above asserted,—that if a great thing can be done at all, it can be done easily; and let them not torment themselves with twisting of compositions this way and that, and repeating, and experimenting, and scene-shifting. If a man can compose at all, he can compose at once, or rather he must compose in spite of himself. And this is the reason of that silence which I have kept in most of my works, on the subject of Composition. Many critics, especially the architects, have found fault with me for not "teaching people how to arrange masses"; for not "attributing sufficient importance to composition." Alas! I attribute far more importance to it than they do;—so much importance, that I should just as soon think of sitting down to teach a man how to write a Divina Commedia, or King Lear, as how to "compose," in the true sense, a single building or picture. The marvellous stupidity of this age of lecturers is, that they do not see that what they call "principles of composition," are mere principles of common sense in everything, as well as in pictures and buildings;—A picture is to have a principal light? Yes; and so a dinner is to have a principal dish, and an oration a principal point, and an air of music a principal note, and every man a principal object. A picture is to have harmony of relations among its parts? Yes; and so is a speech well uttered, and an action well ordered, and a company well chosen, and a ragout well mixed. Composition! As if a man were not composing every moment of his life, well or ill, and would not do it instinctively in his picture as well as elsewhere, if he could. Composition of this lower or common kind is of exactly the same importance in a picture that it is in anything else,—no more. It is well that a man should say what he has to say in good order and sequence, but the main thing is to say it truly. And yet we go on preaching to our pupils as if to have a principal light was every thing, and so cover our academy walls with Shacabac feasts, wherein the courses are indeed well ordered, but the dishes empty.

It is not, however, only in invention that men overwork themselves, but in execution also; and here I have a word to say to the Pre-Raphaelites specially. They are working too hard. There is evidence in failing portions of their pictures, showing that they have wrought so long upon them that their very sight has failed for weariness, and that the hand refused any more to obey the heart.

And, besides this, there are certain qualities of drawing which they miss from over-carefulness. For, let them be assured, there is a great truth lurking in that common desire of men to see things done in what they call a "masterly," or "bold," or "broad," manner: a truth oppressed and abused, like almost every other in this world, but an eternal one nevertheless; and whatever mischief may have followed from men's looking for nothing else but this facility of execution, and supposing that a picture was assuredly all right if only it were done with broad dashes of the brush, still the truth remains the same:—that because it is not intended that men shall torment or weary themselves with any earthly labor, it is appointed that the noblest results should only be attainable by a certain ease and decision of manipulation. I only wish people understood this much of sculpture, as well as of painting, and could see that the finely finished statue is, in ninety-nine cases out of a hundred, a far more vulgar work than that which shows rough signs of the right hand laid to the workman's hammer: but at all events, in painting it is felt by all men, and justly felt. The freedom of the lines of nature can only be represented by a similar freedom in the hand that follows them; there are curves in the flow of the hair, and in the form of the features, and in the muscular outline of the body, which can in no wise be caught but by a sympathetic freedom in the stroke of the pencil. I do not care what example is taken, be it the most subtle and careful work of Leonardo himself, there will be found a play and power and ease in the outlines, which no *slow* effort could ever imitate. And if the Pre-Raphaelites do not understand how this kind of power, in its highest perfection, may be united with the most severe rendering of all other orders of truth, and especially of those with which they themselves have most sympathy, let them look at the drawings of John Lewis.

These then are the principal lessons which we have to learn from Turner, in his second or central period of labor. There is one more, however, to be received; and that is a warning; for towards the close of it, what with doing small conventional vignettes for publishers, making showy drawings from sketches taken by other people of places he had never seen, and touching up the bad engraving from his works submitted to him almost every day,—engravings utterly destitute of animation, and which had to be raised into a specious brilliancy by scratching them over with white, spotty lights, he gradually got inured to many conventionalities, and even falsities; and, having trusted for ten or twelve years almost entirely to his memory and invention, living I believe mostly in London, and receiving a new sensation only from the burning of the Houses of Parliament, he painted many pictures between 1830 and 1840 altogether unworthy of him. But he was not thus to close his career.

In the summer either of 1840 or 1841, he undertook another journey into Switzerland. It was then at least forty years since he had first seen the Alps; (the source of the Arveron, in Mr. Fawkes's collection, which could not have been painted till he had seen the thing itself, bears date 1800,) and the direction of his journey in 1840 marks his fond memory of that earliest one; for, if we look over the Swiss studies and drawings executed in his first period, we shall be struck with his fondness for the pass of the St. Gothard; the most elaborate drawing in the Farnley collection is one of the Lake of Lucerne from Fluelen; and, counting the Liber Studiorum subjects, there are, to my knowledge, six compositions taken at the same period from the pass of St. Gothard, and, probably, several others are in existence. The valleys of Sallenche, and Chamouni, and Lake of Geneva, are the only other Swiss scenes which seem to have made very profound impressions on him.

He returned in 1841 to Lucerne; walked up Mont Pilate on foot, crossed the St. Gothard, and returned by Lausanne and Geneva. He made a large number of colored sketches on this journey, and realised several of them on his return. The drawings thus produced are different from all that had preceded them, and are the first which belong definitely to what I shall henceforth call his Third period.

The perfect repose of his youth had returned to his mind, while the faculties of imagination and execution appeared in renewed strength; all conventionality being done away with by the force of the impression which he had received from the Alps, after his long separation from them. The drawings are marked by a peculiar largeness and simplicity of thought: most of them by deep serenity, passing into melancholy; all by a richness of color, such as he had never before conceived. They, and the works done in following years, bear the same relation to those of the rest of his life that the colors of sunset do to those of the day; and will be recognised, in a few years more, as the noblest landscapes ever yet conceived by human intellect.

Such has been the career of the greatest painter of this century. Many a century may pass away before there rises such another; but what greatness any among us may be capable of, will, at least, be attained by following in his path; by beginning in all quietness and hopefulness to use whatever powers we may possess to represent the things around us as we see and feel them; trusting to the close of life to give the perfect crown to the course of its labors, and knowing assuredly that the determination of the degree in which watchfulness is to be exalted into invention, rests with a higher will than our own. And, if not greatness, at least a certain good, is thus to be achieved; for though I have above spoken of the mission of the more humble artist, as if it were merely to be subservient to that of the antiquarian or the man of science, there is an ulterior aspect in which it is not subservient, but superior. Every archæologist, every natural philosopher, knows that there is a peculiar rigidity of mind brought on by long devotion to logical and analytical inquiries. Weak men, giving themselves to such studies, are utterly hardened by them, and become incapable of understanding anything nobler, or even of feeling the value of the results to which they lead. But even the best men are in a sort injured by them, and pay a definite price, as in most other matters, for definite advantages. They gain a peculiar strength, but lose in tenderness, elasticity, and impressibility. The man who has gone, hammer in hand, over the surface of a romantic country, feels no longer, in the mountain ranges he has so laboriously explored, the sublimity or mystery with which they were veiled when he first beheld them, and with which they are adorned in the mind of the passing traveller. In his more informed conception, they arrange themselves like a dissected model: where another man would be awe struck by the magnificence of the precipice, he sees nothing but the emergence of a fossiliferous rock, familiarised already to his imagination as extending in a shallow stratum, over a perhaps uninteresting district; where the unlearned spectator would be touched with strong emotion by the aspect of the snowy summits which rise in the distance, he sees only the culminating points of a metamorphic formation, with an uncomfortable web of fan-like fissures radiating, in his imagination, through their centres.

That in the grasp he has obtained of the inner relations of all these things to the universe, and to man, that in the views which have been opened to him of natural energies such as no human mind would have ventured to conceive, and of past states of being, each in some new way bearing witness to the unity of purpose and everlastingly consistent providence of the Maker of all things, he has received reward well worthy the sacrifice, I would not for an instant deny; but the sense of the loss is not less painful to him if his mind be rightly constituted; and it would be with infinite gratitude that he would regard the man, who, retaining in his delineation of natural scenery a fidelity to the fact of science so rigid as to make his work at once acceptable and credible to the most sternly critical intellect, should yet invest its features again with the sweet veil of their daily aspect; should make them dazzling with the splendor of wandering light, and involve them in the unsearchableness of stormy obscurity; should restore to the divided anatomy its visible vitality of operation, clothe naked crags with soft forests, enrich the mountain ruins with bright pastures, and lead the thoughts from the monotonous recurrence of the phenomena of the physical world, to the sweet interests and sorrows of human life and death.

John Henry Newman

KNOWLEDGE ITS OWN END

In 1851 Newman delivered a series of philosophical addresses for the new Catholic University of Dublin. In these essays, later published as *The Idea of A University,* his first aim was to mediate between forces within his own church, between the Catholic liberals who hoped to see the physical sciences dominate the new college and the conservative Catholics who wanted the position of theology to remain central. Newman's second aim was to refute his extremely vocal free-thinking Protestant contemporaries.

From *The Idea of a University* (1852).

Insisting upon the fundamental unity of all knowledge, Newman argued that theology should be treated as a science and balanced with the other parts of the curriculum. He observed also that the aim of liberal knowledge is to develop not the "good man" but the "gentleman"—the person equipped to enjoy and understand philosophy, beauty, and science, all with equal disinterestedness. When Newman postulated that the goal of such an education "is nothing more or less than intellectual excellence" (he equated the scholar's "beauty of intellect" with the artist's "beauty of feature and form," the poet's "beauty of mind," and the preacher's "beauty of grace"), he was supplying, though unwittingly, a rationale for the Cyrenaicism of Pater and the aesthetes: Pater's belief that "all beauty is in the long run only *fineness* of truth" parallels Newman; and Pater acknowledged an even closer affinity when he observed that "the perfect handling of a theory like the *Idea of A University*" provides "something of the uses of a religious 'retreat' " for the man of culture seeking to escape "vulgarity in the actual world."

I

I HAVE SAID that all branches of knowledge are connected together, because the subject-matter of knowledge is intimately united in itself, as being the acts and the work of the Creator. Hence it is that the Sciences, into which our knowledge may be said to be cast, have multiplied bearings one on another, and an internal sympathy, and admit, or rather demand, comparison and adjustment. They complete, correct, balance each other. This consideration, if well-founded, must be taken into account, not only as regards the attainment of truth, which is their common end, but as regards the influence which they exercise upon those whose education consists in the study of them. I have said already, that to give undue prominence to one is to be unjust to another; to neglect or supersede these is to divert those from their proper object. It is to unsettle the boundary lines between science and science, to disturb their action, to destroy the harmony which binds them together. Such a proceeding will have a corresponding effect when introduced into a place of education. There is no science but tells a different tale, when viewed as a portion of a whole, from what it is likely to suggest when taken by itself, without the safeguard, as I may call it, of others.

Let me make use of an illustration. In the combination of colours, very different effects are produced by a difference in their selection and juxtaposition; red, green, and white, change their shades, according to the contrast to which they are submitted. And, in like manner, the drift and meaning of a branch of knowledge varies with the company in which it is introduced to the student. If his reading is confined simply to one subject, however such division of labour may favour the advancement of a particular pursuit, a point into which I do not here enter, certainly it has a tendency to contract his mind. If it is incorporated with others, it depends on those others as to the kind of influence which it exerts upon him. Thus the Classics, which in England are the means of refining the taste, have in France subserved the spread of revolutionary and deistical doctrines. In Metaphysics, again, Butler's Analogy of Religion, which has had so much to do with the conversion to the Catholic faith of members of the University of Oxford, appeared to Pitt and others, who had received a different training, to operate only in the direction of infidelity. And so again, Watson, Bishop of Llandaff, as I think he tells us in the narrative of his life, felt the science of Mathematics to indispose the mind to religious belief, while others see in its investigations the best parallel, and thereby defence, of the Christian Mysteries. In like manner, I suppose, Arcesilas would not have handled logic as Aristotle, nor Aristotle have criticised poets as Plato; yet reasoning and poetry are subject to scientific rules.

It is a great point then to enlarge the range of studies which a University professes, even for the sake of the students; and, though they cannot pursue every subject which is open to them, they will be the gainers by living among those and under those who represent the whole circle. This I conceive to be the advantage of a seat of universal learning, considered as a place of education. An assemblage of learned men, zealous for their own sciences, and rivals of each other, are brought, by familiar intercourse and for the sake of intellectual peace, to adjust together the claims and relations of their respective subjects of investigation. They learn to respect, to consult, to aid each other. Thus is created a pure and clear atmosphere of thought, which the student also breathes, though in his own case he only pursues a few sciences out of the multitude. He profits by an intellectual tradition, which is independent of particular teachers, which guides him in his choice of subjects, and duly interprets for him those which he chooses. He apprehends the great outlines of knowledge, the principles on which it rests, the scale of its parts, its lights and its shades, its great points and its little, as he otherwise cannot apprehend them. Hence it is that his education is called "Liberal." A habit of mind is formed which lasts through life, of which the attributes are, freedom, equitableness, calmness, moderation, and wisdom; or what in a former Discourse I have ventured to call a philosophical habit. This then I would assign as the special fruit of the education furnished at a University, as contrasted with other places of teaching or modes of teaching. This is the main purpose of a University in its treatment of its students.

And now the question is asked me, What is the *use* of it? and my answer will constitute the main subject of the Discourses which are to follow.

II

Cautious and practical thinkers, I say, will ask of me, what, after all, is the gain of this Philosophy, of which I make such account, and from which I promise so much. Even supposing it to enable us to exercise the degree of trust exactly due to every science respectively, and to estimate precisely the value of every truth which is anywhere to be found, how are we better for this master view of things, which I have been extolling? Does it not reverse the principle of the division of labour? will practical objects be obtained better or worse by its cultivation? to what then does it lead? where does it end? what does it do? how does it profit? what does it promise? Particular sciences are respectively the basis of definite arts, which carry on to results tangible and beneficial the truths which are the subjects of the knowledge attained; what is the Art of this science of sciences? what is the fruit of such a Philosophy? what are we proposing to effect, what inducements do we hold out to the Catholic community, when we set about the enterprise of founding a University?

I am asked what is the end of University Education, and of the Liberal or Philosophical Knowledge which I conceive it to impart:

I answer, that what I have already said has been sufficient to show that it has a very tangible, real, and sufficient end, though the end cannot be divided from that knowledge itself. Knowledge is capable of being its own end. Such is the constitution of the human mind, that any kind of knowledge, if it be really such, is its own reward. And if this is true of all knowledge, it is true also of that special Philosophy, which I have made to consist in a comprehensive view of truth in all its branches, of the relations of science to science, of their mutual bearings, and their respective values. What the worth of such an acquirement is, compared with other objects which we seek,—wealth or power or honour or the conveniences and comforts of life, I do not profess here to discuss; but I would maintain, and mean to show, that it is an object, in its own nature so really and undeniably good, as to be the compensation of a great deal of thought in the compassing, and a great deal of trouble in the attaining.

Now, when I say that Knowledge is, not merely a means to something beyond it, or the preliminary of certain arts into which it naturally resolves, but an end sufficient to rest in and to pursue for its own sake, surely I am uttering no paradox, for I am stating what is both intelligible in itself, and has ever been the common judgment of philosophers and the ordinary feeling of mankind. I am saying what at least the public opinion of this day ought to be slow to deny, considering how much we have heard of late years, in opposition to Religion, of entertaining, curious, and various knowledge. I am but saying what whole volumes have been written to illustrate, viz., by a "selection from the records of Philosophy, Literature, and Art, in all ages and countries, of a body of examples, to show how the most unpropitious circumstances have been unable to conquer an ardent desire for the acquisition of knowledge." That further advantages accrue to us and redound to others by its possession, over and above what it is in itself, I am very far indeed from denying; but, independent of these, we are satisfying a direct need of our nature in its very acquisition; and, whereas our nature, unlike that of the inferior creation, does not at once reach its perfection, but depends, in order to it, on a number of external aids and appliances, Knowledge, as one of the principal of these, is valuable for what its very presence in us does for us after the manner of a habit, even though it be turned to no further account, nor subserve any direct end.

III

Hence it is that Cicero, in enumerating the various heads of mental excellence, lays down the pursuit of Knowledge for its own sake, as the first of them. "This pertains most of all to human nature," he says, "for we are all of us drawn to the pursuit of Knowledge; in which to excel we consider excellent, whereas to mistake, to err, to be ignorant, to be deceived, is both an evil and a disgrace." And he considers Knowledge the very first object to which we are attracted, after the supply of our physical wants. After the calls and duties of our animal existence, as they may be termed, as regards ourselves, our family, and our neighbours, follows, he tells us, "the search after truth. Accordingly, as soon as we escape from the pressure of necessary cares, forthwith we desire to see, to hear, and to learn; and consider the knowledge of what is hidden or is wonderful a condition of our happiness."

This passage, though it is but one of many similar passages in a multitude of authors, I take for the very reason that it is so familiarly known to us; and I wish you to observe, Gentlemen, how distinctly it separates the pursuit of Knowledge from those ulterior objects to which certainly it can be made to conduce, and which are, I suppose, solely contemplated by the persons who would ask of me the use of a University or Liberal Education. So far from dreaming of the cultivation of Knowledge directly and mainly in order to our physical comfort and enjoyment, for the sake of life and person, of health, of the conjugal and family union, of the social tie and civil security, the great Orator implies, that it is only after our physical and political needs are supplied, and when we are "free from necessary duties and cares," that we are in a condition for "desiring to see, to hear, and to learn." Nor does he contemplate in the least degree the reflex or subsequent action of Knowledge, when acquired, upon those material goods which we set out by securing before we seek it; on the contrary, he expressly denies its bearing upon social life altogether, strange as such a procedure is to those who live after the rise of the Baconian philosophy, and he cautions us against such a cultivation of it as will interfere with our duties to our fellow-creatures. "All these methods," he says, "are engaged in the investigation of truth; by the pursuit of which to be carried off from public occupations is a transgression of duty. For the praise of virtue lies altogether in action; yet intermissions often occur, and then we recur to such pursuits; not to say that the incessant activity of the mind is vigorous enough to carry us on in the pursuit of knowledge, even without any exertion of our own." The idea of benefiting society by means of "the pursuit of science and knowledge" did not enter at all into the motives which he would assign for their cultivation.

This was the ground of the opposition which the elder Cato made to the introduction of Greek Philosophy among his countrymen, when Carneades and his companions, on occasion of their embassy, were charming the Roman youth with their eloquent expositions of it. The fit representative of a practical people, Cato estimated every thing by what it produced; whereas the Pursuit of Knowledge promised nothing beyond Knowledge itself. He despised that refinement or enlargement of mind of which he had no experience.

IV

Things, which can bear to be cut off from every thing else and yet persist in living, must have life in themselves; pursuits, which issue in nothing, and still maintain their ground for ages, which are regarded as admirable, though they have not as yet proved themselves to be useful, must have their sufficient end in themselves, whatever it turn out to be. And we are brought to the same conclusion by considering the force of the epithet, by which the knowledge under consideration is popularly designated. It is common to speak of "*liberal* knowledge," of the "*liberal* arts and studies," and of a "*liberal* education," as the especial characteristic or property of a University and of a gentleman; what is really meant by the word? Now, first, in its grammatical sense it is opposed to *servile;* and by "servile work" is understood, as our catechisms inform us, bodily labour, mechanical employment, and the like, in which the mind has little or no part. Parallel to such servile works are those arts, if they deserve the name, of which the poet speaks, which owe their origin and their methods to hazard, not to skill; as, for instance, the practice and operations of an empiric. As far as this contrast may be considered as a guide into the meaning of the word, liberal education and liberal pursuits are exercises of mind, of reason, of reflection.

But we want something more for its explanation, for there are bodily exercises which are liberal, and mental exercises which are not so. For instance, in ancient times the practitioners in medicine were commonly slaves; yet it was an art as intellectual in its nature, in spite of the pretence, fraud, and quackery with which it might then, as now, be debased, as it was heavenly in its aim. And so in like manner, we contrast a liberal education with a commercial education or a professional; yet no one can deny that commerce and the professions afford scope for the highest and most diversified powers of mind. There is then a great variety of intellectual exercises, which are not technically called "liberal"; on the other hand, I say, there are exercises of the body which do receive that appellation. Such, for instance, was the palæstra, in ancient times; such the Olympic games, in which strength and dexterity of body as well as of mind gained the prize. In Xenophon we read of the young Persian nobility being taught to ride on horseback and to speak the truth; both being among the accomplishments of a gentleman. War, too, however rough a profession, has ever been accounted liberal, unless in cases when it becomes heroic, which would introduce us to another subject.

Now comparing these instances together, we shall have no difficulty in determining the principle of this apparent variation in the application of the term which I am examining. Manly games, or games of skill, or military prowess, though bodily, are, it seems, accounted liberal; on the other hand, what is merely professional, though highly intellectual, nay, though liberal in comparison of trade and manual labour, is not simply called liberal, and mercantile occupations are not liberal at all. Why this distinction? Because that alone is liberal knowledge, which stands on its own pretensions, which is independent of sequel, expects no complement, refuses to be *informed* (as it is called) by any end, or absorbed into any art, in order duly to present itself to our contemplation. The most ordinary pursuits have this specific character, if they are self-sufficient and complete; the highest lose it, when they minister to something beyond them. It is absurd to balance, in point of worth and importance, a treatise on reducing fractures with a game of cricket or a fox-chase; yet of the two the bodily exercise has that quality which we call "liberal," and the intellectual has it not. And so the learned professions altogether, considered merely as professions; although one of them be the most popularly beneficial, and another the most politically important, and the third the most intimately divine of all human pursuits, yet the very greatness of their end, the health of the body, or of the commonwealth, or of the soul, diminishes, not increases, their claim to the appellation "liberal," and that still more, if they are cut down to the strict exigencies of that end. If, for instance, Theology, instead of being cultivated as a contemplation, be limited to the purposes of the pulpit or be represented by the catechism, it loses,—not its usefulness, not its divine character, not its meritoriousness (rather it gains a claim upon these titles by such charitable condescension),—but it does lose the particular attribute which I am illustrating; just as a face worn by tears and fasting loses its beauty, or a labourer's hand loses its delicateness;—for Theology thus exercised is not simple knowledge, but rather is an art or a business making use of Theology. And thus it appears that even what is supernatural need not be liberal, nor need a hero be a gentleman, for the plain reason that one idea is not another idea. And in like manner the Baconian Philosophy, by using its physical sciences in the service of man, does thereby transfer them from the order of Liberal Pursuits to, I do not say the inferior, but the distinct class of the Useful. And, to take a different instance, hence again, as is evident, whenever personal gain is the motive, still more distinctive an effect has it upon the character of a given pursuit; thus racing, which was a liberal exercise in Greece, forfeits its rank in times like these, so far as it is made the occasion of gambling.

All that I have been now saying is summed up in a few characteristic words of the great Philosopher. "Of possessions," he says, "those rather are useful, which bear fruit; those *liberal, which tend to enjoyment.* By fruitful, I mean, which yield revenue; by enjoyable, where *nothing accrues of consequence beyond the using.*"

V

Do not suppose, that in thus appealing to the ancients, I am throwing back the world two thousand years, and fettering Philosophy with the reasonings of paganism. While the world lasts, will Aristotle's doctrine on these matters last, for he is the oracle of nature and of truth. While we are men, we cannot help, to a great extent, being Aristotelians, for the great Master does but analyze the thoughts, feelings, views, and opinions of human kind. He has told us the meaning of our own words and ideas, before we were born. In many subject-matters, to think correctly, is to think like Aristotle; and we are his disciples whether we will or no, though we may not know it. Now, as to the particular instance before us, the word "liberal" as applied to Knowledge and Education, expresses a specific idea, which ever has been, and ever will be, while the nature of man is the same, just as the idea of the Beautiful is specific, or of the Sublime, or of the Ridiculous, or of the Sordid. It is in the world now, it was in the world then; and, as in the case of the dogmas of faith, it is illustrated by a continuous historical tradition, and never was out of the world, from the time it came into it. There have indeed been differences of opinion from time to time, as to what pursuits and what arts came under that idea, but such differences are but an additional evidence of its reality. That idea must have a substance in it, which has maintained its ground amid these conflicts and changes, which has ever served as a standard to measure things withal, which has passed from mind to mind unchanged, when there was so much to colour, so much to influence any notion or thought whatever, which was not founded in our very nature. Were it a mere generalization, it would have varied with the subjects from which it was generalized; but though its subjects vary with the age, it varies not itself. The palæstra may seem a liberal exercise to Lycurgus, and illiberal to Seneca; coach-driving and prize-fighting may be recognized in Elis, and be condemned in England; music may be despicable in the eyes of certain moderns, and be in the highest place with Aristotle and Plato,—(and the case is the same in the particular application of the idea of Beauty, or of Goodness, or of Moral Virtue, there is a difference of tastes, a difference of judgments)—still these variations imply, instead of discrediting, the archetypal idea, which is but a previous hypothesis or condition, by means of which issue is joined between contending opinions, and without which there would be nothing to dispute about.

I consider, then, that I am chargeable with no paradox, when I speak of a Knowledge which is its own end, when I call it liberal knowledge, or a gentleman's knowledge, when I educate for it, and make it the scope of a University. And still less am I incurring such a charge, when I make this acquisition consist, not in Knowledge in a vague and ordinary sense, but in that Knowledge which I have especially called Philosophy or, in an extended sense of the word, Science; for whatever claims Knowledge has to be considered as a good, these it has in a higher degree when it is viewed not vaguely, not popularly, but precisely and transcendently as Philosophy. Knowledge, I say, is then especially liberal, or sufficient for itself, apart from every external and ulterior object, when and so far as it is philosophical, and this I proceed to show.

VI

Now bear with me, Gentlemen, if what I am about to say, has at first sight a fanciful appearance. Philosophy, then, or Science, is related to Knowledge in this way:—Knowledge is called by the name of Science or Philosophy, when it is acted upon, informed, or if I may use a strong figure, impregnated by Reason. Reason is the principle of that intrinsic fecundity of Knowledge, which to those who possess it, is its especial value, and which dispenses with the necessity of their looking abroad for any end to rest upon external to itself. Knowledge, indeed, when thus exalted into a scientific form, is also power; not only is it excellent in itself, but whatever such excellence may be, it is something more, it has a result beyond itself. Doubtless; but that is a further consideration, with which I am not concerned. I only say that, prior to its being a power, it is a good; that it is, not only an instrument, but an end. I know well it may resolve itself into an art, and terminate in a mechanical process, and in tangible fruit; but it also may fall back upon that Reason which informs it, and resolve itself into Philosophy. In one case it is called Useful Knowledge, in the other Liberal. The same person may cultivate it in both ways at once; but this again is a matter foreign to my subject; here I do but say that there are two ways of using Knowledge, and in matter of fact those who use it in one way are not likely to use it in the other, or at least in a very limited measure. You see, here are two methods of Education; the end of the one is to be philosophical, of the other to be mechanical; the one rises towards general ideas, the other is exhausted upon what is particular and external. Let me not be thought to deny the necessity, or to decry the benefit, of such attention to what is particular and practical, as belongs to the useful or mechanical arts; life could not go on without them; we owe our daily welfare to them; their exercise is the duty of the many, and we owe to the many a debt of gratitude for fulfilling that duty. I only say that Knowledge, in proportion as it tends more and more to be particular, ceases to be Knowledge. It is a question whether Knowledge can in any proper sense be predicated of the brute creation; without pretending to metaphysical exactness of phraseology, which would be unsuitable to an occasion like this, I say, it seems to me improper to call that passive sensation, or perception of things, which brutes seem to possess, by the name of Knowledge. When I speak of Knowledge, I mean something intellectual, something which grasps what it perceives through the senses; something which takes a view of things; which sees more than the senses convey; which reasons upon what it sees, and while it sees; which invests it with an idea. It expresses itself, not in a mere enunciation, but by an enthymeme: it is of the nature of science from the first, and in this consists its dignity. The principle of real dignity in Knowledge, its worth, its desirableness, considered irrespectively of its results, is this germ within it of a scientific or a philosophical process. This is how it comes to be an end in itself; this is why it admits of being called Liberal. Not to know the relative disposition of things is the state of slaves or children; to have mapped out the Universe is the boast, or at least the ambition, of Philosophy.

Moreover, such knowledge is not a mere extrinsic or accidental advantage, which is ours today and another's tomorrow, which may be got up from a book, and easily forgotten again, which we can command or communicate at our pleasure, which we can borrow for the occasion, carry about in our hand, and take into the market; it is an acquired illumination, it is a habit, a personal possession, and an inward endowment. And this is the reason, why it is more correct, as well as more usual, to speak of a University as a place of education, than of instruction, though, when knowledge is concerned, instruction would at first sight have seemed the more appropriate word. We are instructed, for instance, in manual exercises, in the fine and useful arts, in trades, and in ways of business; for these are methods, which have little or no effect upon the mind itself, are contained in rules committed to memory, to tradition, or to use, and bear upon an end external to themselves. But education is a higher word; it implies an action upon our mental nature, and the formation of a character; it is something individual and permanent, and is commonly spoken of in connexion with religion and virtue. When, then, we speak of the communication of Knowledge as being Education, we thereby really imply that that Knowledge is a state or condition of mind; and since cultivation of mind is surely worth seeking for its own sake, we are thus brought once more to the conclusion, which the word "Liberal" and the word "Philosophy" have already suggested, that there is a Knowledge, which is desirable, though nothing come of it, as being of itself a treasure, and a sufficient remuneration of years of labour.

VII

This, then, is the answer which I am prepared to give to the question with which I opened this Discourse. Before going on to speak of the object of the Church in taking up Philosophy, and the uses to which she puts it, I am prepared to maintain that Philosophy is its own end, and, as I conceive, I have now begun the proof of it. I am prepared to maintain that there is a knowledge worth possessing for what it is, and not merely for what it does; and what minutes remain to me today I shall devote to the removal of some portion of the indistinctness and confusion with which the subject may in some minds be surrounded.

It may be objected then, that, when we profess to seek Knowledge for some end or other beyond itself, whatever it be, we speak intelligibly; but that, whatever men may have said, however obstinately the idea may have kept its ground from age to age, still it is simply unmeaning to say that we seek Knowledge for its own sake, and for nothing else; for that it ever leads to something beyond itself, which therefore is its end, and the cause why it is desirable;—moreover, that this end is twofold, either of this world or of the next; that all knowledge is cultivated either for secular objects or for eternal; that if it is directed to secular objects, it is called Useful Knowledge, if to eternal, Religious or Christian

Knowledge;—in consequence, that if, as I have allowed, this Liberal Knowledge does not benefit the body or estate, it ought to benefit the soul; but if the fact be really so, that it is neither a physical or a secular good on the one hand, nor a moral good on the other, it cannot be a good at all, and is not worth the trouble which is necessary for its acquisition.

And then I may be reminded that the professors of this Liberal or Philosophical Knowledge have themselves, in every age, recognized this exposition of the matter, and have submitted to the issue in which it terminates; for they have ever been attempting to make men virtuous; or, if not, at least have assumed that refinement of mind was virtue and that they themselves were the virtuous portion of mankind. This they have professed on the one hand; and on the other, they have utterly failed in their professions, so as ever to make themselves a proverb among men, and a laughing-stock both to the grave and the dissipated portion of mankind, in consequence of them. Thus they have furnished against themselves both the ground and the means of their own exposure, without any trouble at all to any one else. In a word, from the time that Athens was the University of the world, what has Philosophy taught men, but to promise without practising, and to aspire without attaining? What has the deep and lofty thought of its disciples ended in but eloquent words? Nay, what has its teaching ever meditated, when it was boldest in its remedies for human ill, beyond charming us to sleep by its lessons, that we might feel nothing at all? like some melodious air, or rather like those strong and transporting perfumes, which at first spread their sweetness over every thing they touch, but in a little while do but offend in proportion as they once pleased us. Did Philosophy support Cicero under the disfavour of the fickle populace, or nerve Seneca to oppose an imperial tyrant? It abandoned Brutus, as he sorrowfully confessed, in his greatest need, and it forced Cato, as his panegyrist strangely boasts, into the false position of defying heaven. How few can be counted among its professors, who like Polemo, were thereby converted from a profligate course, or like Anaxagoras, thought the world well lost in exchange for its possession? The philosopher in Rasselas taught a superhuman doctrine, and then succumbed without an effort to a trial of human affection.

"He discoursed," we are told, "with great energy on the government of the passions. His look was venerable, his action graceful, his pronunciation clear, and his diction elegant. He showed, with great strength of sentiment and variety of illustration, that human nature is degraded and debased, when the lower faculties predominate over the higher. He communicated the various precepts given, from time to time, for the conquest of passion, and displayed the happiness of those who had obtained the important victory, after which man is no longer the slave of fear, nor the fool of hope . . . He enumerated many examples of heroes immoveable by pain or pleasure, who looked with indifference on those modes or accidents to which the vulgar give the names of good and evil."

Rasselas in a few days found the philosopher in a room half darkened, with his eyes misty, and his face pale. "Sir," said he, "you have come at a time when all human friendship is useless; what I suffer cannot be remedied, what I have lost cannot be supplied. My daughter, my only daughter, from whose tenderness I expected all the comforts of my age, died last night of a fever." "Sir," said the prince, "mortality is an event by which a wise man can never be surprised; we know that death is always near, and it should therefore always be expected." "Young man," answered the philosopher, "you speak like one who has never felt the pangs of separation." "Have you, then, forgot the precept," said Rasselas, "which you so powerfully enforced? . . . consider that external things are naturally variable, but truth and reason are always the same." "What comfort," said the mourner, "can truth and reason afford me? Of what effect are they now, but to tell me that my daughter will not be restored?"

VIII

Better, far better, to make no professions, you will say, than to cheat others with what we are not, and to scandalize them with what we are. The sensualist, or the man of the world, at any rate is not the victim of fine words, but pursues a reality and gains it. The Philosophy of Utility, you will say, Gentlemen, has at least done its work; and I grant it,—it aimed low, but it has fulfilled its aim. If that man of great intellect who has been its Prophet in the conduct of life played false to his own professions, he was not bound by his philosophy to be true to his friends or faithful in his trust. Moral virtue was not the line in which he undertook to instruct men; and though, as the poet calls him, he were the 'meanest' of mankind, he was so in what may be called his private capacity and without any prejudice to the theory of induction. He had a right to be so, if he chose, for any thing that the Idols of the den or the theatre had to say to the contrary. His mission was the increase of physical enjoyment and social comfort; and most wonderfully, most awfully has he fulfilled his conception and his design. Almost day by day have we fresh shoots, and buds, and blossoms, which are to ripen into fruit, on that magical tree of Knowledge which he planted, and to which none of us perhaps, except the very poor, but owes, if not his present life, at least his daily food, his health, and general well-being. He was the divinely provided minister of temporal benefits to all of us so great, that whatever I am forced to think of him as a man, I have not the heart, from mere gratitude, to speak of him severely. And, in spite of the tendencies of his philosophy, which are, as we see at this day, to depreciate, or to trample on Theology, he has himself, in his writings, gone out of his way, as if with a prophetic misgiving of those tendencies, to insist on it as the instrument of that beneficent Father, who, when He came on earth in visible form, took on Him first and most prominently the office of assuaging the bodily wounds of human nature. And truly, like the old mediciner in the tale, "he sat diligently at his work, and hummed, with cheerful countenance, a pious song"; and then in turn "went out singing into the meadows so gaily, that those who had seen him from afar might well have thought it was a youth gathering flowers for his beloved, instead of an old physician gathering healing herbs in the morning dew."

Alas, that men, in the action of life or in their heart of hearts, are not what they seem to be in their moments of excitement, or in their trances or intoxications of genius,—so good, so noble, so serene! Alas, that Bacon too in his own way should after all be but the fellow of those heathen philosophers who in their disadvantages had some excuse for their inconsistency, and who surprise us rather in what they did say than in what they did not do! Alas, that he too, like Socrates or Seneca, must be stripped of his holy-day coat, which looks so fair, and should be but a mockery amid his most majestic gravity of phrase; and, for all his vast abilities, should, in the littleness of his own moral being, but typify the intellectual narrowness of his school! However, granting all this, heroism after all was not his philosophy:—I cannot deny he has abundantly achieved what he proposed. His is simply a Method whereby bodily discomforts and temporal wants are to be most effectually removed from the greatest number; and already, before it has shown any signs of exhaustion, the gifts of nature, in their most artificial shapes and luxurious profusion and diversity, from all quarters of the earth, are, it is undeniable, by its means brought even to our doors, and we rejoice in them.

IX

Useful Knowledge then, I grant, has done its work; and Liberal Knowledge as certainly has not done its work,—that is, supposing, as the objectors assume, its direct end, like Religious Knowledge, is to make men better; but this I will not for an instant allow, and unless I allow it, those objectors have said nothing to the purpose. I admit, rather I maintain, what they have been urging, for I consider Knowledge to have its end in itself. For all its friends, or its enemies, may say, I insist upon it, that it is as real a mistake to burden it with virtue or religion as with the mechanical arts. Its direct business is not to steel the soul against temptation or to console it in affliction, any more than to set the loom in motion, or to direct the steam carriage; be it ever so much the means or the condition of both material and moral advancement, still, taken by and in itself, it as little mends our hearts as it improves our temporal circumstances. And if its eulogists claim for it such a power, they commit the very same kind of encroachment on a province not their own as the political economist who should maintain that his science educated him for casuistry or diplomacy. Knowledge is one thing, virtue is another; good sense is not conscience, refinement is not humility, nor is largeness and justness of view faith. Philosophy, however enlightened, however profound, gives no command over the passions, no influential motives, no vivifying principles. Liberal Education makes not the Christian, not the Catholic, but the gentleman. It is well to be a gentleman, it is well to have a cultivated intellect, a delicate taste, a candid, equitable, dispassionate mind, a noble and courteous bearing in the conduct of life,—these are the connatural qualities of a large knowledge; they are the objects of a University; I am advocating, I shall illustrate and insist upon them; but still, I repeat, they are no guarantee for sanctity or even for conscientiousness, they may attach to the man of the world, to the profligate, to the heartless,—pleasant, alas, and attractive as he shows when decked out in them. Taken by themselves, they do but seem to be what they are not; they look like virtue at a distance, but they are detected by close observers, and on the long run; and hence it is that they are popularly accused of pretence and hypocrisy, not, I repeat, from their own fault, but because their professors and their admirers persist in taking them for what they are not, and are officious in arrogating for them a praise to which they have no claim. Quarry the granite rock with razors, or moor the vessel with a thread of silk; then may you hope with such keen and delicate instruments as human knowledge and human reason to contend against those giants, the passion and the pride of man.

Surely we are not driven to theories of this kind, in order to vindicate the value and dignity of Liberal Knowledge. Surely the real grounds on which its pretensions rest are not so very subtle or abstruse, so very strange or improbable. Surely it is very intelligible to say, and that is what I say here, that Liberal Education, viewed in itself, is simply the cultivation of the intellect, as such, and its object is nothing more or less than intellectual excellence. Every thing has its own perfection, be it higher or lower in the scale of things; and the perfection of one is not the perfection of another. Things animate, inanimate, visible, invisible, all are good in their kind, and have a *best* of themselves, which is an object of pursuit. Why do you take such pains with your garden or your park? You see to your walks and turf and shrubberies; to your trees and drives; not as if you meant to make an orchard of the one, or corn or pasture land of the other, but because there is a special beauty in all that is goodly in wood, water, plain, and slope, brought all together by art into one shape, and grouped into one whole. Your cities are beautiful, your palaces, your public buildings, your territorial mansions, your churches; and their beauty leads to nothing beyond itself. There is a physical beauty and a moral: there is a beauty of person, there is a beauty of our moral being, which is natural virtue; and in like manner there is a beauty, there is a perfection, of the intellect. There is an ideal perfection in these various subject-matters, towards which individual instances are seen to rise, and which are the standards for all instances whatever. The Greek divinities and demigods, as the statuary has moulded them, with their symmetry of figure, and their high forehead and their regular features, are the perfection of physical beauty. The heroes, of whom history tells, Alexander, or Cæsar, or Scipio, or Saladin, are the representatives of that magnanimity or self-mastery which is the greatness of human nature. Christianity too has its heroes, and in the supernatural order, and we call them Saints. The artist puts before him beauty of feature and form; the poet, beauty of mind; the preacher, the beauty of grace: then intellect too, I repeat, has its beauty, and it has those who aim at it. To open the mind, to correct it, to refine it, to enable it to know, and to digest, master, rule, and use its knowledge, to give it power over its own faculties, application, flexibility, method, critical exactness, sagacity, resource, address, eloquent expression, is an object as intelligible (for here we are inquiring, not what the object of a Liberal Education is worth, nor what use the Church makes of it, but what it is in itself), I say, an object as intelligible as the cultivation of virtue, while, at the same time, it is absolutely distinct from it.

X

This indeed is but a temporal object, and a transitory possession; but so are other things in themselves which we make much of and pursue. The moralist will tell us that man, in all his functions, is but a flower which blossoms and fades, except so far as a higher principle breathes upon him, and makes him and what he is immortal. Body and mind are carried on into an eternal state of being by the gifts of Divine Munificence; but at first they do but fail in a failing world; and if the powers of intellect decay, the powers of the body have decayed before them, and, as an Hospital or an Almshouse, though its end be ephemeral, may be sanctified to the service of religion, so surely may a University, even were it nothing more than I have as yet described it. We attain to Heaven by using this world well, though it is to pass away; we perfect our nature, not by undoing it, but by adding to it what is more than nature, and directing it towards aims higher than its own.

David Ramsay Hay

"THE RELATION OF SYMMETRICAL TO PICTURESQUE BEAUTY"

DAVID RAMSAY HAY was the founder of the Aesthetic Society of Edinburgh and a prolific writer of treatises on Beauty. Convinced that it was possible to base an "aesthetic science" on "the great harmonic law of nature," he elaborated a "geometry" of beauty suitable for the arts of the human figure, architecture, Greek sculpture, color and design, and music. A program so ambitious would certainly justify founding a school to implement it, and Hay had the character and industry to attract enthusiasts; but his statements were derivative, especially of Ruskin, and his style lacked the high felicity and individual grace to keep his aesthetics alive. One of his more interesting enthusiasms was for the picturesque and the eclectic—a taste he shared with his times.

AS ALL BEAUTY is the result of harmony, it will be requisite here to remark, that harmony is not a simple quality, but, as Aristotle defines it, "the union of contrary principles having a ratio to each other." Harmony thus operates in the production of all that is beautiful in nature, whether in the combinations, in the motions, or in the affinities of the elements of matter.

The contrary principles to which Aristotle alludes, are those of uniformity and variety; for, according to the predominance of the one or the other of these principles, every kind of beauty is characterised. Hence the difference between symmetrical and picturesque beauty:—the first allied to the principle of uniformity,

FROM *The Science of Beauty, as Developed in Nature and Applied in Art* (1856).

in being based upon precise laws that may be taught so as to enable men of ordinary capacity to produce it in their works—the second allied to the principle of variety often to so great a degree that they yield an obedience to the precise principles of harmony so subtilely that they cannot be detected in its constitution, but are only felt in the response by which true genius acknowledges their presence. The generality of mankind may be capable of perceiving this latter kind of beauty, and of feeling its effects upon the mind, but men of genius, only, can impart it to works of art, whether addressed to the eye or the ear. Throughout the sounds, forms, and colours of nature, these two kinds of beauty are found not only in distinct developments, but in every degree of amalgamation. We find in the songs of some birds, such as those of the chaffinch, thrush, &c., a rhythmical division, resembling in some measure the symmetrically precise arrangements of parts which characterises all artistic musical composition; while in the songs of other birds, and in the other numerous melodies with which nature charms and soothes the mind, there is no distinct regularity in the division of their parts. In the forms of nature, too, we find amongst the innumerable flowers with which the surface of the earth is so profusely decorated, an almost endless variety of systematic arrangements of beautiful figures, often so perfectly symmetrical in their combination, that the most careful application of the angleometer could scarcely detect the slightest deviation from geometrical precision; while, amongst the masses of foliage by which the forms of many trees are divided and subdivided into parts, as also amongst the hills and valleys, the mountains and ravines, which divide the earth's surface, we find in every possible variety of aspect the beauty produced by that irregular species of symmetry which characterises the picturesque.

In like manner, we find in wild as well as cultivated flowers the most symmetrical distributions of colours accompanying an equally precise species of harmony in their various kinds of contrasts, often as mathematically regular as the geometric diagrams by which writers upon colour sometimes illustrate their works; while in the general colouring of the picturesque beauties of nature, there is an endless variety in its distributions, its blendings, and its modifications. In the forms and colouring of animals, too, the same endless variety of regular and irregular symmetry is to be found. But the highest degree of beauty in nature is the result of an equal balance of uniformity with variety. Of this the human figure is an example; because, when it is of those proportions universally acknowledged to be the most perfect, its uniformity bears to its variety an apparently equal ratio. The harmony of combination in the normal proportions of its parts, and the beautifully simple harmony of succession in the normal melody of its softly undulating outline, are the perfection of symmetrical beauty, while the innumerable changes upon the contour which arise from the actions and attitudes occasioned by the various emotions of the mind, are calculated to produce every species of picturesque beauty, from the softest and most pleasing to the grandest and most sublime.

Amongst the purely picturesque objects of inanimate nature, I may, as in a former work, instance an ancient oak tree, for its beauty is enhanced by want of apparent symmetry. Thus, the more fantastically crooked its branches, and the greater the dissimilarity and variety it exhibits in its masses of foliage, the more beautiful it appears to the artist and the amateur; and, as in the human figure, any attempt to produce variety in the proportions of its lateral halves would be destructive of its symmetrical beauty, so in the oak tree any attempt to produce palpable similarity between any of its opposite sides would equally deteriorate its picturesque beauty. But picturesque beauty is not the result of the total absence of symmetry; for, as none of the irregularly constructed music of nature could be pleasing to the ear unless there existed in the arrangement of its notes an obedience, however subtle, to the great harmonic law of Nature, so neither could any object be picturesquely beautiful, unless the arrangement of its parts yields, although it may be obscurely, an obedience to the same law.

However symmetrically beautiful any architectural structure may be, when in a complete and perfect state, it must, as it proceeds towards ruin, blend the picturesque with the symmetrical; but the type of its beauty will continue to be the latter, so long as a sufficient portion of it remains to convey an idea of its original perfection. It is the same with the human form and countenance; for age does not destroy their original beauty, but in both only lessens that which is symmetrical, while it increases that which is picturesque.

In short, as a variety of simultaneously produced sounds, which do not relate to each other agreeably to this law, can only convey to the mind a feeling of mere noise; so a variety of forms or colours simultaneously exposed to the eye under similar circumstances, can only convey to the mind a feeling of chaotic confusion, or what may be termed *visible* discord. As, therefore, the two principles of uniformity and variety, or similarity and dissimilarity, are in operation in every harmonious combination of the elements of sound, of form, and of colour, we must first have recourse to numbers in the abstract before we can form a proper basis for a universal science of beauty.

John Stuart Mill

THOUGHTS ON POETRY AND ITS VARIETIES

G. K. Chesterton in a somewhat bemused moment called John Stuart Mill "the final flower" of nineteenth-century utilitarianism. Mill was, said Chesterton, "fresh and delicate and pure," with "all that silver sensitiveness that can be seen in his fine portrait by Watts." In his peculiar way, Chesterton clearly saw Mill's dual nature and the turmoil it had caused: the intense rationalism Mill had acquired from his father and Bentham warred with an equally demanding urge for emotional expression (Mill seems to have had a poet's feeling), and led to a nervous breakdown in 1826. The discovery of Coleridge, Wordsworth, and Carlyle, who helped to feed the cravings of his stifled imagination, was his salvation. Carlyle's work, he said, helped him "not as philosophy to instruct, but as poetry to animate." Although Mill never afterward, in his words, "turned recreant to intellectual culture, or ceased to consider the power and practice of analysis as an essential condition both of individual and of social improvement," he tried to maintain "a due balance," making the cultivation of feeling "one of the cardinal points" in his philosophy. His youthful "Thoughts on

1833 (revised, 1859).

Poetry and Its Varieties," first published in 1833 and revised and expanded in 1859, is a fine, though erratic, examination of the poetic process. At the outset, "poetry" includes nearly any state of enlightened feeling, whether expressed in written form or not, is then narrowed to the several arts, and is finally restricted to its traditional boundaries. The later incisive definitions not only show evidence of a Coleridgean aesthetics, but also are based on an associational psychology derived from David Hume, David Hartley, and the Scotch philosopher, Thomas Brown. Mill's theory of the relation between culture and poetic genius, particularly as it affected the Romantics, interestingly foreshadows Matthew Arnold's similar, but better-known, theory presented nearly thirty years later in "The Function of Criticism."

I

It has often been asked, What is Poetry? And many and various are the answers which have been returned. The vulgarest of all—one with which no person possessed of the faculties to which Poetry addresses itself can ever have been satisfied—is that which confounds poetry with metrical composition: yet to this wretched mockery of a definition, many have been led back, by the failure of all their attempts to find any other that would distinguish what they have been accustomed to call poetry, from much which they have known only under other names.

That, however, the word 'poetry' imports something quite peculiar in its nature, something which may exist in what is called prose as well as in verse, something which does not even require the instrument of words, but can speak through the other audible symbols called musical sounds, and even through the visible ones which are the language of sculpture, painting, and architecture; all this, we believe, is and must be felt, though perhaps indistinctly, by all upon whom poetry in any of its shapes produces any impression beyond that of tickling the ear. The distinction between poetry and what is not poetry, whether explained or not, is felt to be fundamental: and where every one feels a difference, a difference there must be. All other appearances may be fallacious, but the appearance of a difference is a real difference. Appearances, too, like other things, must have a cause, and that which can cause anything, even an illusion, must be a reality. And hence, while a half-philosophy disdains the classifications and distinctions indicated by popular language, philosophy carried to its highest point frames new ones, but rarely sets aside the old, content with correcting and regularizing them. It cuts fresh channels for thought, but does not fill up such as it finds ready-made; it traces, on the contrary, more deeply, broadly, and distinctly, those into which the current has spontaneously flowed.

Let us then attempt, in the way of modest inquiry, not to coerce and confine nature within the bounds of an arbitrary definition, but rather to find the boundaries which she herself has set, and erect a barrier round them; not calling mankind to account for having misapplied the word 'poetry', but attempting to clear up the conception which they already attach to it, and to bring forward as a distinct principle that which, as a vague feeling, has really guided them in their employment of the term.

The object of poetry is confessedly to act upon the emotions; and therein is poetry sufficiently distinguished from what Wordsworth affirms to be its logical opposite, namely, not prose, but matter of fact or science. The one addresses itself to the belief, the other to the feelings. The one does its work by convincing or persuading, the other by moving. The one acts by presenting a proposition to the understanding, the other by offering interesting objects of contemplation to the sensibilities.

This, however, leaves us very far from a definition of poetry. This distinguishes it from one thing, but we are bound to distinguish it from everything. To bring thoughts or images before the mind for the purpose of acting upon the emotions, does not belong to poetry alone. It is equally the province (for example) of the novelist: and yet the faculty of the poet and that of the novelist are as distinct as any other two faculties; as the faculties of the novelist and of the orator, or of the poet and the metaphysician. The two characters may be united, as characters the most disparate may; but they have no natural connexion.

Many of the greatest poems are in the form of fictitious narratives, and in almost all good serious fictions there is true poetry. But there is a radical distinction between the interest felt in a story as such, and the interest excited by poetry; for the one is derived from incident, the other from the representation of feeling. In one, the source of the emotion excited is the exhibition of a state or states of human sensibility; in the other, of a series of states of mere outward circumstances. Now, all minds are capable of being affected more or less by representations of the latter kind, and all, or almost all, by those of the former; yet the two sources of interest correspond to two distinct, and (as respects their greater development) mutally exclusive, characters of mind.

At what age is the passion for a story, for almost any kind of story, merely as a story, the most intense? In childhood. But that also is the age at which poetry, even of the simplest description, is least relished and least understood; because the feelings with which it is especially conversant are yet undeveloped, and not having been even in the slightest degree experienced, cannot be sympathized with. In what stage of the progress of society, again, is story-telling most valued, and the story-teller in greatest request and honour?—In a rude state like that of the Tartars and Arabs at this day, and of almost all nations in the earliest ages. But in this state of society there is little poetry except ballads, which are mostly narrative, that is, essentially stories, and derive their principal interest from the incidents. Considered as poetry, they are of the lowest and most elementary kind: the feelings depicted, or rather indicated, are the simplest our nature has; such joys and griefs as the immediate pressure of some outward event excites in rude minds, which live wholly immersed in outward things, and have never, either from choice or a force they could not resist, turned themselves to the contemplation of the world within. Passing now from childhood, and from the childhood of society, to the grown-up men and women of this most grown-up and unchildlike age—the minds and hearts of greatest depths and elevation are commonly those which take greatest delight in poetry; the shallowest and emptiest, on the contrary, are, at all events, not those least addicted to novel-reading. This accords, too, with all analogous experience of human nature. The sort of persons whom not merely in books but in their lives, we find perpetually engaged in hunting for excitement from without, are invariably those who do not possess, either in the vigour of their intellectual powers or in the depth of their sensibilities, that which would enable them to find ample excitement nearer home. The most idle and frivolous persons take a natural delight in fictitious narrative; the excitement it affords is of the kind which comes from without. Such persons are rarely lovers of poetry, though they may fancy themselves so, because they relish novels in verse. But poetry, which is the delineation of the deeper and more secret workings of human emotion, is interesting only to those to whom it recalls what they have felt, or whose imagination it stirs up to conceive what they could feel, or what they might have been able to feel, had their outward circumstances been different.

Poetry, when it is really such, is truth; and fiction also, if it is good for anything, is truth: but they are different truths. The truth of poetry is to paint the human soul truly: the truth of fiction is to give a true picture of life. The two kinds of knowledge are different, and come by different ways, come mostly to different persons. Great poets are often proverbially ignorant of life. What they know has come by observation of themselves; they have found within them one highly delicate and sensitive specimen of human nature, on which the laws of emotion are written in large characters, such as can be read off without much study. Other knowledge of mankind, such as comes to men of the world by outward experience, is not indispensable to them as poets: but to the novelist such knowledge is all in all; he has to describe outward things, not the inward man; actions and events, not feelings; and it will not do for him to be numbered among those who, as Madame Roland said of Brissot, know man but not *men*.

All this is no bar to the possibility of combining both elements, poetry and narrative or incident, in the same work, and calling it either a novel or a poem; but so may red and white combine on the same human features, or on the same canvas. There is one order of composition which requires the union of poetry and incident, each in its highest kind—the dramatic. Even there the two elements are perfectly distinguishable, and may exist of unequal quality, and in the most various proportion. The incidents of a dramatic poem may be scanty and ineffective, though the delineation of passion and character may be of the highest order; as in Goethe's admirable *Torquato Tasso;* or again, the story as a mere story may be well got up for effect, as is the case with some of the most trashy productions of the Minerva press: it may even be, what those are not, a coherent and probable series of events, though there be scarcely a feeling exhibited which is not represented falsely, or in a manner absolutely commonplace. The combination of the two excellences is what renders Shakespeare so generally acceptable, each sort of readers finding in him what is suitable to their facilities. To the many he is great as a story-teller, to the few as a poet.

In limiting poetry to the delineation of states of feeling, and denying the name where nothing is delineated but outward objects, we may be thought to have done what we promised to avoid—to have not found, but made a definition, in opposition to the usage of language, since it is established by common consent that there is a poetry called descriptive. We deny the charge. Description is not poetry because there is descriptive poetry, no more than science is poetry because there is such a thing as a didactic poem. But an object which admits of being described, or a truth which may fill a place in a scientific treatise, may also furnish an occasion for the generation of poetry, which we thereupon choose to call descriptive or didactic. The poetry is not in the object itself, nor in the scientific truth itself, but in the state of mind in which the one and the other may be contemplated. The mere delineation of the dimensions and colours of external objects is not poetry, no more than a geometrical ground-plan of St. Peter's or Westminster Abbey is painting. Descriptive poetry consists, no doubt, in description, but in description of things as they appear, not as they are; and it paints them not in their bare and natural lineaments, but seen through the medium and arrayed in the colours of the imagination set in action by the feelings. If a poet describes a lion, he does not describe him as a naturalist would, nor even as a traveller would, who was intent upon stating the truth, the whole truth, and nothing but the truth. He describes him by imagery, that is, by suggesting the most striking likenesses and contrasts which might occur to a mind contemplating the lion, in the state of awe, wonder, or terror, which the spectacle naturally excites, or is, on the occasion, supposed to excite. Now this is describing the lion professedly, but the state of excitement of the spectator really. The lion may be described falsely or with exaggeration, and the poetry be all the better; but if the human emotion be not painted with scrupulous truth, the poetry is bad poetry, i. e., is not poetry at all, but a failure.

Thus far our progress towards a clear view of the essentials of poetry has brought us very close to the last two attempts at a definition of poetry which we happen to have seen in print, both of them by poets and men of genius. The one is by Ebenezer Elliott, the author of *Corn-Law Rhymes,* and other poems of still greater merit. 'Poetry', says he, 'is impassioned truth.' The other is by a writer in *Blackwood's Magazine*, and comes, we think, still nearer the mark. He defines poetry, 'man's thoughts tinged by his feelings'. There is in either definition a near approximation to what we are in search of. Every truth which a human being can enunciate, every thought, even every outward impression, which can enter into his consciousness, may become poetry when shown through any impassioned medium, when invested with the colouring of joy, or grief, or pity, or affection, or admiration, or reverence, or awe, or even hatred or terror: and, unless so coloured, nothing, be it as interesting as it may, is poetry. But both these definitions fail to discriminate between poetry and eloquence. Eloquence, as well as poetry, is impassioned truth; eloquence, as well as poetry, is thought coloured by the feelings. Yet common apprehension and philosophic criticism alike recognize a distinction between the two: there is much that every one would call eloquence, which no one would think of classing as poetry. A question will sometimes arise, whether some particular author is a poet; and those who maintain the negative commonly allow that, though not a poet, he is a highly eloquent writer. The distinction between poetry and eloquence appears to us to be equally fundamental with the distinction between poetry and narrative, or between poetry and description, while it is still farther from having been satisfactorily cleared up than either of the others.

Poetry and eloquence are both alike the expression or utterance of feeling. But if we may be excused the antithesis, we should say that eloquence is *heard*, poetry is *over*heard. Eloquence supposes an audience; the peculiarity of poetry appears to us to lie in the poet's utter unconsciousness of a listener. Poetry is feeling confessing itself to itself, in moments of solitude, and embodying itself in symbols which are the nearest possible representations of the feeling in the exact shape in which it exists in the poet's mind. Eloquence is feeling pouring itself out to other minds, courting their sympathy, or endeavouring to influence their belief or move them to passion or to action.

All poetry is of the nature of soliloquy. It may be said that poetry which is printed on hot-pressed paper and sold at a bookseller's shop, is a soliloquy in full dress, and on the stage. It is so; but there is nothing absurd in the idea of such a mode of soliloquizing. What we have said to ourselves, we may tell to others afterwards; what we have said or done in solitude, we may voluntarily reproduce when we know that other eyes are upon us. But no trace of consciousness that any eyes are upon us must be visible in the work itself. The actor knows that there is an audience present; but if he act as though he knew it, he acts ill. A poet may write poetry not only with the intention of printing it, but for the express purpose of being paid for it; that it should *be* poetry, being written under such influences, is less probable; not, however, impossible; but no otherwise possible than if he can succeed in excluding from his work every vestige of such lookings-forth into the outward and everyday world, and can express his emotions exactly as he has felt them in solitude, or as he is conscious that he should feel them though they were to remain for ever unuttered, or (at the lowest) as he knows that others feel them in similar circumstances of solitude. But when he turns round and addresses himself to another person; when the act of utterance is not itself the end, but a means to an end,—viz. by the feelings he himself expresses, to work upon the feelings, or upon the belief, or the will, of another,—when the expression of his emotions, or of his thoughts tinged by his emotions, is tinged also by that purpose, by that desire of making an impression upon another mind, then it ceases to be poetry, and becomes eloquence.

Poetry, accordingly, is the natural fruit of solitude and meditation; eloquence, of intercourse with the world. The persons who have most feeling of their own, if intellectual culture has given them a language in which to express it, have the highest faculty of poetry; those who best understand the feelings of others, are the most eloquent. The persons, and the nations, who commonly excel in poetry, are those whose character and tastes render them least dependent upon the applause, or sympathy, or concurrence of the world in general. Those to whom that applause, that sympathy, that concurrence are most necessary, generally excel most in eloquence. And hence, perhaps, the French, who are the least poetical of all great and intellectual nations, are among the most eloquent: the French, also, being the most sociable, the vainest, and the least self-dependent.

If the above be, as we believe, the true theory of the distinction commonly admitted between eloquence and poetry; or even though it be not so, yet if, as we cannot doubt, the distinction above stated be a real bona fide distinction, it will be found to hold, not merely in the language of words, but in all other language, and to intersect the whole domain of art.

Take, for example, music: we shall find in that art, so peculiarly the expression of passion, two perfectly distinct styles; one of which may be called the poetry, the other the oratory of music. This difference, being seized, would put an end to much musical sectarianism. There has been much contention whether the music of the modern Italian school, that of Rossini and his successors, be impassioned or not. Without doubt, the passion it expresses is not the musing, meditative tenderness, or pathos, or grief of Mozart or Beethoven. Yet it is passion, but garrulous passion—the passion which pours itself into other ears; and therein the better calculated for dramatic effect, having a natural adaptation for dialogue. Mozart also is great in musical oratory; but his most touching compositions are in the opposite style—that of soliloquy. Who can imagine 'Dove sono' *heard?* We imagine it *over*heard.

Purely pathetic music commonly partakes of soliloquy. The soul is absorbed in its distress, and though there may be bystanders, it is not thinking of them. When the mind is looking within, and not without, its state does not often or rapidly vary; and hence the even, uninterrupted flow, approaching almost to monotony, which a good reader, or a good singer, will give to words or music of a pensive or melancholy cast. But grief taking the form of a prayer, or of a complaint, becomes oratorical; no longer low, and even, and subdued, it assumes a more emphatic rhythm, a more rapidly returning accent; instead of a few slow equal notes, following one after another at regular intervals, it crowds note upon note, and often assumes a hurry and bustle like joy. Those who are familiar with some of the best of Rossini's serious compositions, such as the air 'Tu che i miseri conforti', in the opera of *Tancredi*, or the duet 'Ebben per mia memoria', in *La Gazza Ladra*, will at once understand and feel our meaning. Both are highly tragic and passionate; the passion of both is that of oratory, not poetry. The like may be said of that most moving invocation in Beethoven's *Fidelio*—

Komm, Hoffnung, lass letzte Stern
Der Müde nicht erbleichen;

in which Madame Schröder Devrient exhibited such consummate powers of pathetic expression. How different from Winter's beautiful 'Paga fui', the very soul of melancholy exhaling itself in solitude; fuller of meaning, and, therefore, more profoundly poetical than the words for which it was composed—for it seems to express not simple melancholy, but the melancholy of remorse.

If, from vocal music, we now pass to instrumental, we may have a specimen of musical oratory in any fine military symphony or march: while the poetry of music seems to have attained its consummation in Beethoven's Overture to Egmont, so wonderful in its mixed expression of grandeur and melancholy.

In the arts which speak to the eye, the same distinctions will be found to hold, not only between poetry and oratory, but between poetry, oratory, narrative, and simple imitation or description.

Pure description is exemplified in a mere portrait or a mere landscape—productions of art, it is true, but of the mechanical rather than of the fine arts, being works of simple imitation, not creation. We say, a mere portrait, or a mere landscape, because it is possible for a portrait or a landscape, without ceasing to be such, to be also a picture; like Turner's landscapes, and the great portraits by Titian or Vandyke.

Whatever in painting or sculpture expresses human feeling—or character, which is only a certain state of feeling grown habitual—may be called, according to circumstances, the poetry, or the eloquence, of the painter's or the sculptor's art: the poetry, if the feeling declares itself by such signs as escape from us when we are unconscious of being seen; the oratory, if the signs are those we use for the purpose of voluntary communication.

The narrative style answers to what is called historical painting, which it is the fashion among connoisseurs to treat as the climax of the pictorial art. That it is the most difficult branch of the art we do not doubt, because, in its perfection, it includes the perfection of all the other branches: as in like manner an epic poem, though in so far as it is epic (i. e. narrative) it is not poetry at all, is yet esteemed the greatest effort of poetic genius, because there is no kind whatever of poetry which may not appropriately find a place in it. But an historical picture as such, that is, as the representation of an incident, must necessarily, as it seems to us, be poor and ineffective. The narrative powers of painting are extremely limited.

Scarcely any picture, scarcely even any series of pictures, tells its own story without the aid of an interpreter. But it is the single figures which, to us, are the great charm even of an historical picture. It is in these that the power of the art is really seen. In the attempt to narrate, visible and permanent signs are too far behind the fugitive audible ones, which follow so fast one after another, while the faces and figures in a narrative picture, even though they be Titian's, stand still. Who would not prefer one Virgin and Child of Raphael, to all the pictures which Rubens, with his fat, frouzy Dutch Venuses, ever painted? Though Rubens, besides excelling almost every one in his mastery over the mechanical parts of his art, often shows real genius in *grouping* his figures, the peculiar problem of historical painting. But then, who, except a mere student of drawing and colouring, ever cared to look twice at any of the figures themselves? The power of painting lies in poetry, of which Rubens had not the slightest tincture—not in narrative, wherein he might have excelled.

The single figures, however, in an historical picture, are rather the eloquence of painting than the poetry: they mostly (unless they are quite out of place in the picture) express the feelings of one person as modified by the presence of others. Accordingly the minds whose bent leads them rather to eloquence than to poetry, rush to historical painting. The French painters, for instance, seldom attempt, because they could make nothing of, single heads, like those glorious ones of the Italian masters, with which they might feed themselves day after day in their own Louvre. They must all be historical; and they are, almost to a man, attitudinizers. If we wished to give any young artist the most impressive warning our imagination could devise against that kind of vice in the pictorial, which corresponds to rant in the histronic art, we would advise him to walk once up and once down the gallery of the Luxembourg. Every figure in French painting or statuary seems to be showing itself off before spectators; they are not poetical, but in the worst style of corrupted eloquence.

II

Nascitur Poeta is a maxim of classical antiquity, which has passed to these latter days with less questioning than most of the doctrines of that early age. When it originated, the human faculties were occupied, fortunately for posterity, less in examining how the works of genius are created, than in creating them: and the adage, probably, had no higher source than the tendency common among mankind to consider all power which is not visibly the effect of practice, all skill which is not capable of being reduced to mechanical rules, as the result of a peculiar gift. Yet this aphorism, born in the infancy of psychology, will perhaps be found, now when that science is in its adolescence, to be as true as an epigram ever is, that is, to contain some truth: truth, however, which has been so compressed and bent out of shape, in order to tie it up into so small a knot of only two words that it requires an almost infinite amount of unrolling and laying straight, before it will resume its just proportions.

We are not now intending to remark upon the grosser misapplications of this ancient maxim, which have engendered so many races of poetasters. The days are gone by when every raw youth whose borrowed phantasies have set themselves to a borrowed tune, mistaking, as Coleridge says, an ardent desire of poetic reputation for poetic genius, while unable to disguise from himself that he had taken no means whereby he might *become* a poet, could fancy himself a born one. Those who would reap without sowing, and gain the victory without fighting the battle, are ambitious now of another sort of distinction, and are born novelists, or public speakers, not poets. And the wiser thinkers understand and acknowledge that poetic excellence is subject to the same necessary conditions with any other mental endowment; and that to no one of the spiritual benefactors of mankind is a higher or a more assiduous intellectual culture needful than to the poet. It is true, he possesses this advantage over others who use the 'instrument of words', that, of the truths which he utters, a larger proportion are derived from personal consciousness, and a smaller from philosophic investigation. But the power itself of discriminating between what really is consciousness, and what is only a process of inference completed in a single instant—and the capacity of distinguishing whether that of which the mind is conscious be an eternal truth, or but a dream—are among the last results of the most matured and perfect intellect. Not to mention that the poet, no more than any other person who writes, confines himself altogether to intuitive truths, nor has any means of communicating even these but by words, every one of which derives all its power of conveying a meaning, from a whole host of acquired notions, and facts learnt by study and experience.

Nevertheless, it seems undeniable in point of fact, and consistent with the principles of a sound metaphysics, that there are poetic *natures.* There is a mental and physical constitution or temperament, peculiarly fitted for poetry. This temperament will not of itself make a poet, no more than the soil will the fruit; and as good fruit may be raised by culture from indifferent soils, so may good poetry from naturally unpoetical minds. But the poetry of one who is a poet by nature, will be clearly and broadly distinguishable from the poetry of mere culture. It may not be truer; it may not be more useful; but it will be different: fewer will appreciate it, even though many should affect to do so; but in those few it will find a keener sympathy, and will yield them a deeper enjoyment.

One may write genuine poetry, and not be a poet; for whosoever writes out truly any human feeling, writes poetry. All persons, even the most unimaginative, in moments of strong emotion, speak poetry; and hence the drama is poetry, which else were always prose, except when a poet is one of the characters. What *is* poetry, but the thoughts and words in which emotion spontaneously embodies itself? As there are few who are not, at least for some moments and in some situations, capable of some strong feeling, poetry is natural to most persons at some period of their lives. And any one whose feelings are genuine, though but of the average strength,—if he be not diverted by uncongenial thoughts or occupations from the indulgence of them, and if he acquire by culture, as all persons may, the faculty of delineating them correctly,—has it in his power to be a poet, so far as a life passed in writing unquestionable poetry may be considered to confer that title. But *ought* it to do so? Yes, perhaps, in a collection of 'British Poets'. But 'poet' is the name also of a variety of man, not solely of the author of a particular variety of book: now, to have written whole volumes of real poetry is possible to almost all kinds of characters, and implies no greater peculiarity of mental construction, than to be the author of a history, or a novel.

Whom, then, shall we call poets? Those who are so constituted, that emotions are the links of association by which their ideas, both sensuous and spiritual, are connected together. This constitution belongs (within certain limits) to all in whom poetry is a pervading principle. In all others, poetry is something extraneous and superinduced: something out of themselves, foreign to the habitual course of their everyday lives and characters; a world to which they may make occasional visits, but where they are sojourners, not dwellers, and which, when out of it, or even when in it, they think of, peradventure, but as a phantom-world, a place of *ignes fatui* and spectral illusions. Those only who have the peculiarity of association which we have mentioned, and which is a natural though not a universal consquence of intense sensibility, instead of seeming not themselves when they are uttering poetry, scarcely seem themselves when uttering anything to which poetry is foreign. Whatever be the thing which they are contemplating, if it be capable of connecting itself with their emotions, the aspect under which it first and most naturally paints itself to them, is its poetic aspect. The poet of culture sees his object in prose, and describes it in poetry; the poet of nature actually sees it in poetry.

This point is perhaps worth some little illustration; the rather, as metaphysicians (the ultimate arbiters of all philosophical criticism), while they have busied themselves for two thousand years, more or less, about the few *universal* laws of human nature, have strangely neglected the analysis of its *diversities*. Of these, none lie deeper or reach further than the varieties which difference of nature and of education makes in what may be termed the habitual bond of association. In a mind entirely uncultivated, which is also without any strong feelings, objects whether of sense of or intellect arrange themselves in the mere casual order in which they have been seen, heard, or otherwise perceived. Persons of this sort may be said to think chronologically. If they remember a fact, it is by reason of a fortuitous coincidence with some trifling incident or circumstance which took place at the very time. If they have a story to tell, or testimony to deliver in a witness-box, their narrative must follow the exact order in which the events took place: *dodge* them, and the thread of association is broken; they cannot go on. Their associations, to use the language of philosophers, are chiefly of the successive, not the synchronous kind, and whether successive or synchronous, are mostly casual.

To the man of science, again, or of business, objects group themselves according to the artificial classifications which the understanding has voluntarily made for the convenience of thought or of practice. But where any of the impressions are vivid and intense, the associations into which these enter are the ruling ones: it being a well-known law of association, that the stronger a feeling is, the more quickly and strongly it associates itself with any other object or feeling. Where, therefore, nature has given strong feelings, and education has not created factitious tendencies stronger than the natural ones, the prevailing associations will be those which connect objects and ideas with emotions, and with each other through the intervention of emotions. Thoughts and images will be linked together, according to the similarity of the feelings which cling to them. A thought will introduce a thought by first introducing a feeling which is allied with it. At the centre of each group of thoughts or images will be found a feeling; and the thoughts or images will be there only because the feeling was there. The combinations which the mind puts together, the pictures which it paints, the wholes which Imagination constructs out of the materials supplied by Fancy, will be indebted to some dominant *feeling*, not as in other natures to a dominant *thought*, for their unity and consistency of character, for what distinguishes them from incoherencies.

The difference, then, between the poetry of a poet, and the poetry of a cultivated but not naturally poetic mind, is, that in the latter, with however bright a halo of feeling the thought may be surrounded and glorified, the thought itself is always the conspicuous object; while the poetry of a poet is Feeling itself, employing Thought only as the medium of its expression. In the one, feeling waits upon thought; in the other, thought upon feeling. The one writer has a distinct aim, common to him with any other didactic author; he desires to convey the thought, and he conveys it clothed in the feelings which it excites in himself, or which he deems most appropriate to it. The other merely pours forth the overflowing of his feelings; and all the thoughts which those feelings suggest are floated promiscuously along the stream.

It may assist in rendering our meaning intelligible, if we illustrate it by a parallel between the two English authors of our own day who have produced the greatest quantity of true and enduring poetry, Wordsworth and Shelley. Apter instances could not be wished for; the one might be cited as the type, the *exemplar*, of what the poetry of culture may accomplish: the other as perhaps the most striking example ever known of the poetic temperament. How different, accordingly, is the poetry of these two great writers! In Wordsworth, the poetry is almost always the mere setting of a thought. The thought may be more valuable than the setting, or it may be less valuable, but there can be no question as to which was first in his mind: what he is impressed with, and what he is anxious to impress, is some proposition, more or less distinctly conceived; some truth, or something which he deems such. He lets the thought dwell in his mind, till it excites, as is the nature of thought, other thoughts, and also such feelings as the measure of his sensibility is adequate to supply. Among these thoughts and feelings, had he chosen a different walk of authorship (and there are many in which he might equally have excelled), he would probably have made a different selection of media for enforcing the parent thought: his habits, however, being those of poetic composition, he selects in preference the strongest feelings, and the thoughts with which most of feeling is naturally or habitually connected. His poetry, therefore, may be defined to be, his thoughts, coloured by, and impressing themselves by means of, emotions. Such poetry, Wordsworth has occupied a long life in producing. And well and wisely has he so done. Criticisms, no doubt, may be made occasionally both upon the thoughts themselves, and upon the skill he has demonstrated in the choice of his media: for an affair of skill and study, in the most rigorous sense, it evidently was. But he has not laboured in vain; he has exercised, and continues to exercise, a powerful, and mostly a highly beneficial influence over the formation and growth of not a few of the most cultivated and vigorous of the youthful minds of our time, over whose heads poetry of the opposite description would have flown, for want of an original organization, physical or mental, in sympathy with it.

On the other hand, Wordsworth's poetry is never bounding, never ebullient; has little even of the appearance of spontaneousness: the well is never so full that it overflows. There is an air of calm deliberateness about all he writes, which is not characteristic of the poetic temperament: his poetry seems one thing, himself another; he seems to be poetical because he wills to be so, not because he cannot help it: did he will to dismiss poetry, he need never again, it might almost seem, have a poetical thought. He never seems *pos-*

sessed by any feeling; no emotion seems ever so strong as to have entire sway, for the time being, over the current of his thoughts. He never, even for the space of a few stanzas, appears entirely given up to exultation, or grief, or pity, or love, or admiration, or devotion, or even animal spirits. He now and then, though seldom, attempts to write as if he were: and never, we think, without leaving an impression of poverty: as the brook which on nearly level ground quite fills its banks, appears but a thread when running rapidly down a precipitous declivity. He has feeling enough to form a decent, graceful, even beautiful decoration to a thought which is in itself interesting and moving; but not so much as suffices to stir up the soul by mere sympathy with itself in its simplest manifestation, nor enough to summon up that array of 'thoughts of power' which in a richly stored mind always attends the call of really intense feeling. It is for this reason, doubtless, that the genius of Wordsworth is essentially unlyrical. Lyric poetry, as it was the earliest kind, is also, if the view we are now taking of poetry be correct, more eminently and peculiarly poetry than any other: it is the poetry most natural to a really poetic temperament, and least capable of being successfully imitated by one not so endowed by nature.

Shelley is the very reverse of all this. Where Wordsworth is strong, he is weak; where Wordsworth is weak, he is strong. Culture, that culture by which Wordsworth has reared from his own inward nature the richest harvest ever brought forth by a soil of so little depth, is precisely what was wanting to Shelley: or let us rather say, he had not, at the period of his deplorably early death, reached sufficiently far in that intellectual progression of which he was capable, and which, if it has done so much for greatly inferior natures, might have made of him the most perfect, as he was already the most gifted of our poets. For him, voluntary mental discipline had done little: the vividness of his emotions and of his sensations had done all. He seldom follows up an idea; it starts into life, summons from the fairy-land of his inexhaustible fancy some three or four bold images, then vanishes, and straight he is off on the wings of some casual association into quite another sphere. He had scarcely yet acquired the consecutiveness of thought necessary for a long poem; his more ambitious compositions too often resemble the scattered fragments of a mirror; colours brilliant as life, single images without end, but no picture. It is only when under the overruling influence of some one state of feeling, either actually experienced, or summoned up in the vividness of reality by a fervid imagination, that he writes as a great poet; unity of feeling being to him the harmonizing principle which a central idea is to minds of another class, and supplying the coherency and consistency which would else have been wanting. Thus it is in many of his smaller, and especially his lyrical poems. They are obviously written to exhale, perhaps to relieve, a state of feeling, or of conception of feeling, almost oppressive from its vividness. The thoughts and imagery are suggested by the feeling, and are such as it finds unsought. The state of feeling may be either of soul or of sense, or oftener (might we not say invariably?) of both: for the poetic temperament is usually, perhaps always, accompanied by exquisite senses. The exciting cause may be either an object or an idea. But whatever of sensation enters into the feeling, must not be local, or consciously organic; it is a condition of the whole frame, not of a part only. Like the state of sensation produced by a fine climate, or indeed like all strongly pleasurable or painful sensations in an impassioned nature, it pervades the entire nervous system. States of feeling, whether sensuous or spiritual, which thus possess the whole being, are the fountains of that which we have called the poetry of poets; and which is little else than a pouring forth of the thoughts and images that pass across the mind while some permanent state of feeling is occupying it.

To the same original fineness of organization, Shelley was doubtless indebted for another of his rarest gifts, that exuberance of imagery, which when unrepressed, as in many of his poems it is, amounts to a fault. The susceptibility of his nervous system, which made his emotions intense, made also the impressions of his external senses deep and clear; and agreeably to the law of association by which, as already remarked, the strongest impressions are those which associate themselves the most easily and strongly, these vivid sensations were readily recalled to mind by all objects or thoughts which had co-existed with them, and by all feelings which in any degree resembled them. Never did a fancy so teem with sensuous imagery as Shelley's. Wordsworth economizes an image, and detains it until he has distilled all the poetry out of it, and it will not yield a drop more: Shelley lavishes his with a profusion which is unconscious because it is inexhaustible.

If, then, the maxim *Nascitur poeta* mean, either that the power of producing poetical compositions is a peculiar faculty which the poet brings into the world with him, which grows with his growth like any of his bodily powers, and is as independent of culture as his height, and his complexion; or that any natural peculiarity whatever is implied in producing poetry, real poetry, and in any quantity —such poetry too, as, to the majority of educated and intelligent readers, shall appear quite as good as, or even better than, any other; in either sense the doctrine is false. And nevertheless, there *is* poetry which could not emanate but from a mental and physical constitution peculiar, not in the kind, but in the degree of its susceptibility: a constitution which makes its possesser capable of greater happiness than mankind in general, and also of greater unhappiness; and because greater, so also more various. And such poetry, to all who know enough of nature to own it as being in nature, is much more poetry, is poetry in a far higher sense, than any other; since the common element of all poetry, that which constitutes poetry, human feeling, enters far more largely into this than into the poetry of culture. Not only because the natures which we have called poetical, really feel more, and consequently have more feeling to express; but because, the capacity of feeling being so great, feeling, when excited and not voluntarily resisted, seizes the helm of their thoughts, and the succession of ideas and images becomes the mere utterance of an emotion; not, as in other natures, the emotion a mere ornamental colouring of the thought.

Ordinary education and the ordinary course of life are constantly at work counteracting this quality of mind, and substituting habits more suitable to their own ends: if instead of substituting they were content to superadd, there would be nothing to complain of. But when will education consist, not in repressing any mental faculty or power, from the uncontrolled action of which danger is apprehended, but in training up to its proper strength the corrective and antagonist power?

In whomsoever the quality which we have described exists, and is not stifled, that person is a poet. Doubtless he is a greater poet in proportion as the fineness of his perceptions, whether of sense or of internal consciousness, furnishes him with an ampler supply of lovely images—the vigor and richness of his intellect, with a greater abundance of moving thoughts. For it is through these thoughts and images that the feeling speaks, and through their impressiveness that it impresses itself, and finds response in other hearts; and from these media of transmitting it (contrary to the laws of physical nature) increase of intensity is reflected back upon the feeling itself. But all these it is possible to have, and not be a poet; they are mere materials, which the poet shares in common with other people. What constitutes the poet is not the imagery nor the thoughts, nor even the feelings, but the law according to which they are called up. He is a poet, not because he has ideas of any particular kind, but because the succession of his ideas is subordinate to the course of his emotions.

Many who have never acknowledged this in theory, bear testimony to it in their particular judgments. In listening to an oration, or reading a written discourse not professedly poetical, when do we begin to feel that the speaker or author is putting off the character of the orator or the prose writer, and is passing into the poet? Not when he begins to show strong feeling; *then* we merely say, he is in earnest, he feels what he says; still less when he expresses himself in imagery; then, unless illustration be manifestly his sole object, we are apt to say, this is affectation. It is when the feeling (instead of passing away, or, if it continue, letting the train of thoughts run on exactly as they would have done if there were no influence at work but the mere intellect) becomes itself the originator of another train of association, which expels or blends with the former; when (for example) either his words, or the mode of their arrangement, are such as we spontaneously use only when in a state of excitement, proving that the mind is at least as much occupied by a passive state of its own feelings, as by the desire of attaining the premeditated end which the discourse has in view.*

* And this, we may remark by the way, seems to point to the true theory of poetic diction; and to suggest the true answer to as much as is erroneous of Wordsworth's celebrated doctrine on that subject. For on the one hand, *all* language which is the natural expression of feeling, is really poetical, and will be felt as such, apart from conventional associations; but on the other, whenever intellectual culture has afforded a choice between several modes of expressing the same emotion, the stronger the feeling is, the more naturally and certainly will it prefer the language which is most peculiarly appropriated to itself, and kept sacred from the contact of more vulgar objects of contemplation.

Our judgements of authors who lay actual claim to the title of poets, follow the same principle. Whenever, after a writer's meaning is fully understood, it is still a matter of reasoning and discussion whether he is a poet or not, he will be found to be wanting in the characteristic peculiarity of association so often adverted to. When, on the contrary, after reading or hearing one or two passages, we instinctively and without hesitation cry out, 'This is a poet', the probability is, that the passages are strongly marked with this peculiar quality. And we may add that in such case, a critic who, not having sufficient feeling to respond to the poetry, is also without sufficient philosophy to understand it though he feel it not, will be apt to pronounce, not 'this is prose', but 'this is exaggeration', 'this is mysticism', or 'this is nonsense.'

Although a philosopher cannot, by culture, make himself, in the peculiar sense in which we now use the term, a poet, unless at least he have that peculiarity of nature which would probably have made poetry his earliest pursuit; a poet may always, by culture, make himself a philosopher. The poetic laws of association are by no means incompatible with the more ordinary laws; are by no means such as *must* have their course, even though a deliberate purpose require their suspension. If the peculiarities of the poetic temperament were uncontrollable in any poet, they might be supposed so in Shelley; yet how powerfully, in the *Cenci,* does he coerce and restrain all the characteristic qualities of his genius; what severe simplicity, in place of his usual barbaric splendour; how rigidly does he keep the feelings and the imagery in subordination to the thought.

The investigation of nature requires no habits or qualities of mind, but such as may always be acquired by industry and mental activity. Because at one time the mind may be so given up to a state of feeling, that the succession of its ideas is determined by the present enjoyment or suffering which pervades it, this is no reason but that in the calm retirement of study, when under no peculiar excitement either of the outward or of the inward sense, it may form any combinations, or pursue any trains of ideas, which are most conducive to the purposes of philosophic inquiry; and may, while in that state, form deliberate convictions, from which no excitement will afterwards make it swerve. Might we not go even further than this? We shall not pause to ask whether it be not a misunderstanding of the nature of passionate feeling to imagine that it is inconsistent with calmness; whether they who so deem of it, do not mistake passion in the militant or antagonistic state, for the type of passion universally; do not confound passion struggling towards an outward object, with passion brooding over itself. But without entering into this deeper investigation; that capacity of strong feeling, which is supposed necessarily to disturb the judgment, is also the material out of which all *motives* are made; the motives, consequently, which lead human beings to the pursuit of truth. The greater the individual's capability of happiness and of misery, the stronger interest has that individual in arriving at truth; and when once that interest is felt, an impassioned nature is sure to pursue this, as to pursue any other object, with greater ardour; for energy of character is commonly the offspring of strong feeling. If, therefore, the most impassioned natures do not ripen into the most powerful intellects, it is always from defect of culture, or something wrong in the circumstances by which the being has originally or successively been surrounded. Undoubtedly strong feelings require a strong intellect to carry them, as more sail requires more ballast: and when, from neglect, or bad education, that strength is wanting, no wonder if the grandest and swiftest vessels make the most utter wreck.

Where, as in some of our older poets, a poetic nature has been united with logical and scientific culture, the peculiarity of association arising from the finer nature so perpetually alternates with the associations attainable by commoner natures trained to high perfection, that its own particular law is not so conspicuously characteristic of the result produced, as in a poet like Shelley, to whom systematic intellectual culture, in a measure proportioned to the intensity of his own nature, has been wanting. Whether the superiority will naturally be on the side of the philosopher-poet or of the mere poet—whether the writings of the one ought, as a whole, to be truer, and their influence more beneficent, than those of the other—is too obvious in principle to need statement: it would be absurd to doubt whether two endowments are better than one; whether truth is more certainly arrived at by two processes, verifying and correcting each other, than by one alone. Unfortunately, in practice the matter is not quite so simple; there the question often is, which is least prejudicial to the intellect, uncultivation or malcultivation. For, as long as education consists chiefly of the mere inculcation of traditional opinions, many of which, from the mere fact that the human intellect has not yet reached perfection, must necessarily be false; so long as even those who are best taught, are rather taught to know the thoughts of others than to think, it is not always clear that the poet of acquired ideas has the advantage over him whose feeling has been his sole teacher. For the depth and durability of wrong as well as of right impressions is proportional to the fineness of the material; and they who have the greatest capacity of natural feelings are generally those whose artificial feelings are the strongest. Hence, doubtless, among other reasons, it is, that in an age of revolutions in opinion, the co-temporary poets, those at least who deserve the name, those who have any individuality of character, if they are not before their age, are almost sure to be behind it. An observation curiously verified all over Europe in the present century. Nor let it be thought disparaging. However urgent may be the necessity for a breaking up of old modes of belief, the most strong-minded and discerning, next to those who head the movement, are generally those who bring up the rear of it.

Eneas Sweetland Dallas

"THE SECRECY OF ART"

E. S. Dallas was one member of David Hay's Aesthetic Society who was unable to accept the scientific attitudes of the group. Although less sensitive and profound a writer than Hay, he nevertheless gave a forcible statement to his enthusiasm for "subjective" art and his suspicion of the rational. His intense language ("thrill of pleasure," "mental possession," "shock of these touches," "an occult power") foreshadowed the aesthetes. He even hinted at a necessary isolation of the artist from society (an "esoteric

From *The Gay Science* (1866).

mode," he said, is appropriate for the "hidden life within us"), though ultimately he felt, as Ruskin had, that some divine urge prompts the gifted man to spread his good news in the market-place. In his writing there are interesting implications of the life of sensation rather than of thought, and of the "hard, gemlike flame."

WE STARTED with the common doctrine that art is the opposite of science, and that, as the object of science is knowledge, so that of art is pleasure. But if the reader has apprehended what I have tried to convey to him as to the existence within us of two great worlds of thought—a double life, the one known or knowable, the other unknown and for the most part unknowable, he will be prepared, if not to accept, yet to understand this further conception of the difference between science and art that the field of science is the known and the knowable, while the field of art is the unknown and the unknowable. It is a strange paradox that the mind should be described as possessing and compassing the unknown. But my whole argument has been working up to this point, and, I trust, rendering it credible—that the mind may possess and be possessed by thoughts of which nevertheless it is ignorant.

Now, because such a statement as this will appear to be a paradox to those who have not considered it; also, because to say that the field of art is the unknown, is like saying that the object of art is a negation, it is fit that in ordinary speech we should avoid such phrases, and be content with the less paradoxical expression—that the object of art is pleasure. The object of science, we say, is knowledge—a perfect grasp of all the facts which lie within the sphere of consciousness. The object of art is pleasure—a sensible possession or enjoyment of the world beyond consciousness. We do not know that world, yet we feel it—feel it chiefly in pleasure, but sometimes in pain, which is the shadow of pleasure. It is a vast world we have seen; of not less importance to us than the world of knowledge. It is in the hidden sphere of thought, even more than in the open one, that we live, and move, and have our being; and it is in this sense that the idea of art is always a secret. We hear much of the existence of such a secret, and people are apt to say—If a secret exist, and if the artist convey it in his art, why does he not plainly tell us what it is? But here at once we fall into contradictions, for as all language refers to the known, the moment we begin to apply it to the unknown, it fails. Until the existence of an unknown hidden life within us be thoroughly well accepted, not only felt, but also to some extent understood, there will always be an esoteric mode of stating the doctrine, which is not for the multitude. . . .

It was in the last century a commonplace of French criticism and conversation, that what is most lovely, most attractive, in man, in nature, in art, is a certain *je ne sais quoi.* And adopting this phrase, it will not be much of a paradox to assert that, while the object of science is to know and to make known, the object of art is to appropriate and to communicate the nameless grace, the ineffable secret of the know-not-what. If the object of art were to make known and to explain its ideas, it would no longer be art, but science. Its object is very different. The true artist recognises, however dimly, the existence within us of a double world of thought, and his object is, by subtle forms, tones, words, allusions, associations, to establish a connection with the unconscious hemisphere of the mind, and to make us feel a mysterious energy there in the hidden soul. For this purpose he doubtless makes use of the known. He paints what we have seen, he describes what we have heard; but his use of knowledge is ever to suggest something beyond knowledge. If he be merely dealing with the known and making it better known, then it becomes necessary to ask wherein does his work differ from science? Through knowledge, through consciousness, the artist appeals to the unconscious part of us. The poet's words, the artist's touches, are electric; and we feel those words, and the shock of those touches, going through us in a way we cannot define, but always giving us a thrill of pleasure, awakening distant associations, and filling us with the sense of a mental possession beyond that of which we are daily and hourly conscious. Art is poetical in proportion as it has this power of appealing to what I may call the absent mind, as distinct from the present mind, on which falls the great glare of consciousness, and to which alone science appeals. On the temple of art, as on the temple of Isis, might be inscribed—"I am whatsoever is, whatsoever has been, whatsoever shall be; and the veil which is over my face no mortal hand has ever raised."

. . . The art of Shakespeare, be it observed, is complex. It is built on a vast expenditure of facts, on a wonderful exposition of knowledge. Through the splendid collision of facts, we learn to catch at something which is not in the facts; from the conquered world of knowledge we sidle into the unconquered world of hidden thought—"the worlds unrealized" of Wordsworth. But in any attempt to show the greatness of Shakespeare, the proofs are nearly all based on the greatness of his knowledge. It is only this kind of proof that we can logically construe. Who can take the measure of his influence in the hidden world of thought? We can measure his knowledge, we cannot measure all that is comprised in the know-not-what of his influence. Now if we try to put into comparison the mental grasp of Beethoven with that of Shakespeare—what do we find? We find in Beethoven the great master of an art, which is not complex but simple—which acts powerfully and vitally on the unknown realm of thought, but not through the means, or at least very little through the means, of definite knowledge. The definite knowledge which Beethoven or any great musician puts before our minds as a means of gaining access to the hidden soul is very small; compared with that which Shakespeare sets in the glare of consciousness it is as nothing. The standard, therefore, of conscious comparison between the great musician and the great dramatist entirely fails.

When we turn from music and poetry to painting and sculpture, there may be more difficulty in accepting art as in the strictest sense the opposite of science—the keeper of a secret which may be imparted but never known. Music is nothing if not suggestive, and all good poetry has a latency of meaning beyond the simple statement of facts. But in the arts of painting and sculpture there is the precision, the clearsightedness, the accuracy of science; and we admire so much the knowledge of the thing represented, which the artist exhibits, that we are less struck by the something beyond knowledge—the know-not-what which he suggests to the imagination. When the poet makes Perdita babble of the daffodils that come before the swallow dares, and take the winds of March with beauty, he displays a suggestiveness which outruns the whole art of painting. *Qui pingit florem, non pingit floris odorem.* How can a painter in the tinting of a daffodil convey fine suggestions of the confidence and power of beauty in a tender flower? The painter may give us "pale primroses," but how can he convey what Perdita means when she tells us that they die unmarried ere they can behold bright Phoebus in his strength? The painter's art is evidently tied to fact more strictly than that of the poet. We are all familiar with the manner in which truth of drawing, truth of colour, truth of perspective, truth of light and shadow, truth to the minutest hair and filament of fact—in one word, complete science is demanded of the artist who appeals to us through the visual sense; and his scientific mastery of the human forms, or dog-forms, or forms of whatever else is to be pictured, bulks so large in our esteem that we forget often the somewhat more than science which ought to be on his canvas or in his marble, and without which his art is naught. If mere accuracy, if mere matter of fact, were all in all, then the artist would stand a poor chance in competition with the photograph and other mechanical modes of copying nature. It is the artist's business, by the capture of evanescent and almost impalpable expression, by the unfathomable blending of light in shadow, by delicacies of purest colour, by subtleties of lineament, by touches of a grace that is beyond calculation, by all the mysteries that are involved in the one word—tone—to convey to the imagination a something beyond nature, and beyond science—

> The light which never was on sea or land,
> The consecration and the poet's dream.

If there be artists who content themselves with adhesion to bare fact, who are never able to transcend fact and to move the imagination, then we must think of them as of Defoe. We take an interest in what Defoe tells us, but it is not the interest excited by art. He sees things clearly and describes them sharply; but the complaint against him is that he has no imagination—that he never touches the hidden sense, which we have been trying to analyze. And as a man may tell a story well (it is done every day in the newspapers), and yet his clear story-telling is not poetry; so a man may paint a picture well, and yet his picture for all the clearness and fulness of knowledge it exhibits may not be art, because it wants that something which a great artist once described by snapping his fingers. "It wants," said Sir Joshua Reynolds, "it wants *that*."

There is a famous saying of Shakespeare's Ulysses, "that one touch of nature makes the whole world kin;" and in a sense very different from that which our dramatist had in his mind, it is frequently cited as the clearest expression of what art most gloriously achieves, and what the artist ought most steadily to pursue. Whoever will refer to the passage in the original, will see that Shakespeare meant nothing like what his readers divorcing the line from the context now see in it. The supposition is, that when we discover any one touch of nature our hearts are stirred into sympathy with all nature, and we rejoice in the felt grandeur of the bond which links us to the universe. It is a mistake, however, to suppose that any touch of nature will produce this effect, and that the artist has nothing to do but to render nature. It is only by touches of nature that he can move us, but he has to select his touches. Truth of touch is not enough, because every true touch is not in magnetic relation with the hidden life of the mind. The artist may fill his canvas with true touches; and Sir Joshua, snapping his fingers, may have to say—"It wants *that.*"

If the essential quality of art may be expressed by the pantomime of snapping one's fingers, and by saying, " 'tis *that,*" then there is good reason why in a previous chapter I should have refused to limit the scope of art to the true, to the beautiful, or to any one idea within the sphere of knowledge; but there may also seem to be fair grounds for challenging the possibility of a critical science. If the field of art be the unknown and unknowable, where is the room for science? Is it not likely that all our enquiries into the nature of art may end in no better result than the page-boy in one of Lilly's plays gets out of Sir Tophaz? "Tush, boy!" cries the bragging soldier, Sir Tophaz, "I think it but some device of the poet to get money." "A poet!" says Epiton; "what's that?' "Dost thou not know what a poet is?" "No," says the page. "Why, fool," rejoins Sir Tophaz, "a poet is as much as one should say, a poet." If, however, there be aught of which a science is impossible there may still be room for scientific ignorance. Nay, more, Sir William Hamilton,[1] who, notwithstanding Mr. Mill, will hold his place as the greatest thinker of the nineteenth century, maintained, though he did not originate the paradox, "that what we are conscious of is constructed out of what we are not conscious of,—that our whole

[1] Sir William R. Hamilton (1788–1856). See Mill's *An Examination of Sir William Hamilton's Philosophy* (1865) and *Autobiography*, Chapter VII (1873).

knowledge, in fact, is made up of the unknown and incognisable," I do not insist upon this, although it is capable of distinct proof, because to render such a mystery in knowledge plain to the popular mind would be too much of a digression. But it may be enough to say that if we cannot tear the secret from art, we can, at any rate, lay bare the conditions under which it passes current. There is a science of biology, and yet no one can define what is life. The science of life is but a science of the laws and conditions under which it is manifested. So, again, is it essential to the science of electricity that we should know for certain what is electricity? We know not what it is: we only see its effects; and yet relating to these effects of an unknown power there has been built up a great science. Again, we can trace the orbits of comets and reckon upon their visits, though of themselves, their what, their why, their wherefore, we know almost nothing. And so there may be a science of poetry and the fine arts, although the theme of art is the Unknown, and its motive power is the Hidden Soul.

Matthew Arnold

"THE CONTRIBUTION OF THE CELTS TO ENGLISH LITERATURE"

THE SELECTION below is the sixth and concluding lecture in the ambitious, pioneering defense of Celtic literature which Arnold delivered as holder of the Oxford Chair of Poetry in 1867. His intent was propagandistic: from a renewed contact of the two literatures, English and Celtic, he hoped that his Philistine contemporaries would imbibe a "quickness of perception" which would soften their Germanic devotion to fact and their Latin "decisiveness or hardness." Celtic art, he believed, would supply Philistine Britain with passion, delicacy, mystery, and grace. Portions of the earlier lectures seem dated and reveal an occasional unsureness in the somewhat uneasy philologic regions of Angus

FROM *On the Study of Celtic Literature* (1867).

and Taliesen; but in the concluding lecture, where he probes the English cultural temper and finds it lacking, he is on thoroughly familiar ground.

IF I WERE ASKED where English poetry got these three things, its turn for style, its turn for melancholy, and its turn for natural magic, for catching and rendering the charm of nature in a wonderfully near and vivid way,—I should answer, with some doubt, that it got much of its turn for style from a Celtic source, with less doubt, that it got much of its melancholy from a Celtic source; with no doubt at all, that from a Celtic source it got nearly all its natural magic.

Any German with penetration and tact in matters of literary criticism will own that the principal deficiency of German poetry is in style; that for style, in the highest sense, it shows but little feeling. Take the eminent masters of style, the poets who best give the idea of what the peculiar power which lies in style is—Pindar, Virgil, Dante, Milton. An example of the peculiar effect which these poets produce, you can hardly give from German poetry. Examples enough you can give from German poetry of the effect produced by genius, though, and feeling expressing themselves in clear language, simple language, passionate language, eloquent language, with harmony and melody: but not of the peculiar effect exercised by eminent power of style. Every reader of Dante can at once call to mind what the peculiar effect I mean is; I spoke of it in my lectures on translating Homer, and there I took an example of it from Dante, who perhaps manifests it more eminently than any other poet. But from Milton, too, one may take examples of it abundantly; compare this from Milton:—

> . . . nor sometimes forget
> Those other two equal with me in fate,
> So were I equall'd with them in renown,
> Blind Thamyris and blind Mæonides—

with this from Goethe:—

> Es bildet ein Talent sich in der Stille,
> Sich ein Character in dem Strom der Welt.

Nothing can be better in its way than the style in which Goethe there presents his thought, but it is the style of prose as much as of poetry; it is lucid, harmonious, earnest, eloquent, but it has not received that peculiar kneading, heightening, and recasting which is observable in the style of the passage from Milton—a style which seems to have for its cause a certain pressure of emotion, and an ever-surging, yet bridled, excitement in the poet, giving a special intensity to his way of delivering himself. In poetical races and epochs this turn for style is peculiarly observable; and perhaps it is only on condition of having this somewhat heightened and difficult manner, so different from the plain manner of prose, that poetry gets the privilege of being loosed, at its best moments, into that perfectly simple, limpid style, which is the supreme style of all, but the simplicity of which is still not the simplicity of prose. The simplicity of Menander's style is the simplicity of prose, and is the same kind of simplicity as that which Goethe's style, in the passage I have quoted, exhibits; but Menander does not belong to a great poetical moment, he comes too late for it; it is the simple passages in poets like Pindar or Dante which are perfect, being masterpieces of *poetical* simplicity. One may say the same of the simple passages in Shakespeare; they are perfect, their simplicity being a *poetical* simplicity. They are the golden, easeful, crowning moments of a manner which is always pitched in another key from that of prose, a manner changed and heightened; the Elizabethan style, regnant in most of our dramatic poetry to this day, is mainly the continuation of this manner of Shakespeare's. It was a manner much more turbid and strewn with blemishes than the manner of Pindar, Dante, or Milton; often it was detestable; but it owed its existence to Shakespeare's instinctive impulse towards *style* in poetry, to his native sense of the necessity for it; and without the basis of style everywhere, faulty though it may in some places be, we should not have had the beauty of expression, unsurpassable for effectiveness and charm, which is reached in Shakespeare's best passages. The turn for style is perceptible all through English poetry, proving, to my mind, the genuine poetical gift of the race; this turn imparts to our poetry a stamp of high distinction, and sometimes it doubles the force of a poet not by nature of the very highest order, such as Gray, and raises him to a rank beyond what his natural richness and power seem to promise. Goethe, with his fine critical perception, saw clearly enough both the power of style in itself, and the lack of style in the literature of his own country; and perhaps if we regard him solely as a German, not as a European, his great work was that he labored all his life to impart style into German literature, and firmly to establish it there. Hence the immense importance to him of the world of classical art, and of the productions of Greek or Latin genius, where style so eminently manifests its power. Had he found in the German genius and literature an element of style existing by nature and ready to his hand, half his work, one may say, would have been saved him, and he might have done much more in poetry. But as it was, he had to try and create, out of his own powers, a style for German poetry, as well as to provide contents for this style to carry; and thus his labor as a poet was doubled.

It is to be observed that power of style, in the sense in which I am here speaking of style, is something quite different from the power of idiomatic simple, nervous, racy expression, such as the expression of healthy, robust natures so often is, such as Luther's was in a striking degree. Style, in my sense of the word, is a peculiar recasting and heightening, under a certain condition of spiritual excitement, of what a man has to say, in such a manner as to add dignity and distinction to it; and dignity and distinction are not terms which suit many acts or words of Luther. Deeply touched with the *Gemeinheit* which is the bane of his nation, as he is at the same time a grand example of the honesty which is his nation's excellence, he can seldom even show himself brave, resolute, and truthful, without showing a strong dash of coarseness and commonness all the while; the right definition of Luther, as of our own Bunyan, is that he is a Philistine of genius. So Luther's sincere idiomatic German,—such language as this: "Hilf, lieber Gott, wie manchen Jammer habe ich gesehen, dass der gemeine Mann doch so gar nichts weiss von der christlichen Lehre!"—no more proves a power of style in German literature, than Cobbett's sinewy idiomatic English proves it in English literature. Power of style, properly so-called, as manifested in masters of style like Dante or Milton in poetry, Cicero, Bossuet or Bolingbroke in prose, is something quite different, and has, as I have said, for its characteristic effect, this: to add dignity and distinction. . . .

This something is *style*, and the Celts certainly have it in a wonderful measure. Style is the most striking quality of their poetry. Celtic poetry seems to make up to itself for being unable to master the world and give an adequate interpretation of it, by throwing all its force into style, by bending language at any rate to its will, and expressing the ideas it has with unsurpassable intensity, elevation, and effect. It has all through it a sort of intoxication of style—a *Pindarism,* to use a word formed from the name of the poet, on whom, above all other poets, the power of style seems to have exercised an inspiring and intoxicating effect; and not in its great poets only, in Taliesin, or Llywarch Hen, or Ossian, does the Celtic genius show this Pindarism, but in all its productions:—

> The grave of March is this, and this the grave of Gwythyr;
> Here is the grave of Gwgawn Gleddyfreidd;
> But unknown is the grave of Arthur.

That comes from the Welsh *Memorials of the Graves of the Warriors,* and if we compare it with the familiar memorial inscriptions of an English churchyard (for we English have so much Germanism in us that our productions offer abundant examples of German want of style as well as of its opposite):—

> Afflictions sore long time I bore,
> Physicians were in vain,
> Till God did please Death should me seize
> And ease me of my pain—

if, I say, we compare the Welsh memorial lines with the English, which in their *Gemeinheit* of style are truly Germanic, we shall get a clear sense of what that Celtic talent for style I have been speaking of is. . . .

Its chord of penetrating passion and melancholy, again, its *Titanism* as we see it in Byron,—what other European poetry possesses that like the English, and where do we get it from? The Celts, with their vehement reaction against the despotism of fact, with their sensuous nature, their manifold striving, their adverse destiny, their immense calamities, the Celts are the prime authors of this vein of piercing regret and passion,—of this Titanism in poetry. A famous book, Macpherson's *Ossian,*[1] carried in the last

[1] James Macpherson (1736–1796) published anonymously in 1760 his *Fragments of Ancient Poetry, Collected in the Highlands of Scotland and Translated from the Gaelic or Erse language.* An epic, *Fingal,* and other poems followed. Their authenticity was early doubted, and they are now generally held to be forgeries.

century this vein like a flood of lava through Europe. I am not going to criticize Macpherson's *Ossian* here. Make the part of what is forged, modern, tawdry, spurious, in the book, as large as you please; strip Scotland, if you like, of every feather of borrowed plumes which on the strength of Macpherson's *Ossian* she may have stolen from the *vetus et major Scotia,* the true home of the Ossianic poetry, Ireland; I make no objection. But there will still be left in the book a residue with the very soul of the Celtic genius in it, and which has the proud distinction of having brought this soul of the Celtic genius into contact with the genius of the nations of modern Europe, and enriched all our poetry by it. Woody Morven, and echoing Sora, and Selma with its silent halls!—we all owe them a debt of gratitude, and when we are unjust enough to forget it, may the Muse forget us! Choose any one of the better passages in Macpherson's *Ossian* and you can see even at this time of day what an apparition of newness and power such a strain must have been to the eighteenth century:—

"I have seen the walls of Balclutha, but they were desolate. The fox looked out from the windows, the rank grass of the wall waved round her head. Raise the song of mourning, O bards, over the land of strangers. They have but fallen before us, for one day we must fall. Why dost thou build the hall, son of the winged days? Thou lookest from thy towers today; yet a few years, and the blast of the desert comes; it howls in thy empty court, and whistles round thy half-worn shield. Let the blast of the desert come! we shall be renowned in our day."

All Europe felt the power of that melancholy; but what I wish to point out is, that no nation of Europe so caught in its poetry the passionate penetrating accent of the Celtic genius, its strain of Titanism, as the English. Goethe, like Napoleon, felt the spell of Ossian very powerfully, and he quotes a long passage from him in his *Werther*. But what is there Celtic, turbulent, and Titanic about the German Werther, that amiable, cultivated and melancholy young man, having for his sorrow and suicide the perfectly definite motive that Lotte cannot be his? Faust, again, has nothing unaccountable, defiant, and Titanic in him; his knowledge does not bring him the satisfaction he expected from it, and meanwhile he finds himself poor and growing old, and balked of the palpable enjoyment of life; and here is the motive for Faust's discontent. In the most energetic and impetuous of Goethe's creations,—his *Prometheus,*—it is not Celtic self-will and passion, it is rather the Germanic sense of justice and reason, which revolts against the despotism of Zeus. The German *Sehnsucht* itself is a wistful, soft, tearful longing, rather than a struggling, fierce, passionate one. But the Celtic melancholy is struggling, fierce, passionate; to catch its note, listen to Llywarch Hen in old age, addressing his crutch:—

"O my crutch! is it not autumn, when the fern is red, the water-flag yellow? Have I not hated that which I love?

O my crutch! is it not winter-time now, when men talk together after that they have drunken? Is not the side of my bed left desolate?

O my crutch! is it not spring, when the cuckoo passes through the air, when the foam sparkles on the sea? The young maidens no longer love me.

O my crutch! is it not the first day of May? The furrows, are they not shining; the young corn, is it not springing? Ah! the sight of thy handle makes me wroth.

O my crutch! stand straight, thou wilt support me the better; it is very long since I was Llywarch.

Behold old age, which makes sport of me, from the hair of my head to my teeth, to my eyes, which women loved.

The four things I have all my life most hated fall upon me together,—coughing and old age, sickness and sorrow.

I am old, I am alone, shapeliness and warmth are gone from me; the couch of honor shall be no more mine; I am miserable, I am bent on my crutch.

How evil was the lot allotted to Llywarch, the night when he was brought forth! sorrows without end, and no deliverance from his burden."

There is the Titanism of the Celt, his passionate, turbulent, indomitable reaction against the despotism of fact; and of whom does it remind us so much as of Byron?

> The fire which on my bosom preys
> Is lone as some volcanic isle;
> No torch is kindled at its blaze;
> A funeral pile!

Or, again:—

Count o'er the joys thine hours have seen,
Count o'er thy days from anguish free,
And know, whatever thou has been,
'Tis something better not to be.

One has only to let one's memory begin to fetch passages from Byron striking the same note as that passage from Llywarch Hen, and she will not soon stop. And all Byron's heroes, not so much in collision with outward things, as breaking on some rock of revolt and misery in the depths of their own nature; Manfred, self-consumed, fighting blindly and passionately with I know not what, having nothing of the consistent development and intelligible motive of Faust,—Manfred, Lara, Cain, what are they but Titanic? Where in European poetry are we to find this Celtic passion of revolt so warm-breathing, puissant, and sincere; except perhaps in the creation of a yet greater poet than Byron, but an English poet, too, like Byron,—in the Satan of Milton?

. . . What though the field be lost?
All is not lost; the unconquerable will,
And study of revenge, immortal hate,
And courage never to submit or yield,
And what is else not to be overcome.

There, surely, speaks a genius to whose composition the Celtic fibre was not wholly a stranger!

And as, after noting the Celtic Pindarism or power of style present in our poetry, we noted the German flatness coming in our hymns, and found here a proof of our compositeness of nature; so, after noting the Celtic Titanism or power of rebellious passion in our poetry, we may also note the Germanic patience and reasonableness in it, and get in this way a second proof how mixed a spirit we have. After Llywarch Hen's,

How evil was the lot allotted to Llywarch, the night
When he was brought forth—

after Byron's,—

Count o'er the joys thine hours have seen—

take this of Southey's, in answer to the question whether he would like to have his youth over again,—

> Do I regret the past?
> Would I live o'er again
> The morning hours of life?
> Nay, William, nay, not so!
> Praise be to God who made me what I am,
> Other I would not be.

There we have the other side of our being; the Germanic goodness, docility, and fidelity to nature, in place of the Celtic Titanism.

The Celt's quick feeling for what is noble and distinguished gave his poetry style; his indomitable personality gave it pride and passion; his sensibility and nervous exaltation gave it a better gift still, the gift of rendering with wonderful felicity the magical charm of nature. The forest solitude, the bubbling spring, the wild flowers, are everywhere in romance. They have a mysterious life and grace there; they are Nature's own children, and utter her secret in a way which makes them something quite different from the woods, waters, and plants of Greek and Latin poetry. Now of this delicate magic, Celtic romance is so pre-eminent a mistress, that it seems impossible to believe the power did not come into romance from the Celts. Magic is just the word for it,—the magic of nature, not merely the beauty of nature,—that the Greeks and Latins had; not merely an honest smack of the soil, a faithful realism,—that the Germans had; but the intimate life of Nature, her weird power and her fairy charm. As the Saxon names of places, with the pleasant wholesome smack of the soil in them,—Weathersfield, Thaxted, Shalford,—are to the Celtic names of places, with their penetrating, lofty beauty,—Velindra, Tyntagel, Caernarvon,—so is the homely realism of German and Norse nature to the fairy-like loveliness of Celtic nature. Gwydion wants a wife for his pupil: "Well," says Math, "we will seek, I and thou, by charms and illusions, to form a wife for him out of flowers. So they took the blossoms of the oak, and the blossoms of the broom, and the blossoms of the meadow-sweet, and produced from them a maiden, the fairest and most graceful that man ever saw. And they baptized her, and gave her the name of Flower-Aspect." Celtic romance is full of exquisite touches like that, showing the delicacy of the Celt's feeling in these matters, and how deeply Nature lets him come into her secrets. The quick dropping of blood is called "faster than the fall of the dewdrop from the blade of reed-grass upon the earth, when the dew of June is at the heaviest." And thus is Olwen described: "More yellow was her hair than the flower of the broom, and her skin was whiter than the foam of the wave, and fairer were her hands and her fingers than the blossoms of the wood-anemone amidst the spray of the meadow fountains." For loveliness it would be hard to beat that; and for magical clearness and nearness take the following:—

"And in the evening Peredur entered a valley, and at the head of the valley he came to a hermit's cell, and the hermit welcomed him gladly, and there he spent the night. And in the morning he arose, and when he went forth, behold, a shower of snow had fallen the night before, and a hawk had killed a wild-fowl in front of the cell. And the noise of the horse scared the hawk away, and a raven alighted upon the bird. And Peredur stood and compared the blackness of the raven, and the whiteness of the snow, and the redness of the blood, to the hair of the lady whom best he loved, which was blacker than the raven, and to her skin, which was whiter than the snow, and to her two cheeks which were redder than the blood upon the snow appeared to be."

And this, which is perhaps less striking, is not less beautiful:—

"And early in the day Geraint and Enid left the wood, and they came to an open country, with meadows on one hand and mowers mowing the meadows. And there was a river before them, and the horses bent down and drank the water. And they went up out of the river by a steep bank, and there they met a slender stripling with a satchel about his neck; and he had a small blue pitcher in his hand, and a bowl on the mouth of the pitcher."

And here the landscape, up to this point so Greek in its clear beauty, is suddenly magicalized by the romance touch,—

"And they saw a tall tree by the side of the river, one-half of which was in flames from the root to the top, and the other half was green and in full leaf."

Magic is the word to insist upon,—a magically vivid and near interpretation of nature; since it is this which constitutes the special charm and power of the effect I am calling attention to, and it is for this that the Celt's sensibility gives him a peculiar aptitude. But the matter needs rather fine handling, and it is easy to make mistakes here in our criticism. In the first place, Europe tends constantly to become more and more one community, and we tend to become Europeans instead of merely Englishmen, Frenchmen, Germans, Italians; so whatever aptitude or felicity one people imparts into spiritual work, gets imitated by the others, and thus tends to become the common property of all. Therefore anything so beautiful and attractive as the natural magic I am speaking of, is sure, nowadays, if it appears in the productions of the Celts, or of the English, or of the French, to appear in the productions of the Germans also, or in the productions of the Italians; but there will be a stamp of perfectness and inimitableness about it in the literatures where it is native, which it will not have in the literatures where it is not native. Novalis or Rückert, for instance, have their eye fixed on nature, and have undoubtedly a feeling for natural magic; a rough-and-ready critic easily credits them and the Germans with the Celtic fineness of tact, the Celtic nearness to nature and her secret; but the question is whether the strokes in the German's picture of nature have ever the indefinable delicacy, charm, and perfection of the Celt's touch in the pieces I just now quoted, or of Shakespeare's touch in his daffodil, Wordsworth's in his cuckoo, Keats's in his Autumn, Obermann's in his mountain birch-tree, or his Easter-daisy among the Swiss farms. To decide where the gift for natural magic originally lies, whether it is properly Celtic or Germanic, we must decide this question.

In the second place, there are many ways of handling nature, and we are here only concerned with one of them; but a rough-and-ready critic imagines that it is all the same so long as nature is handled at all, and fails to draw the needful distinction between modes of handling her. But these modes are many; I will mention four of them now: there is the conventional way of handling nature, there is the faithful way of handling nature, there is the Greek way of handling nature, there is the magical way of handling nature. In all these three last the eye is on the object, but with a difference; in the faithful way of handling nature, the eye is on the object, and that is all you can say; in the Greek, the eye is on the object, but lightness and brightness are added; in the magical, the eye is on the object, but charm and magic are added. In the conventional way of handling nature, the eye is not on the object; what that means we all know, we have only to think of our eighteenth-century poetry:—

> As when the moon, refulgent lamp of night—

to call up any number of instances. Latin poetry supplies plenty of instances too; if we put this from Propertius's *Hylas:—*

> . . . manus heroum . . .
> Mollia composita litora fronde tegit—

side by side with the line of Theocritus by which it was suggested:—

> λειμὼν γάρ σφιν ἔκειτο μέγας, στιβάδεσσιν ὄνειαρ—

we get at the same moment a good specimen both of the conventional and of the Greek way of handling nature. But from our own poetry we may get specimens of the Greek way of handling nature, as well as of the conventional: for instance, Keats's:—

> What little town by river or seashore,
> Or mountain-built with quiet citadel,
> Is emptied of its folk, this pious morn?

is Greek, as Greek as a thing from Homer or Theocritus; it is composed with the eye on the object, a radiancy and light clearness being added. German poetry abounds in specimens of the faithful way of handling nature; an excellent example is to be found in the stanzas called *Zueignung*, prefixed to Goethe's poems; the morning walk, the mist, the dew, the sun, are as faithful as they can be, they are given with the eye on the object, but there the merit of the work, as a handling of nature, stops; neither Greek radiance nor Celtic magic is added; the power of these is not what gives the poem in question its merit, but a power of quite another kind, a power of moral and spiritual emotion. But the power of Greek radiance Goethe could give to his handling of nature, and nobly too, as any one who will read his *Wanderer,*—the poem in which a wanderer falls in with a peasant woman and her child by their hut, built out of the ruins of a temple near Cuma,—may see. Only the power of natural magic Goethe does not, I think, give; whereas

Keats passes at will from the Greek power to that power which is, as I say, Celtic; from his

> What little town, by river or seashore—

to his

> White hawthorn and the pastoral eglantine,
> Fast-fading violets cover'd up in leaves—

or his

> . . . magic casements, opening on the foam
> Of perilous seas, in fairy lands forlorn—

in which the very same note is struck as in those extracts which I quoted from Celtic romance, and struck with authentic and unmistakable power.

Shakespeare, in handling nature, touches this Celtic note so exquisitely, that perhaps one is inclined to be always looking for the Celtic note in him, and not to recognize his Greek note when it comes. But if one attends well to the difference between the two notes, and bears in mind, to guide one, such things as Virgil's "moss-grown springs and grass softer than sleep:"—

> Muscosi fontes et somno mollior herba—

as his charming flower-gatherer, who—

> Pallentes violas et summa papavera carpens
> Narcissum et florem jungit bene olentis anethi—

as his quinces and chestnuts:—

> . . . cana legam tenera lanugine mala
> Castaneasque nuces . . .

then, I think, we shall be disposed to say that in Shakespeare's

> I know a bank where the wild thyme blows,
> Where oxlips and the nodding violet grows,
> Quite over-canopied with luscious woodbine,
> With sweet musk-roses and with eglantine—

it is mainly a Greek note which is struck. Then, again in his

> . . . look how the floor of heaven
> Is thick inlaid with patines of bright gold!

we are at the very point of transition from the Greek note to the Celtic; there is the Greek clearness and brightness, with the Celtic aërialness and magic coming in. Then we have the sheer, inimitable Celtic note in passages like this:—

> Met we on hill, in dale, forest or mead,
> By paved fountain or by rushy brook,
> Or in the beached margent of the sea—

or this, the last I will quote:—

> The moon shines bright. In such a night as this,
> When the sweet wind did gently kiss the trees,
> And they did make no noise, in such a night
> Troilus, methinks, mounted the Trojan walls—
>
> . . . in such a night
> Did Thisbe fearfully o'ertrip the dew—
>
> . . . in such a night
> Stood Dido, with a willow in her hand,
> Upon the wild sea-banks, and waved her love
> To come again to Carthage.

And those last lines of all are so drenched and intoxicated with the fairy-dew of that natural magic which is our theme, that I cannot do better than end with them.

And now, with the pieces of evidence in our hand, let us go to those who say it is vain to look for Celtic elements in any Englishman, and let us ask them, first, if they seize what we mean by the power of natural magic in Celtic poetry: secondly, if English poetry does not eminently exhibit this power; and, thirdly, where they suppose English poetry got it from?

I perceive that I shall be accused of having rather the air, in what I have said, of denying this and that gift to the Germans, and of establishing our difference from them a little ungraciously and at their expense. The truth is, few people have any real care to analyse closely in their criticism; they merely employ criticism as a means for heaping all praise on what they like, and all blame on what they dislike. Those of us (and there are many) who owe a great debt of gratitude to the German spirit and to German literature, do not like to be told of any powers being lacking there; we are like the young ladies who think the hero of their novel is only half a hero unless he has all perfections united in him. But nature does not work, either in heroes or races, according to the young ladies' notion. We all are what we are, the hero and the great nation are what they are, by our limitations as well as by our powers, by lacking something as well as by possessing something. It is not always gain to possess this or that gift, or loss to lack this or that gift. Our great, our only first-rate body of contemporary poetry is the German; the grand business of modern poetry—a moral interpretation, from an independent point of view, of man and the world—it is only German poetry, Goethe's poetry, that has, since the Greeks, made much way with. Campbell's power of style, and the natural magic of Keats and Wordsworth, and Byron's Titanic personality, may be wanting to this poetry; but see what it has accomplished without them! How much more than Campbell with his power of style, and Keats and Wordsworth with their natural magic, and Byron with his Titanic personality! Why, for the immense serious task it had to perform, the steadiness of German poetry, its going near the ground, its patient fidelity to nature, its using great plainness of speech, poetical drawbacks in one point of view, were safeguards and helps in another. The plainness and earnestness of the two lines I have already quoted from Goethe—

> Es bildet ein Talent sich in der Stille,
> Sich ein Character in dem Strom der Welt—

compared with the play and power of Shakespeare's style or Dante's, suggest at once the difference between Goethe's task and theirs, and the fitness of the faithful laborious German spirit for its own task. Dante's task was to set forth the lesson of the world from the point of view of medieval Catholicism; the basis of spiritual life was given, Dante had not to make this anew. Shakespeare's task was to set forth the spectacle of the world when man's spirit re-awoke to the possession of the world at the Renaissance. The spectacle of human life, left to bear its own significance and tell its own story, but shown in all its fulness, variety, and power, is at that moment the great matter; but, if we are to press deeper, the basis of spiritual life is still at that time the traditional religion, reformed or unreformed, of Christendom, and Shakespeare has not to supply a new basis. But when Goethe came, Europe had lost her basis of spiritual life; she had to find it again; Goethe's task was—the inevitable task for the modern poet henceforth is—as it was for the Greek poet in the days of Pericles, not to preach a sublime sermon on a given text like Dante, not to exhibit all the kingdoms of human life and the glory of them like Shakespeare, but to interpret human life afresh, and to supply a new spiritual basis to it. This is not only a work of style, eloquence, charm, poetry; it is a work for science; and the scientific, serious German spirit, not carried away by this and that intoxication of ear, and eye, and self-will, has peculiar aptitudes for it.

We, on the other hand, do not necessarily gain by the commixture of elements in us; we have seen how the clashing of natures in us hampers and embarrasses our behaviour; we might very likely be more attractive, we might very likely be more successful, if we were all of a piece. Our want of sureness of taste, our eccentricity, come in great measure, no doubt, from our not being all of a piece, from our having no fixed, fatal, spiritual centre of gravity. The Rue de Rivoli is one thing, and Nuremberg is another, and Stonehenge is another; but we have a turn for all three, and lump them all together. Mr. Tom Taylor's translations from Breton poetry offer a good example of this mixing; he has a genuine feeling for these Celtic matters, and often, as in the *Evil Tribute of Nomenoë*, or in *Lord Nann and the Fairy*, he is, both in movement and expression, true and appropriate; but he has a sort of Teutonism and Latinism in him too, and so he cannot forbear mixing with his Celtic strain such disparates as,—

> 'Twas mirk, mirk night, and the water bright
> Troubled and drumlie flowed—

which is evidently Lowland-Scotchy; or as,—

> Foregad, but thou'rt an artful hand!

which is English-stagey; or as,—

To Gradlon's daughter, bright of blee,
Her lover he whispered tenderly—
Bethink thee, sweet Dahut! the key!

which is Anacreontic in the manner of Tom Moore. Yes, it is not a sheer advantage to have several strings to one's bow! if we had been all German, we might have had the science of Germany; if we had been all Celtic we might have been popular and agreeable; if we had been all Latinised, we might have governed Ireland as the French govern Alsace, without getting ourselves detested. But now we have Germanism enough to make us Philistines, and Normanism enough to make us imperious, and Celtism enough to make us self-conscious and awkward; but German fidelity to Nature, and Latin precision and clear reason, and Celtic quick-wittedness and spirituality, we fall short of. Nay, perhaps, if we are doomed to perish (Heaven avert the omen!), we shall perish by our Celtism, by our self-will and want of patience with ideas, our inability to see the way the world is going; and yet those very Celts, by our affinity with whom we are perishing, will be hating and upbraiding us all the time.

This is a somewhat unpleasant view to take of the matter; but if it is true, its being unpleasant does not make it any less true, and we are always the better for seeing the truth. What we here see is not the whole truth, however. So long as this mixed constitution of our nature possesses us, we pay it tribute and serve it; so soon as we possess it, it pays us tribute and serves us. So long as we are blindly and ignorantly rolled about by the forces of our nature, their contradiction baffles us and lames us; so soon as we have clearly discerned what they are, and begun to apply to them a law of measure, control, and guidance, they may be made to work for our good and to carry us forward. Then we may have the good of our German part, the good of our Latin part, the good of our Celtic part; and instead of one part clashing with the other, we may bring it in to continue and perfect the other, when the other has given us all the good it can yield, and by being pressed further, could only give us its faulty excess. Then we may use the German faithfulness to Nature to give us science, and to free us from insolence and self-will; we may use the Celtic quickness of perception to give us delicacy, and to free us from hardness and Philistinism; we may use the Latin decisiveness to give us strenuous clear method and to free us from fumbling and idling. Already, in their untrained state, these elements give signs, in our life and literature, of their being present in us, and a kind of prophecy of what they could do for us if they were properly observed, trained, and applied. But this they have not yet been; we ride one force of our nature to death; we will be nothing but Anglo-Saxons in the Old World or in the New; and when our race has built Bold Street, Liverpool, and pronounced it very good, it hurries across the Atlantic, and builds Nashville, and Jacksonville, and Milledgeville, and thinks it is fulfilling the designs of Providence in an incomparable manner. But true Anglo-Saxons, simply and sincerely rooted in the German nature, we are not and cannot be; all we have accomplished by our onesidedness is to blur and confuse the natural basis in ourselves altogether, and to become something eccentric, unattractive, and inharmonious. . . .

At this moment, when the narrow Philistinism which has long had things its own way in England, is showing its natural fruits, and we are beginning to feel ashamed, and uneasy, and alarmed at it; now, when we are becoming aware that we have sacrificed to Philistinism culture, and insight, and dignity, and acceptance, and weight among the nations, and hold on events that deeply concern us, and control of the future, and yet that it cannot even give us the fool's paradise it promised us, but is apt to break down, and to leave us with Mr. Roebuck's and Mr. Lowe's laudations of our matchless happiness, and the largest circulation in the world assured to the *Daily Telegraph*, for our only comfort; at such a moment it needs some moderation not to be attacking Philistinism by storm, but to mine it through such gradual means as the slow approaches of culture, and the introduction of chairs of Celtic. But the hard unintelligence, which is just now our bane, cannot be conquered by storm; it must be supplied and reduced by culture, by a growth in the variety, fulness, and sweetness of our spiritual life; and this end can only be reached by studying things that are outside of ourselves, and by studying them disinterestedly. Let us reunite ourselves with our better mind and with the world through science; and let it be one of our angelic revenges on the Philistines, who among their other sins are the guilty authors of Fenianism, to found at Oxford a chair of Celtic, and to send, through the gentle ministration of science, a message of peace to Ireland.

Walter Pater

"CRITICISM AND PERSONALITY," "DANTE GABRIEL ROSSETTI," and "THE NEW CYRENAICISM"

PATER'S *Renaissance* was Oscar Wilde's "golden book of spirit and sense," his "holy writ of beauty." Wilde never travelled anywhere without it: "it is the very flower of decadence: the last trumpet should have sounded the moment it was written." Such accolades made Pater more than a little uneasy. He insisted upon his own severe spirituality and never wholly accepted his flamboyant influence on Wilde and his generation. The "Preface," the early work which established Pater's reputation, contains the nucleus of his influential theory of personality; the critic's business is to seek the elusive *virtue,* personality, or "active principle" of each individual work of art.

When he came to explore the *virtue* of Rossetti's poetry, Pater was faithful to the tenets developed ten years before in *The Renaissance.* His good taste, his appreciation of the complexities of the works before him, his preference of the sensuous, critical approach to the abstract, and his fair sensitive judgments are clearly displayed. In time, disturbed by the use Wilde and others were making of his theories, and by the strictures of critics accusing him of an amoral hedonism, in Chapter IX of *Marius,* Pater defended his philosophy and style. Cyrenaicism, he explained in his own baroque manner, is appropriately "religious," and gives the artist an invaluable bulwark against an unaesthetic, materialistic age.

CRITICISM AND PERSONALITY

MANY ATTEMPTS have been made by writers on art and poetry to define beauty in the abstract, to express it in the most general

FROM *Studies in the History of the Renaissance* (1873), *Appreciations* (1889), and *Marius the Epicurean* (1885).

terms, to find a universal formula for it. The value of these attempts has most often been in the suggestive and penetrating things said by the way. Such discussions help us very little to enjoy what has been well done in art or poetry, to discriminate between what is more and what is less excellent in them, or to use words like beauty, excellence, art, poetry, with a more precise meaning than they would otherwise have. Beauty, like all other qualities presented to human experience, is relative; and the definition of it becomes unmeaning and useless in proportion to its abstractness. To define beauty, not in the most abstract, but in the most concrete terms possible, to find, not a universal formula for it, but the formula which expresses most adequately this or that special manifestation of it, is the aim of the true student of aesthetics.

"To see the object as in itself it really is," has been justly said to be the aim of all true criticism whatever; and in aesthetic criticism the first step towards seeing one's object as it really is, is to know one's own impression as it really is, to discriminate it, to realise it distinctly. The objects with which aesthetic criticism deals—music, poetry, artistic and accomplished forms of human life—are indeed receptacles of so many powers or forces: they possess, like the products of nature, so many virtues or qualities. What is this song or picture, this engaging personality presented in life or in a book, to *me?* What effect does it really produce on me? Does it give me pleasure? and if so, what sort or degree of pleasure? How is my nature modified by its presence, and under its influence? The answers to these questions are the original facts with which the aesthetic critic has to do; and, as in the study of light, of morals, of number, one must realise such primary data for one's self, or not at all. And he who experiences these impressions strongly, and drives directly at the discrimination and analysis of them, has no need to trouble himself with the abstract question what beauty is in itself, or what its exact relation to truth or experience—metaphysical questions, as unprofitable as metaphysical questions elsewhere. He may pass them all by as being, answerable or not, of no interest to him.

The aesthetic critic, then, regards all the objects with which he has to do, all works of art, and the fairer forms of nature and human life, as powers or forces producing pleasurable sensations, each of a more or less peculiar or unique kind. This influence he feels, and wishes to explain, by analysing and reducing it to its elements. To him, the picture, the landscape, the engaging personality in life or in a book, *La Gioconda,* the hills of Carrara, Pico of Mirandola,[1] are valuable for their virtues, as we say, in speaking of an herb, a wine, a gem; for the property each has of affecting one with a special, a unique, impression of pleasure. Our education becomes complete in proportion as our susceptibility to these impressions increases in depth and variety. And the function of the aesthetic critic is to distinguish, to analyse, and separate from its adjuncts, the virtue by which a picture, a landscape, a fair personality in life or in a book, produces this special impression of beauty or pleasure, to indicate what the source of that impression is, and under what conditions it is experienced. His end is reached when he has disengaged that virtue, and noted it, as a chemist notes some natural element, for himself and others; and the rule for those who would reach this end is stated with great exactness in the words of a recent critic of Sainte-Beuve:—*De se borner à connaître de près les belles choses, et à s'en nourrir en exquis amateurs, en humanistes accomplis.*

What is important, then, is not that the critic should possess a correct abstract definition of beauty for the intellect, but a certain kind of temperament, the power of being deeply moved by the presence of beautiful objects. He will remember always that beauty exists in many forms. To him all periods, types, schools of taste, are in themselves equal. In all ages there have been some excellent workmen, and some excellent work done. The question he asks is always:—In whom did the stir, the genius, the sentiment of the period find itself? Where was the receptacle of its refinement, its elevation, its taste? "The ages are all equal," says William Blake, "but genius is always above its age."

Often it will require great nicety to disengage this virtue from the commoner elements with which it may be found in combination. Few artists, not Goethe or Byron even, work quite cleanly, casting off all *débris,* and leaving us only what the heat of their imagination has wholly fused and transformed. Take, for instance, the writings of Wordsworth. The heat of his genius, entering into the substance of his work, has crystallised a part, but only a part, of it; and

[1] *La Gioconda,* Leonardo Da Vinci's famous *Mona Lisa;* Pico della Mirandola (1463–1494), an Italian humanist scholar.

in that great mass of verse there is much which might well be forgotten. But scattered up and down it, sometimes fusing and transforming entire compositions, like the Stanzas on *Resolution and Independence*, or the Ode on the *Recollections of Childhood*, sometimes, as if at random, depositing a fine crystal here or there, in a matter it does not wholly search through and transmute, we trace the action of his unique, incommunicable faculty, that strange, mystical sense of a life in natural things, and of man's life as a part of nature, drawing strength and color and character from local influences, from the hills and streams, and from natural sights and sounds. Well! that is the *virtue*, the active principle in Wordsworth's poetry; and then the function of the critic of Wordsworth is to follow up that active principle, to disengage it, to mark the degree in which it penetrates his verse. . . .

DANTE GABRIEL ROSSETTI

It was characteristic of a poet who had ever something about him of mystic isolation, and will still appeal perhaps, though with a name it may seem now established in English literature, to a special and limited audience, that some of his poems had won a kind of exquisite fame before they were in the full sense published. *The Blessed Damozel,* although actually printed twice before the year 1870, was eagerly circulated in manuscript; and the volume which it now opens came at last to satisfy a long-standing curiosity as to the poet, whose pictures [2] also had become an object of the same peculiar kind of interest. For those poems were the work of a painter, understood to belong to, and to be indeed the leader, of a new school then rising into note; and the reader of today may observe already, in *The Blessed Damozel,* written at the age of eighteen, a prefigurement of the chief characteristics of that school, as he will recognise in it also, in proportion as he really knows Rossetti, many of the characteristics which are most markedly personal and his own. Common to that school and to him, and in both alike of primary significance, was the quality of sincerity, already felt as one of the charms of that earliest poem—a perfect sincerity, taking effect in the deliberate use of the most direct and unconventional expression, for the conveyance of a poetic sense which recognised no conventional standard of what poetry

[2] See "Jane Burden as Queen Guenevere" in first group of illustrations.

was called upon to be. At a time when poetic originality in England might seem to have had its utmost play, here was certainly one new poet more, with a structure and music of verse, a vocabulary, an accent, unmistakably novel, yet felt to be no mere tricks of manner adopted with a view to forcing attention—an accent which might rather count as the very seal of reality on one man's own proper speech; as that speech itself was the wholly natural expression of certain wonderful things he really felt and saw. Here was one, who had a matter to present to his readers, to himself at least, in the first instance, so valuable, so real and definite, that his primary aim, as regards form or expression in his verse, would be but its exact equivalence to those *data* within. That he had this gift of transparency in language—the control of a style which did but obediently shift and shape itself to the mental motion, as a well-trained hand can follow on the tracing-paper the outline of an original drawing below it, was proved afterwards by a volume of typically perfect translations from the delightful but difficult "early Italian poets": such transparency being indeed the secret of all genuine style, of all such style as can truly belong to one man and not to another. His own meaning was always personal and even recondite, in a certain sense learned and casuistical, sometimes complex or obscure; but the term was always, one could see, deliberately chosen from many competitors, as the just transcript of that peculiar phase of soul which he alone knew, precisely as he knew it.

One of the peculiarities of *The Blessed Damozel* was a definiteness of sensible imagery, which seemed almost grotesque to some, and was strange, above all, in a theme so profoundly visionary. The gold bar of heaven from which she leaned, her hair yellow like ripe corn, are but examples of a general treatment, as naïvely detailed as the pictures of those early painters contemporary with Dante, who has shown a similar care for minute and definite imagery in his verse; there, too, in the very midst of profoundly mystic vision. Such definition of outline is indeed one among many points in which Rossetti resembles the great Italian poet, of whom, led to him at first by family circumstances, he was ever a lover—a "servant and singer," faithful as Dante, "of Florence and of Beatrice"—with some close inward conformities of genius also, independent of any mere circumstances of education. It was said by a critic of the last century, not wisely though agreeably to the practice of his time, that poetry rejoices in abstractions. For Rossetti, as for Dante, without question on his part, the first condition of the poetic way of seeing and presenting things is particularisation. "Tell me now," he writes, for Villon's

> Dictes-moy où, n'en quel pays,
> Est Flora, la belle Romaine—
>
> Tell me now, in what hidden way is
> Lady Flora, the lovely Roman:

—"way," in which one might actually chance to meet her; the unmistakably poetic effect of the couplet in English being dependent on the definiteness of that single word (though actually lighted on in the search after a difficult double rhyme) for which every one else would have written, like Villon himself, a more general one, just equivalent to place or region.

And this delight in concrete definition is allied with another of his conformities to Dante, the really imaginative vividness, namely, of his personifications—his hold upon them, or rather their hold upon him, with the force of a Frankenstein, when once they have taken life from him. Not Death only and Sleep, for instance, and the winged spirit of Love, but certain particular aspects of them, a whole "populace" of special hours and places, "the hour" even "which might have been, yet might not be," are living creatures, with hands and eyes and articulate voices. . . .

Poetry as a *mania*—one of Plato's two higher forms of "divine" mania—has, in all its species, a mere insanity incidental to it, the "defect of its quality," into which it may lapse in its moment of weakness; and the insanity which follows a vivid poetic anthropomorphism like that of Rossetti may be noted here and there in his work, in a forced and almost grotesque materialising of abstractions, as Dante also became at times a mere subject of the scholastic realism of the Middle Age.

In *Love's Nocturn* and *The Stream's Secret,* congruously perhaps with a certain feverishness of soul in the moods they present, there is at times a near approach (may it be said?) to such insanity of realism—

Pity and love shall burn
In her pressed cheek and cherishing hands;
And from the living spirit of love that stands
Between her lips to soothe and yearn,
Each separate breath shall clasp me round in turn
And loose my spirit's bands.

But even if we concede this; even if we allow, in the very plan of those two compositions, something of the literary conceit—what exquisite, what novel flowers of poetry, we must admit them to be, as they stand! In the one, what a delight in all the natural beauty of water, all its details for the eye of a painter; in the other, how subtle and fine the imaginative hold upon all the secret ways of sleep and dreams! In both of them, with much the same attitude and tone, Love—sick and doubtful Love—would fain inquire of what lies below the surface of sleep, and below the water; stream or dream being forced to speak by Love's powerful "control"; and the poet would have it foretell the fortune, issue, and event of his wasting passion. Such artifices, indeed, were not unknown in the old Provençal poetry of which Dante had learned something. Only, in Rossetti at least, they are redeemed by a serious purpose, by that sincerity of his, which allies itself readily to a serious beauty, a sort of grandeur of literary workmanship, to a great style. One seems to hear there a really new kind of poetic utterance, with effects which have nothing else like them; as there is nothing else, for instance, like the narrative of Jacob's Dream in *Genesis*, or Blake's design of the Singing of the Morning Stars, or Addison's Nineteenth Psalm.

With him indeed, as in some revival of the old mythopoeic age, common things—dawn, noon, night—are full of human or personal expression, full of sentiment. The lovely little sceneries scattered up and down his poems, glimpses of a landscape, not indeed of broad open-air effects, but rather that of a painter concentrated upon the picturesque effect of one or two selected objects at a time—the "hollow brimmed with mist," or the "ruined weir," as he sees it from one of the windows, or reflected in one of the mirrors of his "house of life" (the vignettes for instance seen by Rose Mary in the magic beryl) attest, by their very freshness and simplicity, to a pictorial or descriptive power in dealing with the inanimate world, which is certainly also one half of the charm, in that other, more remote and mystic, use of it. For with Rossetti this sense of lifeless nature, after all, is translated to a higher service, in which it does but incorporate itself with some phase of strong emotion. Every one understands how this may happen at critical moments of life; what a weirdly expressive soul may have crept, even in full noonday, into "the white-flower'd elder-thicket," when Godiva saw it "gleam through the Gothic archways in the wall," at the end of her terrible ride. To Rossetti it is so always, because to him life is a crisis at every moment. A sustained impressibility towards the mysterious conditions of man's everyday life, towards the very mystery itself in it, gives a singular gravity to all his work: those matters never became trite to him. But throughout, it is the ideal intensity of love—of love based upon a perfect yet peculiar type of physical or material beauty—which is enthroned in the midst of those mysterious powers; Youth and Death, Destiny and Fortune, Fame, Poetic Fame, Memory, Oblivion, and the like. Rossetti is one of those who, in the words of Mérimée *se passionnent pour la passion*, one of Love's lovers.

And yet, again as with Dante, to speak of his ideal type of beauty as material, is partly misleading. Spirit and matter, indeed, have been for the most part opposed with a false contrast or antagonism by schoolmen, whose artificial creation those abstractions really are. In our actual concrete experience, the two trains of phenomena which the words *matter* and *spirit* do but roughly distinguish, play inextricably into each other. Practically, the church of the Middle Age by its aesthetic worship, its sacramentalism, its real faith in the resurrection of the flesh, had set itself against the Manichean opposition of spirit and matter, and its results in men's way of taking life; and in this, Dante is the central representative of its spirit. To him, in the vehement and impassioned heat of his conceptions, the material and the spiritual are fused and blent: if the spiritual attains the definite visibility of a crystal, what is material loses its earthiness and impurity. And here again, by force of instinct, Rossetti is one with him. His chosen type of beauty is one,

> Whose speech Truth knows not from her thought,
> Nor Love her body from her soul.

Like Dante, he knows no region of spirit which shall not be sensuous also, or material. The shadowy world, which he realises so powerfully, has still the ways and houses, the land and water, the light and darkness, the fire and flowers, that had so much to do in the moulding of those bodily powers and aspects which counted for so large a part of the soul, here.

For Rossetti, then, the great affections of persons to each other, swayed and determined, in the case of his highly pictorial genius, mainly by that so-called material loveliness, formed the great undeniable reality in things, the solid resisting substance, in a world where all beside might be but shadow. The fortunes of those affections—of the great love so determined; its casuistries, its languor sometimes; above all, its sorrows; its fortunate or unfortunate collisions with those other great matters; how it looks, as the long day of life goes round, in the light and shadow of them: all this, conceived with an abundant imagination, and a deep, a philosophic, reflectiveness, is the matter of his verse, and especially of what he designed as his chief poetic work, "a work to be called *The House of Life,*" towards which the majority of his sonnets and songs were contributions.

The dwelling-place in which one finds oneself by chance or destiny, yet can partly fashion for oneself; never properly one's own at all, if it be changed too lightly; in which every object has its associations—the dim mirrors, the portraits, the lamps, the books, the hair-tresses of the dead, any visionary magic crystals in the secret drawers, the names and words scratched on the windows, windows open upon prospects the saddest or the sweetest; the house one must quit, yet taking perhaps, how much of its quietly active light and colour along with us!—grown now to be a kind of raiment to one's body, as the body, according to Swedenborg, is but the raiment of the soul—under that image, the whole of Rossetti's work might count as a *House of Life,* of which he is but the "Interpreter." And it is a "haunted" house. A sense of power in love, defying distance, and those barriers which are so much more than physical distance of unutterable desire penetrating into the world of sleep, however "lead-bound," was one of those anticipative notes obscurely struck in *The Blessed Damozel,* and, in his later work, makes him speak sometimes almost like a believer in mesmerism. Dreamland, as we said, with its "phantoms of the body," deftly coming and going on love's service, is to him, in no mere fancy or figure of speech, a real country, a veritable expansion of, or addition to, our waking life; and he did well perhaps to wait carefully upon sleep, for the lack of it became mortal disease with him. One may even recognize a sort of morbid and over-hasty making-ready for death itself, which increases on him; thoughts concerning it, its imageries, coming with a frequency and importunity, in excess, one might think, of even the very saddest, quite wholesome wisdom.

And indeed the publication of his second volume of *Ballads and Sonnets* preceded his death by scarcely a twelvemonth. That volume bears witness to the reverse of any failure of power, or falling-off from his early standard of literary perfection, in every one of his then accustomed forms of poetry—the song, the sonnet, and the ballad. The newly printed sonnets, now completing the *House of Life,* certainly advanced beyond those earlier ones, in clearness; his dramatic power in the ballad, was here at its height; while one monumental, gnomic piece, *Soothsay,* testifies, more clearly even than the *Nineveh* of his first volume, to the reflective force, the dry reason, always at work behind his imaginative creations, which at no time dispensed with a genuine intellectual structure. For in matters of pure reflection also, Rossetti maintained the painter's sensuous clearness of conception; and this has something to do with the capacity, largely illustrated by his ballads, of telling some red-hearted story of impassioned action with effect. . . .

Perhaps, if one had to name a single composition of his to readers desiring to make acquaintance with him for the first time, one would select: *The King's Tragedy*—that poem so moving, so popularly dramatic, and lifelike. Notwithstanding this, his work, it must be conceded, certainly through no narrowness or egotism, but in the faithfulness of a true workman to a vocation so emphatic, was mainly of the esoteric order. But poetry, at all times, exercises two distinct functions: it may reveal, it may unveil to every eye, the ideal aspects of common things, after Gray's way (though Gray too, it is well to remember, seemed in his own day, seemed even to Johnson, obscure) or it may actually add to the number of motives poetic and uncommon in themselves, by the imaginative creation of things that are ideal from their very birth. Rossetti did something, something excellent, of the former kind; but his characteristic, his really revealing work, lay in the adding to poetry of fresh poetic material, of a new order of phenomena, in the creation of a new ideal.

THE NEW CYRENAICISM

SUCH WERE the practical conclusions drawn for himself by Marius, when somewhat later he had outgrown the mastery of others, from the principle that "all is vanity." If he could but count upon the present, if a life brief at best could not certainly be shown to conduct one anywhere beyond itself, if men's highest curiosity was indeed so persistently baffled—then, with the Cyrenaics of all ages, he would at least fill up the measure of that present with vivid sensations, and such intellectual apprehensions, as, in strength and directness and their immediately realized values at the bar of an actual experience, are most like sensations. So some have spoken in every age; for, like all theories which really express a strong natural tendency of the human mind or even one of its characteristic modes of weakness, this vein of reflection is a constant tradition in philosophy. Every age of European thought has had its Cyrenaics or Epicureans, under many disguises: even under the hood of the monk. But—*Let us eat and drink, for to-morrow we die!*—is a proposal, the real import of which differs immensely, according to the natural taste, and the acquired judgment, of the guests who sit at the table. It may express nothing better than the instinct of Dante's Ciacco, the accomplished glutton, in the mud of the *Inferno;* or, since on no hypothesis does man "live by bread alone," may come to be identical with—"My meat is to do what is just and kind;" while the soul, which can make no sincere claim to have apprehended anything beyond the veil of immediate experience, yet never loses a sense of happiness in conforming to the highest moral ideal it can clearly define for itself; and actually, though but with so faint hope, does the "Father's business."

In that age of Marcus Aurelius, so completely disabused of the metaphysical ambition to pass beyond "the flaming ramparts of the world," but, on the other hand, possessed of so vast an accumulation of intellectual treasure, with so wide a view before it over all varieties of what is powerful or attractive in man and his works, the thoughts of Marius did but follow the line taken by the majority of educated persons, though to a different issue. Pitched to a really high and serious key, the precept—*Be perfect in regard to what is here and now*: the precept of "culture," as it is called, or of a complete education—might at least save him from the vulgarity and heaviness of a generation, certainly of no general fineness of temper, though with a material well-being abundant enough. Conceded that what is secure in our existence is but the sharp apex of the present moment between two hypothetical eternities, and all that is real in our experience but a series of fleeting impressions:—so Marius continued the skeptical argument he had condensed, as the matter to hold by, from his various philosophical reading:—given, that we are never to get beyond the walls of the closely shut cell of one's own personality; that the ideas we are somehow impelled to form of an outer world, and of other minds akin to our own, are, it may be, but a day-dream, and the thought of any world beyond, a day-dream perhaps idler still: then, he, at least, in whom those fleeting impressions—faces, voices, material sunshine—were very real and imperious, might well set himself to the consideration, how such actual moments as they passed might be made to yield their utmost, by the most dexterous training of capacity. Amid abstract metaphysical doubts, as to what might lie one step only beyond that experience, reënforcing, the deep original materialism or earthliness of human nature itself, bound so intimately to the sensuous world, let him at least make the most of what was "here and now." In the actual dimness of ways from means to ends—ends in themselves desirable, yet for the most part distant and for him, certainly, below the visible horizon—he would at all events be sure that the means, to use the well-worn terminology, should have something of finality or perfection aboout them, and themselves partake, in a measure, of the more excellent nature of ends—that the means should justify the end.

With this view he would demand culture, παιδεα, as the Cyrenaics said, or, in other words, a wide, a complete, education—an education partly negative, as ascertaining the true limits of man's capacities, but for the most part positive, and directed especially to the expansion and refinement of the power of reception; of those powers, above all, which are immediately relative to fleeting phenomena, the powers of emotion and sense. In such an education, an "esthetic" education, as it might now be termed, and certainly occupied very largely with those aspects of things which affect us pleasurably through sensation, art, of course, including all the finer sorts of literature, would have a great part to play. The study of music, in that wider Platonic sense, according to which, *music* comprehends all those matters over which the Muses of Greek mythology preside, would conduct one to an exquisite appreciation of all the finer traits of nature and of man. Nay! the products of the imagination must themselves be held to present the most perfect forms of life—spirit and matter alike under their purest and most perfect conditions—the most strictly appropriate objects of that impassioned contemplation, which, in the world of intellectual discipline, as in the highest forms of morality and religion, must be held to be the essential function of the "perfect." Such manner of life might come even to seem a kind of religion—an inward, visionary mystic piety, or religion, by virtue of its effort to live days "lovely and pleasant" in themselves, here and now, and with an all-sufficiency of well-being in the immediate sense of the object contemplated, independently of any faith, or hope that might be entertained as to their ulterior tendency. In this way, the true esthetic culture would be realizable as a new form of the contemplative life, founding its claim on the intrinsic "blessedness" of "vision"—the vision of perfect men and things. One's human nature, indeed, would fain reckon on an assured and endless future, pleasing itself with the dream of a final home, to be attained at some still remote date, yet with a conscious, delightful home-coming at last, as depicted in many an old poetic Elysium. On the other hand, the world of perfected sensation, intelligence, emotion, is so close to us, and so attractive, that the most visionary of spirits must needs represent the world unseen in colors, and under a form really borrowed from it. Let me be sure then—might he not plausibly say?—that I miss no detail of this life of realized consciousness in the present! Here at least is a vision, a theory, θεωρία, which reposes on no basis of unverified hypothesis, which makes no call upon a future after all somewhat problematic; as it would be unaffected by any discovery of an Empedocles (improving on the old story of Prometheus) as to what had really been the origin, and course of development, of man's actually attained faculties and that seemingly divine particle of reason or spirit in him. Such a doctrine, at more leisurable moments, would of course have its precepts to deliver on the embellishment, generally, of what is near at hand, on the adornment of life, till, in a not impracticable rule of conduct, one's existence, from day to day, came to be like a well-executed piece of music; that "perpetual motion" in things (so Marius figured the matter to himself, under the old Greek imageries) according itself to a kind of cadence or harmony.

It was intelligible that this "esthetic" philosophy might find itself (theoretically, at least, and by way of a curious question in casuistry, legitimate from its own point of view) weighing the claims of that eager, concentrated, impassioned realization of experience, against those of the received morality. Conceiving its own function in a somewhat desperate temper, and becoming, as every high-strung form of sentiment, as the religious sentiment itself, may become, somewhat antinomian, when, in its effort towards the order of experiences it prefers, it is confronted with the traditional and popular morality, at points where that morality may look very like a convention, or a mere stage-property of the world, it would be found, from time to time, breaking beyond the limits of the actual moral order; perhaps not without some pleasurable excitement in so bold a venture.

With the possibility of some such hazard as this, in thought or even in practice—that it might be, though refining, or tonic even, in the case of those strong and in health, yet, as Pascal says of the kindly and temperate wisdom of Montaigne, "pernicious for those who have any natural tendency to impiety or vice," the line of reflection traced out above, was fairly chargeable.—Not, however, with "hedonism" and its supposed consequences. The blood, the heart, of Marius were still pure. He knew that his carefully considered theory of practice braced him, with the effect of a moral principle duly recurring to mind every morning, towards the work of a student, for which he might seem intended. Yet there were some among his acquaintance who jumped to the conclusion that, with the "Epicurean style," he was making pleasure—pleasure, as they so poorly conceived it—the sole motive of life; and they precluded any exacter estimate of the situation by covering it with a high-sounding general term, through the vagueness of which they were enabled to see the severe and laborious youth in the vulgar company of Lais. Words like "hedonism"—terms of large and vague comprehension—above all when used for a purpose avowedly controversial, have ever been the worst examples of what are called "question-begging terms;" and in that late age in which Marius lived, amid the dust of so many centuries of philosophical debate, the air was full of them. Yet those who used that reproachful Greek term for the philosophy of pleasure, were hardly more likely than the old Greeks themselves (on whom regarding this very subject of the theory of pleasure, their masters in the art of thinking had so emphatically to impress the necessity of "making distinctions") to come to any very delicately correct ethical conclusions by a reasoning, which began with a general term, comprehensive enough to cover pleasures so different in quality, in their causes and effects, as the pleasures of wine and love, of art and science, of religious enthusiasm and political enterprise, and of that taste or curiosity which satisfied itself with long days of serious study. Yet, in truth, each of those pleasurable modes of activity, may, in its turn, fairly become the ideal of the "hedonistic" doctrine. Really, to the phase of reflection through which Marius was then passing, the charge of "hedonism," whatever its true weight might be, was not properly applicable at all. Not pleasure, but fullness of life, and "insight" as conducting to that fullness—energy, variety, and choice of experience, including noble pain and sorrow even, loves such as those in the exquisite old story of Apuleius, sincere and strenuous forms of the moral life, such as Seneca and Epictetus—whatever form of human life, in short, might be heroic, impassioned, ideal: from these the "new Cyrenaicism" of Marius took its criterion of values. It was a theory, indeed, which might properly be regarded as in great degree coincident with the main principle of the Stoics themselves, and an older version of the precept "Whatsoever thy hand findeth to do, do it with thy might"—a doctrine so widely acceptable among the nobler spirits of that time. And, as with that, its mistaken tendency would lie in the direction of a kind of idolatry of mere life, or natural gift, or strength—*l'idôlatrie des talents.*

To understand the various forms of ancient art and thought, the various forms of actual human feeling (the only new thing, in a world almost too opulent in what was old) to satisfy, with a kind of scrupulous equity, the claims of these concrete and actual objects on his sympathy, his intelligence, his senses—to "pluck out the heart of their mystery," and in turn become the interpreter of them to others: this had now defined itself for Marius as a very narrowly practical design: it determined his choice of a vocation to live by. It was the era of the *rhetoricians,* or *sophists,* as they were sometimes called; of men who came in some instances to great fame and fortune, by way of a literary cultivation of "science." That science, it has been often said, must have been wholly an affair of words. But in a world, confessedly so opulent in what was old, the work even of genius must necessarily consist very much in criticism; and, in the case of the more excellent specimens of his class, the rhetorician was, after all, the eloquent and effective interpreter, for the delighted ears of others, of what understanding himself had come by, in years of travel and study, of the beautiful house of art and thought which was the inheritance of the age. The emperor Marcus Aurelius, to whose service Marius had now been called, was himself, more or less openly a "lecturer." That late world, amid many curiously vivid modern traits, had this spectacle, so familiar to ourselves, of the public lecturer or essayist; in some cases adding to his other gifts that of the Christian preacher, who knows how to touch people's sensibilities on behalf of the suffering. To follow in the way of these successes, was the natural instinct of youthful ambition; and it was with no vulgar egotism that Marius, at the age of nineteen, determined, like many another young man of parts, to enter as a student of rhetoric at Rome.

Though the manner of his work was changed formally from poetry to prose, he remained, and must always be, of the poetic temper: by which, I mean, among other things, that quite independently of the general habit of that pensive age he lived much, and as it were by system, in reminiscence. Amid his eager grasping at the sensation, the consciousness of the present, he had come to see that, after all, the main point of economy in the conduct of the present, was the question:—How will it look to me, at what shall I value it, this day next year?—that in any given day or month one's main concern was its impression for the memory. A strange trick memory sometimes played him; for, with no natural gradation, what was of last month, or of yesterday, of to-day even, would seem as far off, as entirely detached from him, as things of ten years ago. Detached from him, yet very real, there lay certain spaces of his life, in delicate perspective, under a favorable light; and, somehow, all the less fortunate detail and circumstance had parted from them. Such hours were oftenest those in which he had been helped by work of others to the pleasurable apprehension of art, of nature, or of life. "Not what I do, but what I am, under the power of this vision"—he would say to himself—"is what were indeed pleasing to the gods!"

And yet, with a kind of inconsistency in one who had taken for his philosophic ideal the *μονόχρονος ἡδονή* of Aristippus—the pleasure of the ideal present, of the mystic *now*—there would come, together with that precipitate sinking of things into the past, a desire, after all, to retain "what was so transitive." Could he but arrest, for others also, certain clauses of experience, as the imaginative memory presented them to himself! In those grand, hot summers, he would have imprisoned the very perfume of the flowers. To create, to live, perhaps, a little while beyond the allotted hours, if it were but in a fragment of perfect expression:—it was thus his longing defined itself for something to hold by amid the "perpetual flux." With men of his vocation, people were apt to say, words were things. Well! with him, words should be indeed things,—the word, the phrase, valuable in exact proportion to the transparency with which it conveyed to others the apprehension, the emotion, the mood, so vividly real within himself. *Verbaque provisam rem non invita sequentur:* Virile apprehension of the true nature of things, of the true nature of one's own impression, first of all!—words would follow that naturally, a true understanding of one's self being ever the first condition of genuine style. Language delicate and measured, the delicate Attic phrase, for instance, in which the eminent Aristeides could speak, was then a power to which people's hearts, and sometimes even their purses, readily responded. And there were many points, as Marius thought, on which the heart of that age greatly needed to be touched. He hardly knew how strong that old religious sense of responsibility, the conscience, as we call it, still was within him—a body of inward impressions, as real as those so highly valued outward ones—to offend against which, brought with it a strange feeling of disloyalty, as to a person. And the determination, adhered to with no misgiving, to add nothing, not so much as a transient sigh, to the great total of men's unhappiness, in his way through the world:—that too was something to rest on, in the drift of mere "appearances."

All this would involve a life of industry, of industrious study, only possible through healthy rule, keeping clear the eye alike of body and soul. For the male element, the logical conscience asserted itself now, with opening manhood—asserted itself, even in his literary style, by a certain firmness of outline, that touch of the worker in metal, amid its richness. Already he blamed instinctively alike in his work and in himself, as youth so seldom does, all that had not passed a long and liberal process of erasure. The happy phrase or sentence was really modeled upon a cleanly finished structure of scrupulous thought. The suggestive force of the one master of his development, who had battled so hard with imaginative prose; the utterance, the golden utterance, of the other, so content with its living power of persuasion that he had never written at all,—in the commixture of these two qualities he set up his literary ideal, and this rare blending of grace with an intellectual rigor or astringency, was the secret of a singular expressiveness in it.

He acquired at this time a certain bookish air, the somewhat somber habitude of the avowed scholar, which though it never interfered with the perfect tone, "fresh and serenely disposed," of the Roman gentleman, yet qualified it as by an interesting oblique trait, and frightened away some of his equals in age and rank. The sober discretion of his thoughts, his sustained habit of meditation, the sense of those negative conclusions enabling him to concentrate himself, with an absorption so entire, upon what is immediately *here* and *now*, gave him a peculiar manner of intellectual confidence, as of one who had indeed been initiated into a great secret. —Though with an air so disengaged, he seemed to be living so intently in the visible world! And now, in revolt against that preoccupation with other persons, which had so often perturbed his spirit, his wistful speculations as to what the real, the greater experience might be, determined in him, not as the longing for love—to be with Cynthia, or Aspasia—but as a thirst for existence in exquisite places. The veil that was to be lifted for him lay over the works of the old masters of art, in places where nature also had used her mastery. And it was just at this moment that a summons to Rome reached him.

James McNeill Whistler

"THE TEN O'CLOCK"

None of the criticisms of Victorian middle-class taste achieved quite the ironic public success of Whistler's "Ten O'Clock," delivered after appropriate heralding in St. James's Hall, Picadilly. The hour was chosen by the artist to allow the gentlemen time to finish their after-dinner port and cigars. This witty, epigrammatic lecture struck the fashionable audience very well indeed and was repeated on four occasions the following year, once in 1888, and again in 1891. It was published separately in 1888; then in 1890 it appeared as a section of *The Gentle Art of Making Enemies*. Although Whistler's immediate purpose was to censure popular taste, on the positive side he acclaimed the artist as an arranger of harmonies and a creator of effects based on subtle hints from nature. The creator must work "severed" and apart, with no commitment to reform society.

It is not surprising that Whistler, who was fond of picturing himself as a butterfly with a sting in its tail, has proved one of the most durable of the Victorian figures: his talent, verve, and eccentric courage would be striking in any age.

Ladies and Gentlemen:

It is with great hesitation and much misgiving that I appear before you, in the character of The Preacher.

If timidity be at all allied to the virtue modesty, and can find favour in your eyes, I pray you, for the sake of that virtue, accord me your utmost indulgence.

I would plead for my want of habit, did it not seem preposterous, judging from precedent, that aught save the most efficient effrontery could be ever expected in connection with my subject—for I will not conceal from you that I mean to talk about Art. Yes, Art—that

Lecture first delivered February 20, 1885.

has of late become, as far as much discussion and writing can make it, a sort of common topic for the tea-table.

Art is upon the Town!—to be chucked under the chin by the passing gallant—to be enticed within the gates of the householder—to be coaxed into company, as a proof of culture and refinement.

If familiarity can breed contempt, certainly Art—or what is currently taken for it—has been brought to its lowest stage of intimacy.

The people have been harassed with Art in every guise, and vexed with many methods as to its endurance. They have been told how they shall love Art, and live with it. Their homes have been invaded, their walls covered with paper, their very dress taken to task—until, roused at last, bewildered and filled with the doubts and discomforts of senseless suggestion, they resent such intrusion, and cast forth the false prophets, who have brought the very name of the beautiful into disrepute, and derision upon themselves.

Alas! ladies and gentlemen, Art has been maligned. She has naught in common with such practices. She is a goddess of dainty thought—reticent of habit, abjuring all obtrusiveness, purposing in no way to better others.

She is, withal, selfishly occupied with her own perfection only—having no desire to teach—seeking and finding the beautiful in all conditions and in all times, as did her high priest, Rembrandt, when he saw picturesque grandeur and noble dignity in the Jews' quarter of Amsterdam, and lamented not that its inhabitants were not Greeks.

As did Tintoret and Paul Veronese, among the Venetians, while not halting to change the brocaded silks for the classic draperies of Athens.

As did, at the Court of Philip, Velasquez, whose Infantas, clad in inæsthetic hoops, are, as works of Art, of the same quality as the Elgin marbles.

No reformers were these great men—no improvers of the way of others! Their productions alone were their occupation, and, filled with the poetry of their science, they required not to alter their surroundings—for, as the laws of their Art were revealed to them they saw, in the development of their work, that real beauty which, to them, was as much a matter of certainty and triumph as is to the astronomer the verification of the result, foreseen with the light given to him alone. In all this, their world was completely severed from that of their fellow-creatures with whom sentiment is mistaken for poetry; and for whom there is no perfect work that shall not be explained by the benefit conferred upon themselves.

Humanity takes the place of Art, and God's creations are excused by their usefulness. Beauty is confounded with virtue, and, before a work of Art, it is asked: "What good shall it do?"

Hence it is that nobility of action, in this life, is hopelessly linked with the merit of the work that portrays it! and thus the people have acquired the habit of looking, as who should say, not *at* a picture, but *through* it, at some human fact, that shall, or shall not, from a social point of view, better their mental or moral state. So we have come to hear of the painting that elevates, and of the duty of the painter—of the picture that is full of thought, and of the panel that merely decorates.

A favourite faith, dear to those who teach, is that certain periods were especially artistic, and that nations, readily named, were notably lovers of Art.

So we are told that the Greeks were, as a people, worshippers of the beautiful, and that in the fifteenth century Art was engrained in the multitude.

That the great masters lived in common understanding with their patrons—that the early Italians were artists—all—and that the demand for the lovely thing produced it.

That we, of to-day, in gross contrast to this Arcadian purity, call for the ungainly, and obtain the ugly.

That, could we but change our habits and climate—were we willing to wander in groves—could we be roasted out of broadcloth—were we to do without haste, and journey without speed, we should again *require* the spoon of Queen Anne, and pick at our peas with the fork of two prongs. And so, for the flock, little hamlets grow near Hammersmith, and the steam horse is scorned.

Useless! Quite hopeless and false is the effort!—built upon fable, and all because "a wise man has uttered a vain thing and filled his belly with the East wind."

Listen! There never was an artistic period.

There never was an Art-loving nation.

In the beginning, man went forth each day—some to do battle, some to the chase; others, again, to dig and to delve in the field—all that they might gain and live, or lose and die. Until there was found among them one, differing from the rest, whose pursuits attracted him not, and so he stayed by the tents with the women, and traced strange devices with a burnt stick upon a gourd.

This man, who took no joy in the ways of his brethren—who cared not for conquest, and fretted in the field—this designer of quaint patterns—this deviser of the beautiful—who perceived in Nature about him curious curvings, as faces are seen in the fire—this dreamer apart, was the first artist.

And when, from the field and from afar, there came back the people, they took the gourd—and drank from out of it.

And presently there came to this man another—and, in time, others—of like nature, chosen by the Gods—and so they worked together; and soon they fashioned, from the moistened earth, forms resembling the gourd. And with the power of creation, the heirloom of the artist, presently they went beyond the slovenly suggestion of Nature, and the first vase was born, in beautiful proportion.

And the toilers tilled, and were athirst; and the heroes returned from fresh victories, to rejoice and to feast; and all drank alike from the artists' goblets, fashioned cunningly, taking no note the while of the craftsman's pride, and understanding not his glory in his work; drinking at the cup, not from choice, not from a consciousness that it was beautiful, but because, forsooth, there was none other!

And time, with more state, brought more capacity for luxury, and it became well that men should dwell in large houses, and rest upon couches, and eat at tables; whereupon the artist, with his artificers, built palaces, and filled them with furniture, beautiful in proportion and lovely to look upon.

And the people lived in marvels of art—and ate and drank out of masterpieces—for there was nothing else to eat and to drink out of, and no bad building to live in; no article of daily life, of luxury, or of necessity, that had not been handed down from the design of the master, and made by his workmen.

And the people questioned not, *and had nothing to say in the matter.*

So Greece was in its splendour, and Art reigned supreme—by

force of fact, not by election—and there was no meddling from the outsider. The mighty warrior would no more have ventured to offer a design for the temple of Pallas Athene than would the sacred poet have proffered a plan for constructing the catapult.

And the Amateur was unknown—and the Dilettante undreamed of!

And history wrote on, and conquest accompanied civilization, and Art spread, or rather its products were carried by the victors among the vanquished from one country to another. And the customs of cultivation covered the face of the earth, so that all peoples continued to use what *the artist alone produced.*

And centuries passed in this using, and the world was flooded with all that was beautiful, until there arose a new class, who discovered the cheap, and foresaw fortune in the facture of the sham.

Then sprang into existence the tawdry, the common, the gewgaw.

The taste of the tradesman supplanted the science of the artist, and what was born of the million went back to them, and charmed them, for it was after their own heart; and the great and the small, the statesman and the slave, took to themselves the abomination that was tendered, and preferred it—and have lived with it ever since!

And the artist's occupation was gone, and the manufacturer and the huckster took his place.

And now the heroes filled from the jugs and drank from the bowls—with understanding—noting the glare of their new bravery, and taking pride in its worth.

And the people—this time—had much to say in the matter—and all were satisfied. And Birmingham and Manchester arose in their might—and Art was relegated to the curiosity shop.

Nature contains the elements, in colour and form, of all pictures, as the keyboard contains the notes of all music.

But the artist is born to pick, and choose, and group with science, these elements, that the result may be beautiful—as the musician gathers his notes, and forms his chords, until he bring forth from chaos glorious harmony.

To say to the painter, that Nature is to be taken as she is, is to say to the player, that he may sit on the piano.

That Nature is always right, is an assertion, artistically, as untrue, as it is one whose truth is universally taken for granted. Nature is very rarely right, to such an extent even, that it might almost be said that Nature is usually wrong: that is to say, the condition of things that shall bring about the perfection of harmony worthy a picture is rare, and not common at all.

This would seem, to even the most intelligent, a doctrine almost blasphemous. So incorporated with our education has the supposed aphorism become, that its belief is held to be part of our moral being, and the words themselves have, in our ear, the ring of religion. Still, seldom does Nature succeed in producing a picture.

The sun blares, the wind blows from the east, the sky is bereft of cloud, and without, all is of iron. The windows of the Crystal Palace are seen from all points of London. The holiday-maker rejoices in the glorious day, and the painter turns aside to shut his eyes.

How little this is understood, and how dutifully the casual in Nature is accepted as sublime, may be gathered from the unlimited admiration daily produced by a very foolish sunset.

The dignity of the snow-capped mountain is lost in distinctness, but the joy of the tourist is to recognise the traveller on the top. The desire to see, for the sake of seeing it, is, with the mass, alone the one to be gratified, hence the delight in detail.

And when the evening mist clothes the riverside with poetry, as with a veil, and the poor buildings lose themselves in the dim sky, and the tall chimneys become campanili, and the warehouses are palaces in the night, and the whole city hangs in the heavens, and fairy-land is before us—then the wayfarer hastens home; the working man and the cultured one, the wise man and the one of pleasure, cease to understand, as they have ceased to see, and Nature, who, for once, has sung in tune, sings her exquisite song to the artist alone, her son and her master—her son in that he loves her, her master in that he knows her.

To him her secrets are unfolded, to him her lessons have become gradually clear. He looks at her flower, not with the enlarging lens, that he may gather facts for the botanist, but with the light of the one who sees in her choice selection of brilliant tones and delicate tints, suggestions of future harmonies.

He does not confine himself to purposeless copying, without thought, each blade of grass, as commended by the inconsequent, but, in the long curve of the narrow leaf, corrected by the straight tall stem, he learns how grace is wedded to dignity, how strength enhances sweetness, that elegance shall be the result.

In the citron wing of the pale butterfly, with its dainty spots of orange, he sees before him the stately halls of fair gold, with their slender saffron pillars, and is taught how the delicate drawing high upon the walls shall be traced in tender tones of orpiment, and repeated by the base in notes of graver hue.

In all that is dainty and lovable he finds hints for his own combinations, and *thus* is Nature ever his resource and always at his service, and to him is naught refused.

Through his brain, as through the last alembic, is distilled the refined essence of that thought which began with the Gods, and which they left him to carry out.

Oscar Wilde

"THE DECAY OF LYING"

Oscar Wilde, who like Whistler was a zealous antiliteralist, detested the emasculative influence of "fact" on art. "The Decay of Lying," one of his finest essays, is primarily an attack on nineteenth-century Realism; and Wilde's highly aphoristic, scintillating manner conceals deeply-felt aesthetic principles. His basic contention is that all true art, all inspired "lying," transcends time; its communicative power is constant and immutable. By insisting upon fidelity to the raw materials of nature and life, the Realist denies the universality of creative art.

Whistler was annoyed by Wilde's essay. Not only were there echoes of his own "Ten O'Clock" (Wilde's fog passage is a parody of Whistler's famous one), but a man thought to be a disciple had arrogantly taken the defense of art and style upon his own shoulders, freely borrowing from the master's tone and ideas. The truth

From *The Nineteenth Century* (January, 1889).

is that Wilde's essay is much more cohesive stylistically than Whistler's, better organized, and not as derivative as Whistler imagined. The selection opens shortly after the beginning of the dialogue.

VIVIAN. Shall I read you what I have written? It might do you a great deal of good.

CYRIL. Certainly, if you give me a cigarette. Thanks. By the way, what magazine do you intend it for?

VIVIAN. For the *Retrospective Review*. I think I told you that the elect had revived it.

CYRIL. Whom do you mean by "the elect"?

VIVIAN. Oh, the Tired Hedonists, of course. It is a club to which I belong. We are supposed to wear faded roses in our button-holes when we meet, and to have a sort of cult for Domitian. I am afraid you are not eligible. You are too fond of simple pleasures.

CYRIL. I should be black-balled on the ground of animal spirits, I suppose?

VIVIAN. Probably. Besides you are a little too old. We don't admit anybody who is of the usual age.

CYRIL. Well, I should fancy you are all a good deal bored with each other.

VIVIAN. We are. That is one of the objects of the club. Now, if you promise not to interrupt too often, I will read you my article.

CYRIL. You will find me all attention.

VIVIAN (*reading in a very clear, musical voice*). "THE DECAY OF LYING: A PROTEST.—One of the chief causes that can be assigned for the curiously commonplace character of most of the literature of our age is undoubtedly the decay of Lying as an art, a science, and a social pleasure. The ancient historians gave us delightful fiction in the form of fact; the modern novelist presents us with dull facts under the guise of fiction. The Blue-Book is rapidly becoming his ideal both for method and manner. He has his tedious '*document humain*,' his miserable little '*coin de la création*,' into which he peers with his microscope. He is to be found at the Librarie Nationale, or at the British Museum, shamelessly reading up his subject. He has not even the courage of other people's ideas, but insists on going directly to life for everything, and ultimately, between encyclopaedias and personal experience, he comes to the ground, having drawn his types from the family circle or from the weekly washerwoman, and having acquired an amount of useful information from which never, even in his most meditative moments, can he thoroughly free himself.

"The loss that results to literature in general from this false ideal of our time can hardly be over-estimated. People have a careless way of talking about a 'born liar,' just as they talk about a 'born poet.' But in both cases they are wrong. Lying and poetry are arts—arts, as Plato saw, not unconnected with each other—and they require the most careful study, the most disinterested devotion. Indeed, they have their technique, just as the more material arts of painting and sculpture have, their subtle secrets of form and colour, their craft-mysteries, their deliberate artistic methods. As one knows the poet by his fine music, so one can recognize the liar by his rich rhythmic utterance, and in neither case will the casual inspiration of the moment suffice. Here, as elsewhere, practice must precede perfection. But in modern days while the fashion of writing poetry has become far too common, and should, if possible, be discouraged, the fashion of lying has almost fallen into disrepute. Many a young man starts in life with a natural gift for exaggeration which, if nurtured in congenial and sympathetic surroundings, or by the imitation of the best models, might grow into something really great and wonderful. But, as a rule, he comes to nothing. He either falls into careless habits of accuracy——"

CYRIL. My dear fellow!

VIVIAN. Please don't interrupt in the middle of a sentence. "He either falls into careless habits of accuracy, or takes to frequenting the society of the aged and the well-informed. Both things are equally fatal to his imagination, as indeed they would be fatal to the imagination of anybody, and in a short time he develops a morbid and unhealthy faculty of truth-telling, begins to verify all statements made in his presence, has no hesitation in contradicting people who are much younger than himself, and often ends by writing novels which are so like life that no one can possibly believe in their probability. This is no isolated instance that we are giving. It is simply one example out of many; and if something cannot be done to check, or at least to modify, our monstrous worship of facts, Art will become sterile, and Beauty will pass away from the land.

"Even Mr. Robert Louis Stevenson, that delightful master of delicate and fanciful prose, is tainted with this modern vice, for we know positively no other name for it. There is such a thing as robbing a story of its reality by trying to make it too true, and *The Black Arrow* is so inartistic as not to contain a single anachronism to boast of, while the transformation of Dr. Jekyll reads dangerously like an experiment out of the *Lancet*. As for Mr. Rider Haggard, who really has, or had once, the makings of a perfectly magnificent liar, he is now so afraid of being suspected of genius that when he does tell us anything marvellous, he feels bound to invent a personal reminiscence, and to put it into a footnote as a kind of cowardly corroboration. Nor are our other novelists much better. Mr. Henry James writes fiction as if it were a painful duty, and wastes upon mean motives and imperceptible 'points of view' his neat literary style, his felicitous phrases, his swift and caustic satire. Mr. Hall Caine, it is true, aims at the grandiose, but then he writes at the top of his voice. He is so loud that one cannot hear what he says. Mr. James Payn is an adept in the art of concealing what is not worth finding. He hunts down the obvious with the enthusiasm of a short-sighted detective. As one turns over the pages, the suspense of the author becomes almost unbearable. The horses of Mr. William Black's phaeton do not soar towards the sun. They merely frighten the sky at evening into violent chromolithographic effects. On seeing them approach, the peasants take refuge in dialect. Mrs. Oliphant prattles pleasantly about curates, lawn-tennis parties, domesticity, and other wearisome things. Mr. Marion Crawford has immolated himself upon the altar of local colour. . . . *Robert Elsmere* is of course a masterpiece—a masterpiece of the 'genre ennuyeux,' the one form of literature that the English people seem to thoroughly enjoy. A thoughtful young friend of ours once told us that it reminded him of the sort of conversation that goes on at a meat tea in the house of a serious Nonconformist family, and we can quite believe it. Indeed it is only in England that such a book could be produced. England is the home of lost ideas. As for that great and daily increasing school of novelists for whom the sun always rises in the East-End, the only thing that can be said about them is that they find life crude, and leave it raw.

"In France, though nothing so deliberately tedious as *Robert Elsmere* has been produced, things are not much better. M. Guy de Maupassant, with his keen mordant irony and his hard vivid style, strips life of the few poor rags that still cover her, and shows us foul sore and festering wound. He writes lurid little tragedies in which everybody is ridiculous; bitter comedies at which one cannot laugh for very tears. M. Zola, true to the lofty principle that he lays down in one of his pronunciamentos on literature, 'L'homme de génie n'a jamais d'esprit,' is determined to show that, if he has not got genius, he can at least be dull. And how well he succeeds! He is not without power. Indeed at times, as in *Germinal*, there is something almost epic in his work. But his work is entirely wrong from beginning to end, and wrong not on the ground of morals, but on the ground of art. From any ethical standpoint it is just what it should be. The author is perfectly truthful, and describes things exactly as they happen. What more can any moralist desire? We have no sympathy at all with the moral indignation of our time against M. Zola. It is simply the indignation of Tartuffe on being exposed. But from the standpoint of art, what can be said in favour of the author of *L'Assommoir*, *Nana*, and *Pot-Bouille*? Nothing. Mr. Ruskin once described the characters in George Eliot's novels as being like the sweepings of a Pentonville omnibus, but M. Zola's characters are much worse. They have their dreary vices, and their drearier virtues. The record of their lives is absolutely without interest. Who cares what happens to them? In literature we require distinction, charm, beauty, and imaginative power. We don't want to be harrowed and disgusted with an account of the doings of the lower orders. M. Daudet is better. He has wit, a light touch, and an amusing style. But he has lately committed literary suicide. Nobody can possibly care for Delobelle with his 'Il faut lutter pour l'art,' or for Valmajour with his eternal refrain about the nightingale, or for the poet in *Jack* with his 'mots cruels,' now that we have learned from *Vingt Ans de ma Vie littéraire* that these characters were taken directly from life. To us they seem to have suddenly lost all their vitality, all the few qualities they ever possessed. The only real people are the people who never existed, and if a novelist is base enough to go to life for his personages he should at least pretend that they are creations, and not boast of them as copies. The justification of a character in a novel is not that other persons are what they are, but that the author is what he is. Otherwise the novel is not a work of art. . . ." However, my dear Cyril, I will not detain you any further here. I quite admit that modern novels have many good points. All I insist on is that, as a class, they are quite unreadable.

CYRIL. That is certainly a very grave qualification, but I must say that I think you are rather unfair in some of your strictures. I like *The Deemster,* and *The Daughter of Heth,* and *Le Disciple,* and *Mr. Isaacs,* and as for *Robert Elsmere* I am quite devoted to it. Not that I can look upon it as a serious work. As a statement of the problems that confront the earnest Christian it is ridiculous and antiquated. It is simply Arnold's *Literature and Dogma* with the literature left out. It is as much behind the age as Paley's *Evidences,* or Colenso's method of Biblical exegesis. Nor could anything be less impressive than the unfortunate hero gravely heralding a dawn that rose long ago, and so completely missing its true significance that he proposes to carry on the business of the old firm under the new name. On the other hand, it contains several clever caricatures, and a heap of delightful quotations, and Green's philosophy very pleasantly sugars the somewhat bitter pill of the author's fiction. I also cannot help expressing my surprise that you have said nothing about the two novelists whom you are always reading, Balzac and George Meredith. Surely they are realists, both of them?

VIVIAN. Ah! Meredith! Who can define him? His style is chaos illumined by flashes of lightning. As a writer he has mastered everything except language: as a novelist he can do everything, except tell a story: as an artist he is everything, except articulate. Somebody in Shakespeare—Touchstone, I think—talks about a man who is always breaking his shins over his own wit, and it seems to me that this might serve as the basis for a criticism of Meredith's method. But whatever he is, he is not a realist. Or rather I would say that he is a child of realism who is not on speaking terms with his father. By deliberate choice he has made himself a romanticist. He has refused to bow the knee to Baal, and after all, even if the man's fine spirit did not revolt against the noisy assertions of realism, his style would be quite sufficient of itself to keep life at a respectful distance. By its means he has planted round his garden a hedge full of thorns, and red with wonderful roses. As for Balzac, he was a most remarkable combination of the artistic temperament with the scientific spirit. The latter he bequeathed to his disciples: the former was entirely his own. The difference between such a book as M. Zola's *L'Assommoir* and Balzac's *Illusions Perdues* is the difference between unimaginative realism and imaginative reality. "All Balzac's characters," said Baudelaire, "are gifted with the same ardour of life that animated himself. All his fictions are as deeply coloured as dreams. Each mind is a weapon loaded to the muzzle with will. The very scullions have genius." A steady course of Balzac reduces our living friends to shadows, and our acquaintances to the shadows of shades. His characters have a kind of fervent fiery-coloured existence. They dominate us, and defy scepticism. One of the greatest tragedies of my life is the death of Lucien de Rubempré. It is a grief from which I have never been able to completely rid myself. It haunts me in my moments of pleasure. I remember it when I laugh. But Balzac is no more a realist than Holbein was. He created life, he did not copy it. I admit, however, that he set far too high a value on modernity of form, and that, consequently, there is no book of his that, as an artistic masterpiece, can rank with *Salammbô* or *Esmond*, or *The Cloister and the Hearth*, or the *Vicomte de Bragelonne*.

CYRIL. Do you object to modernity of form, then?

VIVIAN. Yes. It is a huge price to pay for a very poor result. Pure modernity of form is always somewhat vulgarising. It cannot help being so. The public imagine that, because they are interested in their immediate surroundings, Art should be interested in them also, and should take them as her subject-matter. But the mere fact that they are interested in these things makes them unsuitable subjects for Art. The only beautiful things, as somebody once said, are the things that do not concern us. As long as a thing is useful or necessary to us, or affects us in any way, either for pain or for pleasure, or appeals strongly to our sympathies, or is a vital part of the environment in which we live, it is outside the proper sphere of art. To art's subject-matter we should be more or less indifferent. We should, at any rate, have no preferences, no prejudices, no partisan feeling of any kind. It is exactly because Hecuba is nothing to us that her sorrows are such an admirable motive for a tragedy. I do not know anything in the whole history of literature sadder than the artistic career of Charles Reade. He wrote one beautiful book, *The Cloister and the Hearth,* a book as much above *Romola* as *Romola* is above *Daniel Deronda,* and wasted the rest of his life in a foolish attempt to be modern, to draw public attention to the state of our convict prisons, and the management of our private lunatic asylums. Charles Dickens was depressing enough in all conscience when he tried to arouse our sympathy for the victims of the poor-law administration; but Charles Reade, an artist, a scholar, a man with a true sense of beauty, raging and roaring over the abuses of contemporary life like a common pamphleteer or a sensational journalist, is really a sight for the angels to weep over. Believe me, my dear Cyril, modernity of form and modernity of subject-matter are entirely and absolutely wrong. We have mistaken the common livery of the age for the vesture of the Muses, and spend our days in the sordid streets and hideous suburbs of our vile cities when we should be out on the hillside with Apollo. Certainly we are a degraded race, and have sold our birthright for a mess of facts.

CYRIL. There is something in what you say, and there is no doubt that whatever amusement we may find in reading a purely modern novel, we have rarely any artistic pleasure in re-reading it. And this is perhaps the best rough test of what is literature and what is not. If one cannot enjoy reading a book over and over again, there is no use reading it at all. But what do you say about the return to Life and Nature? This is the panacea that is always being recommended to us.

VIVIAN. I will read you what I say on that subject. The passage comes later on in the article, but I may as well give it to you now:—

"The popular cry of our time is 'Let us return to Life and Nature; they will recreate Art for us, and send the red blood coursing through her veins; they will shoe her feet with swiftness and make her hand strong.' But, alas! we are mistaken in our amiable and well-meaning efforts. Nature is always behind the age. And as for Life, she is the solvent that breaks up Art, the enemy that lays waste her house."

CYRIL. What do you mean by saying that Nature is always behind the age?

VIVIAN. Well, perhaps that is rather cryptic. What I mean is this. If we take Nature to mean natural simple instinct as opposed to self-conscious culture, the work produced under this influence is always old-fashioned, antiquated, and out of date. One touch of Nature may make the whole world kin, but two touches of Nature will destroy any work of Art. If, on the other hand, we regard Nature as the collection of phenomena external to man, people only discover in her what they bring to her. She has no suggestions of her own. Wordsworth went to the lakes, but he was never a lake poet. He found in stones the sermons he had already hidden there. He went moralising about the district, but his good work was produced when he returned, not to Nature but to poetry. Poetry gave him "Laodamia," and the fine sonnets, and the great Ode, such as it is. Nature gave him "Martha Ray" and "Peter Bell," and the address to Mr. Wilkinson's spade.

CYRIL. I think that view might be questioned. I am rather inclined to believe in the "impulse from a vernal wood," though of course the artistic value of such an impulse depends entirely on the kind of temperament that receives it, so that the return to Nature would come to mean simply the advance to a great personality. You would agree with that, I fancy. However, proceed with your article.

VIVIAN (*reading*). "Art begins with abstract decoration with purely imaginative and pleasurable work dealing with what is unreal and non-existent. This is the first stage. Then Life becomes fascinated with this new wonder, and asks to be admitted into the charmed circle. Art takes life as part of her rough material, recreates it, and refashions it in fresh forms, is absolutely indifferent to fact, invents, imagines, dreams, and keeps between herself and reality the impenetrable barrier of beautiful style, of decorative or ideal treatment. The third stage is when Life gets the upper hand, and drives Art out into the wilderness. This is the true decadence, and it is from this that we are now suffering.

"Take the case of the English drama. At first in the hands of the monks Dramatic Art was abstract, decorative, and mythological. Then she enlisted Life in her service, and using some of life's external forms, she created an entirely new race of beings, whose sorrows were more terrible than any sorrow man has ever felt, whose joys were keener than lovers' joys, who had the rage of the Titans and the calm of the gods, who had monstrous and marvellous sins, monstrous and marvelous virtues. To them she gave a language different from that of actual use, a language full of resonant music and sweet rhythm, made stately by solemn cadence, or made delicate by fanciful rhyme, jewelled with wonderful words, and enriched with lofty diction. She clothed her children in strange raiment and gave them masks, and at her bidding the antique world rose from its marble tomb. A new Cæsar stalked through the streets of risen Rome, and with purple sail and flute-led oars another Cleopatra passed up the river to Antioch. Old myth and legend and dream took shape and substance. History was entirely re-written, and there was hardly one of the dramatists who did not recognize that the object of Art is not simple truth but complex beauty. In this they were perfectly right. Art itself is really a form of exaggeration; and selection, which is the very spirit of art, is nothing more than an intensified mode of over-emphasis.

"But Life soon shattered the perfection of the form. Even in Shakespeare we can see the beginning of the end. It shows itself by the gradual breaking up of the blank-verse in the later plays, by the predominance given to prose, and by the over-importance assigned to characterisation. The passages in Shakespeare—and they are many—where the language is uncouth, vulgar, exaggerated, fantastic, obscene even, are entirely due to Life calling for an echo of her own voice, and rejecting the intervention of beautiful style, through which alone should Life be suffered to find expression. Shakespeare is not by any means a flawless artist. He is too fond of going directly to life, and borrowing life's natural utterance. He forgets that when Art surrenders her imaginative medium she surrenders everything. . . .

"What is true about the drama and the novel is no less true about those arts that we call the decorative arts. The whole history of these arts in Europe is the record of the struggle between Orientalism, with its frank rejection of imitation, its love of artistic convention, its dislike to the actual representation of any object in Nature, and our own imitative spirit. Wherever the former has been paramount, as in Byzantium, Sicily, and Spain, by actual contact, or in the rest of Europe by the influence of the Crusades, we have had beautiful and imaginative work in which the visible things of life are transmuted into artistic conventions, and the things that Life has not are invented and fashioned for her delight. But wherever we have returned to Life and Nature, our work has always become vulgar, common, and uninteresting. Modern tapestry, with its aërial effects, its elaborate perspective, its broad expanses of waste sky, its faithful and laborious realism, has no beauty whatsoever. The pictorial glass of Germany is absolutely detestable. We are beginning to weave possible carpets in England, but only because we have returned to the method and spirit of the East. Our rugs and carpets of twenty years ago, with their solemn depressing truths, their inane worship of Nature, their sordid reproductions of visible objects, have become, even to the Philistine, a source of laughter. A cultured Mahomedan once remarked to us, 'You Christians are so occupied in misinterpreting the fourth commandment that you have never thought of making an artistic application of the second.' He was perfectly right, and the whole truth of the matter is this: The proper school to learn art in is not Life but Art."

And now let me read you a passage which seems to me to settle the question very completely.

"It was not always thus. We need not say anything about the poets, for they, with the unfortunate exception of Mr. Wordsworth, have been really faithful to their high mission, and are universally recognized as being absolutely unreliable. But in the works of Herodotus, who, in spite of the shallow and ungenerous attempts of modern sciolists to verify his history, may justly be called the 'Father of Lies'; in the published speeches of Cicero and the biographies of Suetonius; in Tacitus at his best; in Pliny's *Natural History;* in Hanno's *Periplus;* in all the early chronicles; in the Lives of the Saints; in Froissart and Sir Thomas Mallory; in the travels of Marco Polo; in Olaus Magnus, and Aldrovandus, and Conrad Lycosthenes, with his magnificent *Prodigiorum et Ostentorum Chronicon;* in the autobiography of Benvenuto Cellini; in the memoirs of Casanuova; in Defoe's *History of the Plague;* in Boswell's *Life of Johnson;* in Napoleon's despatches, and in the works of our own Carlyle, whose *French Revolution* is one of the most fascinating historical novels ever written, facts are either kept in their proper subordinate position, or else entirely excluded on the general ground of dulness. Now, everything is changed. Facts are not merely finding a footing-place in history, but they are usurping the domain of Fancy, and have invaded the kingdom of Romance. Their chilling touch is over everything. They are vulgarising mankind. The crude commercialism of America, its materialising spirit, its indifference to the poetical side of things, and its lack of imagination and of high unattainable ideals, are entirely due to that country having adopted for its national hero a man, who according to his own confession, was incapable of telling a lie, and it is not too much to say that the story of George Washington and the cherry-tree has done more harm, and in a shorter space of time, than any other moral tale in the whole of literature."

CYRIL. My dear boy!

VIVIAN. I assure you it is the case, and the amusing part of the whole thing is that the story of the cherry-tree is an absolute myth. However, you must not think that I am too despondent about the artistic future either of America or of our own country. Listen to this:—

"That some change will take place before this century has drawn to its close we have no doubt whatsoever. Bored by the tedious and improving conversation of those who have neither the wit to exaggerate nor the genius to romance, tired of the intelligent person whose reminiscences are always based upon memory, whose statements are invariably limited by probability, and who is at any time liable to be corroborated by the merest Philistine who happens to be present, Society sooner or later must return to its lost leader, the cultured and fascinating liar. Who he was who first, without ever having gone out to the rude chase, told the wondering cavemen at sunset how he had dragged the Megatherium from the purple darkness of its jasper cave, or slain the Mammoth in single combat and brought back its gilded tusks, we cannot tell, and not one of our modern anthropologists, for all their much-boasted science, has had the ordinary courage to tell us. Whatever was his name or race, he certainly was the true founder of social intercourse. For the aim of the liar is simply to charm, to delight, to give pleasure. He is the very basis of civilised society, and without him a dinner party, even at the mansions of the great, is as dull as a lecture at the Royal Society, or a debate at the Incorporated Authors, or one of Mr. Burnand's farcical comedies.

"Nor will he be welcomed by society alone. Art, breaking from the prison-house of realism, will run to greet him, and will kiss his false, beautiful lips, knowing that he alone is in possession of the great secret of all her manifestations, the secret that Truth is entirely and absolutely a matter of style; while Life—poor, probable, uninteresting human life—tired of repeating herself for the benefit of Mr. Herbert Spencer, scientific historians, and the compilers of statistics in general, will follow meekly after him, and try to reproduce, in her own simple and untutored way, some of the marvels of which he talks.

"No doubt there will always be critics who, like a certain writer in the *Saturday Review*, will gravely censure the teller of fairy tales for his defective knowledge of natural history, who will measure imaginative work by their own lack of any imaginative faculty, and will hold up their inkstained hands in horror if some honest gentleman, who has never been farther than the yew-trees of his own garden, pens a fascinating book of travels like Sir John Mandeville, or, like great Raleigh, writes a whole history of the world, without knowing anything whatsoever about the past. To excuse themselves they will try and shelter under the shield of him who made Prospero the magician, and gave him Caliban and Ariel as his servants, who heard the Tritons blowing their horns round the coral reefs of the Enchanted Isle, and the fairies singing to each other in a wood near Athens, who led the phantom kings in dim procession across the misty Scottish heath, and hid Hecate in a cave with the weird sisters. They will call upon Shakespeare—they always do—and will quote that hackneyed passage about Art holding the mirror up to Nature, forgetting that this unfortunate aphorism is deliberately said by Hamlet in order to convince the bystanders of his absolute insanity in all art-matters."

CYRIL. Ahem! Another cigarette, please.

VIVIAN. My dear fellow, whatever you may say, it is merely a dramatic utterance, and no more represents Shakespeare's real views upon art than the speeches of Iago represent his real views upon morals. But let me get to the end of the passage:

"Art finds her own perfection within, and not outside of, herself. She is not to be judged by any external standard of resemblance. She is a veil, rather than a mirror. She has flowers that no forests know of, birds that no woodland possesses. She makes and unmakes many worlds, and can draw the moon from heaven with a scarlet thread. Hers are the 'forms more real than living man,' and hers the great archetypes of which things that have existence are but unfinished copies. Nature has, in her eyes, no laws, no uniformity. She can work miracles at her will, and when she calls monsters from the deep they come. She can bid the almond tree blossom in winter, and send the snow upon the ripe cornfield. At her word the frost lays its silver finger on the burning mouth of June, and the winged lions creep out from the hollows of the Lydian hills. The dryads peer from the thicket as she passes by, and the brown fauns smile strangely at her when she comes near them. She has hawk-faced gods that worship her, and the centaurs gallop at her side."

CYRIL. I like that. I can see it. Is that the end?

VIVIAN. No. There is one more passage, but it is purely practical. It simply suggests some methods by which we could revive this lost art of Lying.

CYRIL. Well, before you read it to me, I should like to ask you a question. What do you mean by saying that life, "poor, probable, uninteresting human life," will try to reproduce the marvels of art? I can quite understand your objection to art being treated as a mirror. You think it would reduce genius to the position of a cracked looking-glass. But you don't mean to say that you seriously believe that Life imitates Art, that Life in fact is the mirror, and Art the reality?

VIVIAN. Certainly I do. Paradox though it may seem—and paradoxes are always dangerous things—it is none the less true that Life imitates art far more than Art imitates life. We have all seen in our own day in England how a certain curious and fascinating type of beauty, invented and emphasised by two imaginative painters, has so influenced Life that whenever one goes to a private view or to an artistic salon one sees, here the mystic eyes of Rossetti's dream, the long ivory throat, the strange square-cut jaw, the loosened shadowy hair that he so ardently loved, there the sweet maidenhood of "The Golden Stair," the blossom-like mouth and weary loveliness of the "Laus Amoris," the passion-pale face of Andromeda, the thin hands and lithe beauty of the Vivien in "Merlin's Dream." And it has always been so. A great artist invents a type, and Life tries to copy it, to reproduce it in a popular form, like an enterprising publisher. . . .

However, I do not wish to dwell any further upon individual instances. Personal experience is a most vicious and limited circle. All that I desire to point out is the general principle that Life imitates Art far more than Art imitates Life, and I feel sure that if you think seriously about it you will find that it is true. Life holds the mirror up to Art, and either reproduces some strange type imagined by painter or sculptor, or realises in fact what has been dreamed in fiction. Scientifically speaking, the basis of life—the energy of life, as Aristotle would call it—is simply the desire for expression, and Art is always presenting various forms through which this expression can be attained. Life seizes on them and uses them, even if they be to her own hurt. Young men have committed suicide because Rolla did so, have died by their own hand because by his own hand Werther died. Think of what we owe to the imitation of Christ, of what we owe to the imitation of Cæsar.

Cyril. The theory is certainly a very curious one, but to make it complete you must show that Nature, no less than Life, is an imitation of Art. Are you prepared to prove that?

Vivian. My dear fellow, I am prepared to prove anything.

William Butler Yeats and *John Eglinton* (pseudonym of *William Kirkpatrick Magee*)

LITERARY IDEALS IN IRELAND

The following essays by Yeats and Eglinton, members of the Celtic Revival, were part of a series which appeared in Saturday numbers of the Dublin *Daily Express* in 1898. Thinking they might furnish "a possible chapter of Irish literary history,"

From *Literary Ideals in Ireland* (1898).

T. Fisher Unwin published them (along with essays by George Russell and W. Larmine) the following year under the title *Literary Ideals in Ireland.* The essays were ostensibly concerned with a national literature, but they discussed also the relation of the artist to his time.

In a postscript Yeats appended to a review of the work of Nora Hopper, he took issue with an earlier statement by Eglinton, who had remarked that it was impossible for a dramatist to transform ancient legends into a living national art; such legends, Eglinton said, "obstinately refuse to be taken up out of their old environment and be transplanted into the world of modern sympathies": since we have lost the "proper mode" of treating them, they must remain culturally atypical. In dissenting, Yeats referred to Ibsen and Wagner, whose works based on folk materials were nationally important. The relevant fact, said Yeats, is the genius of the writer and not the age of the subject matter; a gifted writer can transform any material into art.

Eglinton's reply, "National Drama and Contemporary Life," was courteous. It is possible, he said, for a genius to transmute folk materials into art; but the result will be modern, and no longer "pure." Moreover, Yeats was mistaken about Wagner and Ibsen: Wagner's dramas are not "ideal" in a Greek sense; the music is imperfect, and the dramaturgy depends as much upon passion of sound and stage paraphernalia as upon dramatic force. Nor does Ibsen's *Peer Gynt* have the poetical form and "dominating ideas" claimed for it. Eglinton concluded his essay with observations on the tone of nineteenth-century poetry. This paragraph appears below. It is followed by Yeat's reply, Eglinton's further response, and finally by Yeats's "The Autumn of the Flesh," a luxurious description of the decadent mode in literature. Yeats's essay was later published under the slightly less nervous title "The Autumn of the Body."

John Eglinton

NATIONAL DRAMA AND CONTEMPORARY LIFE

There are two conceptions of poetry, mutually antagonistic so far, and not to be reconciled except in the life-work of another great poet, of which one may be called Wordsworthian, which regards the poetic consciousness as acting from within outward and able to confer on even common things the radiance of the imagination; the other, to which those who are rather in sympathy with art than with philosophy are inclined, regards the poet as passive to elect influences and endowing old material with new form. The first regards the poet as a seer and a spiritual force; the second as an aristocratic craftsman. The first looks to man himself as the source of inspiration; the second to tradition, to the forms and images in which old conceptions have been embodied—old faiths, myths, dreams. The weakness of the first is an inclination to indifference toward the form and comeliness of art, as in Whitman; while the second, if it hold aloof from the first, cuts itself asunder from the source of all regeneration in art. The bias of the first is toward naked statement, hard fact, dogmatism; the bias of the second toward theory, diffuseness, insincerity. The latter appears to me to be the bias of belles lettres at present. The poet looks too much away from himself and from his age, does not feel the facts of life enough, but seeks in art an escape from them. Consequently, the art he achieves cannot be the expression of the age and of himself—cannot be representative or national. . . .

W. B. Yeats

JOHN EGLINTON AND SPIRITUAL ART

MR. JOHN EGLINTON wrote recently that though "the ancient legends of Ireland undoubtedly contain situations and characters as well suited for drama as most of those used in Greek tragedies," yet "these subjects," meaning old legends in general, "refuse to be taken up out of their old environment, and be transplanted into the world of modern sympathies. The proper mode of treating them is a secret lost with the subjects themselves." I might have replied by naming a good part of modern literature; but as he spoke particularly of drama I named Ibsen's "Peer Gynt," which is admittedly the chief among the national poems of modern Norway; and Wagner's musical dramas, which I compared with the Greek tragedies, not merely because of the mythological substance of "The Ring" and of "Parsifal," but because of the influence both words and music are beginning to have upon the intellect of Germany and of Europe, which begins to see the German soul in them.

He replied by saying that he preferred Ibsen's dramas, which are "not ideal," which is nothing to the point, and that "the crowd of elect persons seated in curiously devised seats at Bayreuth does not seem very like the whole Athenian democracy thronging into their places for a couple of obols supplied by the State, and witnessing in good faith the deeds of their ancestors." He is mistaken about the facts, for Wagner's musical dramas are not acted only or principally at Bayreuth, but before large crowds of not particularly elect persons at Vienna and at Munich and in many places in Germany and other countries. I do not think the point important, however, for when I spoke of their influence I thought less of the crowds at Vienna or at Munich than of the best intellects of our day, of men like Count Villiers de L'Isle Adam, (*sic.*), the principal founder of the symbolist movement, of whom M. Remy de Gourmont has written, "He opened the doors of the unknown with a crash, and a generation has gone through them to the infinite." The crowds may applaud good art for a time, but they will forget it when vulgarity invents some new thing, for the only permanent influence of any art is an influence that flows down gradually and imperceptibly, as if through orders and hierarchies.

His second article abandons the opinion—an opinion that I thought from the beginning a petulance of rapid writing—that ancient legends "cannot be transplanted into the world of modern sympathies," and thinks that a poet "may be inspired by the legends of his country," but goes on to distinguish between "two conceptions of poetry mutually antagonistic, two ways of treating legends and other things." I am glad to discuss these distinctions with him, for I think it a misfortune that Mr. John Eglinton, whose influence on Irish opinion may yet be great, should believe, as I understand him to believe, in popular music, popular painting, and popular literature. He describes the "conception" of poetry, he believes me to prefer, as preferred "by those who are rather in sympathy with art than with philosophy," as regarding the poet as "an aristocratic craftsman" looking for "the source of inspiration" to "the forms and images, in which old conceptions have been embodied—old faiths, myths, dreams," and as seeking "'in poetry an escape from the facts of life;" and he describes the "conception" he himself prefers and calls Wordsworthian as looking "to man himself as the source of inspiration," and as desiring a poetry that expresses "its age" and "the facts of life," and is yet, strange to say, "a spiritual force" and the work of "a seer."

I will restate these distinctions in the words of the younger Hallam, in his essay on Tennyson; one of the most profound criticisms in the English language. Arthur Hallam described Tennyson, who had then written his earlier and greater, but less popular poems, as belonging to "the aesthetic school," founded by Keats and Shelley —"A poetry of sensation rather than of reflection," "a sort of magic producing a number of impressions too multiplied, too minute, and too diversified to allow of our tracing them to the causes, because just such was the effect, even so boundless and so bewildering, produced" on the imagination of the poet "by the real appearance of nature." This poetry, the work of men whose "fine organs" "have trembled with emotion at colours and sounds and movements unperceived by duller temperaments," must always, he thinks, be unpopular because dull temperaments shrink from, or are incapable of the patient sympathy and exaltation of feeling needful for its understanding. He contrasts it with the popular school, the school he thinks Wordsworth belonged to, in all but his highest moments, which "mixes up'" anecdotes and opinions and moral maxims for their own sake—the things dull temperaments can understand—with what is sometimes the poetry of a fine temperament, but is more often an imitation.

This poetry of the popular school is the poetry of those "who are rather in sympathy" with philosophy than with art, and resembles those paintings one finds in every Royal Academy surrounded by crowds, which "are rather in sympathy" with anecdotes or pretty faces of babies than with good painting. It is the poetry of the utilitarian and the rhetorician and the sentimentalist and the popular journalist and the popular preacher, but it is not the poetry of "the seer," the most "aristocratic" of men, who tells what he alone has tasted and touched and seen amid the exaltation of his senses; and it is not a "spiritual force," though it may talk of nothing but spiritual forces, for a spiritual force is as immaterial and as imperceptible as the falling of dew or as the first greyness of dawn. Why, too, should Mr. John Eglinton, who is a profound transcendentalist, prefer a poetry which is, like all the lusts of the market place, "an expression of its age" and of "the facts of life," the very phrases of the utilitarian criticism of the middle century—to a poetry which seeks to express great passions that are not in nature, though "the real appearance of nature" awakens them; "ideas" that "lie burningly on the divine hand," as Browning calls them, "the beauty that is beyond the grave," as Poe calls them?

The Belgian poet, M. Verhaeren, has also discussed these "two conceptions of poetry," and has described the one as founded on physical science and the other as founded upon transcendental science, and has shown that "the bias of belles lettres at present," of which Mr. John Eglinton complains, has accompanied a renewed interest in transcendental science. And it may well be that men are only able to fashion into beautiful shapes the most delicate emotions of the soul, spending their days with a patience like the patience of the middle ages in the perfect rounding of a verse, or in the perfect carving of a flower, when they are certain that the soul will not die with the body and that the gates of peace are wide, and that the watchers are at their places upon the wall.

I believe that the renewal of belief, which is the great movement of our time, will more and more liberate the arts from "their age" and from life, and leave them more and more free to lose themselves in beauty, and to busy themselves, like all the great poetry of the past and like religions of all times, with "old faiths, myths, dreams," the accumulated beauty of the age. I believe that all men will more and more reject the opinion that poetry is "a criticism of life," and be more and more convinced that it is a revelation of a hidden life, and that they may even come to think "painting, poetry, and music" "the only means of conversing with eternity left to man on earth." I believe, too, that though a Homer or a Dante or a Shakespeare may have used all knowledge, whether of life or of philosophy, or of mythology or of history, he did so, not for the sake of the knowledge, but to shape to a familiar and intelligible body something he had seen or experienced in the exaltation of his senses. I believe, too, that the difference between good and bad poetry is not in its preference for legendary, or for unlegendary subjects, or for a modern or for an archaic treatment, but in the volume and intensity of its passion for beauty, and in the perfection of its workmanship; and that all criticism that forgets these things is mischievous, and doubly mischievous in a country of unsettled opinion.

John Eglinton

MR. YEATS AND POPULAR POETRY

The remark criticised by Mr. Yeats, that "these subjects (ancient legends) refuse to be taken up out of their old environment and be transplanted into the world of modern sympathies," and that "the proper mode of treating them, as they exist in tradition, is a secret lost with the subjects themselves," was not exactly a "petulance of rapid writing," but, on the whole, I am ready to accept responsibility for it. At any rate, its falsity is not apparent in the light of the examples he mentions—Ibsen's "Peer Gynt" and Wagner's musical dramas. When a great legend or narrative comes down to us from antiquity—as, for instance, the Biblical story of David—it does so in a certain form, the form in which it has spontaneously clothed itself, and which fits it as the body fits the soul. No one could improve upon the story of David, unless, by a miracle, he could introduce some new and transforming element into his conception of it. In like manner, the Irish legends have come down to us in a certain form and language, proper to the original conception of them, and they can only be made to live again by something new added to them out of the author's age and personality. As an instance of an old legend or narrative so transformed in the mind of a great and serious artist we might mention Milton's "Samson," which is thus the utterance of Milton's age as much as if the whole conception were original. On the other hand, Morris's "Sigurd" or Ferguson's "Congal," to whatever praise either of them is entitled, is not in the same way an original poem or the utterance of the author's age, as the highest poetry always is. To emphasize this truth is not "mischievous," but serviceable in this or in any country where a serious desire for a truly original literature exists.

The facts of life with which poetry is concerned are not the complex and conventional facts, but the simple and universal. This age cannot have a realistic poet, as it fondly dreams, because poetry is ideal and not realistic. The kinematograph, the bicycle, electric tramcars, labour-saving contrivances, etc., are not susceptible of poetic treatment, but are, in fact, themselves the poetry, not without a kind of suggestiveness, of a scientific age, with which the poetry of Greek and Hebrew tradition vainly endeavors to vie. It is no wonder that an age which has achieved this concrete type of poetry should be content with an attitude of simple politeness toward those dreamers who walk with their heads in a cloud of vision; we can understand its being so better than we can its genial invitation to our poetic dreamers to apply their visionary faculty and quaint rhythmic trick to a treatment of the mechanical triumphs of modern life, as Homer treated the manners and customs of an heroic age. The epics of the present are the steam-engine and the dynamo, its lyrics the kinematograph, photograph, etc., and these bear with them the hearts of men as the Iliad and Odyssey of former days uplifted the youth of antiquity, or as the old English ballads expressed the mind of a nation in its childhood. When the poetic and mythopoeic faculty deserted the disillusioned Greeks they began to speculate on the nature of poetry, and when the moderns, perceiving a certain void in their lives, have begun to ask for an ideal poetic art springing directly out of modern life, it has been found necessary to investigate the origin and nature of poetry. The further these investigations are carried, the greater confirmation will that theory of poetry receive which is so honourably associated with the name of Wordsworth, and which has been adopted and carried forward by Carlyle, Ruskin, Emerson, Whitman, and others; a theory for the statement of which we may refer to the fragment prefixed by Wordsworth to the "Excursion." It is to give the cause of idealism into the hands of the Philistines to allow for a moment that poetry is less a "fact of life" than business or engine-screeching. Far better fall into a ridiculous attitude of hostility toward modern tendencies, like Ruskin or the grim Carlyle, who refused to consider as poetry what was not rooted in the facts of life, or to regard such facts of life as could not be illustrated by poetry as other than "phantasms."

It is curious that the poetry which has been most a fact of the life of the nineteenth century in England, and has been most universal in its appeal, should be called with some propriety "Wordsworthian"—after a man who was certainly without great poetic talent or artistic faculty, but who, simply because he was right, and by virtue of his simplicity and seriousness, reached, as Emerson rightly said, the high-water mark of poetry in this century. With Wordsworth, except at his best, we need not concern ourselves. If, at his best, he is a popular poet, which is doubtful, it is surely in the sense in which Shakespeare and the Bible are popular rather than as Hall Caine and Marie Corelli, or even Byron and Swinburne, are so; and it is not clear that such a popularity need be considered as greatly to his discredit. It is rather a sign that poetry is much more of a fact of life than is commonly supposed, and that a man has only to be original to be universal. The poetry of thought in this century—the poetry of Wordsworth, Tennyson, Browning—is more important than the poetry of art and artifice—the poetry of Coleridge, Rossetti, Swinburne—because of its higher seriousness and more universal appeal; because it is more concerned with the facts of life and is more inspired by faith and hope; because it expresses its age better and what is best in the age.

"I fear," said Blake to Crabb Robinson, "that Wordsworth loves nature," and Mr. Yeats, as a philosopher, though not, we are glad to believe, as a poet, would no doubt sympathise with that solicitude. The writer whom he so greatly admires, Villiers de l'Isle Adam, cherished a particular objection to the sun and daylight; and Paul Verlaine, whose influence Mr. Yeats would perhaps consider less baneful in this country than that of Wordsworth, acknowledged that he "hated to hear the laugh of a healthy man." But really, what do the symbolists, who talk so much of the "exaltation of the senses," mean exactly by saying that the "poetic passion is not in nature," and that art is to be "liberated from life"? Life is nothing but what we make it, and we do not alter its substance by twisting it into an abnormality. If the transcendent realities do not exist in the normal human consciousness, they do not exist in "poetry, music, and painting," or at all. Mr. Yeats thinks that Shakespeare interested himself in life and humanity consciously for the sake of his art. This is a matter of opinion; but we think it more likely that Shakespeare's interest in life was a broadly human and representative interest, and that this was the source and power of his art. Art which only interests itself in life and humanity for the sake of art may achieve the occult triumphs of the symbolist school, but humanity will return its indifference in kind, and leave it to the dignity and consolation of "unpopularity."

William Butler Yeats

THE AUTUMN OF THE FLESH

OUR THOUGHTS and emotions are often but spray flung up from hidden tides that follow a moon no eye can see. I remember that when I first began to write I desired to describe outward things as vividly as possible, and took pleasure, in which there was, perhaps, a little discontent, in picturesque and declamatory books. And then, quite suddenly, I lost the desire of describing outward things, and found that I took little pleasure in a book unless it was spiritual and unemphatic. I did not then understand that the change was from beyond my own mind, but I understand now that writers are struggling all over Europe, though not often, with a philosophic understanding of their struggle, against that picturesque and declamatory way of writing, against that 'externality' which a time of scientific and political thought has brought into literature. This struggle has been going on for some years, but it has only just become strong enough to draw within itself the little inner world which alone seeks more than amusement in the arts. In France, where movements are more marked, because the people are pre-eminently logical, "The Temptation of S. Anthony," the last great dramatic invention of the old romanticism, contrasts very plainly with "Axël," the first great dramatic invention of the new; and Maeterlinck has followed Count Villiers de L'Isle Adam (*sic.*). Flaubert wrote unforgettable descriptions of grotesque, bizarre, and beautiful scenes and persons, as they show to the ear and to the eye, and crowded them with historic and ethnographical details; but Count Villiers de L'Isle Adam swept together, by what seemed a sudden energy, words, behind which glimmered a spiritual and passionate mood, as the flame glimmers behind the dusky blue and red glass in an Eastern lamp; and created persons from whom has fallen all even of personal characteristic except a thirst for that hour when all things shall pass away like a vapour, and a pride like that of the Magi following their star over many mountains; while Maeterlinck has plucked away even this thirst and this pride and set before us faint souls, naked and pathetic shadows already half vapour and sighing to one another upon the border of the last abyss. There has been, as I think, a like change in French painting, for one sees everywhere, instead of the dramatic stories, and picturesque moments of an older school, frail and tremulous bodies unfitted for the labour of life, and landscape where subtle rhythms of colour and of form have overcome the clear outline of things as we see them in the labour of life.

There has been a like change in England, but it has come more gradually and is more mixed with lesser changes than in France. The poetry which found its expression in the poems of writers like Browning and of Tennyson, and even of writers, who are seldom classed with them, like Swinburne, and like Shelley in his earlier years, pushed its limits as far as possible, and tried to absorb into itself the science and politics, the philosophy and morality of its time; but a new poetry, which is always contracting its limits, has grown up under the shadow of the old. Rossetti began it, but was too much of a painter in his poetry to follow it with a perfect devotion; and it became a movement when Mr. Lang and Mr. Gosse and Mr. Dobson devoted themselves to the most condensed of lyric forms, and when Mr. Bridges, a more considerable poet, elaborated a rhythm too delicate for any but an almost bodiless emotion, and repeated over and over the most ancient notes of poetry, and none but these. The poets who followed have either, like Mr. Kipling, turned from serious poetry altogether, and so passed out of the processional order, or speak out of some personal or spiritual passion in words and types and metaphors that draw one's imagination as far as possible from the complexities of modern life and thought. The change has been more marked in English painting, which, when intense enough to belong to the processional order, began to cast out things, as we see them in the labour of life, so much before French painting, that ideal art is sometimes called English art upon the Continent.

I see, indeed, in the arts of every country those faint lights and faint colours and faint outlines and faint energies which many call "the decadence," and which I, because I believe that the arts lie dreaming of things to come, prefer to call the autumn of the flesh. An Irish poet whose rhythms are like the cry of a sea-bird in autumn twilight has told its meaning in the line, "The very sunlight's weary, and it's time to quit the plough." Its importance is the greater because it comes to us at the moment when we are beginning to be interested in many things which positive science, the interpreter of exterior law, has always denied: communion of mind with mind in thought and without words, foreknowledge in dreams and in visions, and the coming amongst us of the dead, and of much else. We are, it may be, at a crowning crisis of the world, at the moment when man is about to ascend, with his arms full of the wealth he has been so long gathering, the stairway he has been descending from the first days. The first poets, if one may find their images in the Kalevala, had not Homer's preoccupation with things, and he was not so full of their excitement as Virgil. Dante added to poetry a dialectic which, although he made it serve his laborious ecstasy, was the invention of minds trained by the labour of life, by a traffic among many things, and not a spontaneous expression of an interior life; while Shakespeare shattered the symmetry of verse and of drama that he might fill them with things and their accidental relations.

Each of these writers had come further down the stairway than those who had lived before him, but it was only with the modern poets, with Goethe and Wordsworth and Browning, that poetry gave up the right to consider all things in the world as a dictionary of types and symbols and began to call itself a critic of life and an interpreter of things as they are. Painting, music, science, politics, and even religion, because they have felt a growing belief that we know nothing but the fading and flowering of the world, have changed in numberless elaborate ways. Man has wooed and won the world, and has fallen weary, and not, I think, for a time, but with a weariness that will not end until the last autumn, when the stars shall be blown away like withered leaves. He grew weary when he said—"These things that I touch and see and hear are alone real," for he saw them without illusion at last, and found them but air and dust and moisture. And now he must be philosophical about everything, even about the arts, for he can only return the way he came, and so escape from weariness, by philosophy. The arts are, I believe, about to take upon their shoulders the burdens that have fallen from the shoulders of priests, and to lead us back upon our journey by filling our thoughts with the essences of things, and not with things. We are about to substitute once more the distillation of alchemy for the analyses of chemistry and for the method of some other sciences; and certain of us are looking everywhere for the perfect alembic that no silver or golden drop may escape. Mr. Symons has written lately on M. Mallarmé's method, and has quoted him as saying that we should "abolish the pretension, æsthetically an error, despite its dominion over almost all the masterpieces, to enclose within the subtle pages other than —for example—the horror of the forest or the silent thunder in the leaves, not the intrinsic dense wood of the trees," and as desiring to substitute for "the old lyric afflatus or the enthusiastic personal direction of the phrase" words "that take light from mutual reflection, like an actual trail of fire over precious stones," and "to make an entire word hitherto unknown to the language" "out of many vocables." Mr. Symons understands these and other sentences to mean that poetry will henceforth be a poetry of essences, separated one from another in little and intense poems. I think there will be much poetry of this kind, because of an ever more arduous search for an almost disembodied ecstasy, but I think we will not cease to write long poems, but rather that we will write them more and more as our new belief makes the world plastic under our hands again. I think that we will learn again how to describe at great length an old man wandering among enchanted islands, his return home at last, his slow-gathering vengeance, a flitting shape of a goddess, and a flight of arrows, and yet to make all of these so different things "take light by mutual reflection, like an actual trail of fire over precious stones," and become "an entire word," the signature or symbol of a mood of the divine imagination as imponderable as "the horror of the forest or the silent thunder in the leaves."

Our traditions are unfortunate. The public taste is with the idle laughers, and still inclines to follow them.

George Meredith, "An Essay on Comedy"

Why do artists no longer paint sign-boards for our pleasure? They should really do so.

Max Beerbohm, "Sign-Boards"

Ernest . . . It seems that a lady once gravely asked the remorseful Academician, as you call him, if his celebrated picture of "A Spring-Day at Whiteley's," or "Waiting for the Last Omnibus," or some subject of that kind, was all painted by hand.

Gilbert. And was it?

Oscar Wilde, "The Critic As Artist"

I would rather for my own part that no architects had ever condescended to adopt one of the views suggested in this book. I have had indirect influence on nearly every cheap villa builder between this and Bromley, and there is scarcely a public-house near the Crystal Palace but sells its gin and bitters under pseudo-Victorian capitals copied from the Church of the Madonna of Health of the Miracles. And one of my principal motives for leaving my present house is that it is surrounded everywhere by the accursed Frankenstein monsters of, indirectly, my own making.

John Ruskin, *Stones of Venice*

William Makepeace Thackeray

"MICHAEL ANGELO TITMARSH IN THE GALLERIES"

THACKERAY's enthusiasm for art, as the following selection reveals, was a lively one. His criticism tended to be rambling, journalistic, and kindly—he called it "gossip" about art—and his judgments have not all stood the test of time. He admired Mulready, Biard, and Danby, painters seldom mentioned today; he was insensitive to the works of Turner's last period (but so was Ruskin, it should be recalled). On the other hand, some of his statements and attitudes have worn well. His suspicions of the grand history picture, one of the most formidable of Victorian genres, distinguished his taste from the main enthusiasms of the time; and he was satiric of the "milk and water" aesthetics which inspired acres of insipid Academy art. At one time he himself had studied art in Paris, and he later employed his talents to illustrate many of his own novels. His pseudonym, *Michael Angelo Titmarsh,* was one of several he used during the early years before his success as a novelist (Théophile Wagstaff, Goliah Gahagan, George Savage, Mr. Snob, and Fitz-Boodle are other delightful ones). "May Gambols," before its close, moves sprightly past many more pictures than the three representative ones described below.

ONE DAY, by custom, no doubt, the public taste will grow better, and as the man who begins by intoxicating himself with a glass of gin finishes sometimes by easily absorbing a bottle; as the law-student, who at first is tired with a chapter of Blackstone, will presently swallow you down with pleasure a whole volume of Chitty; as education, in a word, advances, it is humbly to be hoped that the great and generous British public will not be so easily satisfied as at present, and will ask for a better article for its money.

Meanwhile, their taste being pitiable, the artists supply them with poor stuff—pretty cheap tawdry toys and gimcracks in place

FROM "May Gambols; or Titmarsh in the Picture Galleries" (June, 1844).

of august and beautiful objects of art. It is always the case. I do not mean to say that the literary men are a bit better. Poor fellows of the pen and pencil! We must live. The public likes light literature and we write it. Here am I writing magazine jokes and follies, and why? Because the public like such, will purchase no other. Otherwise, as Mr. Nickisson, and all who are acquainted with M. A. Titmarsh, in private know, my real inclinations would lead me to write works upon mathematics, geology, and chemistry, varying them in my lighter hours with little playful treatises on questions of political economy, epic poems, and essays on the Æolic digamma. So, in fact, these severe rebukes with which I am about to belabour my neighbour must be taken, as they are given, in a humble and friendly spirit; they are not actuated by pride, but by deep sympathy. Just as we read in holy Mr. Newman's life of Saint Stephen Harding, that it was the custom among the godly Cistercian monks (in the good old times, which holy Newman would restore) to assemble every morning in full chapter; and there, after each monk had made his confession, it was free to—nay, it was strictly enjoined on—any other brother to rise and say, "Brother So-and-so hath not told all his sins; our dear brother has forgotten that yesterday he ate his split-pease with too much gormandize;" or, "This morning he did indecently rejoice over his water-gruel," or what not. These real Christians were called upon to inform, not only of themselves, but to be informers over each other; and, the information being given, the brother informed against thanked his brother the informer, and laid himself down on the desk, and was flagellated with gratitude. Sweet friends! be you like the Cistercians! Brother Michael Angelo is going to inform against you. Get ready your garments and prepare for flagellation. Brother Michael Angelo is about to lay on and spare not.

Brother Michael lifts up his voice against the young painters collectively in the first place, afterwards individually, when he will also take leave to tickle them with the wholesome stripes of the flagellum. In the first place, then (and my heart is so tender that, rather than begin the operation, I have been beating about the bush for more than a page, of which page the reader is cordially requested to omit the perusal, as it is not the least to the purpose), I say that the young painters of England, whose uprise this

Magazine[1] and this critic were the first to hail, asserting loudly their superiority over the pompous old sham-classical big-wigs of the Academy, the young painters of England *are not doing their duty*. They are going backwards, or rather, they are flinging themselves under the wheels of that great golden Juggernaut of an Art-Union. The thought of the money is leading them astray; they are poets no longer, but money-hunters. They paint down to the level of the public intelligence, rather than seek to elevate the public to them. Why do these great geniuses fail in their duty of instruction? Why, knowing better things, do they serve out such awful twaddle as we have from them? Alas! it is not for art they paint, but for the Art-Union.

The first dear brother I shall take the liberty to request to get ready for operation is brother Charles Landseer.[2] Brother Charles has sinned. He has grievously sinned. And we will begin with this miserable sinner, and administer to him admonition in a friendly, though most fierce and cutting manner.

The subject of brother Charles Landseer's crime is this. The sinner has said to himself, "The British public likes domestic pieces. They will have nothing *but* domestic pieces. I will give them one, and of a new sort. Suppose I paint a picture that must have a hit. My picture will have every sort of interest. It shall interest the domestic public; it shall interest the amateur for the cleverness of its painting; it shall interest little boys and girls, for I will introduce no end of animals: camels, monkeys, elephants, and cockatoos; it shall interest sentimental young ladies, for I will take care to have a pretty little episode for them. I will take the town by storm, in a word." This is what I conceive was passing in brother Charles Landseer's sinful soul when he conceived and executed his "Noah's Ark In a Domestic Point of View."

Noah and his family (with some supplemental young children, very sweetly painted) are seated in the ark, and a port-hole is opened, out of which one of the sons is looking at the now peaceful waters. The sunshine enters the huge repository of the life of the world, and the dove has just flown in with an olive branch and nestles in the bosom of one of the daughters of Noah; the patriarch and his aged partner are lifting up their venerable eyes in thank-

[1] *Fraser's Magazine.*
[2] Charles Landseer (1799–1879), brother of Sir Edwin Landseer.

fulness; the children stand around, the peaceful labourer and the brown huntsman each testifying his devotion after his fashion. The animals round about participate in the joyful nature of the scene; their instinct seems to tell them that the hour of their deliverance is near.

There, the picture is described romantically and in the best of language. Now let us proceed to examine the poetry critically and to see what its claims are. Well, the ark is a great subject. The history from which we have our account of it, from a poet, surely demands a reverent treatment; a blacksmith roaring from the desk of a conventicle may treat it familiarly, but an educated artist ought surely to approach such a theme with respect. The point here is only urged aesthetically. As a matter of *taste,* then (and the present humble writer has no business to speak on any other), such a manner of treating the subject is certainly reprehensible. The ark is vulgarized here and reduced to the proportions of a Calais steamer. The passengers are rejoicing: they are glad to get away. Their live animals are about them no more nor less sublime than so many cattle or horses in loose boxes. The parrots perched on the hoop yonder have as little signification as a set of birds in a cage at the Zoological Gardens; the very dove becomes neither more nor less than the *pet* of the pretty girl represented in the centre of the picture. All the greatness of the subject is lost; and, putting the historical nature of the personages out of the question, they have little more interest than a group of any emigrants in the hold of a ship, who rouse and rally at the sound of "Land ho!"

Why, if all great themes of poetry are to be treated in this way, the art would be easy. We might have Hector shaving himself before going out to fight Achilles, as undoubtedly the Trojan hero did; Priam in a cotton nightcap asleep in a four-poster on the night of the sack of Troy, Hecuba, of course, by his side, with curl papers, and her *tour de tête* on the toilet-glass. We might have Dido's maid coming after her mistress in the shower with pattens and an umbrella; or Cleopatra's page guttling the figs in the basket which had brought the asp that killed the mistress of Antony. Absurd trivialities, or pretty trivialities, are nothing to the question; those I have adduced here are absurd, but they are just as poetical as prettiness, not a whit less degrading and commonplace. No painter has a right to treat great historical subjects in such a fashion: and though the public are sure to admire, and young ladies, in raptures, look on at the daring of a dove, and little boys in delight cry, "Look, papa, at the parroquets!"—"Law, ma, what big trunks the elephants have!" it yet behoves the critic to say this is an unpoetical piece, and severely to reprehend the unhappy perpetrator thereof.

I know brother Charles will appeal. I know it will be pleaded in his favour that the picture is capitally painted, some of the figures very pretty; two, that of the old woman and the boy looking out, quite grand in drawing and colour; the picture charming for its silvery tone and agreeable pleasantry of colour. All this is true. BUT he has sinned, he has greatly sinned; let him acknowledge his fault in the presence of the chapter, and receive the customary and wholesome reward thereof—.

Frater Redgrave [3] is the next malefactor whose sins deserve a reprobation. In the namby-pamby line his errors are very sad. Has he not been already warned in this very miscellany of his propensity to small sentiment? Has he corrected himself of that grievous tendency? No; his weakness grows more and more upon him, and he is now more sinful than ever. One of his pictures is taken from the most startling lyric in our language, the "Song of the Shirt," a song as bitter and manly as it is exquisitely soft and tender, a song of which the humour draws tears.[4]

Mr. Redgrave has illustrated everything except the humour, the manliness, and the bitterness of the song. He has only depicted the tender, good-natured part of it. It is impossible to quarrel with the philanthropy of the painter. His shirt-maker sits by her little neat bed, work, working away. You may see how late it is, for the candle is nearly burnt out, the clock (capital poetic notion!) says what o'clock it is, the grey-streaked dawn is rising over the opposite house seen through the cheerless casement, and where (from a light which it has in its window) you may imagine that another poor shirt-maker is toiling too. The one before us is pretty, pale, and wan; she turns up the whites of her fine, fatigued eyes to the little ceiling. She is ill, as the artist has shown

[3] Richard Redgrave, R.A. (1804–1888).

[4] How is it that none of the papers have noticed the astonishing poem by Mr. Hood in the May number of his magazine, to which our language contains no parallel?—Thackeray's note.

us by a fine stroke of genius—a parcel of medicine bottles on the mantelpiece! The picture is carefully and cleverly painted—extremely popular—gazed at with vast interest by most spectators. Is it, however, a poetical subject? Yes, Hood has shown that it can be made one, but by surprising turns of thought brought to bear upon it, strange, terrible unexpected lights of humour which he has flung upon it. And, to "trump" this tremendous card, Mr. Redgrave gives us this picture; his points being the clock, which tells the time of day, the vials which show the poor girl takes physic, and such other vast labours of intellect!

Mr. Redgrave's other picture, the "Marriage Morning," is also inspired by that milk-and-water of human kindness, the flavour of which is so insipid to the roast-beef intellect. This is . . . a picture in which there is much clever and conscientious painting, from which, however, I must confess I derive little pleasure. The sentiment and colour of the picture somehow coincide; the eye rests upon a variety of neat tints of pale drab, pale green, pale brown, pale puce colour, of a sickly warmth, not pleasant to the eye. The drawing is feeble, the expression of the face pretty, but lackadaisical. The penance I would order Mr. Redgrave should be a pint of port wine to be taken daily, and a devilled kidney every morning for breakfast before beginning to paint.

Charles Kingsley

"THE WORKER IN THE NATIONAL GALLERY"

KINGSLEY's effort to improve the British workingman's sensitivity to great art, to reveal some of the unique serenity and beauty existent in his "paradise," the National Gallery, is free of the condescension one might expect of the earnest Victorian instructing members of an inferior class. His "Parson Lot" speaks with sympathy and dignity as he introduces the Bellini portrait of the

FROM *Politics for the People* (May 6, 1848 and May 20, 1848).

Doge. Although the interpretation of the picture is mainly literary, Kingsley does attempt to awaken his viewer to its mood; in other words, he meets the painting on something of its own terms.

THE NATIONAL GALLERY.—NO. I.

Picture-galleries should be the workman's paradise, and garden of pleasure, to which he goes to refresh his eyes and heart with beautiful shapes and sweet colouring, when they are wearied with dull bricks and mortar, and the ugly colourless things which fill the workshop and the factory. For believe me, there is many a road into our hearts besides our ears and brains; many a sight, and sound, and scent, even, of which we have never *thought* at all, sinks into our memory, and helps to shape our characters; and thus children brought up among beautiful sights and sweet sounds will most likely show the fruits of their nursing, by thoughtfulness, and affection, and nobleness of mind, even by the expression of the countenance. The poet Wordsworth, talking of training up a beautiful country girl, says—

> The floating clouds their state shall lend
> To her—for her the willow bend;
> Nor shall she fail to see,
> Even in the motions of the storm,
> *Grace which shall mould the maiden's form,*
> *By silent sympathy.*
>
> * * * * *
>
> And she shall bend her ear
> In many a secret place
> Where rivulets dance their wayward round,
> *And beauty, born of murmuring sound,*
> *Shall pass into her face.*

Those who live in towns should carefully remember this, for their own sakes, for their wives' sakes, for their children's sakes. *Never lose an opportunity of seeing anything beautiful.* Beauty is God's hand-writing—a way-side sacrament; welcome it in every fair face, every fair sky, every fair flower, and thank for it *Him,* the fountain of all loveliness, and drink it in, simply and earnestly, with all your eyes; it is a charmed draught, a cup of blessing.

Therefore I said that picture-galleries should be the townsman's paradise of refreshment. Of course, if he can get the real air, the real trees, even for an hour, let him take it, in God's name; but how many a man who cannot spare time for a daily country walk, may well slip into the National Gallery, or any other collection of pictures, for ten minutes. *That* garden, at least, flowers as gaily in winter as in summer. Those noble faces on the wall are never disfigured by grief or passion. There, in the space of a single room, the townsman may take his country walk—a walk beneath mountain peaks, blushing sunsets, with broad woodlands spreading out below it; a walk through green meadows, under cool mellow shades, and overhanging rocks, by rushing brooks, where he watches and watches till he seems to *hear* the foam whisper, and to *see* the fishes leap; and his hardworn heart wanders out free, beyond the grim city—world of stone and iron, smoky chimneys and roaring wheels, into the world of beautiful things—*the world which shall be hereafter!*—ay, which shall be! Believe it, toil-worn workers, in spite of thy foul alley, thy crowded lodging, thy grimed clothing, thy ill-fed children, thy thin, pale wife—believe it, thou, too, and thine, will some day have *your* share of beauty. God made you love beautiful things only because He intends hereafter to give you your fill of them. That pictured face on the wall is lovely —but lovelier still may the wife of thy bosom be when she meets thee on the resurrection morn! Those baby cherubs in the old Italian painting—how gracefully they flutter and sport among the soft clouds, full of rich young life and baby joy!—Yes, beautiful indeed, but just such a one at this very moment is that once pining, deformed child of thine, over whose death-cradle thou wast weeping a month ago; now a child-angel, whom thou shalt meet again, never to part! Those landscapes, too, painted by loving, wise, old Claude, two hundred years ago, are still as fresh as ever.—How still the meadows are! how pure and free that vault of deep blue sky! No wonder that thy worn heart, as thou lookest, sighs aloud, 'Oh, that I had wings as a dove, then would I flee away and be at rest!' Ay, but gayer meadows and bluer skies await thee in the *world to come*—that fairy-land made real—'The new heavens and the new earth,' which God has prepared for the pure and the loving, the just and the brave, who have conquered in this sore fight of life!

Courtesy of A. & F. Pears, Ltd.

BUBBLES

After a painting by John Everett Millais, 1885

Courtesy of the Trustees of the Tate Gallery, London

DIGNITY AND IMPUDENCE

Painting by Sir Edwin Landseer, 1839

Courtesy of the Detroit Institute of Arts

A GREYHOUND, EOS, BELONGING TO HER MAJESTY, QUEEN VICTORIA

An engraving by Victoria of a drawing by Albert, 1834, 1840

Courtesy of the Detroit Institute of Arts

NOCTURNE IN BLACK AND GOLD: THE FALLING ROCKET

Painting by James McNeill Whistler, 1875

Courtesy of the Trustees of the Tate Gallery, London

OLD BATTERSEA BRIDGE: NOCTURNE IN BLUE AND GOLD

Painting by James McNeill Whistler, 1877

THE DREAM

Drawing by Aubrey Beardsley for Pope's "Rape of the Lock," 1896

Courtesy of R. A. Walker, Esq.

ENTER HERODIAS

Drawing by Aubrey Beardsley, 1893

Courtesy of the Detroit Institute of Arts

THE PASSING OF VENUS

Tapestry after a design of Sir Edward Burne-Jones, woven by the Morris and Co. Merton Abbey looms (1901-1907; 1923-1926)

These thoughts may seem all too far-fetched to spring up in a man's head from merely looking at pictures; but it is not so in practice. See, now, such thoughts have sprung up in *my* head; else how did I write them down here? And why should not they, and better ones, too, spring up in your heads, friends? It is delightful to watch in a picture-gallery some streetboy enjoying himself; how first wonder creeps over his rough face, and then a sweeter, more earnest, awe-struck look, till his countenance seems to grow handsomer and nobler on the spot, and drink in and reflect unknowingly, the beauty of the picture he is studying. See how some labourer's face will light up before the painting which tells him a noble story of by-gone days. And why? because he feels as if he himself had a share in the story at which he looks. They may be noble and glorious men who are painted there; but they are still *men* of like passions with himself, and his man's heart understands them and glories in them; and he begins, and rightly, to respect himself the more when he finds that he, too, has a fellow-feeling with noble men and noble deeds.

I say, pictures raise blessed thoughts in me—why not in you, my brothers? Your hearts are fresh, thoughtful, kindly; you only want to have these pictures *explained* to you, that you may know *why* and *how* they are beautiful, and what feelings they ought to stir in your minds; and therefore I wish, with your good will, to explain, one by one, in future numbers, some of the best pictures in the National Gallery, and the statues in the British Museum. I shall begin by a portrait or two; they are simpler than large pictures, and they speak of real men and women who once lived on this earth of ours—generally of remarkable and noble men—and man should be always interesting to man. And as these papers go on, if any one of you, in any part of England, will be so kind as to mention *well-known* statues and pictures of any sort which you wish explained, I, Parson Lot, shall be most happy to tell you as much about them as God shall give me wits to find out.

PARSON LOT

THE NATIONAL GALLERY.–NO. II

ANY ONE who goes to the National Gallery in Trafalgar-square, and passes right through it into the furthest room of all, cannot help seeing at the left-hand corner two large and beautiful pictures—the nearer of the two labelled Titian, representing Bacchus leaping from a car drawn by leopards. The other, labelled Francia, representing the Holy Family seated on a sort of throne, with several figures arranged below—one of them a man pierced with arrows. Between these two, low down, hangs a small picture, about two feet square, containing only the portrait of an old man, in a white cap and robe, and labelled on the picture itself, *Joannes Bellinus*. Now, this old man is a very ancient friend of mine, and has comforted my heart, and preached me a sharp sermon too, many a time. I never enter that Gallery without having five minutes' converse with him; and yet he has been dead at least three hundred years; and, what is more, I don't even know his name. I believe I might have found out if I had taken the trouble to ask, but how much should I have been the wiser? What more do I know of a man by knowing his name? It amuses me much, in the world, when one asks, 'Who is that man?' to be answered, 'Oh don't you know? that's Mr. Brown, who married Mrs. Smith's daughter;' and so on. Bah! Whether the man's name be Brown, or whether he has as many names and titles as a Spanish grandee, what does that tell me about the *man*?—the spirit and character of the man—what the man will say when he is asked—what the man will do when he is stirred up to action? The man's name is part of his clothes—his shell—his husk. Change his name and all his titles, you don't change *him*—'a man's a man for a' that,' as Burns says, and a goose a goose. Other men gave him his name—but his heart and his spirit—his love and his hatred—his wisdom and his folly—his power to do well and ill—those God and himself gave him. I must know those, and then I know the *man*.

Let us see what we can make out from the picture itself, about the man whom it represents. In the first place, we may see by his dress that he was in his day the Doge (or chief magistrate) of Venice, the island city, the queen of the seas. So we may guess that he had many a stirring time of it, and many a delicate game to play, among those tyrannous and covetous old merchant-princes who had elected him—who were keeping up their own power at the expense of every one's liberty, by spies and nameless accusers, and secret councils, tortures and prisons, whose horrors no one ever returned to describe. Nay, we may guess just the very men with whom he had to deal—the very battles he may have seen fought—for the painter's name on the picture shows when he lived.

But all these are *circumstances,* things which *stand round* the man, (as the word means,) and not the old man himself,—not the character and heart of the man,—*that* we must get from the portrait; and if the portrait is a truly *noble* portrait, we *shall* get it. If it is a merely vulgar or *naturalist* picture, like most that are painted now-a-days, we shall get the man's dress and general shape of his face, but little or no expression; if it is a *pathetic* portrait, or picture of passion we shall get one particular temporary expression of his face,—perhaps joy, sorrow, anger, disgust,—but still one which may have passed any moment, and left his face quite different; but if the full expression of the man's picture is of the noblest kind, an *ideal* or *high-art* picture, we shall get the *whole* spirit, we shall read his whole character there; just all his strength and weakness, his kindliness or his sternness, his thoughtfulness or his carelessness, written there once and for ever;—what he would be, though all the world passed away,—what his immortal and eternal soul will be, unless God or the devil changed his heart, to all eternity.

This is a deep matter; we shall get at it step by step, by many examples. Let us see, now, whether this is an *ideal* portrait; in short, if it gives us a full *idea* of a complete character, so that we should know him if any one talked to us of his character, even without telling us his likeness.

We may see at once that he has been very handsome, but it is a peculiar sort of beauty. How delicate and graceful all the lines in his face are! he is a gentleman of God's own making, and not of the tailor's making. He is such a gentleman as I have seen among working-men and nine-shilling-a-week labourers, often and often; his nobleness is in his heart,—it is God's gift, therefore it shows in his noble-looking face. No matter whether he were poor or rich; all the rags in the world, all the finery in the world, could not have made him look like a snob or a swell. He was a thoughtful man, too; no one with such a forehead could have been a trifler: a kindly man, too, and honest, one that may have played merrily enough with his grand-children, and put his hand in his purse for many a widow and orphan. Look what a bright, clear, straightforward, gentle look he has,—almost a smile; but he has gone through too many sad hours to smile much; he is a man of many sorrows, like all true and noble rulers; and, like a high mountainside, his face bears the furrows of many storms. He has had a stern life of it, what with tyrant noblemen, and wayward snobs, and the cares of a great nation on his shoulders. He has seen that in this world there is no rest for those who live like true men. You may see it by the wrinkles in his brow, and the sharp-cut furrows in his cheeks, and those firm-set, determined lips. His eyes almost show the marks of many noble tears,—tears such as good men shed over their nation's sins; but that, too, is past now. He has found out his path, and he will keep it; and he has no misgiving now about what God would have him do,—or about the reward which God has laid up for the brave and just,—and that is what makes his forehead so clear and bright, while his very teeth are clenched with calm determination. And by the look of those high cheek bones, and that large square jaw, he is a strong-willed man enough, and not one to be easily turned aside from his purpose by any man alive, or by any woman either, or by his own passions and tempers. One fault of character, I think, he may perhaps have had much trouble with,—I mean bitterness and contemptuousness. His lips are very thin; he may have sneered many a time, when he was younger, at the follies of the world, which that great, lofty, thoughtful brain and clear eye of his told him were follies; but he seems to have got past that too. Such is the man's character,—a noble, simple, commanding old man, who has conquered many hard things, and, hardest of all, has conquered himself, and now is waiting calm for his everlasting rest. God send us all the same.

Now consider the deep insight of old John Bellini, who could see all this,—and put it down there for us with pencil and paint,—better far, more livingly and speakingly, than I could describe it to you in a dozen letters.

No doubt there was something in old John's own character which made him especially able to paint such a man; for, as I have read, he was much such a man himself, and we always understand those best who are most like ourselves; and therefore you may tell pretty nearly a painter's own character by seeing what sort of subjects he paints, and what his style of painting is. And a noble, simple, brave, godly man was old John Bellini, and never lost his head, though princes were flattering him, and mobs following him with shouts and blessings for his noble pictures of the Venetian victories, as if he had been a man sent from God Himself, as indeed he was,—as all great painters are: for who but God makes beauty? Who gives the loving heart, and the clear eye, and the graceful taste to see beauty and to copy it, and to set forth on canvas, or in stone, the noble deeds of patriots dying for their country? To paint truly patriotic pictures well, a man must have his heart in his work—he must be a true patriot himself, as John Bellini was (if I mistake not, he had fought for his country himself in more than one shrewd fight). And what makes men patriots, or artists, or anything noble at all, but the spirit of the living God? Those great pictures of Bellini's are no more; they were burnt a few years afterwards, with the magnificent National Hall in which they hung; but the spirit of them is not passed away. Even now, Venice, Bellini's beloved mother-land, is rising, new-born, from long weary years of Austrian slavery, and trying to be free and great once more; and young Italian hearts are lighting up with the thought of her old fleets and her old victories, her merchants and her statesmen, whom John Bellini drew. Venice sinned and fell; and sorely has she paid for her sins, through 200 years of shame, and profligacy, and slavery. And now she has broken the oppressor's yoke by a strange and unexpected chance. The fall of Louis-Philippe has proved the salvation of Venice. God send her a new life! May she learn by her ancient sins! May she learn by her ancient glories!

You will forgive me for forgetting my picture to talk of such things? But we must return. Look back at what I said about the old portrait—the clear, calm, victorious character of the old man's face, and see how all the rest of the picture agrees with it, in a complete harmony, as all things in a first-rate picture should. The dress, the scenery, the light and shade, the general 'tone' of colour, should all agree with the character of the face—all help to bring our minds into that state in which we may best feel and sympathise with the human beings painted. Now here, because the face is calm and grand, the colour and the outlines are quiet and grand likewise. How different these colours are from that glorious Holy Family of Francia's, next to it on the right—or from that equally glorious Bacchus and Ariadne of Titian's on the left! Yet all three are right, each for its own subject. Here you have no brilliant reds, no rich warm browns, or luscious greens. The white robe and cap give us the thought of purity and simplicity; the very golden embroidery on them, which marks his rank, is carefully kept back from being too gaudy. Everything is *sober* here. And the lines of the dress, how simple they all are—no rich curves, no fluttering drapery. They would be quite stiff if it were not for that waving line of round tassels in front, which break the extreme straightness and heaviness of the splendid robe; and all pointing upwards towards that solemn, thin, calm face, with its high white cap, rising like the peak of a snow mountain against the dark, deep, boundless, blue sky behind.

Punch, or the London Charivari

"THE OPENING OF THE GREAT EXHIBITION"

No MID-CENTURY EVENT better illustrated, focused, and intensified Victorian taste than the Great Exhibition of 1851. *Punch's* account of the opening, despite a few rather dismal puns, manages quite well to convey the excitement of the event, the great popularity of the Queen, and the function of the exhibition as a social leveller.

MAY HAS OFTEN belied its character for merriment by occasional fits of gloom, and by appearing in the wooly paletôt or over-coat of fleecy clouds; but the first of May in the present year has sufficed to retrieve all former faults of that frequently fickle month, and render it for ever famous in the annals of glorious sunshine and cheerfulness. We had intended to get up with the lark, but there being no local lark to regulate our movements, we accepted as a substitute for the early bird, those well known London blackbirds, the sweeps, whose cry was the signal for our rising.

Volume XX (1851).

Everything seemed auspicious. Even our razor was in excellent temper, which was fortunate, for had it been obstinate, we should have had a terribly close shave to join in sufficient time the line of equipages, which already, before eight o'clock, extended in one rank—a rank in which no aristocratic distinctions were observed—from the doors of the Crystal Palace to the very centre of the Metropolis. The proudest equipage of the peer was obliged to fall in behind the humblest fly or the ugliest Hansom; there being no privileged order, but the order of arrival. The student in armorial bearings would have had a miscellaneous feast in examining the panels of the various vehicles, which combined all the brilliant blazonry of BURKE, with all the mysterious heraldry of the cab-stand.

During the time of waiting for the opening of the doors, good-humour kept up the spirits of all, except some of those who, being driven impatiently by the side of the line, found themselves obliged to retrace their steps on arriving at the park gates, and take their places at the back of the whole string, which had lengthened a mile or so since they had foolishly quitted it. The contents—or rather the non-contents—of the vehicles in this dilemma afforded amusement to those who had fallen in at once with the regulations, and, as the former were seen returning a good deal farther back than the place they came from, it was clear that the occupants of each carriage were throwing, sometimes upon each other, but more often on the unfortunate driver, the blame of their failure. Nevertheless, the arrangements were so excellent, and every foot of ground was so well apportioned, that scarcely any one had room for complaint, except, perhaps, when a passing coal-wagon made every one wish the Wall's-end at the World's End, or when the carts of a suburban milk company, returning from the morning supply of their customers, intruded with their "pure milk" among many who thought themselves for the moment the cream of elegance, and turned somewhat sour at the contact.

The doors were at length reached, and the crowd waiting the arrival of HER MAJESTY, furnished an exhibition of various kinds of industry not represented within the doors of the Crystal Palace. Every available place for catching a sight of the procession had been taken possession of in every available manner. Our friends, the Bedouins, who, according to the Astleian views of their habits, run about piled on each others' shoulders in pyramids, four or five human stories high, were equalled, if not surpassed, by our native acrobats. Looking at the doubtful security of those forming the capitals of these strangely constructed pillars, we could not help philosophising inwardly on the danger of a high position, even when resting on the shoulders of the people. The trees opposite the principal door seemed to have burst out suddenly into a crop of eager boys, who, in spite of the warnings of the police against the forbidden fruits of juvenile industry, seemed to think every tree a legitimate tree of knowledge, if anything could be learned or seen by climbing it.

In vain did the constable look up at the trees and threaten the juvenile branches, who felt there was little fear of their being taken up, as long as their being got down was impracticable. Here and there an adventurous policeman would climb after the contumacious urchin; but the latter, with provoking levity, would scramble on to some bough too slender to bear the weight of the civil authority, who, however, on this occasion, seldom lost his temper, though sometimes losing his balance.

We now enter the building, and our first care is to find for the beloved *Judy* one of those seats said to have been reserved for ladies.

With our usual good fortune, we secured a front place; and, indeed, where should *Punch* be, but in the foremost ranks of those desirous of showing loyalty and affection to the Sovereign? Having taken up our quarters, we had leisure, for the first time, to admire the wondrous magnificence—the grandeur enhanced by the simplicity—of Mr. PAXTON's building. We will not enlarge upon its merits; for *Punch* disdains to echo the general voice; which, in this instance, is, in fact, the echo of the approval *Punch* himself was pleased to bestow on the first design of the architect. Where were the croakers and detractors who knew the building was unsafe, though it was strong enough to bear the weight of their stupidity and malignity combined?—and where, oh where, were the formidable sparrows which we had been told had got irremedially into the building; but which, if they inhabit any nest at all, must occupy some mare's nest or other, of which, happily, no trace is visible?

At length a cheer without, and a flourish of trumpets within, announce the arrival of the QUEEN—and the PRINCE, who, by the idea of this Exhibition, has given to Royal Consortship a new glory, or, rather, has rendered for ever illustrious, in his own case, a position too often vibrating between the mischievous and the insignificant. PRINCE ALBERT has done a grand service to humanity, and earned imperishable fame for himself by an idea, the greatness of which, instead of becoming less, will appear still greater as it recedes from us. We are as yet too completely face to face with the object to see at once all its grandeur; but it will be more perceptible as we advance, just as the height and extent of the mountain are but partially developed to the traveller who has not yet quitted it.

During the ceremonial, which was of a solemn and imposing nature—and for which we refer to our merely matter-of-fact contemporaries,—it was not surprising that several eyes, including the Royal one, were slightly crystallised in a graceful harmony with the Crystal Palace. While the proceedings were going on, the attempt to keep the ladies off the seats was given up as hopeless, and it was a pardonable instance of the weakness of human nature, even in that stern piece of stuff, a metropolitan policeman, that the constable, gradually growing absorbed in the overwhelming interest of the scene, appeared to think that the country would excuse him for attending more to the throbbings of his heart than his ordinary beat, and that England would not be too rigorous in expecting every man—that is to say, every policeman—at such a moment to do his duty. Nevertheless, so admirable were the arrangements, that there was at the time specified really no duty to do.

At the conclusion of the ceremonial, a Chinese, carried away, or rather pushed forward, by his enthusiasm, performed suddenly, before HER MAJESTY, an elaborate salaam, consisting of a sudden act of prostration on his face, and when the individual rose up, the custom at once occurred to us as the cause of the general flatness of feature and particular squareness of nose of that flowery people, who, from their countenance, appear to have been sown broad-cast over a large tract of country.

Beyond comparison, the most gratifying incident of the day was the promenade of the QUEEN and PRINCE, holding by the hand their two eldest children, through the whole of the lower range of the building. It was a magnificent lesson for foreigners—and especially for the Prussian princes, who cannot stir abroad without an armed escort—to see how securely and confidently a young female Sovereign and her family could walk in the closest possible contact, near enough to be touched by almost everyone, with five-and-twenty thousand people, selected from no class, and requiring only the sum of forty-two shillings as a qualification for the nearest proximity with royalty. Here was a splendid example of that real freedom on the one hand, and perfect security on the other, which are the result of our constitutional monarchy, and which all the despotism and republicanism of the world cannot obtain elsewhere, let them go on as long as they may, executing each other in the name of order, or cutting each other's throats in the name of liberty. It was delightful to see the smiling confidence of the QUEEN, as—leaning on her husband's arm, the father and the mother each holding by the hand one of the royal children—she acknowledged the heartfelt cheerings of the enthusiastic but perfectly orderly multitude.

The only blot, as we thought, upon the whole proceedings, were the unnatural and crab-like movements of one of our wealthiest peers, the MARQUESS OF WESTMINSTER, and his fellow-official, the LORD CHAMBERLAIN, whose part in the pageant consisted of the difficult, but not very dignified, feat of walking backwards, during the progress of the procession. We hope the time is not far distant when, among the other sensible arrangements of the present reign, a wealthy nobleman may be released from the humiliation of having to perform before the Sovereign and the public a series of awkward evolutions, which not all the skill of the posture-master can redeem from the absurdity attaching to the contortions of the mountebank.

Not the least interesting incident of the day was a little bit of by-play between the DUKE OF WELLINGTON and the MARQUESS OF ANGLESEY, who, when preparing to form the procession, engaged in a slight contest, or rather passage of arms, one attempting to pass the arm of the other through his own as the privilege due to seniority. The Duke eventually succeeded in causing the Marquess to surrender his arm, which the latter never did before; and the two veterans, who had been often side by side on the field of battle, proceeded side by side among the triumphs of the peaceful contest of Industry.

We have left ourselves no space, had our emotions left us inclination, to notice all, or any, of the wonders of the Great Exposition, to which we hope often to go, for the profit, not of ourselves alone, but of the public, whom we mean to make our constant companions in our numerous anticipated visits. We could not help, however, being struck by the glaring contrast between large pretension and little performance, as exemplified in the dreary and empty aspect of the large space claimed by and allotted to America. An enormous banner betokened the whole of the east end as devoted to the United States; but what was our astonishment, on arriving there, to find that their contribution to the world's industry consists as yet of a few wine-glasses, a square or two of soap, and a pair of salt-cellars! For a calculating people, our friends the Americans are thus far terribly out in their calculations.

Prince Albert
"TENDER PLANTS"

Punch, or the London Charivari
"PRINCE ALBERT AND THE CRITICS"

GOOD INTENTIONS inform the address of the Prince Consort to the Royal Academy. Couched in a conciliatory tone, Albert's understanding of the ready hostility of critics towards the artists and their "tender plants" is nebulous; and his style is lugubriously

Prince Albert at the Dinner of the Royal Academy, May 3, 1851.
Punch, Volume XX (1851).

respectable. *Punch* found in his speech an opportunity for some rousing irony. The occasion for the dinner was the inauguration of Sir Charles Eastlake as president of the Academy.

TENDER PLANTS

Mr. President,
My Lords and Gentlemen—

You have been very kind in responding with so much warmth to the toast which your President has just proposed to you, and he will allow me to thank him very cordially for the flattering expressions which he used towards myself in introducing to you that toast.

I shall feel very happy if the future should prove that the Great Exhibition, to which all nations have so generously contributed, should, amongst other advantages which I firmly hope will result from it, likewise tend to assist in the promotion of the Fine Arts in this country, of which you are the representatives; and I feel proud that we can show to the many foreigners who are now visiting our shores specimens of British art such as these walls display.

Although I have, since my first arrival in this country, never once missed visiting the Exhibition of the Royal Academy, and have always derived the greatest pleasure and instruction from these visits, it is but seldom that my engagements will allow me to join in your festive dinner. I have, however, upon this occasion, made it a point to do so, in order to assist in what may be considered the inauguration festival of your newly-elected President, at whose election I have heartily rejoiced, not only on account of my high estimate of his qualities, but also on account of my feelings of regard towards him personally.

It would be presumptuous in me to speak to you of his talent as an artist, for that is well known to you, and of it you are the best judges; or of his merits as an author, for you are all familiar with his works, or at least ought to be so; or of his amiable character as a man, for that also you must have had opportunities to estimate: but my connection with him, now for nine years, on Her Majesty's Commission of the Fine Arts, has enabled me to know what you can know less, and what is of the greatest value in a President of the Royal Academy—I mean that kindness of heart and refinement of feeling which guided him in all his communications, often most difficult and delicate, with the different artists whom we had to invite to competition, whose works we had to criticise, whom we had to employ or to reject.

Gentlemen, the production of all works in art or poetry requires, in their conception and execution, not only an exercise of the intellect, skill, and patience, but particularly *a concurrent warmth of feeling* and a free flow of imagination. This renders them most tender plants, which will thrive only in an atmosphere calculated to maintain that warmth, and that atmosphere is one of *kindness*—kindness towards the artist personally as well as towards his production. An unkind word of criticism passes like a cold blast over their tender shoots, and shrivels them up, checking the flow of the sap, which was rising to produce, perhaps, multitudes of flowers and fruit. But still criticism is absolutely necessary to the development of art, and the injudicious praise of an inferior work becomes an insult to superior genius.

In this respect our times are peculiarly unfavorable when compared with those when Madonnas were painted in the seclusion of convents; for we have now on the one hand the eager competition of a vast array of artists of every degree of talent and skill, and on the other, as judge, a great public, for the greater part wholly uneducated in art, and thus led by professional writers, who often strive to impress the public with a great idea of their own artistic knowledge by the merciless manner in which they treat works which cost those who produced them the highest efforts of mind or feeling.

The works of art, by being publicly exhibited and offered for sale, are becoming articles of trade, following as such the unreasoning laws of markets and fashion; and public and even private patronage is swayed by their tyrannical influence.

It is, then, to an institution like this, gentlemen, that we must look for a counterpoise to these evils. Here young artists are educated and taught the mysteries of their profession; those who have distinguished themselves, and given proof of their talent and power, receive a badge of acknowledgment from their professional brethren by being elected Associates of the Academy; and are at last, after long toil and continued exertion, received into a select aristocracy of a limited number, and shielded in any further struggle by their well-established reputation, of which the letters R.A. attached to their names give a pledge to the public.

If this body is often assailed from without, it shares only the fate of every aristocracy; if more than another, this only proves that it is even more difficult to sustain an aristocracy of merit than one of birth or of wealth, and may serve as a useful check upon yourselves when tempted at your elections to let personal predilection compete with real merit.

Of one thing, however, you may rest assured, and that is the continued favour of the Crown. The same feelings which actuated George the Third in founding this institution, still actuate the Crown in continuing to it its patronage and support, recognizing in you a constitutional link, as it were, between the Crown itself and the artistic body. And when I look at the assemblage of guests at this table, I may infer that the Crown does not stand alone in this respect, but that its feelings are shared also by the great and noble in the land.

May the Academy long flourish, and continue its career of usefulness!

PRINCE ALBERT AND THE CRITICS

ACCORDING TO VOLTAIRE, "Honest criticism is the tenth muse." But this saying is only another venomous falsehood of the philosopher; only one of the huge sheaf of poisoned arrows still flying downward. We are much grieved to find PRINCE ALBERT inclined to a fallacy—happily not very popular—that the claims of literature and art should be considered with good temper, and even with delicacy. This is a weakness. Mere common ink, good enough to make an entry in a ledger, or even to chronicle a dreadful accident, a daring robbery, or an ingenious act of swindling, is not the sort of fluid to drop upon a book, or to spatter on a picture. Treat the author as something only a little above a begging letter-writer; consider the artist as merely bent upon obtaining money under false pretences, and—nineteen times out of twenty—writers and painters are fitly entertained. This is an axiom of certain fast critics; an axiom valorously carried out upon the opening of the Royal Academy. For instance, a day or two since, how gallantly was MACLISE bespattered—how nobly was he bullied before all the faces of the seven hundred subscribers of the *Morning Chronicle!* And if we suppose that every *Chronicle* is read by three persons, why here is an R.A. made to look very small and very dirty indeed, in the eyes of one thousand one hundred of the population and visitors to Great Britain; Is this nothing?

However, come we to the opinions of PRINCE ALBERT, delivered a few days since at the Royal Academy Dinner. The speeches of the Prince have ever been distinguished by such fine sense, such delicacy of appreciation, and such deep, unostentatious humanity—wide away from the tinkling philanthropy, the brassy benevolence of many platforms—that we the more especially regret the short-coming of His Royal Highness when addressing the R.A.s. He said:—

> Gentlemen, the production of all works in art or poetry requires, in their conception or execution, not only an exercise of the intellect, skill, and patience, but particularly a concurrent warmth of feeling, and a free flow of imagination.

Now, if these opinions of the Prince become widely acknowledged, what will be the fate of "fast" criticism? Your fast critic should look upon a picture as he would look upon an iron pot-hook—a thing hammered out to order, and to be done by the hundred by the mere hand of man; his heart and brain having just as much, and no more, to do with the picture, than has the farrier, who whistles while he rounds a horse-shoe. Again, for literature: a book is to be considered as an attempt to beguile the good-will of the reader, and to be treated, nine times out of ten, as the petition of an imposter. Nevertheless, hear what the good-hearted, but mistaken, Prince says of the claims of art and letters. They are produced by feeling and imagination, and—

> This renders them most tender plants, which will thrive only in an atmosphere calculated to maintain that warmth; and that atmosphere is one of kindness—kindness towards the artist personally, as well *as towards his production.* An unkind word of criticism passes like a cold blast over their tender shoots, and shrinks them up, checking the flow of the sap which was rising to produce, perhaps, multitudes of flowers and fruit.

What mistaken benevolence is this! Art, like a foot-ball, bounds the higher the more you kick it: and for the effect of "cold blasts" on "tender shoots," why, the colder and more cutting the wind, the more luxuriant the blossoms. We believe that artists and authors are persons of a peculiar organisation, with a good deal of walnut-sap in their frames; the more you thrash them, the better they flourish. And we think it the especial duty of the critic, in order to test the vital strength of flowers in the bud, and fruit in the blossom, to drench them well with a solution of vitriol, or, what may be readier at hand, a copious flow of Day and Martin. It is also an excellent custom—as geese are sometimes turned in to bite down vegetation that promises to become rank—to put a "fast" critic on a young painter's picture, or young author's book, to bite the thing to the heart. We have also read it to be the custom in certain vineyards to send in an ass or two to feed off the too luxuriant shoots. And thus they were pruned; or rather criticised—"fast" criticised. Happy we are to find, for the true interests of art, that the *Chronicle* keeps a donkey!

In conclusion, we trust that PRINCE ALBERT will reconsider his opinions: in their mistaken benevolence, they may tend to an effeminate consideration of the claims of art and letters. No, no; let us still dab mud on the palette of the painter; let us still mix dirt in the ink of the writer.

Wild and rank indeed would be the vineyards of art and letters, but for the judicious asses—both fast and slow—that prune the shoots!

Herbert Spencer

"HEALTH AND ART"

HERBERT SPENCER was a prolific writer who articulated and summed up many of the central socio-ethical doctrines of Victorian liberalism. His major work, the vast *Synthetic Philosophy,*

FROM *Education* (1861).

was developed from his comprehension of the laws of evolution and took thirty-six years in the writing (1860–1896). Simply to name his works is to indicate the grand scope of his interests: *Progress: Its Law and Cause* (1857), *First Principles* (1862), *The Principles of Biology* (1864–1867), *The Principles of Psychology* (1855–1872), *The Principles of Sociology* (1876–1896), *The Principles of Ethics* (1879–1893), *Education* (1861), *The Man versus the States* (1884), the suppressed *The Nature and Reality of Religion* (1885), and the posthumous *Autobiography* (1904). His reputation, in spite of all his industry, is now in eclipse; but he was not without originality and depth. As the following selection reveals, however, his approach to art easily invited the suspicions of the Hellenists. He acknowledged the elevating power of works of the imagination, but insisted nonetheless that before a society can be ready for art its citizens must be housed, fed, and educated.

AND NOW we come to that remaining division of human life which includes the relaxations and amusements filling leisure hours. After considering what training best fits for self-preservation, for the obtainment of sustenance, for the discharge of parental duties, and for the regulation of social and political conduct, we have now to consider what training best fits for the miscellaneous ends not included in these—for the enjoyments of Nature, of Literature, and of the Fine Arts, in all their forms. Postponing them as we do to things that bear more vitally upon human welfare; and bringing everything, as we have, to the test of actual value; it will perhaps be inferred that we are inclined to slight these less essential things. No greater mistake could be made, however. We yield to none in the value we attach to aesthetic culture and its pleasures. Without painting, sculpture, music, poetry, and the emotions produced by natural beauty of every kind, life would lose half its charm. So far from regarding the training and gratification of the tastes as unimportant, we believe that in time to come they will occupy a much larger share of human life than now. When the forces of Nature have been fully conquered to man's use—when the means of production have been brought to perfection—when labour has been economized to the highest degree—when education has been so systematized that a preparation for the more essential activities may be made with comparative rapidity—and when, consequently, there is a great increase of spare time; then will the beautiful, both in Art and Nature, rightly fill a large space in the minds of all.

But it is one thing to approve of aesthetic culture as largely conducive to human happiness; and another thing to admit that it is a fundamental requisite to human happiness. However important it may be, it must yield precedence to those kinds of culture which bear directly upon daily duties. As before hinted, literature and the fine arts are made possible by those activities which make individual and social life possible; and manifestly, that which is made possible must be postponed to that which makes it possible. A florist cultivates a plant for the sake of its flower; and regards the roots and leaves as of value, chiefly because they are instrumental in producing the flower. But while, as an ultimate product, the flower is the thing to which everything else is subordinate, the florist has learnt that the root and leaves are intrinsically of greater importance; because on them the evolution of the flower depends. He bestows every care in rearing a healthy plant; and knows it would be folly if, in his anxiety to obtain the flower, he were to neglect the plant. Similarly in the case before us. Architecture, sculpture, painting, music, and poetry, may truly be called the efflorescence of civilized life. But even supposing they are of such transcendent worth as to subordinate the civilized life out of which they grow (which can hardly be asserted), it will still be admitted that the production of a healthy civilized life must be the first condition; and that culture sub-serving this must occupy the highest place.

And here we see most distinctly the vice of our educational system. It neglects the plant for the sake of the flower. In anxiety for elegance, it forgets substance. While it gives no knowledge conducive to self-preservation—while of knowledge that facilitates gaining a livelihood it gives but the rudiments, and leaves the greater part to be picked up anyhow in after life—while for the discharge of parental functions it makes not the slightest provision—and while for the duties of citizenship it prepares by imparting a mass of facts, most of which are irrelevant, and the rest without a key; it is diligent in teaching whatever adds to refinement, polish, *éclat*. Fully as we may admit that extensive acquaintance with modern languages is a valuable accomplishment, which through reading, conversation, and travel, aids in giving a certain finish; it by no means follows that this result is rightly purchased at the cost of the vitally important knowledge sacrificed to it. Supposing it true that classical education conduces to elegance and correctness of style; it cannot be said that elegance and correctness of style are comparable in importance to a familiarity with the principles that should guide the rearing of children. Grant that the taste may be improved by reading the poetry written in extinct languages; yet it is not to be inferred that such improvement of taste is equivalent in value to an acquaintance with the laws of health. Accomplishments, the fine arts, *belles-lettres*, and all those things which, as we say, constitute the efflorescence of civilization, should be wholly subordinate to that instruction and discipline on which civilization rests. *As they occupy the leisure part of life, so should they occupy the leisure part of education.*

John Ruskin

"TRAFFIC"

"TRAFFIC" has the immediacy of being the record of an actual address, and its Olympian view is its own. Ruskin spoke as a seer, informing his listeners of the right morality of architectural taste; and in the process he arraigned his whole culture for its intense materialism. It is important to note how accurately Ruskin has suited his style to public invective and to practical rather than theoretic criticism. Few of his later polemics are as animated or as inclusive of themes related to public taste as is "Traffic." In the "Wharnside" passage and in the satiric bite of his fantastic "Goddess-of-Getting-On" he is at his homiletic best.

MY GOOD YORKSHIRE FRIENDS, you asked me down here among your hills that I might talk to you about this Exchange you are going to build: but earnestly and seriously asking you to pardon me, I

Delivered in the Town Hall, Bradford, April 21, 1864; published in 1866 as the second lecture of *The Crown of Wild Olive.*

am going to do nothing of the kind. I cannot talk, or at least can say very little, about this same Exchange. I must talk of quite other things, though not willingly;—I could not deserve your pardon, if when you invited me to speak on one subject, I wilfully spoke on another. But I cannot speak, to purpose, of anything about which I do not care; and most simply and sorrowfully I have to tell you, in the outset, that I do *not* care about this Exchange of yours.

If, however, when you sent me your invitation, I had answered, 'I won't come, I don't care about the Exchange of Bradford,' you would have been justly offended with me, not knowing the reasons of so blunt a carelessness. So I have come down, hoping that you will patiently let me tell you why, on this, and many other such occasions, I now remain silent, when formerly I should have caught at the opportunity of speaking to a gracious audience.

In a word, then, I do not care about this Exchange,—because *you* don't; and because you know perfectly well I cannot make you. Look at the essential circumstances of the case, which you, as business men, know perfectly well, though perhaps you think I forget them. You are going to spend 30,000*l.*, which to you, collectively, is nothing; the buying a new coat is, as to the cost of it, a much more important matter of consideration to me than building a new Exchange is to you. But you think you may as well have the right thing for your money. You know there are a great many odd styles of architecture about; you don't want to do anything ridiculous; you hear of me, among others, as a respectable architectural man-milliner; and you send for me, that I may tell you the leading fashion; and what is, in our shops, for the moment, the newest and sweetest thing in pinnacles.

Now, pardon me for telling you frankly, you cannot have good architecture merely by asking people's advice on occasion. All good architecture is the expression of national life and character; and it is produced by a prevalent and eager national taste, or desire for beauty. And I want you to think a little of the deep significance of this word 'taste;' for no statement of mine has been more earnestly or oftener controverted than that good taste is essentially a moral quality. 'No,' say many of my antagonists, 'taste is one thing, morality is another. Tell us what is pretty; we shall be glad to know that; but preach no sermons to us.'

Permit me, therefore, to fortify this old dogma of mine somewhat. Taste is not only a part and an index of morality—it is the ONLY morality. The first, and last, and closest trial question to any living creature is, 'What do you like?' Tell me what you like, and I'll tell you what you are. Go out into the street, and ask the first man or woman you meet, what their 'taste' is, and if they answer candidly, you know them, body and soul. 'You, my friend in the rags, with the unsteady gait, what do *you* like?' 'A pipe and a quartern of gin.' I know you. 'You, good woman, with the quick step and tidy bonnet, what do you like?' 'A swept hearth and a clean tea-table, and my husband opposite me, and a baby at my breast.' Good, I know you also. 'You, little girl with the golden hair and the soft eyes, what do you like?' 'My canary, and a run among the wood hyacinths.' 'You, little boy with the dirty hands and the low forehead, what do you like?' 'A shy at the sparrows, and a game at pitch-farthing.' Good; we know them all now. What more need we ask?

'Nay,' perhaps you answer: 'we need rather to ask what these people and children do, than what they like. If they *do* right, it is no matter that they like what is wrong; and if they do wrong, it is no matter that they like what is right. Doing is the great thing; and it does not matter that the man likes drinking, so that he does not drink; nor that the little girl likes to be kind to her canary, if she will not learn her lessons; nor that the little boy likes throwing stones at the sparrows, if he goes to the Sunday school.' Indeed, for a short time, and in a provisional sense, this is true. For if, resolutely, people do what is right, in time they come to like doing it. But they only are in a right moral state when they *have* come to like doing it; and as long as they don't like it, they are still in a vicious state. The man is not in health of body who is always thirsting for the bottle in the cupboard, though he bravely bears his thirst; but the man who heartily enjoys water in the morning and wine in the evening, each in its proper quantity and time. And the entire object of true education is to make people not merely *do* the right things, but *enjoy* the right things— not merely industrious, but to love industry—not merely learned, but to love knowledge—not merely pure, but to love purity—not merely just, but to hunger and thirst after justice.

But you may answer or think, 'Is the liking for outside ornaments,—for pictures, or statues, or furniture, or architecture,—a moral quality?' Yes, most surely, if a rightly set liking. Taste for *any* pictures or statues is not a moral quality, but taste for good ones is. Only here again we have to define the word 'good.' I don't mean by 'good,' clever—or learned—or difficult in the doing. Take a picture by Teniers, of sots quarrelling over their dice: it is an entirely clever picture; so clever that nothing in its kind has ever been done equal to it; but it is also an entirely base and evil picture. It is an expression of delight in the prolonged contemplation of a vile thing, and delight in that is an 'unmannered,' or 'immoral' quality. It is 'bad taste' in the profoundest sense—it is the taste of the devils. On the other hand, a picture of Titian's, or a Greek statue, or a Greek coin, or a Turner landscape, expresses delight in the perpetual contemplation of a good and perfect thing. That is an entirely moral quality—it is the taste of the angels. And all delight in art, and all love of it, resolve themselves into simple love of that which deserves love. That deserving is the quality which we call 'loveliness'—(We ought to have an opposite word, hateliness, to be said of the things which deserve to be hated); and it is not an indifferent nor optional thing whether we love this or that; but it is just the vital function of all our being. What we *like* determines what we *are*, and is the sign of what we are; and to teach taste is inevitably to form character. As I was thinking over this, in walking up Fleet Street the other day, my eye caught the title of a book standing open in a bookseller's window. It was—'On the necessity of the diffusion of taste among all classes.' 'Ah,' I thought to myself, 'my classifying friend, when you have diffused your taste, where will your classes be? The man who likes what you like, belongs to the same class with you, I think. Inevitably so. You may put him to other work if you choose; but, by the condition you have brought him into, he will dislike the other work as much as you would yourself. You get hold of a scavenger, or a costermonger, who enjoyed the Newgate Calendar for literature, and "Pop goes the Weasel" for music. You think you can make him like Dante and Beethoven? I wish you joy of your lessons; but if you do, you have made a gentleman of him:—he won't like to go back to his costermongering.'

And so completely and unexceptionally is this so, that, if I had time to-night, I could show you that a nation cannot be affected by any vice, or weakness, without expressing it, legibly, and for ever, either in bad art, or by want of art; and that there is no national virtue, small or great, which is not manifestly expressed in all the art which circumstances enable the people possessing that virtue to produce. Take, for instance, your great English virtue of enduring and patient courage. You have at present in England only one art of any consequence—that is, iron-working. You know thoroughly well how to cast and hammer iron. Now, do you think in those masses of lava which you build volcanic cones to melt, and which you forge at the mouths of the Infernos you have created; do you think, on those iron plates, your courage and endurance are not written for ever—not merely with an iron pen, but on iron parchment? And take also your great English vice—European vice—vice of all the world—vice of all other worlds that roll or shine in heaven, bearing with them yet the atmosphere of hell—the vice of jealousy, which brings competition into your commerce, treachery into your councils, and dishonour into your wars—that vice which has rendered for you, and for your next neighbouring nation, the daily occupations of existence no longer possible, but with the mail upon your breasts and the sword loose in its sheath; so that, at last, you have realised for all the multitudes of the two great peoples who lead the so-called civilisation of the earth,—you have realised for them all, I say, in person and in policy, what was once true only of the rough Border riders of your Cheviot hills—

> They carved at the meal
> With gloves of steel,
> And they drank the red wine through the helmet barr'd;—

do you think that this national shame and dastardliness of heart are not written as legibly on every rivet of your iron armour as the strength of the right hands that forged it? Friends, I know not whether this thing be the more ludicrous or the more melancholy. It is quite unspeakably both. Suppose, instead of being now sent for by you, I had been sent for by some private gentleman, living in a suburban house, with his garden separated only by a fruit-wall from his next door neighbour's; and he had called me to consult with him on the furnishing of his drawing room. I begin looking about me, and find the walls rather bare; I think such and such a paper might be desirable—perhaps a little fresco here and there on the ceiling—a damask curtain or so at the windows. 'Ah,' says my employer, 'damask curtains, indeed! That's all very fine, but you know I can't afford that kind of thing just now!' 'Yet the world credits you with a splendid income!' 'Ah, yes,' says my friend, 'but do you know, at present, I am obliged to spend it nearly all in steel-traps?' 'Steel-traps! for whom?' 'Why, for that fellow on the other side the wall, you know: we're very good friends, capital friends; but we are obliged to keep our traps set on both sides of the wall; we could not possibly keep on friendly terms without them, and our spring guns. The worst of it is, we are both clever fellows enough; and there's never a day passes that we don't find out a new trap, or a new gun-barrel, or something; we spend about fifteen millions a year each in our traps, take it all together; and I don't see how we're to do with less.' A highly comic state of life for two private gentlemen! but for two nations, it seems to me, not wholly comic? Bedlam would be comic, perhaps, if there were only one madman in it; and your Christmas pantomime is comic, when there is only one clown in it; but when the whole world turns clown, and paints itself red with its own heart's blood instead of vermilion, it is something else than comic, I think.

Mind, I know a great deal of this is play, and willingly allow for that. You don't know what to do with yourselves for a sensation: fox-hunting and cricketing will not carry you through the whole of this unendurably long mortal life: you liked pop-guns when you were schoolboys, and rifles and Armstrongs are only the same things better made: but then the worst of it is, that what was play to you when boys, was not play to the sparrows; and what is play to you now, is not play to the small birds of State neither; and for the black eagles, you are somewhat shy of taking shots at them, if I mistake not.

I must get back to the matter in hand, however. Believe me, without farther instance, I could show you, in all time, that every nation's vice, or virtue, was written in its art: the soldiership of early Greece; the sensuality of late Italy; the visionary religion of Tuscany; the splendid human energy and beauty of Venice. I have no time to do this to-night (I have done it elsewhere before now); but I proceed to apply the principle to ourselves in a more searching manner.

I notice that among all the new buildings that cover your once wild hills, churches and schools are mixed in due, that is to say, in large proportion, with your mills and mansions; and I notice also that the churches and schools are almost always Gothic, and the mansions and mills are never Gothic. Will you allow me to ask precisely the meaning of this? For, remember, it is peculiarly a modern phenomenon. When Gothic was invented, houses were Gothic as well as churches; and when the Italian style superseded the Gothic, churches were Italian as well as houses. If there is a Gothic spire to the cathedral of Antwerp, there is a Gothic belfry to the Hôtel de Ville at Brussels; if Inigo Jones builds an Italian Whitehall, Sir Christopher Wren builds an Italian St. Paul's. But now you live under one school of architecture, and worship under another. What do you mean by doing this? Am I to understand that you are thinking of changing your architecture back to Gothic; and that you treat your churches experimentally, because it does not matter what mistakes you make in a church? Or am I to understand that you consider Gothic a pre-eminently sacred and beautiful mode of building, which you think, like the fine frankincense, should be mixed for the tabernacle only, and reserved for your religious services? For if this be the feeling, though it may seem at first as if it were graceful and reverent, you will find that, at the root of the matter, it signifies neither more nor less than that you have separated your religion from your life.

For consider what a wide significance this fact has; and remember that it is not you only, but all the people of England, who are behaving thus just now.

You have all got into the habit of calling the church 'the house of God.' I have seen, over the doors of many churches, the legend actually carved, '*This* is the house of God, and this is the gate of heaven.' Now, note where that legend comes from, and of what place it was first spoken. A boy leaves his father's house to go on a long journey on foot, to visit his uncle; he has to cross a wild hill-desert; just as if one of your own boys had to cross the wolds of Westmoreland, to visit an uncle at Carlisle. The second or third day your boy finds himself somewhere between Hawes and Brough, in the midst of the moors, at sunset. It is stony ground, and boggy; he cannot go one foot farther that night. Down he lies, to sleep, on Wharnside, where best he may, gathering a few of the stones together to put under his head;—so wild the place is, he cannot get anything but stones. And there, lying under the broad night, he has a dream; and he sees a ladder set up on the earth, and the top of it reaches to heaven, and the angels of God are ascending and descending upon it. And when he wakes out of his sleep, he says, 'How dreadful is this place; surely, this is none other than the house of God, and this is the gate of heaven.' This PLACE, observe; not this church; not this city; not this stone, even, which he puts up for a memorial—the piece of flint on which his head has lain. But this *place;* this windy slope of Wharnside; this moorland hollow, torrent-bitten, snow-blighted; this *any* place where God lets down the ladder. And how are you to know where that will be? or how are you to determine where it may be, but by being ready for it always? Do you know where the lightning is to fall next? You *do* know that, partly; you can guide the lightning; but you cannot guide the going forth of the Spirit, which is that lightning when it shines from the east to the west.

But the perpetual and insolent warping of that strong verse to serve a merely ecclesiastical purpose, is only one of the thousand instances in which we sink back into gross Judaism. We call our churches 'temples.' Now, you know, or ought to know, they are *not* temples. They have never had, never can have, anything whatever to do with temples. They are 'synagogues'—'gathering places'—where you gather yourselves together as an assembly; and by not calling them so, you again miss the force of another mighty text—'Thou, when thou prayest, shalt not be as the hypocrites are; for they love to pray standing in the *churches*' [we should translate it], 'that they may be seen of men. But thou, when thou prayest, enter into thy closet, and when thou hast shut thy door, pray to thy Father,'—which is, not in chancel nor in aisle, but 'in secret.'

Now, you feel, as I say this to you—I know you feel—as if I were trying to take away the honour of your churches. Not so; I am trying to prove to you the honour of your houses and your hills; I am trying to show you—not that the Church is not sacred—but that the whole Earth IS. I would have you feel, what careless, what constant, what infectious sin there is in all modes of thought, whereby, in calling your churches only 'holy,' you call your hearts and homes profane; and have separated yourselves from the heathen by casting all your household gods to the ground, instead of recognising, in the place of their many and feeble Lares, the presence of your One and Mighty Lord and Lar.

'But what has all this to do with our Exchange?' you ask me, impatiently. My dear friends, it has just everything to do with it; on these inner and great questions depend all the outer and little ones; and if you have asked me down here to speak to you, because you had before been interested in anything I have written, you must know that all I have yet said about architecture was to show this. The book I called 'The Seven Lamps' was to show that certain right states of temper and moral feeling were the magic powers by which all good architecture, without exception, had been produced. 'The Stones of Venice,' had, from beginning to end, no other aim than to show that the Gothic architecture of Venice had arisen out of, and indicated in all its features, a state of pure national faith, and of domestic virtue; and that its Renaissance architecture had arisen out of, and in all its features indicated, a state of concealed national infidelity, and of domestic corruption. And now, you ask me what style is best to build in; and how can I answer, knowing the meaning of the two styles, but by another question—do you mean to build as Christians or as as Infidels? And still more—do you mean to build as honest Christians or as honest Infidels? as thoroughly and confessedly either one or the other? You don't like to be asked such rude questions. I cannot help it; they are of much more importance than this Exchange business; and if they can be at once answered, the Exchange business settles itself in a moment. But, before I press them farther, I must ask leave to explain one point clearly. In all my past work, my endeavour has been to show that good architecture is essentially religious—the production of a faithful and virtuous, not of an infidel and corrupted people. But in the course of doing this, I have had also to show that good architecture is not *ecclesiastical*. People are so apt to look upon religion as the business of the clergy, not their own, that the moment they hear of anything depending on 'religion,' they think it must also have depended on the priesthood; and I have had to take what place was to be occupied between these two errors, and fight both, often with seeming contradiction. Good architecture is the work of good and believing men; therefore, you say, at least some people say, 'Good architecture must essentially have been the work of the clergy, not of the laity.'

No—a thousand times no; good architecture has always been the work of the commonalty, *not* of the clergy. What, you say, those glorious cathedrals—the pride of Europe—did their builders not form Gothic architecture? No; they corrupted Gothic architecture. Gothic was formed in the baron's castle, and the burgher's street. It was formed by the thoughts, and hands, and powers of free citizens and soldier kings. By the monk it was used as an instrument for the aid of his superstition; when that superstition became a beautiful madness, and the best hearts of Europe vainly dreamed and pined in the cloister, and vainly raged and perished in the crusade—through that fury of perverted faith and wasted war, the Gothic rose also to its loveliest, most fantastic, and, finally, most foolish dreams; and, in those dreams, was lost. . . .

You know we are speaking always of the real, active, continual, national worship; that by which men act while they live; not that which they talk of when they die. Now, we have, indeed, a nominal religion, to which we pay tithes of property, and sevenths of time; but we have also a practical and earnest religion, to which we devote nine-tenths of our property and six-sevenths of our time. And we dispute a great deal about the nominal religion; but we are all unanimous about this practical one, of which I think you will admit that the ruling goddess may be best generally described as the 'Goddess of Getting-on,' or 'Britannia of the Market.' The Athenians had an 'Athena Agoraia,' or Minerva of the Market; but she was a subordinate type of their goddess, while our Britannia Agoraia is the principal type of ours. And all your great architectural works, are, of course, built to her. It is long since you built a great cathedral; and how you would laugh at me, if I proposed building a cathedral on the top of one of these hills of yours, taking it for an Acropolis! But your railroad mounds, prolonged masses of Acropolis; your railroad stations, vaster than the Parthenon, and innumerable; your chimneys, how much more mighty and costly than cathedral spires! your harbour-piers; your warehouses; your exchanges!—all these are built to your great Goddess of 'Getting-on!' and she has formed, and will continue to form, your architecture, as long as you worship her; and it is quite vain to ask me to tell you how to build to *her;* you know far better than I.

There might indeed, on some theories, be a conceivably good

architecture for Exchanges—that is to say if there were any heroism in the fact or deed of exchange, which might be typically carved on the outside of your building. For, you know, all beautiful architecture must be adorned with sculpture or painting; and for sculpture or painting, you must have a subject. And hitherto it has been a received opinion among the nations of the world that the only right subjects for either, were *heroisms* of some sort. Even on his pots and his flagons, the Greek put a Hercules slaying lions, or an Apollo slaying serpents, or Bacchus slaying melancholy giants, and earth-born despondencies. On his temples, the Greek put contests of great warriors in founding states, or of gods with evil spirits. On his houses and temples alike, the Christian put carvings of angels conquering devils; or of hero-martyrs exchanging this world for another; subject inappropriate, I think, to our manner of exchange here. And the Master of Christians not only left his followers without any orders as to the sculpture of affairs of exchange on the outside of buildings, but gave some strong evidence of his dislike of affairs of exchange within them. And yet there might surely be a heroism in such affairs; and all commerce become a kind of selling of doves, not impious. The wonder has always been great to me, that heroism has never been supposed to be in anywise consistent with the practice of supplying people with food, or clothes; but rather with that of quartering oneself upon them for food, and stripping them of their clothes. Spoiling of armour is an heroic deed in all ages; but the selling of clothes, old, or new, has never taken any colour of magnanimity. Yet one does not see why feeding the hungry and clothing the naked should ever become base businesses, even when engaged in on a large scale. If one could contrive to attach the notion of conquest to them anyhow? so that, supposing there were anywhere an obstinate race, who refused to be comforted, one might take some pride in giving them compulsory comfort; and as it were, 'occupying a country' with one's gifts, instead of one's armies? If one could only consider it as much a victory to get a barren field sown, as to get an eared field stripped; and contend who should build villages, instead of who should 'carry' them. Are not all forms of heroism, conceivable in doing these serviceable deeds? You doubt who is strongest? It might be ascertained by push of spade, as well as push of sword. Who is wisest? There are witty things to be thought of in planning other business than campaigns. Who is bravest? There are always the elements to fight with, stronger than men; and nearly as merciless. The only absolutely and unapproachably heroic element in the soldier's work seems to be—that he is paid little for it—and regularly: while you traffickers, and exchangers, and others occupied in presumably benevolent business, like to be paid much for it—and by chance. I never can make out how it is that a knight-errant does not expect to be paid for his trouble; but a pedlar-errant always does;—that people are willing to take hard knocks for nothing, but never to sell ribands cheap;—that they are ready to go on fervent crusades to recover the tomb of a buried God, never on any travels to fulfil the orders of a living God;—that they will go anywhere barefoot to preach their faith, but must be well bribed to practice it, and are perfectly ready to give the Gospel gratis, but never the loaves and fishes. If you chose to take the matter up on any such soldierly principle, to do your commerce, and your feeding of nations, for fixed salaries; and to be as particular about giving people the best food, and the best cloth, as soldiers are about giving them the best gunpowder, I could carve something for you on your exchange worth looking at. But I can only at present suggest decorating its frieze with pendant purses; and making its pillars broad at the base for the sticking of bills. And in the innermost chambers of it there might be a statue of Britannia of the Market, who may have, perhaps advisably, a partridge for her crest, typical at once of her courage in fighting for noble ideas; and of her interest in game; and round its neck the inscription in golden letters, 'Perdix fovit quæ non peperit.' * Then, for her spear, she might have a weaver's beam; and on her shield, instead of her Cross, the Milanese boar, semi-fleeced, with the town of Gennesaret proper, in the field and the legend 'In the best market,' and her corslet, of leather, folded over her heart in the shape of a purse, with thirty slits in it for a piece of money to go in at, on each day of the month. And I doubt not but that people would come to see your exchange, and its goddess, with applause.

Nevertheless, I want to point out to you certain strange char-

* Jerem. xvii. 11 (best in Septuagint and Vulgate). "As the partridge, fostering what she brought not forth, so he that getteth riches, not by right shall leave them in the midst of his days, and at his end shall be a fool."

acters in this goddess of yours. She differs from the great Greek and Mediæval deities essentially in two things—first, as to the continuance of her presumed power; secondly, as to the extent of it.

1st, as to the Continuance.

The Greek Goddess of Wisdom gave continual increase of wisdom, as the Christian Spirit of Comfort (or Comforter) continual increase of comfort. There was no question, with these, of any limit or cessation of function. But with your Agora Goddess, that is just the most important question. Getting on—but where to? Gathering together—but how much? Do you mean to gather always—never to spend? If so, I wish you joy of your goddess, for I am just as well off as you, without the trouble of worshipping her at all. But if you do not spend, somebody else will—somebody else must. And it is because of this (among many other such errors) that I have fearlessly declared your so-called science of Political Economy to be no science; because, namely, it has omitted the study of exactly the most important branch of the business—the study of *spending*. For spend you must, and as much as you make, ultimately. You gather corn:—will you bury England under a heap of grain; or will you, when you have gathered, finally eat? You gather gold:—will you make your house-roofs of it, or pave your streets with it? That is still one way of spending it. But if you keep it, that you may get more, I'll give you more; I'll give you all the gold you want—all you can imagine—if you can tell me what you'll do with it. You shall have thousands of gold pieces;—thousands of thousands—millions—mountains, of gold: where will you keep them? Will you put an Olympus of silver upon a golden Pelion—make Ossa like a wart? Do you think the rain and dew would then come down to you, in the streams from such mountains, more blessedly than they will down the mountains which God has made for you, of moss and whinstone? But it is not gold that you want to gather! What is it? greenbacks? No; not those neither. What is it then—is it ciphers after a capital I? Cannot you practice writing ciphers, and write as many as you want? Write ciphers for an hour every morning, in a big book, and say every evening, I am worth all those noughts more than I was yesterday. Won't that do? Well, what in the name of Plutus is it you want? Not gold, not greenbacks, not ciphers after a capital I? You will have to answer, after all, 'No; we want, somehow or other, money's *worth.*' Well, what is that? Let your Goddess of Getting-on discover it, and let her learn to stay therein.

II. But there is yet another question to be asked respecting this Goddess of Getting-on. The first was of the continuance of her power; the second is of its extent.

Pallas and the Madonna were supposed to be all the world's Pallas, and all the world's Madonna. They could teach all men, and they could comfort all men. But, look strictly into the nature of the power of your Goddess of Getting-on; and you will find she is the Goddess—not of everybody's getting on—but only of somebody's getting on. This is a vital, or rather deathful distinction. Examine it in your own ideal of the state of national life which this Goddess is to evoke and maintain. I asked you what it was, when I was last here;—you have never told me. Now, shall I try to tell you?

Your ideal of human life then is, I think, that it should be passed in a pleasant undulating world, with iron and coal everywhere underneath it. On each pleasant bank of this world is to be a beautiful mansion, with two wings; and stables, and coach-houses; a moderately sized park; a large garden and hot houses; and pleasant carriage drives through the shrubberies. In this mansion are to live the favoured votaries of the Goddess; the English gentleman, with his gracious wife, and his beautiful family; always able to have the boudoir and the jewels for the wife, and the beautiful ball dresses for the daughters, and hunters for the sons, and a shooting in the Highlands for himself. At the bottom of the bank, is to be the mill; not less than a quarter of a mile long, with a steam engine at each end, and two in the middle, and a chimney three hundred feet high. In this mill are to be in constant employment from eight hundred to a thousand workers, who never drink, never strike, always go to church on Sunday, and always express themselves in respectful language.

Is not that, broadly, and in the main features, the kind of thing you propose to yourselves? It is very pretty indeed seen from above; not at all so pretty, seen from below. For, observe, while to one family this deity is indeed the Goddess of Getting on, to a thousand families she is the Goddess of *not* Getting on. 'Nay,' you say, 'they have all their chance.' Yes, so has every one in a lottery, but there must always be the same number of blanks. 'Ah! but in a lottery it is not skill and intelligence which take the lead, but blind chance.' What then! do you think the old practice, that 'they should take who have the power, and they should keep who can,' is less iniquitous, when the power has become power of brains instead of fist? and that, though we may not take advantage of a child's or a woman's weakness, we may of a man's foolishness? 'Nay, but finally, work must be done, and some one must be at the top, some one at the bottom.' Granted, my friends. Work must always be, and captains of work must always be; and if you in the least remember the tone of any of my writings, you must know that they are thought unfit for this age, because they are always insisting on need of government, and speaking with scorn of liberty. But I beg you to observe that there is a wide difference between being captains or governors of work, and taking the profits of it. It does not follow, because you are general of an army, that you are to take all the treasure, or land, it wins (if it fight for treasure or land); neither, because you are king of a nation, that you are to consume all the profits of the nation's work. Real kings, on the contrary, are known invariably by their doing quite the reverse of this,—by their taking the least possible quantity of the nation's work for themselves. There is no test of real kinghood so infallible as that. Does the crowned creature live simply, bravely, unostentatiously? probably he *is* a King. Does he cover his body with jewels, and his table with delicates? in all probability he is *not* a King. It is possible he may be, as Solomon was; but that is when the nation shares his splendour with him. Solomon made gold, not only to be in his own palace as stones, but to be in Jerusalem as stones. But even so, for the most part, these splendid kinghoods expire in ruin, and only the true kinghoods live, which are of royal labourers governing loyal labourers; who, both leading rough lives, establish the true dynasties. Conclusively you will find that because you are king of a nation, it does not follow that you are to gather for yourself all the wealth of that nation; neither, because you are king of a small part of the nation, and lord over the means of its maintenance—over field, or mill, or mine, are you to take all the produce of that piece of the foundation of national existence for yourself.

You will tell me I need not preach against these things, for I cannot mend them. No, good friends, I cannot; but you can, and you will; or something else can and will. Do you think these phenomena are to stay always in their present power or aspect? All history shows, on the contrary, that to be the exact thing they never can do. Change *must* come; but it is ours to determine whether change of growth, or change of death. Shall the Parthenon be in ruins on its rock, and Bolton priory in its meadow, but these mills of yours be the consummation of the buildings of the earth, and their wheels be as the wheels of eternity? Think you that 'men may come, and men may go,' but—mills—go on forever? Not so; out of these, better or worse shall come; and it is for you to choose which.

I know that none of this wrong is done with deliberate purpose. I know, on the contrary, that you wish your workmen well; that you do much for them, and that you desire to do more for them, if you saw your way to it safely. I know that many of you have done, and are every day doing, whatever you feel to be in your power; and that even all this wrong and misery are brought about by a warped sense of duty, each of you striving to do his best, without noticing that this best is essentially and centrally the best for himself, not for others. And all this has come of the spreading of that accursed, thrice impious doctrine of the modern economist, that 'To do the best for yourself, is finally to do the best for others.' Friends, our great Master said not so; and most absolutely we shall find this world is not made so. Indeed, to do the best for others, is finally to do the best for ourselves; but it will not do to have our eyes fixed on that issue. The Pagans had got beyond that. Hear what a Pagan says of this matter; hear what were, perhaps, the last written words of Plato,—if not the last actually written (for this we cannot know), yet assuredly in fact and power his parting words—in which, endeavouring to give full crowning and harmonious close to all his thoughts, and to speak the sum of them by the imagined sentence of the Great Spirit, his strength and his heart fail him, and the words cease; broken off for ever. It is the close of the dialogue called 'Critias,' in which he describes, partly from real tradition, partly in ideal dream, the early state of Athens; and the genesis, and order, and religion, of the fabled isle of Atlantis; in which genesis he conceives the same first perfection and final degeneracy of man, which in our own Scriptural tradition is expressed by saying that the Sons of God intermarried with the daughters of men, for he supposes the earliest race to have been indeed the children of God; and to have corrupted themselves, until 'their spot was not the spot of his children.' And this, he says, was the end; that indeed 'through many generations, so long as the God's nature in them yet was full, they were submissive to the sacred laws, and carried themselves lovingly to all that had kindred with them in divineness; for their uttermost spirit was faithful and true, and in every wise great; so that, in all meekness of wisdom, they dealt with each other, and took all the chances of life; and despising all things except virtue, they cared little what happened day by day, and *bore lightly the burden* of gold and of possessions; for they saw that, if only their common love and virtue increased, all these things would be increased together with them; but to set their esteem and ardent pursuit upon material possession would be to lose that first, and their virtue and affection together with it. And by such reasoning, and what of the divine nature remained in them, they gained all this greatness of which we have already told, but when the God's part of them faded and became extinct, being mixed again and again, and effaced by the prevalent mortality; and the human nature at last exceeded, they then became unable to endure the courses of fortune; and fell into shapelessness of life, and baseness in the sight of him who could see, having lost everything that was fairest of their honour; while to the blind hearts which could not discern the true life, tending to happiness, it seemed that they were then chiefly noble and happy, being filled with all iniquity of inordinate possession and power. Whereupon, the God of God's, whose Kinghood is in laws, beholding a once just nation thus cast into misery, and desiring to lay such punishment upon them as might make them repent into restraining, gathered together all the gods into his dwelling-place, which from heaven's centre overlooks whatever has part in creation; and having assembled them, he said'——

The rest is silence. So ended are the last words of the chief wisdom of the heathen, spoken of this idol of riches; this idol of yours; this golden image high by measureless cubits, set up where your green fields of England are furnace-burnt into the likeness of the plain of Dura: this idol, forbidden to us, first of all idols, by our own Master and faith; forbidden to us also by every human lip that has ever, in any age or people, been accounted of as able to speak according to the purposes of God. Continue to make that forbidden deity your principal one, and soon no more art, no more science, no more pleasure will be possible. Catastrophe will come; or worse than catastrophe, slow mouldering and withering into Hades. But if you can fix some conception of a true human state of life to be striven for—life for all men as for yourselves—if you can determine some honest and simple order of existence; following those trodden ways of wisdom, which are pleasantness, and seeking her quiet and withdrawn paths, which are peace;—then, and so sanctifying wealth into 'commonwealth,' all your art, your literature, your daily labours, your domestic affection, and citizen's duty, will join and increase into one magnificent harmony. You will know then how to build, well enough; you will build with stone well, but with flesh better; temples not made with hands, but riveted of hearts; and that kind of marble, crimson-veined, is indeed eternal.

Algernon Charles Swinburne

"NOTES ON POEMS AND REVIEWS"

Few Victorian writers, with the possible exception of Rossetti, had Swinburne's talent for arousing the middle-class critics. Equipped with an exceptional rhetoric and invective, he was more than a match for the majority of his enemies. Fortunately, he did not wither under the virulent attacks he endured throughout his early career. Contemptuously dismissing the prevailing notion that Victorian morality should limit the artist's "world of work," he freely scorned journalist-critic spokesmen of "propriety" in art. His *bête noir* was, in essence, *Respectability* in literature, religion, and manners—the same creature George Moore tried later to cage so that it would no longer threaten creative spirits. Under the only true morality, Swinburne insisted, the artist freely confronts and shapes the range of man's experience: historical, cultural, and thematic.

Published as a pamphlet in 1866.

"Notes on Poems and Reviews" was a reply to the host of critics who greeted his *Poems and Ballads* with scandalized derision. The outcry had been so pronounced that Moxon, his publisher, was prevailed upon to withdraw the edition. Incensed, Swinburne transferred the work to John Camden Hotten; and it was at the latter's urging that he fashioned a "defense" in order to help prepare for the re-release of the suspended volume. Swinburne's letters reveal how hard he worked on the essay. His mood ranges from finely controlled calm to scathing irony; his style is flexible, carefully wrought, and characteristically energetic. He called the work "a quiet little pamphlet" (in a letter to F. G. Waugh), adding that it was both "sarcastic and elucidative"—which it is; and he allowed himself the tongue-in-cheek boast to William Michael Rossetti that he had "proved Dolores to be little less than a second Sermon on the Mount, and Anactoria than an archdeacon's charge."

It is by no wish of my own that I accept the task now proposed to me. To vindicate or defend myself from the assault or the charge of men whom, but for their attacks, I might never have heard of, is an office which I, or any writer who respects his work, cannot without reluctance stoop to undertake. As long as the attacks on my books—I have seen a few, I am told there are many—were confined within the usual limits of the anonymous press, I let them pass without the notice to which they appeared to aspire. Sincere or insincere, insolent or respectful, I let my assailants say out their say unheeded.

I have now undertaken to write a few words on this affair, not by way of apology or vindication, of answer or appeal. I have none such to offer. Much of the criticism I have seen is as usual, in the words of Shakespeare's greatest follower,

> As if a man should spit against the wind;
> The filth returns in 's face.

In recognition of his fair dealing with me in this matter, I am bound by my own sense of right to accede to the wish of my present publisher, and to the wishes of friends whose advice I value, that on his account, if not on mine, I should make some reply to the charges brought against me—as far as I understand them. The work is not fruitful of pleasure, of honour, or of profit; but, like other such tasks, it may be none the less useful and necessary. I am aware that it cannot be accomplished without some show of egotism; and I am perforce prepared to incur the consequent charge of arrogance. The office of commentator of my own works has been forced upon me by circumstances connected with the issue and re-issue of my last book. I am compelled to look sharply into it, and inquire what passage, what allusion, or what phrase can have drawn down such sudden thunder from the serene heavens of public virtue. A mere libeller I have no wish to encounter; I leave it to the saints to fight with beasts at Ephesus or nearer. "For in these strifes, and on such persons, it were as wretched to affect a victory, as it is unhappy to be committed with them."

Certain poems of mine, it appears, have been impugned by judges, with or without a name, as indecent or as blasphemous. To me, as I have intimated, their verdict is a matter of infinite indifference: it is of equally small moment to me whether in such eyes as theirs I appear moral or immoral, Christian or pagan. But, remembering that science must not scorn to investigate animalcules and infusoria, I am ready for once to play the anatomist.

With regard to any opinion implied or expressed throughout my book, I desire that one thing should be remembered: the book is dramatic, many-faced, multifarious; and no utterance of enjoyment or despair, belief or unbelief, can properly be assumed as the assertion of its author's personal feeling or faith. Were each poem to be accepted as the deliberate outcome and result of the writer's conviction, not mine alone but most other men's verses would leave nothing behind them but a sense of cloudy chaos and suicidal contradiction. Byron and Shelley, speaking in their own persons, and with what sublime effect we know, openly and insultingly mocked and reviled what the English of their day held most sacred. I have not done this. I do not say that, if I chose, I would not do so to the best of my power; I do say that hitherto I have seen fit to do nothing of the kind.

It remains then to inquire what in that book can be reasonably offensive to the English reader. In order to resolve this problem, I will not fish up any of the ephemeral scurrilities born only to sting if they can, and sink as they must. I will take the one article [1]

[1] "Mr. Swinburne's New Poems: *Poems and Ballads,*" by John Morley (1838–1923), which appeared in the *Saturday Review* for August 4, 1866.

that lies before me; the work (I admit) of an enemy, but the work (I acknowledge) of a gentleman. I cannot accept it as accurate; but I readily and gladly allow that it neither contains nor suggests anything false or filthy. To him therefore, rather than to another, I address my declamation. Two among my poems, it appears, are in his opinion "especially horrible." Good. Though the phrase be somewhat "inexpressive," I am content to meet him on this ground. It is something—nay, it is much—to find an antagonist who has sufficient sense of honesty and honour to mark out the lists in which he, the challenger, is desirous to encounter the challenged.

The first, it appears, of these especially horrible poems is "Anactoria." I am informed, and have not cared to verify the assertion, that this poem has excited, among the chaste and candid critics of the day or hour or minute, a more vehement reprobation, a more virtuous horror, a more passionate appeal, than any other of my writing. Proud and glad as I must be of this distinction, I must yet, however reluctantly, inquire what merit or demerit has incurred such unexpected honour. I was not ambitious of it; I am not ashamed of it; but I am overcome by it. I have never lusted after the praise of reviewers; I have never feared their abuse; but I would fain know why the vultures should gather here of all places; what congenial carrion they smell, who can discern such (it is alleged) in any rosebed. And after a little reflection I do know, or conjecture. Virtue, as she appears incarnate in British journalism and voluble through that unsavoury organ, is something of a compound creature:

> A lump neither alive nor dead,
> Dog-headed, bosom-eyed, and bird-footed;

nor have any dragon's jaws been known to emit or occasion stronger and stranger sounds and odours. But having, not without astonishment and disgust, inhaled these odours, I find myself at last able to analyse their component parts. What my poem means, if any reader should want that explained, I am ready to explain, though perplexed by the hint that explanation may be required. What certain reviewers have imagined it to imply, I am incompetent to explain, and unwilling to imagine. I am evidently not virtuous enough to understand them. I thank Heaven that I am not. *Ma corruption rougirait de leur pudeur*. I have not studied in those schools whence that full-fledged phoenix, the "virtue" of professional press-men, rises chuckling and crowing from the dunghill, its birthplace and its deathbed. But there are birds of alien feather, if not of higher flight; and these I would now recall into no hencoop or preserve of mine, but into the open and general field where all may find pasture and sunshine and fresh air; into places whither the prurient prudery and the virulent virtue of press-men and prostitutes cannot follow; into an atmosphere where calumny cannot speak, and fatuity cannot breathe; in a word, where backbiters and imbeciles become impossible. I neither hope nor wish to change the unchangeable, to purify the impure. To conciliate them, to vindicate myself in their eyes, is a task which I should not condescend to attempt, even were I sure to accomplish.

In this poem I have simply expressed, or tried to express, that violence of affection between one and another which hardens into rage and deepens into despair. The keynote which I have here touched was struck long since by Sappho. We in England are taught, are compelled under penalties to learn, to construe, and to repeat, as schoolboys, the imperishable and incomparable verses of that supreme poet; and I at least am grateful for the training. I have wished, and I have even ventured to hope that I might be in time competent to translate into a baser and later language the divine words which even as a boy I could not but recognise as divine. That hope, if indeed I dared ever entertain such a hope, I soon found fallacious. To translate the two odes and the remaining fragments of Sappho is the one impossible task; and as witness of this I will call up one of the greatest among poets. Catullus "translated"—or as his countrymen would now say "traduced"—the "Ode to Anactoria"—a more beautiful translation there never was and will never be; but compared with the Greek, it is colourless and bloodless, puffed out by additions and enfeebled by alterations. Let any one set against each other the two first stanzas, Latin and Greek, and pronounce. (This would be too much to ask of all of my critics; but some among the journalists of England may be capable of achieving the not exorbitant task.) Where Catullus failed I could not hope to succeed; I tried instead to reproduce in a diluted and dilated form the spirit of a poem which could not be reproduced in the body.

Now the "Ode to Anactoria" (as it is named by tradition)—the poem which English boys have to get by heart—the poem (and this is more important) which has in the whole world of verse no companion and no rival but the "Ode to Aphrodite," has been twice at least translated or "traduced." I am not aware that Mr. Ambrose Phillips, or M. Nicolas Boileau-Despréaux, was ever impeached before any jury of moralists for his sufficiently grievous offense. By any jury of poets both would assuredly have been convicted. Now, what they did I have not done. To the best (and bad is the best) of their ability, they have "done into" bad French and bad English the very words of Sappho. Feeling that although I might do it better I could not do it well, I abandoned the idea of translation.

I tried, then, to write some paraphrase of the fragment which the Fates and the Christians have spared us. I have not said, as Boileau and Phillips have, that the speaker sweats and swoons at sight of her favourite by the side of a man. I have abstained from touching on such details, for this reason: that I felt myself incompetent to give adequate expression in English to the literal and absolute words of Sappho; and would not debase and degrade them into a viler form. No one can feel more deeply than I do the inadequacy of my work. "That is not Sappho," a friend said once to me. I could not reply, "It is as near as I can come; and no man can come close to her." Her remaining verses are the supreme success, the final achievement, of the poetic art.

But this, it may be, is not to the point. I will try to draw thither; though the descent is immeasurable from Sappho's verse to mine, or to any man's. I have striven to cast my spirit into the mould of hers, to express and represent not the poem but the poet. I did not think it requisite to disfigure the page with a footnote wherever I had fallen back upon the original text. Here and there, I need not say, I have rendered into English the very words of Sappho. I have tried also to work into words of my own some expression of their effect: to bear witness how, more than any other's, her verses strike and sting the memory in lonely places, or at sea, among all loftier sights and sounds—how they seem akin to fire and air, being themselves "all air and fire"; other element there is none in them. As to the angry appeal against the supreme mystery of oppressive heaven, which I have ventured to put into her mouth at that point only where pleasure culminates in pain, affection in anger, and desire in despair—as to the "blasphemies" against God or Gods of which here and elsewhere I stand accused—they are to be taken as the first outcome or outburst of foiled and fruitless passion recoiling on itself. After this, the spirit finds time to breathe and repose above all vexed senses of the weary body, all bitter labours of the revolted soul; the poet's pride of place is resumed, the lofty conscience of invincible immortality in the memories and the mouths of men.

What is there now of horrible in this? The expressions of fierce fondness, the ardours of passionate despair? Are these so unnatural as to affright or disgust? Where is there an unclean detail? where an obscene allusion? A writer as impure as my critics might of course have written, on this or on any subject, an impure poem; I have not. And if to translate or paraphrase Sappho be an offence, indict the heavier offenders who have handled and rehandled this matter in their wretched versions of the ode. Is my poem more passionate in detail, more unmistakable in subject? I affirm that it is less; and what I affirm I have proved.

Next on the list of accusation stands the poem of Dolores. The gist and bearing of this I should have thought evident enough, viewed by the light of others which precede and follow it. I have striven here to express that transient state of spirit through which a man may be supposed to pass, foiled in love and weary of loving, but not yet in sight of rest; seeking refuge in those "violent delights" which "have violent ends," in fierce and frank sensualities which at least profess to be no more than they are. This poem, like *Faustine,* is so distinctly symbolic and fanciful that it cannot justly be amenable to judgment as a study in the school of realism. The spirit, bowed and discoloured by suffering and by passion (which are indeed the same thing and the same word), plays for awhile with its pleasures and its pains, mixes and distorts them with a sense half-humorous and half-mournful, exults in bitter and doubtful emotions:

> Moods of fantastic sadness, nothing worth.

It sports with sorrow, and jests against itself; cries out for freedom and confesses the chain; decorates with the name of goddess, crowns anew as the mystical Cotytto, some woman, real or ideal, in whom the pride of life with its companion lusts is incarnate. In her lover's half-shut eyes, her fierce unchaste beauty is transfigured, her cruel sensual eyes have a meaning and a message; there are memories and secrets in the kisses of her lips. She is the darker Venus, fed with burnt-offering and blood-sacrifice; the veiled image of that pleasure which men impelled by satiety and perverted by power have sought through ways as strange as Nero's before and since his time; the daughter of lust and death, and holding of both her parents; Our Lady of Pain, antagonist alike of trivial sins and virtues: no Virgin, and unblessed of men; no mother of the Gods or God; no Cybele, served by sexless priests or monks, adored of Origen or Atys; no likeness of her in Dindymus or Loreto.

The next act in this lyrical monodrama of passion represents a new stage and scene. The worship of desire has ceased; the mad commotion of sense has stormed itself out; the spirit, clear of the old regret that drove it upon such violent ways for a respite, healed of the fever that wasted it in the search for relief among fierce fancies and tempestuous pleasures, dreams now of truth discovered and repose attained. Not the martyr's ardour of selfless love, an unprofitable flame that burnt out and did no service—not the rapid rage of pleasure that seemed for a little to make the flesh divine, to clothe the naked senses with the fiery raiment of faith; but a stingless love, an innocuous desire. "Hesperia," the tenderest type of woman or of dream, born in the westward "islands of the blest," where the shadows of all happy and holy things live beyond the sunset a sacred and a sleepless life, dawns upon his eyes a western dawn, risen as the fiery day of passion goes down, and risen where it sank. Here, between moonrise and sunset, lives the love that is gentle and faithful, neither giving too much nor asking—a bride rather than a mistress, a sister rather than a bride. But not at once, or not for ever, can the past be killed and buried; hither also the huntress follows her flying prey, wounded and weakened, still fresh from the fangs of passion; the cruel hands, the amorous eyes, still glitter and allure. *Qui a bu boira:* the feet are drawn back towards the ancient ways. Only by lifelong flight, side by side with the goddess that redeems, shall her slave of old escape from the goddess that consumes: if even thus one may be saved, even thus distance the bloodhounds.

This is the myth or fable of my poem; and it is not without design that I have slipped in, between the first and the second part, the verses called *The Garden of Proserpine,* expressive, as I meant they should be, of that brief total pause of passion and of thought, when the spirit, without fear or hope of good things or evil, hungers and thirsts only after the perfect sleep. Now what there is in all this unfit to be written—what there is here indecent in manner or repulsive in matter—I at least do not yet see; and before I can see it, my eyes must be purged with the euphrasy and rue which keep clear the purer eyes of professional virtue. The insight into evil of chaste and critical pressmen, their sharp scent for possible or impossible impurities, their delicate ear for a sound or a whisper of wrong—all this knowledge "is too wonderful and excellent for me; I cannot attain unto it." In one thing, indeed, it seems I have erred: I have forgotten to prefix to my work the timely warning of a great poet and humorist:

> J'en previens les meres des familles,
> Ce que j'écries n'est pas pour les petites filles
> Dont on coupe le pain en tartines; mes vers
> Sont des vers de jeune homme.

I have overlooked the evidence which every day makes clearer, that our time has room only for such as are content to write for children and girls. But this oversight is the sum of my offence.

It would seem indeed as though to publish a book were equivalent to thrusting it with violence into the hands of every mother and nurse in the kingdom as fit and necessary food for female infancy. Happily there is no fear that the supply of milk for babes will fall short of the demand for some time yet. There are moral milkmen enough, in all conscience, crying their ware about the streets and byways; fresh or stale, sour or sweet, the requisite fluid runs from a sufficiently copious issue. In due time, perhaps, the critical doctors may prescibe a stronger diet for their hypochondriac patient, the reading world; or the gigantic *malade imaginaire* called the public may rebel against the weekly draught or the daily drug of MM. Purgon and Diafoirus. We, meanwhile, who profess to deal neither in poison nor in pap, may not unwillingly stand aside. Let those read who will, and let those who will abstain from reading. *Caveat emptor.* No one wishes to force men's food down the throats of babes and sucklings. The verses last analysed were assuredly written with no moral or immoral design; but the upshot seems to me moral rather than immoral, if it must needs be one or the other, and if (which I cannot be sure of) I construe aright those somewhat misty and changeable terms.

These poems thus disposed of are (I am told) those which have given most offence and scandal to the venal virtue of journalism. As I have not to review my reviewers, I need not be at pains to refute at length every wilful error or unconscious lie which a workman that way inclined might drag into light. To me, as to all others who may read what I write, the whole matter must continue to seem too pitiable and trivial to waste a word or thought on it which we can help wasting. But having begun this task, I will add yet a word or two of annotation. I have heard that even the little poem of 'Faustine' has been to some readers a thing to make the scalp creep and the blood freeze. It was issued with no such intent. Nor do I remember that any man's voice or heel was lifted against it when it first appeared, a new-born and virgin poem, in the *Spectator* newspaper for 1862. Virtue, it would seem, has shot up surprisingly in the space of four years or less—a rank and rapid growth, barren of blossom and rotten at root. 'Faustine' is the reverie of a man gazing on the bitter and vicious loveliness of a face as common and as cheap as the morality of reviewers, and dreaming of past lives in which this fair face may have held a nobler or fitter station; the imperial profile may have been Faustina's, the thirsty lips a Mænad's, when first she learnt to drink blood or wine, to waste the loves and ruin the lives of men; through Greece and again through Rome she may have passed with the same face which now comes before us dishonoured and discrowned. Whatever of merit or demerit there may be in the verses, the idea that gives them such life as they have is simple enough; the transmigration of a single soul, doomed as though by accident from the first to all evil and no good, through many ages and forms, but clad always in the same type of fleshly beauty. The chance which suggested to me this poem was one which may happen any day to any man—the sudden sight of a living face which recalled the well-known likeness of another dead for centuries: in this instance, the noble and faultless type of the elder Faustina, as seen in coin and bust. Out of that casual glimpse and sudden recollection these verses sprang and grew.

Of the poem in which I have attempted once more to embody the legend of Venus and her knight, I need say only that my first aim was to rehandle the old story in a new fashion. To me it seemed that the tragedy began with the knight's return to Venus—began at the point where hitherto it had seemed to leave off. The immortal agony of a man lost after all repentance—cast down from fearful hope into fearless despair—believing in Christ and bound to Venus—desirous of penitential pain, and damned to joyless pleasure—this, in my eyes, was the kernel and nucleus of a myth comparable only to that of the foolish virgins and bearing the same burden. The tragic touch of the story is this: that the knight who has renounced Christ believes in him; the lover who has embraced Venus disbelieves in her. Vainly and in despair would he make the best of that which is the worst—vainly remonstrate with God, and argue on the side he would fain desert. Once accept or admit the least admixture of pagan worship, or of modern thought, and the whole story collapses into froth and smoke. It was not till my poem was completed that I received from the hands of its author the admirable pamphlet of Charles Baudelaire on Wagner's *Tannhäuser*. If any one desires to see, expressed in better words than I can command, the conception of the mediæval Venus which it was my aim to put into verse, let him turn to the magnificent passage in which M. Baudelaire describes the fallen goddess, grown diabolic among ages that would not accept her as divine. In another point, as I then found, I concur with the great musician and his great panegyrist. I have made Venus the one love of her knight's whole life, as Mary Stuart of Chastelard's; I have sent him, poet and soldier, fresh to her fierce embrace. Thus only both legend and symbol appear to me noble and significant. Light loves and harmless errors must not touch the elect of heaven or of hell. The queen of evil, the lady of lust, will endure no rival but God; and when the vicar of God rejects him, to her only can he return to abide the day of judgment in weariness and sorrow and fear.

These poems do not seem to me condemnable, unless it be on the ground of bad verse; and to any charge of that kind I should of course be as unable as reluctant to reply. But I certainly was even less prepared to hear the batteries of virtue open fire in another quarter. Sculpture I knew was a dead art; buried centuries deep out of sight, with no angel keeping watch over the sepulchre; its very grave-clothes divided by wrangling and impotent sectaries, and no chance anywhere visible of a resurrection. I knew that belief in the body was the secret of sculpture, and that a past age of ascetics could no more attempt or attain it than the present age of hypocrites; I knew that modern moralities and recent religions were, if possible, more averse and alien to this purely physical and pagan art than to the others; but how far averse I did not know. There is nothing lovelier, as there is nothing more famous, in later Hellenic art, than the statue of Hermaphroditus. No one would compare it with the greatest works of Greek sculpture. No one would lift Keats on a level with Shakespeare. But the Fates have allowed us to possess at once Othello and Hyperion, Theseus and Hermaphroditus. At Paris, at Florence, at Naples, the delicate divinity of this work has always drawn towards it the eyes of artists and poets. A creature at once foul and dull enough to extract from a sight so lovely, from a thing so noble, the faintest, the most fleeting idea of impurity, must be, and must remain, below comprehension and below remark. It is incredible that the meanest of men should derive from it any other than the sense of high and grateful pleasure. Odour and colour and music are not more tender or more pure. How favourite and frequent a vision among the Greeks was this of the union of sexes in one body of perfect beauty, none need be told. In Plato the legend has fallen into a form coarse, hard, and absurd. The theory of God splitting in two the double archetype of man and woman, the original hermaphrodite which had to get itself bisected into female and male, is repulsive and ridiculous enough. But the idea thus incarnate, literal or symbolic, is merely beautiful. I am not the first who has translated into written verse this sculptured poem: another before me, as he says, has more than once 'caressed it with a sculptor's love.' It is indeed, among statues as a lyric among tragedies; it stands below the Niobe as Simonides below Æschylus, as Correggio beneath Titian. The sad and subtle moral of this myth, which I have desired to indicate in verse, is that perfection once attained on all sides is a thing thenceforward barren of use or fruit; whereas the divided beauty of separate woman and man—a thing inferior and imperfect—can serve all turns of life. Ideal beauty, like ideal genius, dwells apart, as though by compulsion; supremacy is solitude. But leaving this symbolic side of the matter, I cannot see why this statue should not be the text for yet another poem. Treated in the grave and chaste manner as a serious 'thing of beauty,' to be for ever applauded and enjoyed, it can give no offence but to the purblind and the prurient. For neither of these classes have I ever written or will I ever write. 'Loathsome and abominable' and full of 'unspeakable foulnesses' must be that man's mind who could here discern evil; unclean and inhuman the animal which could suck from this mystical rose of ancient loveliness the foul and rancid juices of an obscene fancy. It were a scavenger's office to descend with torch or spade into such depths of mental sewerage, to plunge or peer into subterranean sloughs of mind impossible alike to enlighten or to cleanse.

I have now gone over the poems which, as I hear, have incurred most blame; whether deservedly or not, I have shown. For the terms in which certain critics have clothed their sentiments I bear them no ill-will: they are welcome for me to write unmolested, as long as they keep to simple ribaldry. I hope it gives them amusement; I presume it brings them profit; I know it does not affect me. Absolute falsehood may, if it be worth while, draw down contradiction and disproof; but the mere calling of bad names is a child's trick, for which the small fry of the press should have a child's correction at the hands of able editors; standing as these gentlemen ought to do in a parental or pedagogic relation to their tender charges. They have, by all I see and hear, been sufficiently scurrilous—one or two in particular:

> However, from one crime they are exempt;
> They do not strike a brother, striking *me*.

I will only throw them one crumb of advice in return: I fear the alms will be of no avail, but it shall not be withheld:

> Why grudge them lotus-leaf and laurel,
> O toothless mouth or swinish maw,
> Who never grudged you bells and coral,
> Who never grudged you troughs and straw?

Lie still in kennel, sleek in stable,
Good creatures of the stall or sty;
Shove snouts for crumbs below the table;
Lie still; and rise not up to lie.

To all this, however, there is a grave side. The question at issue is wider than any between a single writer and his critics, or it might well be allowed to drop. It is this: whether or not the first and last requisite of art is to give no offence; whether or not all that cannot be lisped in the nursery or fingered in the schoolroom is therefore to be cast out of the library; whether or not the domestic circle is to be for all men and writers the outer limit and extreme horizon of their world of work. For to this we have come; and all students of art must face the matter as it stands. Who has not heard it asked, in a final and triumphant tone, whether this book or that can be read aloud by her mother to a young girl? whether such and such a picture can properly be exposed to the eyes of young persons? If you reply that this is nothing to the point, you fall at once into the ranks of the immoral. Never till now, and nowhere but in England, could so monstrous an absurdity rear for one moment its deformed and eyeless head. In no past century were artists ever bidden to work on these terms; nor are they now, except among us. The disease, of course, afflicts the meanest members of the body with most virulence. Nowhere is cant at once so foul-mouthed and so tight-laced as in the penny, twopenny, threepenny, or sixpenny press. Nothing is so favourable to the undergrowth of real indecency as this overshadowing foliage of fictions, this artificial network of proprieties. *L'Arioste rit au soleil, l'Arétin ricane à l'ombre.* The whiter the sepulchre without, the ranker the rottenness within. Every touch of plaster is a sign of advancing decay. The virtue of our critical journals is a dowager of somewhat dubious antecedents: every day that thins and shrivels her cheek thickens and hardens the paint on it; she consumes more chalk and ceruse than would serve a whole courtful of crones. 'It is to be presumed,' certainly, that in her case 'all is not sweet, all is not sound.' The taint on her fly-blown reputation is hard to overcome by patches and perfumery. Literature, to be worthy of men, must be large, liberal, sincere; and cannot be chaste if it be prudish. Purity and prudery cannot keep house together.

Where free speech and fair play are interdicted, foul hints and evil suggestions are hatched into fetid life. And if literature indeed is not to deal with the full life of man and the whole nature of things, let it be cast aside with the rods and rattles of childhood. Whether it affect to teach or to amuse, it is equally trivial and contemptible to us; only less so than the charge of immorality. Against how few really great names has not this small and dirt-encrusted pebble been thrown! A reputation seems imperfect without this tribute also: one jewel is wanting to the crown. It is good to be praised by those whom all men should praise; it is better to be reviled by those whom all men should scorn.

Various chances and causes must have combined to produce a state of faith or feeling which would turn all art and literature 'into the line of children.' One among others may be this: where the heaven of invention holds many stars at once, there is no fear that the highest and largest will either efface or draw aside into its orbit all lesser lights. Each of these takes its own way and sheds its proper lustre. But where one alone is dominant in heaven, it is encircled by a pale procession of satellite moons, filled with shallow and stolen radiance. Thus, with English versifiers now, the idyllic form is alone in fashion. The one great and prosperous poet [2] of the time has given out the tune, and the hoarser choir takes it up. His highest lyrical work remains unimitated, being in the main inimitable. But the trick of tone which suits an idyl is easier to assume; and the note has been struck so often that the shrillest songsters can affect to catch it up. We have idyls good and bad, ugly and pretty; idyls of the farm and the mill; idyls of the dining-room and the deanery; idyls of the gutter and the gibbet. If the Muse of the minute will not feast with 'gig-men' and their wives, she must mourn with costermongers and their trulls. I fear the more ancient Muses are guests at neither house of mourning nor house of feasting.

For myself, I begrudge no man his taste or his success; I can enjoy and applaud all good work, and would always, when possible, have the workman paid in full. There is much excellent and some admirable verse among the poems of the day: to none has it given more pleasure than to me, and from none, had I been a man of letters to whom the ways were open, would it have won heartier applause. I have never been able to see what should at-

[2] Tennyson.

tract men to the profession of criticism but the noble pleasure of praising. But I have no right to claim a place in the silver flock of idyllic swans. I have never worked for praise or pay, but simply by impulse, and to please myself; I must therefore, it is to be feared, remain where I am, shut out from the communion of these. At all events, I shall not be hounded into emulation of other men's work by the baying of unleashed beagles. There are those with whom I do not wish to share the praise of their praisers. I am content to abide a far different judgment:

> I write as others wrote
> On Sunium's height.

I need not be over-careful to justify my ways in other men's eyes; it is enough for me that they also work after their kind, and earn the suffrage, as they labour after the law, of their own people. The idyllic form is best for domestic and pastoral poetry. It is naturally on a lower level than that of tragic or lyric verse. Its gentle and maidenly lips are somewhat narrow for the stream and somewhat cold for the fire of song. It is very fit for the sole diet of girls; not very fit for the sole sustenance of men.

When England has again such a school of poetry, so headed and so followed, as she has had at least twice before, or as France has now; when all higher forms of the various arts are included within the larger limits of a stronger race; then, if such a day should ever rise or return upon us, it will be once more remembered that the office of adult art is neither puerile nor feminine, but virile; that its purity is not that of the cloister or the harem; that all things are good in its sight, out of which good work may be produced. Then the press will be as impotent as the pulpit to dictate the laws and remove the landmarks of art; and those will be laughed at who demand from one thing the qualities of another—who seek for sermons in sonnets and morality in music. Then all accepted work will be noble and chaste in the wider masculine sense, not truncated and curtailed, but outspoken and full-grown; art will be pure by instinct and fruitful by nature, no clipped and forced growth of unhealthy heat and unnatural air; all baseness and all triviality will fall off from it, and be forgotten; and no one will then need to assert, in defence of work done for the work's sake, the simple laws of his art which no one will then be permitted to impugn.

Matthew Arnold

"BARBARIANS, PHILISTINES, POPULACE"

In Chapters I and II of *Culture and Anarchy* Arnold focused primarily on the middle class, and its insensitivity to the sweetness and light of true culture. In Chapter III he scrutinizes the aristocratic or "Barbarian" class and finds it almost equally wanting; though they possess sweetness to a degree, its members are hardly champions of culture and provide scant support for the serious, progressive artist. Arnold's sympathies are clearly with a fourth group, lovers of perfection, "aliens" from the three major classes, who follow a "general *humane* spirit" rather than the dictates of either Philistines, Barbarians, or Populace. To this enlightened band, of course, Arnold himself belonged.

From a man without a philosophy no one can expect philosophical completeness. Therefore I may observe without shame, that in trying to get a distinct notion of our aristocratic, our middle, and our working class, with a view of testing the claims of each of these classes to become a centre of authority, I have omitted, I find, to complete the old-fashioned analysis which I had the fancy of applying, and have not shown in these classes, as well as the virtuous mean and the excess, the defect also. I do not know that the omission very much matters. Still, as clearness is the merit which a plain, unsystematic writer, without a philosophy, can hope to have, and as our notion of the three great English classes may perhaps be made clearer if we see their distinctive qualities in the defect, as well as in the excess and in the mean, let us try, before proceeding further, to remedy this omission.

It is manifest, if the perfect and virtuous mean of that fine spirit which is the distinctive quality of aristocracies, is to be found in a high, chivalrous style, and its excess in a fierce turn for resistance, that its defect must lie in a spirit not bold and high enough, and

From *Culture and Anarchy*, Chapter III (1869).

in an excessive and pusillanimous unaptness for resistance. If, again, the perfect and virtuous mean of that force by which our middle class has done its great works, and of that self-reliance with which it contemplates itself and them, is to be seen in the performances and speeches of our commercial member of Parliament, and the excess of that force and of that self-reliance in the performances and speeches of our fanatical Dissenting minister, then it is manifest that their defect must lie in a helpless inaptitude for the great works of the middle class, and in a poor and despicable lack of its self-satisfaction.

To be chosen to exemplify the happy mean of a good quality, or set of good qualities, is evidently a praise to a man; nay, to be chosen to exemplify even their excess, is a kind of praise. Therefore I could have no hesitation in taking actual personages to exemplify, respectively, the mean and the excess of aristocratic and middle-class qualities. But perhaps there might be a want of urbanity in singling out this or that personage as the representative of defect. Therefore I shall leave the defect of aristocracy unillustrated by any representative man. But with oneself one may always, without impropriety, deal quite freely; and, indeed, this sort of plain-dealing with oneself has in it, as all the moralists tell us, something very wholesome. So I will venture to humbly offer myself as an illustration of defect in those forces and qualities which make our middle class what it is. The too well-founded reproaches of my opponents declare how little I have lent a hand to the great works of the middle class; for it is evidently these works, and my slackness at them, which are meant, when I am said to "refuse to lend a hand to the humble operation of uprooting certain definite evils" (such as church-rates and others), and that therefore "the believers in action grow impatient" with me. The line, again, of a still unsatisfied seeker which I have followed, the idea of self-transformation, of growing towards some measure of sweetness and light not yet reached, is evidently at clean variance with the perfect self-satisfaction current in my class, the middle class, and may serve to indicate in me, therefore, the extreme defect of this feeling. But these confessions, though salutary, are bitter and unpleasant.

To pass, then, to the working class. The defect of this class would be the falling short in what Mr. Frederic Harrison calls those "bright powers of sympathy and ready powers of action," of which we saw in Mr. Odger the virtuous mean, and in Mr. Bradlaugh the excess. The working class is so fast growing and rising at the present time, that instances of this defect cannot well be now very common. Perhaps Canning's "Needy Knife-Grinder" (who is dead, and therefore cannot be pained at my taking him for an illustration) may serve to give us the notion of defect in the essential quality of a working class; or I might even cite (since, though he is alive in the flesh, he is dead to all heed of criticism) my poor old poaching friend, Zephaniah Diggs, who, between his hare-snaring and his gin-drinking, has got his powers of sympathy quite dulled and his powers of action in any great movement of his class hopelessly impaired. But examples of this defect belong, as I have said, to a bygone age rather than to the present.

The same desire for clearness, which has led me thus to extend a little my first analysis of the three great classes of English society, prompts me also to improve my nomenclature for them a little, with a view to making it thereby more manageable. It is awkward and tiresome to be always saying the aristocratic class, the middle class, the working class. For the middle class, for that great body which, as we know, "has done all the great things that have been done in all departments," and which is to be conceived as moving between its two cardinal points of our commercial member of Parliament and our fanatical Protestant Dissenter,—for this class we have a designation which now has become pretty well known, and which we may as well still keep for them, the designation of Philistines. What this term means I have so often explained that I need not repeat it here. For the aristocratic class, conceived mainly as a body moving between the two cardinal points of our chivalrous lord and our defiant baronet, we have as yet got no special designation. Almost all my attention has naturally been concentrated on my own class, the middle class, with which I am in closest sympathy, and which has been, besides, the great power of our day, and has had its praises sung by all speakers and newspapers.

Still the aristocratic class is so important in itself, and the weighty functions which Mr. Carlyle proposes at the present critical time to commit to it, must add so much to its importance, that it seems neglectful, and a strong instance of that want of coherent philosophic method for which Mr. Frederic Harrison blames me, to leave the aristocratic class so much without notice and denomination. It may be thought that the characteristic which I have occasionally mentioned as proper to aristocracies,—their natural inaccessibility, as children of the established fact, to ideas, —points to our extending to this class also the designation of Philistines; the Philistine being, as it is well known, the enemy of the children of light or servants of the idea. Nevertheless, there seems to be an inconvenience in this giving one and the same designation to two very different classes; and besides, if we look into the thing closely, we shall find that the term Philistine conveys a sense which makes it more peculiarly appropriate to our middle class than to our aristocratic. For *Philistine* gives the notion of something particularly stiff-necked and perverse in the resistance to light and its children; and therein it specially suits our middle class, who not only do not pursue sweetness and light, but who even prefer to them that sort of machinery of business, chapels, tea-meetings, and addresses from Mr. Murphy, which makes up the dismal and illiberal life on which I have so often touched. But the aristocratic class has actually, as we have seen, in its well-known politeness, a kind of image or shadow of sweetness; and as for light, if it does not pursue light, it is not that it perversely cherishes some dismal and illiberal existence in preference to light, but it is lured off from following light by those mighty and eternal seducers of our race which weave for this class their most irresistible charms,—by worldly splendour, security, power, and pleasure. These seducers are exterior goods, but in a way they are goods; and he who is hindered by them from caring for light and ideas, is not so much doing what is perverse as what is too natural.

Keeping this in view, I have in my own mind often indulged myself with the fancy of employing, in order to designate our aristocratic class, the name of *The Barbarians*. The Barbarians, to whom we all owe so much, and who reinvigorated and renewed our worn-out Europe, had, as is well-known, eminent merits; and in this country, where we are for the most part sprung from the Barbarians, we have never had the prejudice against them which prevails among the races of Latin origin. The Barbarians brought with them that staunch individualism, as the modern phrase is, and that passion for doing as one likes, for the assertion of personal liberty, which appears to Mr. Bright the central idea of English life, and of which we have, at any rate, a very rich supply. The stronghold and natural seat of this passion was in the nobles of whom our aristocratic class are inheritors; and this class, accordingly, have signally manifested it, and have done much by their example to recommend it to the body of the nation, who already, indeed, had it in their blood. The Barbarians, again, had the passion for field-sports; and they have handed it on to our aristocratic class, who of this passion too, as of the passion for asserting one's personal liberty, are the great natural stronghold. The care of the Barbarians for the body, and for all manly exercises; the vigour, good looks, and fine complexion which they acquired and perpetuated in their families by these means,—all this may be observed still in our aristocratic class. The chivalry of the Barbarians, with its characteristics of high spirit, choice manners, and distinguished bearing,—what is this but the attractive commencement of the politeness of our aristocratic class? In some Barbarian noble, no doubt, one would have admired, if one could have been then alive to see it, the rudiments of our politest peer. Only, all this culture (to call it by that name) of the Barbarians was an exterior culture mainly. It consisted principally in outward gifts and graces, in looks, manners, accomplishments, prowess. The chief inward gifts which had part in it were the most exterior, so to speak, of inward gifts, those which come nearest to outward ones; they were courage, a high spirit, self-confidence. Far within, and unawakened, lay a whole range of powers of thought and feeling, to which these interesting productions of nature had, from the circumstances of their life, no access. Making allowances for the difference of the times, surely we can observe precisely the same thing now in our aristocratic class. In general its culture is exterior chiefly; all the exterior graces and accomplishments, and the more external of the inward virtues, seem to be principally its portion. It now, of course, cannot but be often in contact with those studies by which, from the world of thought and feeling, true culture teaches us to fetch sweetness and light; but its hold upon these very studies appears remarkably external and unable to exert any deep power upon its spirit. Therefore the one insufficiency which we noted in the perfect mean of this class was an insufficiency of light. And owing to the same causes, does not a subtle criticism lead us to make, even on the good looks and politeness of our aristocratic class, and of even the most fascinating half of that class, the feminine half, the one qualifying remark, that in these charming gifts there should perhaps be, for ideal perfection, a shade more *soul*?

I often, therefore, when I want to distinguish clearly the aristocratic class from the Philistines proper, or middle class, name the former, in my own mind, *the Barbarians*. And when I go through the country, and see this and that beautiful and imposing seat of theirs crowning the landscape, "There," I say to myself, "is a great fortified post of the Barbarians."

It is obvious that that part of the working class which, working diligently by the light of Mrs. Gooch's Golden Rule, looks forward to the happy day when it will sit on thrones with commercial members of Parliament and other middle-class potentates, to survey, as Mr. Bright beautifully says, "the cities it has built, the railroads it has made, the manufactures it has produced, the cargoes which freight the ships of the greatest mercantile navy the world has ever seen,"—it is obvious, I say, that this part of the working class is, or is in a fair way to be, one in spirit with the industrial middle class. It is notorious that our middle-class Liberals have long looked forward to this consummation, when the working class shall join forces with them, aid them heartily to carry forward their great works, go in a body to their tea-meetings, and, in short, enable them to bring about their millennium. That part of the working class, therefore, which does really seem to lend itself to these great aims, may, with propriety, be numbered by us among the Philistines. That part of it, again, which so much occupies the attention of philanthropists at present,—the part which gives all its energies to organising itself, through trades' unions and other means, so as to constitute, first, a great working-class power independent of the middle and aristocratic classes, and then, by dint of numbers, give the law to them and itself reign absolutely,—this lively and promising part must also, according to our definition, go with the Philistines; because it is its class and its class instinct which it seeks to affirm—its ordinary self, not its best self; and it is a machinery, an industrial machinery, and power and pre-eminence and other external goods, which fill its thoughts, and not an inward perfection. It is wholly occupied, according to Plato's subtle expression, with the things of itself and not its real self, with the things of the State and not the real State. But that vast portion, lastly, of the working class which, raw and half-developed, has long lain half-hidden amidst its poverty and squalor, and is now issuing from its hiding-place to assert an Englishman's heaven-born privilege of doing as he likes, and is beginning to perplex us by marching where it likes, meeting where it likes, bawling what it likes, breaking what it likes,—to this vast residuum we may with great propriety give the name of *Populace.*

Thus we have got three distinct terms, *Barbarians, Philistines, Populace,* to denote roughly the three great classes into which our society is divided; and though this humble attempt at a scientific nomenclature falls, no doubt, very far short in precision of what might be required from a writer equipped with a complete and coherent philosophy, yet, from a notoriously unsystematic and unpretending writer, it will, I trust, be accepted as sufficient.

But in using this new, and, I hope, convenient division of English society, two things are to be borne in mind. The first is, that since, under all our class divisions, there is a common basis of human nature, therefore, in every one of us, whether we be properly Barbarians, Philistines, or Populace, there exists, sometimes only in germ and potentially, sometimes more or less developed, the same tendencies and passions which have made our fellow-citizens of other classes what they are. This consideration is very important, because it has great influence in begetting that spirit of indulgence which is a necessary part of sweetness, and which, indeed, when our culture is complete, is, as I have said, inexhaustible. Thus, an English Barbarian who examines himself will, in general, find himself to be not so entirely a Barbarian but that he has in him, also, something of the Philistine, and even something of the Populace as well. And the same with Englishmen of the two other classes.

This is an experience which we may all verify every day. For instance, I myself (I again take myself as a sort of *corpus vile* to serve for illustration in a matter where serving for illustration may not by every one be thought agreeable), I myself am properly a Philistine,—Mr. Swinburne would add, the son of a Philistine. And although, through circumstances which will perhaps one day be known if ever the affecting history of my conversion comes to be written, I have, for the most part, broken with the ideas and the tea-meetings of my own class, yet I have not, on that account, been brought much the nearer to the ideas and works of the Barbarians or of the Populace. Nevertheless, I never take a gun or a fishing-rod in my hands without feeling that I have in the ground of my nature the self-same seeds which, fostered by circumstances, do so much to make the Barbarian; and that, with the Barbarian's advantages, I might have rivalled him. Place me in one of his great fortified posts, with these seeds of a love for field-sports sown in my nature, with all the means of developing them, with all pleasures at my command, with most whom I met deferring to me, every one I met smiling on me, and with every appearance of permanence and security before me and behind me,—then I too might have grown, I feel, into a very passable child of the established fact, of commendable spirit and politeness, and, at the same time, a little inaccessible to ideas and light; not, of course, with either the eminent fine spirit of our type of aristocratic perfection, or the eminent turn for resistance of our type of aristocratic excess, but, according to the measure of the common run of mankind, something between the two. And as to the Populace, who, whether he be Barbarian or Philistine, can look at them without sympathy, when he remembers how often,—every time that we snatch up a vehement opinion in ignorance and passion, every time that we long to crush an adversary by sheer violence, every time that we are envious, every time that we are brutal, every time that we adore mere power or success, every time that we add our voice to swell a blind clamour against some unpopular personage, every time that we trample savagely on the fallen,—he has found in his own bosom the eternal spirit of the Populace, and that there needs only a little help from circumstances to make it triumph in him untamably.

The second thing to be borne in mind I have indicated several times already. It is this. All of us, so far as we are Barbarians, Philistines, or Populace, imagine happiness to consist in doing what one's ordinary self likes. What one's ordinary self likes differs according to the class to which one belongs, and has its severer and its lighter side; always, however, remaining machinery, and nothing more. The graver self of the Barbarian likes honours and consideration; his more relaxed self, field-sports and pleasure.

The graver self of one kind of Philistine likes fanaticism, business, and money-making; his more relaxed self, comfort and tea-meetings. Of another kind of Philistine, the graver self likes rattening; the relaxed self, deputations, or hearing Mr. Odger speak. The sterner self of the Populace likes bawling, hustling, and smashing; the lighter self, beer. But in each class there are born a certain number of natures with a curiosity about their best self, with a bent for seeing things as they are, for disentangling themselves from machinery, for simply concerning themselves with reason and the will of God, and doing their best to make these prevail;—for the pursuit, in a word, of perfection. To certain manifestations of this love for perfection mankind have accustomed themselves to give the name of genius; implying, by this name, something original and heaven-bestowed in the passion. But the passion is to be found far beyond those manifestations of it to which the world usually gives the name of genius, and in which there is, for the most part, a *talent* of some kind or other, a special and striking faculty of execution, informed by the heaven-bestowed ardour, or genius. It is to be found in many manifestations besides these, and may best be called, as we have called it, the love and pursuit of perfection; culture being the true nurse of the pursuing love, and sweetness and light the true character of the pursued perfection. Natures with this bent emerge in all classes,—among the Barbarians, among the Philistines, among the Populace. And this bent always tends to take them out of their class, and to make their distinguishing characteristic not their Barbarianism or their Philistinism, but their *humanity*. They have, in general, a rough time of it in their lives; but they are sown more abundantly than one might think, they appear where and when one least expects it, they set up a fire which enfilades, so to speak, the class with which they are ranked; and, in general, by the extrication of their best self as the self to develop, and by the simplicity of the ends fixed by them as paramount, they hinder the unchecked predominance of that class-life which is the affirmation of our ordinary self, and seasonably disconcert mankind in their worship of machinery.

Therefore, when we speak of ourselves as divided into Barbarians, Philistines, and Populace, we must be understood always to imply that within each of these classes there are a certain number of *aliens,* if we may so call them,—persons who are mainly led, not by their class spirit, but by a general *humane* spirit, by the love of human perfection; and that this number is capable of being diminished or augmented. I mean, the number of those who will succeed in developing this happy instinct will be greater or smaller, in proportion both to the force of the original instinct within them, and to the hindrance or encouragement which it meets with from without. In almost all who have it, it is mixed with some infusion of the spirit of an ordinary self, some quantity of class-instinct, and even, as has been shown, of more than one class-instinct at the same time; so that, in general, the extrication of the best self, the predominance of the *humane* instinct, will very much depend upon its meeting, or not, with what is fitted to help and elicit it. At a moment, therefore, when it is agreed that we want a source of authority, and when it seems probable that the right source is our best self, it becomes of vast importance to see whether or not the things around us are, in general, such as to help and elicit our best self, and if they are not, to see why they are not, and the most promising way of mending them.

Now, it is clear that the very absence of any powerful authority amongst us, and the prevalent doctrine of the duty and happiness of doing as one likes, and asserting our personal liberty, must tend to prevent the erection of any very strict standard of excellence, the belief in any very paramount authority of right reason, the recognition of our best self as anything very recondite and hard to come at. It may be, as I have said, a proof of our honesty that we do not attempt to give to our ordinary self, as we have it in action, predominant authority, and to impose its rule upon other people. But it is evident also, that it is not easy, with our style of proceeding, to get beyond the notion of an ordinary self at all, or to get the paramount authority of a commanding best self, or right reason, recognised. The learned Martinus Scriblerus well says:—"the taste of the bathos is implanted by nature itself in the soul of man; till, perverted by custom or example, he is taught, or rather compelled, to relish the sublime." But with us everything seems directed to prevent any such perversion of us by custom or example as might compel us to relish the sublime; by all means we are encouraged to keep our natural taste for the bathos unimpaired.

Robert Buchanan

"THE FLESHLY SCHOOL OF POETRY"

BUCHANAN'S "The Fleshly School" is one of the most notorious attacks ever leveled by one poet against another. Critics have generally agreed that its virulence was irresponsible and exhibitionistic, and it had the unfortunate effect of deepening Rossetti's paranoia. Both Rossetti and Swinburne were attacked by Buchanan, who signed himself "Thomas Maitland" for the first version of this review. Swinburne's response, "Under the Microscope," and not Rossetti's cautious "The Stealthy School of Criticism," contained the pugnacity and force to counter Buchanan's neuroticism; Rossetti was too afraid of a lawsuit. Later Buchanan sycophantically renounced his attack, dedicating his romance *God and Man* (1881) to the "blameless," "pure," "sweet" poet he had wronged; and in the *Academy* (July 1, 1882) he "freely" admitted that Rossetti "never was a Fleshly Poet at all." The damage to Rossetti had of course been done. The captions, "Rossetti" and "Swinburne," are supplied for emphasis; both sections appear in the same essay.

ROSSETTI

HERE IS a full-grown man, presumably intelligent and cultivated, putting on record for other full-grown men to read, the most secret mysteries of sexual connection, and that with so sickening a desire to reproduce the sensual mood, so careful a choice of epithet to convey mere animal sensations, that we merely shudder at the shameless nakedness.[1] We are no purists in such matters. We hold the sensual part of our nature to be as holy as the spiritual or intellectual part, and we believe that such things must find their equivalent in all; but it is neither poetic, nor manly, nor even hu-

FROM *The Fleshly School of Poetry and Other Phenomena of the Day* (1872). First appeared in *The Contemporary Review* (October, 1871).

[1] Buchanan refers to Rossetti's "Nuptial Sleep" which he has just quoted.

man to obtrude such things as the themes of whole poems. It is simply nasty. Nasty as it is, we are very mistaken if many readers do not think it nice. English society of one kind purchases the *Day's Doings.* English society of another kind goes into ecstasy over Mr. Solomon's pictures—pretty pieces of morality, such as "Love dying by the breath of Lust." There is not much to choose between the two objects of admiration, except that painters like Mr. Solomon lend actual genius to worthless subjects, and thereby produce veritable monsters—like the lovely devils that danced round Saint Anthony. Mr. Rossetti owes his so-called success to the same causes. In poems like "Nuptial Sleep," the man who is too sensitive to exhibit his pictures, and so modest that it takes him years to make up his mind to publish his poems, parades his private sensations before a coarse public, and is gratified by their applause.

It must not be supposed that all Mr. Rossetti's poems are made up of trash like this. Some of them are as noteworthy for delicacy of touch as others are for shamelessness of exposition. They contain some exquisite pictures of nature, occasional passages of real meaning, much beautiful phraseology, lines of peculiar sweetness, and epithets chosen with true literary cunning. But the fleshly feeling is everywhere. Sometimes, as in "The Stream's Secret," it is deliciously modulated, and adds greatly to our emotion of pleasure at perusing a finely-wrought poem; at other times, as in the "Last Confession," it is fiercely held in check by the exigencies of a powerful situation and the strength of a dramatic speaker; but it is generally in the foreground, flushing the whole poem with unhealthy rose-colour, stifling the senses with overpowering sickliness, as of too much civet. Mr. Rossetti is never dramatic, never impersonal—always attitudinizing, posturing, and describing his own exquisite emotions. He is the Blessed Damozel, leaning over the "gold bar of heaven," and seeing

> Time like a pulse shake fierce
> Thro' all the worlds,

he is "heaven-born Helen, Sparta's queen," whose "each twin breast is an apple sweet;" he is Lilith the first wife of Adam; he is the rosy Virgin of the poem called "Ave," and the Queen in the "Staff and Scrip;" he is "Sister Helen" melting her waxen man; he is all these, just as surely as he is Mr. Rossetti soliloquizing over

Jenny in her London lodging, or the very nuptial person writing erotic sonnets to his wife. In petticoats or pantaloons, in modern times or in the middle ages, he is just Mr. Rossetti, a fleshly person, with nothing particular to tell us or teach us, with extreme self-control, a strong sense of colour, and a careful choice of diction. Amid all his "affluence of jewel-coloured words," he has not given us one rounded and noteworthy piece of art, though his verses are all art; not one poem which is memorable for its own sake, and quite separable from the displeasing identity of the composer. The nearest approach to a perfect whole is the "Blessed Damozel," a peculiar poem, placed first in the book, perhaps by accident, perhaps because it is a key to the poems which follow. This poem appeared in a rough shape many years ago in the *Germ*, an unwholesome periodical started by the Pre-Raphaelites, and suffered, after gasping through a few feeble numbers, to die the death of all such publications. In spite of its affected title, and of numberless affectations throughout the text, the "Blessed Damozel" has great merits of its own, and a few lines of real genius. We have heard it described as the record of actual grief and love, or, in simple words, the apotheosis of one actually lost by the writer; but, without having any private knowledge of the circumstance of its composition, we feel that such an account of the poem is inadmissible. It does not contain one single note of sorrow. It is a "composition," and a clever one. Read the opening stanzas:—

The blessed damozel leaned out
  From the gold bar of Heaven;
Her eyes were deeper than the depth
  Of water stilled at even;
She had three lilies in her hand,
  And the stars in her hair were seven.

Her robe, ungirt from clasp to hem,
  No wrought flowers did adorn,
But a white rose of Mary's gift,
  For service meetly worn;
Her hair that lay along her back
  Was yellow like ripe corn.

This is a careful sketch for a picture, which, worked into actual colour by a master, might have been worth seeing. The steadiness of hand lessens as the poem proceeds, and although there are several passages of considerable power,—such as that where, far down the void,

this earth
Spins like a fretful midge

or that other, describing how

the curled moon
Was like a little feather
Fluttering far down the gulf—

the general effect is that of a queer old painting in a missal, very affected and very odd. What moved the British critic to ecstasy in this poem seems to us very sad nonsense indeed, or, if not sad nonsense, very meretricious affectation. Thus, we have seen the following verses quoted with enthusiasm, as italicized—

And still she bowed herself and stooped
Out of the circling charm;
Until her bosom must have made
The bar she leaned on warm,
And the lilies lay as if asleep
Along her bended arm.

From the fixed place of Heaven she saw
Time like a pulse shake fierce
Thro' all the worlds. Her gaze still strove
Within the gulf to pierce
Its path; and now she spoke as when
The stars sang in their spheres.

It seems to us that all these lines are very bad, with the exception of the two admirable lines ending the first verse, and that the italicized portions are quite without merit, and almost without meaning. On the whole, one feels disheartened and amazed at the poet who, in the nineteenth century, talks about "damozels," "citherns," and "citoles," and addresses the mother of Christ as the "Lady Mary,"—

With her five handmaidens, whose names
Are five sweet symphonies,
Cecily, Gertrude, Magdalen,
Margaret and Rosalys.

A suspicion is awakened that the writer is laughing at us. We hover uncertainly between picturesqueness and namby-pamby, and the effect, as Artemus Ward would express it, is "weakening to the intellect." The thing would have been almost too much in the shape of a picture, though the workmanship might have made amends. The truth is that literature, and more particularly poetry, is in a very bad way when one art gets hold of another, and imposes upon it its conditions and limitations. In the first few verses of the "Damozel" we have the subject, or part of the subject, of a picture, and the inventor should either have painted it or left it alone altogether; and, had he done the latter, the world would have lost nothing. Poetry is something more than painting; and an idea will not become a poem, because it is too smudgy for a picture.

In a short notice from a well-known pen, giving the best estimate we have seen of Mr. Rossetti's powers as a poet, the *North American Review* offers a certain explanation for affectation such as that of Mr. Rossetti. The writer suggests that "it may probably be the expression of genuine moods of mind in natures too little comprehensive." We would rather believe that Mr. Rossetti lacks comprehension than that he is deficient in sincerity; yet really, to paraphrase the words which Johnson applied to Thomas Sheridan, Mr. Rossetti is affected, naturally affected, but it must have taken him a great deal of trouble to become what we now see him —such an excess of affectation is not in nature. There is very little writing in the volume spontaneous in the sense that some of Swinburne's verses are spontaneous; the poems all look as if they had taken a great deal of trouble. The grotesque mediaevalism of "Stratton Water" and "Sister Helen," the mediaeval classicism of "Troy Town," the false and shallow mysticism of "Eden Bower," are one and all essentially imitative, and must have caused the writer much pains. It is time, indeed, to point out that Mr. Rossetti is a poet possessing great powers of assimilation and some faculty for concealing the nutriment on which he feeds. Setting aside the "Vita Nuova" and the early Italian poems, which are familiar to many readers by his own excellent translations, Mr. Rossetti may be described as a writer who has yielded, to an unusual extent, to the complex influences of the literature surrounding him at the present moment. He has the painter's imitative power developed in proportion to his lack of the poet's conceiving imagination. He reproduces to a nicety the manner of an old ballad, a trick in which Mr. Swinburne is also an adept. Cultivated readers, moreover, will recognize in every one of these poems the tone of Mr. Tennyson broken up by the style of Mr. and Mrs. Browning, and disguised here and there by the eccentricities of the Pre-Raphaelites. The "Burden of Nineveh" is a philosophical edition of "Recollections of the Arabian Nights;" "A Last Confession" and "Dante at Verona" are, in the minutest trick and form of thought, suggestive of Mr. Browning; and that the sonnets have been largely moulded and inspired by Mrs. Browning, especially in points of phraseology, can be ascertained by any critic who will compare them with the "Sonnets from the Portuguese." Much remains, nevertheless, that is Mr. Rossetti's own. I at once recognise as his own property such passages as this:—

> I looked up
> And saw where a brown-shouldered harlot leaned
> Half through a tavern window thick with vine.
> Some man had come behind her in the room
> And caught her by the arms, and she had turned
> With that coarse empty laugh on him, as now
> He *munched her neck with kisses, while the vine*
> *Crawled in her back.*

Or this:—

> As I stooped, her own lips rising there
> *Bubbled with brimming kisses* at my mouth.

Or this:—

> Have seen your lifted silken skirt
> Advertise dainties through the dirt!

Or this:—

> What more prize than love to impel thee,
> *Grip* and *lip* my limbs as I tell thee!*

* Mr. Rossetti accuses me of garbling these four extracts, and alleges that they have a totally different effect when read with their context. In reply to this, let me observe that the four poems which supply these four extracts are full of coarseness from the first line to the last, and that no extract can fitly convey their unwholesomeness and indecency.

Passages like these are the common stock of the walking gentlemen of the Fleshly School. I cannot forbear expressing my wonder, by the way, at the kind of women whom it seems the unhappy lot of these gentlemen to encounter. I have lived nearly as long in the world as they have, but never yet came across persons of the other sex who conduct themselves in the manner described. Females who bite, scratch, scream, bubble, munch, sweat, writhe, twist, wriggle, foam, and in a general way slaver over their lovers, must surely possess some extraordinary qualities to counteract their otherwise most offensive mode of conducting themselves. It appears, however, on examination, that their poet-lovers conduct themselves in a similar manner. They, too, bite, scratch, scream, bubble, munch, sweat, writhe, twist, wriggle, foam, and slaver, in a style frightful to hear of. At times, in reading such books as this, one cannot help wishing that things had remained for ever in the asexual state described in Mr. Darwin's great chapter on Palingenesis. We get very weary of this protracted hankering after a person of the other sex; it seems meat, drink, thought, sinew, religion, for the Fleshly School. There is no limit to the fleshliness, and Mr. Rossetti finds in it its own religious justification much in the same way as Holy Willie:—

> Maybe thou let'st this fleshly thorn
> Perplex thy servant night and morn,
>   'Cause he's so gifted.
> If so, thy hand must e'en be borne,
>   Until thou lift it.

Whether he is writing of the holy Damozel, or of the Virgin herself, or of Lilith, or of Helen, or of Dante, or of Jenny the street-walker, he is fleshly all over, from the roots of his hair to the tip of his toes; never a true lover merging his identity into that of the beloved one; never spiritual, never tender; always self-conscious and æsthetic. "Nothing in human life," says a modern writer, "is so utterly remorseless—not love, not hate, not ambition, not vanity—as the artistic or æsthetic instinct morbidly developed to the supression of conscience and feeling;" and at no time do we feel more fully impressed with this truth than after the perusal of "Jenny," in some respects the cleverest poem in the volume, and in all respects the poem best indicative of the true quality of the writer's humanity. It is a production which bears signs of having been suggested by my own quasi-lyrical poems, which it copies in the style of title, and particularly by "Artist and Model;" but certainly Mr. Rossetti cannot be accused, as I have been accused, of maudlin sentiment and affected tenderness. The first two lines are perfect:—

> Lazy laughing languid Jenny,
> Fond of a kiss and fond of a guinea;

and the poem is a soliloquy of the poet—who has been spending the evening in dancing at a casino—over his partner, whom he has accompanied home to the usual style of lodgings occupied by such ladies, and who has fallen asleep with her head upon his knee, while he wonders, in a wretched pun—

> Whose person or whose purse may be
> The lodestar of your reverie?

The soliloquy is long, and in some parts beautiful, despite a very constant suspicion that we are listening to an emasculated Mr. Browning, whose whole tone and gesture, so to speak, is occasionally introduced with startling fidelity; and there are here and there glimpses of actual thought and insight, over and above the picturesque touches which belong to the writer's true profession, such as that where, at daybreak—

> lights creep in
> Past the gauze curtains half drawn-to,
> And *the lamp's doubled shade grows blue.*

What I object to in this poem is not the subject, which any writer may be fairly left to choose for himself; nor anything particularly vicious in the poetic treatment of it; nor any bad blood bursting through in special passages. But the whole tone, without being more than usually coarse, seems heartless. There is not a drop of piteousness in Mr. Rossetti. He is just to the outcast, even generous; severe to the seducer; sad even at the spectacle of lust in dimity and fine ribbons. Notwithstanding all this, and a certain delicacy and refinement of treatment unusual with this poet, the poem is repelling, and one likes Mr. Rossetti least after its perusal. The "Blessed Damozel" is puzzling, the "Song of the Bower" is amusing, the love-sonnet is depressing and sickening, but "Jenny," though distinguished by less special viciousness of thought and style than any of these, fairly makes the reader lose patience: Its fleshliness is apparent at a glance; one perceives that the scene was fascinating less through its human tenderness than because it, like all the others, possessed an *inherent* quality of Animalism. "The whole work," ("Jenny,") writes Mr. Swinburne, "is worthy to fill its place for ever as one of the most perfect poems of an age or generation. There is just the same life-blood and breadth of poetic interest in this episode of a London street and lodging as in the song of "Troy Town' and the song of 'Eden Bower;' just as much, and no jot more,"—to which last statement I cordially assent; for there is bad blood in all, and breadth of poetic interest in none. "Vengeance of Jenny's case," indeed!—when such a poet as this comes fawning over her; with tender compassion in one eye and æsthetic enjoyment in the other!

SWINBURNE

ALL THAT IS WORST in Mr. Swinburne belongs to Baudelaire. The offensive choice of subject, the obtrusion of unnatural passion, the blasphemy, the wretched animalism, are all taken intact out of the *Fleurs de Mal.* Pitiful! that any sane man, least of all any English poet, should think this dunghill worthy of importation! In the center of his collection Baudelaire placed the most horrid poem ever written by man, a poem unmatched for simple hideousness even in Rome during the decadence—a piece worthy to be spoken by Ascyltos in Petronius Arbiter—and entitled "Femmes Damnées." The interlocutors in this piece are two women, who have just been guilty of the vilest act conceivable in human debauchery, but the theme and the treatment are too loathsome for description. Encouraged by the hideousness of "Femmes Damnées," Mr. Swinburne attempted to beat it in "Anactoria," a poem the subject of which is again that branch of crime which is generally known as the Sapphic passion. It would be tedious, apart from the unsavouriness of the subject, to pursue the analogy much further through individual poems. Perhaps the best plan is to give a few specimens of Baudelaire's quality, and leave the reader to compare them with Mr. Swinburne's book at leisure. . . .

I close Mr. Swinburne's volumes. I try to gather some definite impression, some thought, some light, from what I have been reading. I find my mind jaded, my whole body sick and distressed, a dull pain lurking in the region of the *medulla oblongata.* I try to picture up Mr. Rossetti's poetry, and I am dazzled by conceits in sixteenth-century costume,—"rosy hours," "Loves" with "gonfalons," damsels with "citherns," "soft-complexioned" skies; flowers, fruits, jewels, vases, apple-blossoms, lutes: I see no gleam of nature, not a sign of humanity; I hear only the heated ravings of an affected lover, indecent for the most part, and often blasphemous. I attempt to describe Mr. Swinburne; and lo! the Bacchanal screams, the sterile Dolores sweats, serpents dance, men and women wrench, wriggle, and foam in an endless alliteration (quite in Gascoigne's manner) of heated and meaningless words, the veriest garbage of Baudelaire flowered over with the epithets of the Della Cruscans.

Algernon Charles Swinburne

"UNDER THE MICROSCOPE"

SWINBURNE's satiric exposure of the paramecia among the critics and hack-poets moves skillfully towards its final climatic sections, where Robert Buchanan-*Thomas Maitland* becomes the archetype of the species. Until these sections Swinburne manages to control his repugnance, though along the way he does have some impious things to say about Tennyson's treatment of Arthurian material. Implicit in the essay is the view shared later by Moore, Whistler, Wilde, and others that the genuine artist must be free from unenlightened public morality. In *St. Paul's Magazine* (August 1872) Buchanan managed a feeble reply, called "The Monkey and the Microscope."

IN THAT SINGULARLY interesting essay on "his own tentatives" from which we have already taken occasion to glean certain flowers of

Published as a pamphlet in 1872.

comparative criticism, Mr. Buchanan remarks of this contemporary that he seems rather fond of throwing stones in his (Mr. Buchanan's) direction. This contemporary however is not in the habit of throwing stones; it is a pastime which he leaves to the smaller fry of the literary gutter. These it is sometimes not unamusing to watch as they dodge and shirk round the street-corner after the discharge of their popgun pellet, with the ready plea on their lips that it was not this boy but that—not the good boy Robert, for instance, but the rude boy Thomas. But there is probably only one man living who could imagine it worth his contemporary's while to launch the smallest stone from his sling in such a direction as that—who could conceive the very idlest of marksmen to be capable of taking aim unprovoked at so pitiful a target. Mr. Buchanan and his nursing journals have informed us that to his other laurels he is entitled to add those of an accomplished sportsman. Surely he must know that there are animals which no one counts as game—which are classed under quite another head than that. Their proper designation it is needless here to repeat; it is one that suffices to exempt them from the honour and the danger common to creatures of a higher kind. Of their natural history I did not know enough till now to remark without surprise that specimens of the race may be found which are ambitious to be ranked among objects of sport. For my part, as long as I am not suspected of any inclination to join in the chase, such an one should be welcome to lay that flattering unction to his soul, and believe himself in secret one of the nobler beasts of game; even though it were but a weasel that would fain pass muster as a hart or grice. It must no doubt be "very soothing" to Mr. Buchanan's modesty to imagine himself the object of such notice as he claims to have received; but we may observe from how small a seed so large a growth of self-esteem may shoot up:

σμικρον γενοιτ ἀν σπερματος μεγας πυθμην

From a slight passing mention of 'idyls of the gutter and the gibbet,' in a passage referring to the idyllic schools of our day, Mr. Buchanan has built up this fabric of induction; he is led by even so much notice as this to infer that his work must be to the writer an object of especial attention, and even (God save the mark!) of especial attack. He is welcome to hug himself in that fond belief, and fool himself to the top of his bent; but he will hardly persuade any one else that to find his "neck-verse" merely repulsive; to feel no responsive vibration to "the intense loving tenderness" of his street-walker, as she neighs and brays over her "gallows-carrion;" is the same thing as to deny the infinite value, the incalculable significance, to a great poet, of such matters as this luckless poeticule has here taken into his "hangman's hands." Neither the work nor the workman is to be judged by the casual preferences of social convention. It is not more praiseworthy or more pardonable to write bad verse about costermongers and gaol-birds than to write bad verse about kings and knights; nor (as would otherwise naturally be the case) is it to be expected that because some among the greatest of poets have been born among the poorest of men, therefore the literature of a nation is to suffer joyfully an inundation or eruption of rubbish from all threshers, cobblers, and milkwomen who now, as in the age of Pope, of Johnson, or of Byron, may be stung to madness by the gadfly of poetic ambition. As in one rank we find for a single Byron a score of Roscommons, Mulgraves, and Winchilseas, so in another rank we find for a single Burns a score of Ducks, Bloomfields, and Yearsleys. And if it does not follow that a poet must be great if he be but of low birth, neither does it follow that a poem must be good if it be but written on a subject of low life. The sins and sorrows of all that suffer wrong, the oppressions that are done under the sun, the dark days and shining deeds of the poor whom society casts out and crushes down, are assuredly material for poetry of a most high order; for the heroic passion of Victor Hugo's, for the angelic passion of Mrs. Browning's. Let another such arise to do such work as "Les Pauvres Gens" or the "Cry of the Children," and there will be no lack of response to that singing. But they who can only "grate on their scrannel-pipes of wretched straw" some pitiful "idyl" to milk the maudlin eyes of the nursing journals, must be content with such applause as their own; for in higher latitudes they will find none.

It is not my purpose in this little scientific-excursion to remark further than may be necessary on the symptoms of a poetical sort which the skillful eye may discern in the immediate objects of examination. To play the critic of their idyllic or satirical verse is not an office to which my ambition can aspire. Nevertheless, in the process of research, it may be useful to take note of the casual secretions observable in a fine live specimen of the breed in which we are interested, as well as of its general properties; for thus we may be the better able to determine, if we find that worth while, its special and differential attributes. I have therefore given a first and last glance to the poetic excretions of the present subject. Even from such things as these there might be something to learn, if men would bring to a task so unpromising and uninviting the patient eye and humble spirit of investigation by experiment. Such investigation would secure them against the common critical fallacy of assuming that a poem must be good because written on a subject, and it may be written with an aim, not unworthy of a better man than the writer; that a bad poem, for instance, on the life of our own day and the sorrows of our own people can only be condemned by those who would equally condemn a good poem on the same subject; who would admit nothing as fit matter for artistic handling, which was not of a more remote and ideal kind than this: a theory invaluable to all worthless and ambitious journeymen of verse, who, were it once admitted as a law, would have only the trouble left them of selecting the subject whereon to emit their superfluity of metrical matter. Akin to this is a fallacy more amiable if not less absurd; the exact converse of the old superstition that anything written "by a person of quality" must be precious and praiseworthy. The same unreasoning and valueless admiration is now poured out at the feet of almost any one who comes forward under the contrary plea, as a poet of the people; and men forget that by this promiscuous effusion of praise they betray as complete a disbelief in any real equality of natural rank as did those who fell down before their idols of the other class. Such critics seem bent on verifying the worn old jest of the Irish reformer: "Is not one man as good as another; ay, and a deal better too?" No one now writes or speaks as if he supposed that every man born in what is called the aristocratic class must needs and naturally, if he should make verses, take his place beside Shelley or Byron; the assumption would be felt on all hands as an impertinence rather than a compliment offered to that class; and how can it be other than an impertinence offered to a larger class to assume, or pretend to assume, that any one born in the opposite rank who may be put forward as a poet must naturally be the equal of Béranger or of Burns? Such an assumption is simply an inverted form of tuft-hunting; it implies at once the arrogant condescension of the patron to his parasite and the lurking contempt of the parasite for his patron; not a beautiful or profitable combination of qualities.

A critic in the Contemporary Review, but neither Robert Maitland nor Thomas Buchanan, once took occasion to inquire with emphatic sarcasm, what did Shelley care, or what does another writer whom he did the honour to call the second Shelley—how undeservedly no one can be more conscious than the person so unduly exalted—care for the people, for the sufferings and the cause of the poor? To be accused of caring no more for the people than Shelley did may seem to some men much the same thing as to be accused of caring no more for France than Victor Hugo does, or for Italy than did one whose name I will not now bring into such a paper as this. But to some men, on the other hand, it may appear that this cruel charge will serve to explain the jealous acrimony with which the writer thus condemned and dismissed in such evil company "seems" incessantly and secretly to have assailed the fame of Mr. Buchanan—the rancorous malignity with which he must have long looked up from the hiding-place of a furtive obscurity towards the unapproachable heights, the unattainable honours, of the mountains climbed and the prizes grasped by the Poet of the Poor. It mattered little that his disguise was impenetrable to every other eye; that those nearest him had no suspicion of the villainous design which must ever have been at work in his brain, even when itself unconscious of itself; that his left hand knew not what his right hand was doing (as it most certainly did not) when it cast stones at the sweet lyrist of the slums; masked and cloaked, under the thickest muffler of anonymous or pseudonymous counterfeit, the stealthy and cowering felon stood revealed to the naked eye of honesty—stood detected, convicted, exposed to the frank and fearless gaze of Mr. Buchanan. Can a figure more pitiful or more shameful be conceived? The only atonement that can ever be made for such a rascally form of malevolence is that which is here offered in the way of confession and penance;

the only excuse that can be advanced for such a viperous method of attack is that envy and hatred of his betters have ever been the natural signs and the inevitable appanages of a bad poet, whether he had studied in the fleshly or the skinny school. Remembering this, we can but too easily understand how Mr. Buchanan may have excited the general ill-will of his inferiors; we may deplore, but we cannot wonder, that the author of "Liz" and "Nell" should have aroused a sense of impotent envy in the author of "Jenny" and "Sister Helen"; it would not surprise though it could not but grieve us to hear that the author of "The Earthly Paradise" was inwardly consumed by the canker of jealousy when he thought of the "Legends of Inverburn;" while with burning cheeks and downcast eyes it must be confessed that the author of "Atalanta in Calydon" may well be the prey of rancour yet more keen than theirs when he looks on the laurels that naturally prevent him from sleeping—the classic chaplets that crown the author of "Undertones."

It is but too well known that the three minor minstrels above named, who may perhaps be taken as collectively equivalent in station and intelligence to the single Buchanan, have long been banded together in a dark and unscrupulous league to decry all works and all reputations but their own. In the first and third persons of this unholy trinity the reptile passions of selfishness and envy have constantly broken out in every variety of ugliness; in the leprous eruption of naked insult, in the cancerous process of that rank and rotten malevolence which works its infectious way by hints and indications, in the nervous spasm of epileptic agony which convulses the whole frame of the soul at another's praise, and ends in a sort of moral tetanus at sight of another's triumph. That thus, and thus only, have their wretched spirits been affected by the spectacle of good and great things done by other men, the whole course of their artistic life and the whole tenor of their critical or illustrative work may be cited against them to bear witness. The least reference to the latter will suffice to show the narrow range and the insincere assumption of their hollow and self-centred sympathies, the poisonous bitterness and the rancorous meanness of their furtive and virulent antipathies. Thomas Maitland, in his character of the loyal detective, has also done the state of letters some service by exposing the shameless reciprocity of systematic applause kept up on all hands by this "mutual admiration society." Especial attention should be given to the candid and clear-sighted remarks of the critic on the "puffing" reviews of his accomplices by the senior member of the gang, and of the third party to this plot by both his colleagues in corruption and conspiracy. If any one outside their obscure and restricted circle of reciprocal intrigue and malignant secrecy has ever won from any of them the slightest dole of reluctant and grudging commendation, it has been easily traceable to the muddy source of self-interest or of sycophancy. To men of such long-established eminence and influence that it must evidently bring more of immediate profit to applaud them than to revile, there are writers who will ever be at hand to pour the nauseous libations of a parasite. Envy itself in such natures will change places on alternate days with self-interest; and a hand which the poor cur's tooth would otherwise be fain to bite, his tongue will then be fain to beslaver. More especially when there is a chance of discharging its natural venom in the very act of that servile caress; when the obsequious lip finds a way to insinuate by flattery of one superior some stealthy calumny of another. "Ah, my lord and master," says the jackal to the lion (or for that matter to any other animal from whose charity or contempt it may hope for toleration and a stray bone or so now and then), "observe how all other living creatures belong but to some sub-leonine class, some school of dependants and subordinates such as the poor slave who has now the honour to lick your foot!" This is a somewhat ignoble attitude on the poor slave's part, though excusable perhaps in a hungry four-footed brute; but if any such biped as a minor poet were to play such a game as this of the jackal's, what word could we properly apply to him? and what inference should we be justified in drawing as to the origin of his vicious antipathy to other names not less eminent than his chosen patron's? Might we not imagine that some of the men at whose heels he now snaps instead of cringing have found it necessary before now to "spurn him like a cur out of their way"? It is of course possible that a man may honestly admire Mr. Tennyson who feels nothing but scorn and distaste for Mr. Carlyle or Mr. Thackeray; but if the latter feeling, expressed as it may be with bare-faced and open-mouthed insolence, be as genuine and natural to him as the former, sprung from no petty grudge or privy spite, but reared in the normal soil or manured with the native compost of his mind,—the admiration of such an one is hardly a thing to be desired.

If however any one of that envious and currish triumvirate whom the open voice of honest criticism has already stigmatised should think in future of setting a trap for the illustrious object of their common malice, he will, it is to be hoped, take heed that his feet be not caught in his own snare. He will remember that the judgment of men now or hereafter on the work of an artist in any kind does not wholly depend on the evidence or the opinions of any Jack Alias or Tom Alibi who may sneak into court and out again when detected. He will not think to protect himself from the degradation of public exposure by the assumption of some such pseudonym as Joseph Surface or Seth Pecksniff. He will not feel that all is safe when he has assured the public that a review article alternating between covert praise of himself and overt abuse of his superiors was only through the merest inadvertence not issued in his own name; that it never would have appeared under the signature of Mr. Alias but that Mr. Alibi happened by the most untoward of accidents to be just then away "in his yacht" on a cruise among "the Western Hebrides;" otherwise, and but for the blundering oversight of some unhappy publisher or editor, the passages which refer with more or less stealthy and suggestive insinuation of preference or of praise to the avowed publications of Mr. Alibi would have come before us with the warrant of that gentleman's honoured name. *Credat Judæus Appella!* but even the foolishest of our furtive triumvirate will hardly, I should imagine, expect that any son of circumcision or of uncircumcision would believe such a "legend" or give ear to such an "idyl" as that. Rather will he be inclined to meditate somewhat thus, after the fashion of the American poetess at Elijah Pogram's levee: "To be presented to a Maitland," he will reflect, "by a Buchanan, indeed, an impressive moment is it on what we call our feelings. But why we call them so, or why impressed they are, or if impressed they are at all, or if at all we are, or if there really is, oh gasping one! a Maitland or a Buchanan, or any active principle to which we give those titles, is a topic spirit-searching, light-abandoned, much too vast to enter on at this unlooked-for crisis." Or it may be he will call to mind an old couplet of some such fashion as this:—

> A man of letters would Crispinus be;
> He is a man of letters; yes, of three.

How many names he may have on hand it might not be so easy to resolve: nor which of these, if any, may be genuine; but for the three letters he need look no further than his Latin dictionary; if such a reference be not something more than superfluous for a writer of "epiludes" who renders "domus exilis Plutonia" by "a Plutonian house of exiles": a version not properly to be criticised in any "school" by simple application of goose-quill to paper. The disciple on whom "the deep delicious stream of the Latinity" of Petronius has made such an impression that he finds also a deep delicious morality in the pure and sincere pages of a book from which less pure-minded readers and writers less sincere than himself are compelled to turn away sick and silent with disgust after a second vain attempt to look it over—this loving student and satellite so ready to shift a trencher at the banquet of Trimalchio —has less of tolerance, we are scarcely surprised to find, for Æschylean Greece than for Neronian Rome. Among the imperfect and obsolete productions of the Greek stage he does indeed assign a marked pre-eminence over all others to the *Persæ.* To the famous epitaph of Æschylus which tells only in four terse lines of his service as a soldier against the Persians, there should now be added a couplet in commemoration of the precedence granted to his play by a poet who would not stoop to imitate and a student who need not hesitate to pass sentence. Against this good opinion, however, we are bound to set on record the memorable expression of that deep and thoughtful contempt which a mind so enlightened and a soul so exalted must naturally feel for "the shallow and barbarous myth of Prometheus." Well may this incomparable critic, this unique and sovereign arbiter of thought and letters ancient and modern, remark with compassion and condemnation how inevitably a training in Grecian literature must tend to "emasculate" the student so trained: and well may we congratulate ourselves that no such process as robbed of all strength and manhood the intelligence of Milton has had power to impair the virility of Mr.

Buchanan's robust and masculine genius. To that strong and severe figure we turn from the sexless and nerveless company of shrill-voiced singers who share with Milton the curse of enforced effeminacy; from the pitiful soprano notes of such dubious creatures as Marlowe, Jonson, Chapman, Gray, Coleridge, Shelley, Landor, "cum semiviro comitatu," we avert our ears to catch the higher and manlier harmonies of a poet with all his natural parts and powers complete. For truly, if love or knowledge of ancient art and wisdom be the sure mark of "emasculation," and the absence of any taint of such love or any tincture of such knowledge (as then in consistency it must be) the supreme sign of perfect manhood, Mr. Robert Buchanan should be amply competent to renew the thirteenth labour of Hercules.

> One would not be a young maid in his way
> For more than blushing comes to.

Nevertheless, in a country where (as Mr. Carlyle says in his essay on Diderot) indecent exposure is an offence cognisable at police-offices, it might have been as well for him to uncover with less immodest publicity the gigantic nakedness of his ignorance. Any sense of shame must probably be as alien to the Heracleidan blood as any sense of fear; but the spectators of such an exhibition may be excused if they could wish that at least the shirt of Nessus or another were happily at hand to fling over the more than human display of that massive and muscular impudence, in all the abnormal development of its monstrous proportions. It is possible that our Scottish demigod of song has made too long a sojourn in "the land of Lorne," and learnt from his Highland comrades to dispense in public with what is not usually discarded in any British latitude far south of "the western Hebrides."

At this point, and even after this incomparable windfall in the way of entomology, I begin to doubt whether after all I shall ever make any way as a scientific student. The savours, the forms, the sounds, the contortions, of the singular living things which this science commands us to submit to examination, need a stouter stomach to cope with them than mine. No doubt they have their reasons for being; they were probably meant for some momentary action and passion of their own, harmful or harmless; and how can the naturalist suppose that merely by accurate analysis of their phenomena he has gauged the secret of their mysterious existence? It is so hard to see the reason why they should be, that we are compelled to think the reason must be very grave.

And if once we cease to regard such things scientifically, there is assuredly no reason why we should regard them at all. Historically considered, they have no interest whatever; the historian discerns no perceptible variation in their tribe for centuries on centuries. It is only because this age is not unlike other ages that the children of Zoilus whet their teeth against your epic, the children of Rymer against your play; the children—no, not the children; let us at least be accurate—the successors of Fréron and Desfontaines lift up their throats against your worship of women:

Monsieur Veuillot t'appelle avec esprit citrouille.

Mr. Buchanan indicates to all Hebridean eyes the flaws and affectations in your style, as in that of an amatory foreigner; Mr. Lowell assures his market that the best coin you have to offer is brass, and more than hints that it is stolen brass—whether from his own or another forehead, he scorns to specify; and the Montrouge Jesuit, the Grub Street poet, the Mayflower Puritan, finds each his perfect echo in his natural child; in the first voice you catch the twang of Garasse and Nonotte, in the second of Flecknoe and Dennis, in the third of Tribulation Wholesome and Zeal-of-the-Land Busy. Perhaps then after all their use is to show that the age is not a bastard, but the legitimate heir and representative of other centuries; degenerate, if so it please you to say— all ages have been degenerate in their turn—as to its poets and workers, but surely not degenerate as to these. Poor then as it may be in other things, the very lapse of years which has left it weak may help it more surely to determine than stronger ages could the nature of the critical animal. Has not popular opinion passed through well-nigh the same stages with regard to the critic and to the toad? What was thought in the time of Shakespeare by dukes as well as peasants, we may all find written in his verse; but we know now on taking up a Buchanan that, though very ugly, it is not in the least venomous, and assuredly wears no precious jewel in its head. Yet it is rather like a newt or blind-worm than a toad; there is a mendacious air of the old serpent about it at first sight; and the thing is not even viperous; its sting is as false as its tongue is; its very venom is a lie. But when once we have seen the fang, though innocuous, protrude from a mouth which would fain distil poison and can only distil froth, we need no revelation to assure us that the doom of the creature is to go upon its belly and eat dust all the days of its life.

James McNeill Whistler

THE WHISTLER-RUSKIN TRIAL

WHISTLER's biting account of his famous lawsuit for libel against Ruskin, which took place on November 25 and 26, 1878, sharply reveals the dichotomy in art between the literalists and antiliteralists. Ruskin (through his counsel), Edward Burne-Jones, W. P. Frith, and Tom Taylor,[1] popular public figures all, appeared at the trial to testify for identifiable subject matter in painting, while Whistler alone stood for his special *avant garde* impressionism. Though the immediate question was whether or not Ruskin was guilty of libel, the trial faced the deeper issue of the authority of public taste, which was overwhelmingly on the side of recognizable subject matter. The ridiculous award of a farthing's damages to Whistler indicated that the sentiments of the court were really against the painter, though the presiding officer could hardly subvert justice. Whistler more evenly settled his score with Ruskin when he printed his own witty account of the proceedings: accompanying his text were liberal quotations from Ruskin's works which revealed amusing lapses in the sage's taste, as well as Whistler's personal reflections upon the course of events.

IN THE COURT OF EXCHEQUER DIVISION on Monday, before Baron Huddleston and a special jury, the case of Whistler, *v.* Ruskin

First published as *Whistler* v. *Ruskin* (1878).

[1] Burne-Jones (1833–1898) and Frith (1819–1909) were well-known painters; Taylor was editor of *Punch* and had been a pompous art critic for the *Times*.

came on for hearing. In this action the plaintiff claimed £1000 damages.

Mr. Serjeant Parry and Mr. Petheram appeared for the plaintiff; and the Attorney-General and Mr. Bowen represented the defendant.

Mr. SERJEANT PARRY, in opening the case on behalf of the plaintiff, said that Mr. Whistler had followed the profession of an artist for many years, both in this and other countries. Mr. Ruskin, as would be probably known to the gentlemen of the jury, held perhaps the highest position in Europe and America as an art critic, and some of his works were, he might say, destined to immortality. He was, in fact, a gentleman of the highest reputation. In the July number of *Fors Clavigera* there appeared passages in which Mr. Ruskin criticised what he called "the modern school," and then followed the paragraph of which Mr. Whistler now complained, and which was: "For Mr. Whistler's own sake, no less than for the protection of the purchaser, Sir Coutts Lindsay ought not to have admitted works into the gallery in which the ill-educated conceit of the artist so nearly approached the aspect of wilful imposture. I have seen, and heard, much of cockney impudence before now; but never expected to hear a coxcomb ask two hundred guineas for flinging a pot of paint in the public's face." That passage, no doubt, had been read by thousands, and so it had gone forth to the world that Mr. Whistler was an ill-educated man, an impostor, a cockney pretender, and an impudent coxcomb.

Mr. WHISTLER, cross-examined by the ATTORNEY-GENERAL, said: "I have sent pictures to the Academy which have not been received. I believe that is the experience of all artists. . . . The nocturne in black and gold [2] is a night piece, and represents the fireworks at Cremorne."

"Not a view of Cremorne?"

"If it were called a view of Cremorne, it would certainly bring about nothing but disappointment on the part of the beholders. (*Laughter.*) It is an artistic arrangement. It was marked two hundred guineas."

"Is not that what we, who are not artists, would call a stiffish price?"

"I think it very likely that that may be so."

[2] See second group of illustrations.

"But artists always give good value for their money, don't they?"

"I am glad to hear that so well established. (*A laugh.*) I do not know Mr. Ruskin, or that he holds the view that a picture should only be exhibited when it is finished, when nothing can be done to improve it, but that is a correct view; the arrangement in black and gold was a finished picture, I did not intend to do anything more to it."

"Now, Mr. Whistler. Can you tell me how long it took you to knock off that nocturne?"

. . . "I beg your pardon?" (*Laughter.*)

"Oh! I am afraid that I am using a term that applies rather perhaps to my own work. I should have said, 'How long did you take to paint that picture?' "

"Oh, no! permit me, I am too greatly flattered to think that you apply, to work of mine, any term that you are in the habit of using with reference to your own. Let us say then how long did I take to—'knock off,' I think that is it—to knock off that nocturne; well, as well as I remember, about a day."

"Only a day?"

"Well, I won't be quite positive; I may have still put a few more touches to it the next day if the painting were not dry. I had better say then, that I was two days at work on it."

"Oh, two days! The labour of two days, then, is that for which you ask two hundred guineas!"

"No;—I ask it for the knowledge of a lifetime." (*Applause.*)

"You have been told that your pictures exhibit some eccentricities?"

"Yes; often." (*Laughter.*)

"You send them to the galleries to incite the admiration of the public?"

"That would be such vast absurdity on my part, that I don't think I could." (*Laughter.*)

"You know that many critics entirely disagree with your views as to these pictures?"

"It would be beyond me to agree with the critics."

"You don't approve of criticism then?"

"I should not disapprove in any way of technical criticism by a man whose whole life is passed in the practice of the science which he criticises; but for the opinion of a man whose life is not so passed I would have as little regard as you would, if he expressed an opinion on law."

"You expect to be criticised?"

"Yes; certainly. And I do not expect to be affected by it, until it becomes a case of this kind. It is not only when criticism is inimical that I object to it, but also when it is incompetent. I hold that none but an artist can be a competent critic."

"You put your pictures upon the garden wall, Mr. Whistler, or hang them on the clothes-line, don't you—to mellow?"

"I do not understand."

"Do you not put your paintings out into the garden?"

"Oh! I understand now. I thought, at first, that you were perhaps again using a term that you are accustomed to yourself. Yes; I certainly do put the canvases into the garden that they may dry in the open air while I am painting, but I should be sorry to see them 'mellowed.'"

"Why do you call Mr. Irving 'an arrangement in black'?" (*Laughter.*)

Mr. BARON HUDDLESTON: "It is the picture, and not Mr. Irving, that is the arrangement."

A discussion ensued as to the inspection of the pictures, and incidentally Baron Huddleston remarked that a critic must be competent to form an opinion, and bold enough to express that opinion in strong terms if necessary.

The ATTORNEY-GENERAL complained that no answer was given to a written application by the defendant's solicitors for leave to inspect the pictures which the plaintiff had been called upon to produce at the trial. The WITNESS replied that Mr. Arthur Severn had been to his studio to inspect the paintings, on behalf of the defendant, for the purpose of passing his final judgment upon them and settling that question for ever.

Cross-examination continued: "What was the subject of the nocturne in blue and silver belonging to Mr. Grahame?"

"A moonlight effect on the river near old Battersea Bridge." [3]

"What has become of the nocturne in black and gold?"

"I believe it is before you." (*Laughter.*)

The picture called the nocturne in blue and silver was now produced in Court.

[3] For one version, see second group of illustrations.

"That is Mr. Grahame's picture. It represents Battersea Bridge by moonlight."

Baron Huddleston: "Which part of the picture is the bridge?" (*Laughter.*)

His Lordship earnestly rebuked those who laughed. And witness explained to his Lordship the composition of the picture.

"Do you say that this is a correct representation of Battersea Bridge?"

"I did not intend it to be a 'correct' portrait of the bridge. It is only a moonlight scene, and the pier in the centre of the picture may not be like the piers at Battersea Bridge as you know them in broad daylight. As to what the picture represents, that depends upon who looks at it. To some persons it may represent all that is intended; to others it may represent nothing."

"The prevailing colour is blue?"

"Perhaps."

"Are those figures on the top of the bridge intended for people?"

"They are just what you like."

"Is that a barge beneath?"

"Yes. I am very much encouraged at your perceiving that. My whole scheme was only to bring about a certain harmony of colour."

"What is that gold-coloured mark on the right of the picture like a cascade?"

"The 'cascade of gold' is a firework."

A second nocturne in blue and silver was then produced.

Witness: "That represents another moonlight scene on the Thames looking up Battersea Reach. I completed the mass of the picture in one day."

The Court then adjourned. During the interval the jury visited the Probate Court to view the pictures which had been collected in the Westminster Palace Hotel.

After the Court had re-assembled the "Nocturne in Black and Gold" was again produced, and Mr. Whistler was further cross-examined by the Attorney-General: "The picture represents a distant view of Cremorne with a falling rocket and other fireworks. It occupied two days, and is a finished picture. The black monogram on the frame was placed in its position with reference to the proper decorative balance of the whole."

"You have made the study of Art your study of a lifetime. Now, do you think that anybody looking at that picture might fairly come to the conclusion that it had no peculiar beauty?"

"I have strong evidence that Mr. Ruskin did come to that conclusion."

"Do you think it fair that Mr. Ruskin should come to that conclusion?"

"What might be fair to Mr. Ruskin I cannot answer."

"Then you mean, Mr. Whistler, that the initiated in technical matters might have no difficulty in understanding your work. But do you think now that you could make *me* see the beauty of that picture?"

The witness then paused, and examining attentively the Attorney-General's face and looking at the picture alternately, said, after apparently giving the subject much thought, while the Court waited in silence for his answer:

"No! Do you know I fear it would be as hopeless as for the musician to pour his notes into the ear of a deaf man. (*Laughter.*)

"I offer the picture, which I have conscientiously painted, as being worth two hundred guineas. I have known unbiased people express the opinion that it represents fireworks in a night-scene. I would not complain of any person who might simply take a different view."

The Court then adjourned.

The ATTORNEY-GENERAL, in resuming his address on behalf of the defendant on Tuesday, said he hoped to convince the jury, before his case closed, that Mr. Ruskin's criticism upon the plaintiff's pictures was perfectly fair and *bonâ fide;*[1] and that, however severe it might be, there was nothing that could reasonably be complained of. . . . Let them examine the nocturne in blue and silver, said to represent Battersea Bridge. What was that structure in the middle? Was it a telescope or a fire-escape? Was it like Battersea Bridge? What were the figures at the top of the bridge? And if they were horses and carts, how in the name of fortune were they to get off? Now, about these pictures, if the plaintiff's argument was to avail, they must not venture publicly to express an

[1] "Enter now the great room with the Veronese at the end of it, for which the painter (*quite rightly*) was summoned before the Inquisition of State." —Prof. JOHN RUSKIN: *Guide to Principal Pictures, Academy of Fine Arts, Venice.*

opinion, or they would have brought against them an action for damages.

After all, Critics had their uses.[2] He should like to know what would become of Poetry, of Politics, of Painting, if Critics were to be extinguished? Every Painter struggled to obtain fame.

No artist could obtain fame, except through criticism.[3]

. . . As to these pictures, they could only come to the conclusion that they were strange fantastical conceits not worthy to be called works of Art.

. . . Coming to the libel, the Attorney-General said it had been contended that Mr. Ruskin was not justified in interfering with a

[2] "I have now given up ten years of my life to the single purpose of enabling myself to judge rightly of art . . . earnestly desiring to ascertain, and *to be able to teach,* the truth respecting art; also knowing that this truth was *by time and labour* definitely ascertainable."— Prof. RUSKIN: *Modern Painters,* Vol. III.

"Thirdly, that TRUTHS OF COLOUR ARE THE LEAST IMPORTANT OF ALL TRUTHS."—Mr. RUSKIN, Prof. of Art: *Modern Painters,* Vol. I. Chap. V.

"And that colour is indeed a most unimportant characteristic of objects, would be further evident on the slightest consideration. The colour of plants is constantly changing with the season . . . but the nature and essence of the thing are independent of these changes. An oak is an oak, whether green with spring, or red with winter; a dahlia is a dahlia, whether it be yellow or crimson; and if some monster hunting florist should ever frighten the flower blue, still it will be a dahlia; but not so if the same arbitrary changes could be effected in its form. Let the roughness of the bark and the angles of the boughs be smoothed or diminished, and the oak ceases to be an oak; but let it retain its universal structure and outward form, and though its leaves grow white, or pink, or blue, or tri-colour, it would be a white oak, or a pink oak, or a republican oak, but an oak still."—JOHN RUSKIN, Esq., M.A., Teacher and Slade Prof. of Fine Arts: *Modern Painters.*

Reflection:

In conduct and in conversation,
It did a sinner good to hear
Him deal in ratiocination!

(In the original printed record of the trial, a reproduction of Whistler's celebrated butterfly "signature" was inserted after each *Reflection.*)

[3] "Canaletto, had he been a great painter, might have cast his reflections wherever he chose . . . but he is a little and a bad painter."—Mr. RUSKIN, Art Critic.

"I repeat there is nothing but the work of Prout which is true, living, or right in its general impression, and nothing, therefore, so inexhaustively *agreeable*" (sic).—J. RUSKIN, Art Professor: *Modern Painters.*

man's livelihood. But why not? Then it was said, "Oh! you have ridiculed Mr. Whistler's pictures." If Mr. Whistler disliked ridicule, he should not have subjected himself to it by exhibiting publicly such productions. If a man thought a picture was a daub [4] he had a right to say so, without subjecting himself to a risk of an action.

He would not be able to call Mr. Ruskin, as he was far too ill to attend; but, if he had been able to appear, he would have given his opinion of Mr. Whistler's work in the witness-box.

He had the highest appreciation for *completed pictures;*[5] and he required from an artist that he should possess something more than a few flashes of genius! [6]

Mr. Ruskin entertaining those views, it was not wonderful that his attention should be attracted to Mr. Whistler's pictures. He subjected the pictures; if they chose,[7] to ridicule and contempt. Then Mr. Ruskin spoke of "the ill-educated [8] conceit of the artist, so nearly approaching the action of imposture." If his pictures were mere extravagances, how could it redound to the credit of Mr. Whistler to send them to the Grosvenor Gallery to be exhibited? Some artistic gentleman from Manchester, Leeds, or Sheffield might perhaps be induced to buy one of the pictures because it was a Whistler, and what Mr. Ruskin meant was that he might better have remained in Manchester, Sheffield, or Leeds, with his money in his pocket. It was said that the term "ill-educated conceit" ought never to have been applied to Mr. Whistler, who had devoted the

[4] "Now it is evident that in Rembrandt's system, while the contrasts are not more right than with Veronese, the colours are all wrong from beginning to end."—JOHN RUSKIN, Art Authority.

[5] "I was pleased by a little unpretending modern German picture at Dusseldorf, by Bosch, representing a boy carving a model of his sheep dog in wood." —J. RUSKIN: *Modern Painters.*

[6] "I have just said that every class of rock, earth, and cloud must be known by the painter with geologic and meteorologic accuracy."—Slade Prof. RUSKIN: *Modern Painters.*

[7] "Vulgarity, dulness, or impiety will indeed always express themselves through art, in brown and gray, as in Rembrandt."—Prof. JOHN RUSKIN: *Modern Painters.*

[8] "It is physically impossible, for instance, rightly to draw certain forms of the upper clouds with a brush; nothing will do it but the palette knife with loaded white after the blue ground is prepared."—JOHN RUSKIN, Prof. of Painting.

whole of his life to educating himself in Art;[9] but Mr. Ruskin's views [10] as to his success did not accord with those of Mr. Whistler. The libel complained of said also, "I never expected to hear a coxcomb ask two hundred guineas for flinging a pot of paint in the public's face." What was a coxcomb? He had looked the word up, and found that it came from the old idea of the licensed jester who wore a cap and bells with a cock's comb in it, who went about making jests for the amusement of his master and family. If that were the true definition, then Mr. Whistler should not complain, because his pictures had afforded a most amusing jest! *He did not know when so much amusement had been afforded to the* [11] *British Public as by Mr. Whistler's pictures.* He had now finished. Mr. Ruskin had lived a long life without being attacked, and no one had attempted to control his pen through the medium of a jury. Mr. Ruskin said, through him, as his counsel, that he did not retract one syllable of his criticism, believing it was right. Of course, if they found a verdict against Mr. Ruskin, he would have to cease writing,[12] but it would be an evil day for Art, in this country, when

[9] "And thus we are guided, almost forced, by the laws of nature, to do right in art. Had granite been white and marble speckled (and why should this not have been, but by the definite Divine appointment for the good of man?), the huge figures of the Egyptian would have been as oppressive to the sight as cliffs of snow, and the Venus de Medicis would have looked like some exquisitely graceful species of frog."—Slade Professor JOHN RUSKIN.

Reflection:

"Be not righteous overmuch, neither make thyself overwise; why shouldest thou destroy thyself?"

[10] "The principal object in the foreground of Turner's 'Building of Carthage' is a group of children sailing toy boats. The exquisite choice of this incident . . . is quite as appreciable when it is told, as when it is seen—it has nothing to do with the technicalities of painting; . . . such a thought as this is something far above all art."—JOHN RUSKIN, Art Professor: *Modern Painters.*

[11] "It is especially to be remembered that drawings of this simple character [Prout's and W. Hunt's] were made for these same middle classes, exclusively; and even for the second order of middle classes, more accurately expressed by the term 'bourgeoisie.' They gave an unquestionable tone of liberal-mindedness to a suburban villa, and were the cheerfullest possible decorations for a moderate-sized breakfast parlour, opening on a nicely mown lawn."—JOHN RUSKIN, Art Professor: *Notes on S. Prout and W. Hunt.*

[12] "It seems to me, and seemed always probable, that I might have done much more good in some other way."—Prof. JOHN RUSKIN, Art Teacher: *Modern Painters,* Vol. V.

Mr. Ruskin would be prevented from indulging in legitimate and proper criticism, by pointing out what was beautiful and what was not.[13]

Evidence was then called on behalf of the defendant. Witnesses for the defendant, Messrs. Edward Burne-Jones, Frith, and Tom Taylor.

Mr. EDWARD BURNE-JONES called.

Mr. BOWEN, by way of presenting him properly to the consideration of the Court, proceeded to read extracts of eulogistic appreciation of this artist from the defendant's own writings.[14]

The examination of witness then commenced; and in answer to Mr. BOWEN, Mr. JONES said: "I am a painter,* and have devoted about twenty years to the study. I have painted various works, including the 'Days of Creation' and 'Venus's Mirror,' both of which were exhibited at the Grosvenor Gallery in 1877. I have also exhibited 'Deferentia,' 'Fides,' 'St. George,' and 'Sybil.' I have one work, 'Merlin and Vivian,' now being exhibited in Paris. In my opinion complete finish ought to be the object of all artists. A picture ought not to fall short of what has been for ages considered complete finish.

Mr. BOWEN: "Do you see any art quality in that nocturne, Mr. Jones?"

Mr. JONES: "Yes . . . I must speak the truth, you know" . . . . (*Emotion.*)

[13] "Give thorough examination to the wonderful painting, *as such*, in the great Veronese . . . and then, for contrast with its reckless power, and for final image to be remembered of sweet Italian art in its earnestness . . . the Beata Catherine Vigri's St. Ursula, . . . I will only say in closing, as I said of the Vicar's picture in beginning, that it would be well if any of us could do such things nowadays;— and more especially if our vicars and young ladies could." —JOHN RUSKIN, Prof. of Fine Art: *Guide to Principal Pictures, Academy of Fine Arts, Venice.*

[14] "Of the estimate which shall be formed of Mr. Jones's own work . . .
"His work, first, is simply the only art-work at present produced in England which will be received by the future as 'classic' in its kind—the best that has been or could be."—Prof. RUSKIN: *Fors Clavigera,* July 2, 1877.

"The action or imagination of the highest power in Burne-Jones, under the conditions of scholarship, of social beauty, and of social distress, which necessarily aid, thwart, and colour it in the nineteenth century, are alone in art,—unrivalled in their kind; and I *know* that these will be immortal, as the best things the mid-nineteenth century in England could do, in such true relations as it had, through all confusion, retained with the paternal and everlasting Art of the world."—JOHN RUSKIN, LL.D.: *Fors Clavigera,* July 2, 1877.

* See tapestry, "The Passing of Venus," in second group of illustrations.

Mr. Bowen: ! . . "Yes. Well, Mr. Jones, what quality do you see in it?"

Mr. Jones: "Colour. It has fine colour, and atmosphere."

Mr. Bowen: "Ah. Well, do you consider detail and composition essential to a work of Art?"

Mr. Jones: "Most certainly I do."

Mr. Bowen: "Then what detail and composition do you find in this nocturne?"

Mr. Jones: "Absolutely none." [15]

Mr. Bowen: "Do you think two hundred guineas a large price for that picture?"

Mr. Jones: "Yes. When you think of the amount of earnest work done for a smaller sum."

Examination continued: "Does it show the finish of a complete work of art?"

"Not in any sense whatever. The picture representing a night scene on Battersea Bridge is good in colour, but bewildering in form; and it has no composition and detail. A day or a day and a half seems a reasonable time within which to paint it. It shows no finish—it is simply a sketch. The nocturne in black and gold has not the merit of the other two pictures, and it would be impossible to call it a serious work of art. Mr. Whistler's picture is only one of the thousand failures to paint night. The picture is not worth two hundred guineas."

Mr. Bowen here proposed to ask the witness to look at a picture of Titian,[16] in order to show what finish was.[17]

[15] *Reflection:* There is a cunning condition of mind that *requires to know.* On the Stock Exchange this insures safe investment. In the painting trade this would induce certain picture-makers to cross the river at noon, in a boat, before negotiating a Nocturne, in order to make sure of detail on the bank, that honestly the purchaser might exact, and out of which he might have been tricked by the Night!

[16] "I believe the world may see another Titian, and another Raffaelle, before it sees another Rubens."—Mr. Ruskin.

[17] "The Butcher's Dog, in the corner of Mr. Mulready's 'Butt,' displays, perhaps, the most wonderful, because the most dignified, finish . . . and assuredly the most perfect unity of drawing and colour which the entire range of ancient and modern art can exhibit. Albert Durer is, indeed, the only rival who might be suggested."—John Ruskin. Slade Professor of Art: *Modern Painters.*

Mr. Serjeant Parry objected.

Mr. Baron Huddleston: "You will have to prove that it is a Titian."

Mr. Bowen: "I shall be able to do that."

Mr. Baron Huddleston: "That can only be by repute. I do not want to raise a laugh, but there is a well-known case of 'an undoubted' Titian being purchased with a view to enabling students and others to find out how to produce his wonderful colours. With that object the picture was rubbed down, and they found a red surface, beneath which they thought was the secret, but on continuing the rubbing they discovered a full-length portrait of George III in uniform!"

The witness was then asked to look at the picture, and he said: "It is a portrait of Doge Andrea Gritti, and I believe it is a real Titian. It shows finish. It is a very perfect sample of the highest finish of ancient art.[18] The flesh is perfect, the modelling of the face is round and good. That is an 'arrangement in flesh and blood!'"

The witness having pointed out the excellences of that portrait, said: "I think Mr. Whistler had great powers at first, which he has not since justified. He has evaded the difficulties of his art, because the difficulty of an artist increases every day of his professional life."

Cross-examined: "What is the value of this picture of Titian?"—"That is a mere accident of the sale-room."

"Is it worth one thousand guineas?"—"It would be worth many thousands to me."

[18] "I feel entitled to point out that the picture by Titian, produced in the case of Whistler *v.* Ruskin, is an early specimen of that master, and does not represent adequately the style and qualities which have obtained for him his great reputation—one obvious point of difference between this and his more mature work being the far greater amount of finish—I do not say completeness—exhibited in it . . . and as the picture was brought forward with a view to inform the jury as to the nature of the work of the greatest painter, and more especially as to the high finish introduced in it, it is evident that it was calculated to produce an erroneous impression on their minds, if indeed any one present at the inquiry can hold that those gentlemen were in any way fitted to understand the issues raised therein.—I am, Sir, your obedient servant,

"A. Moore.

"Nov. 28."

Extract of a letter to the Editor of the *Echo*.

Mr. FRITH was then examined: "I am an R.A.; and have devoted my life to painting.[19] I am a member of the Academies of various countries. I am the author of the 'Railway Station,' 'Derby Day,' and 'Rake's Progress.' I have seen Mr. Whistler's pictures, and in my opinion they are not serious works of art. The nocturne in black and gold is not a serious work to me. I cannot see anything of the true representation of water and atmosphere in the painting of 'Battersea Bridge.' There is a pretty colour which pleases the eye, but there is nothing more. To my thinking, the description of moonlight is not true. The picture is not worth two hundred guineas. Composition and detail are most important matters in a picture. In our profession men of equal merit differ as to the character of a picture. One may blame, while another praises, a work. I have not exhibited at the Grosvenor Gallery. I have read Mr. Ruskin's works."

Mr. Frith here got down.[20]

Mr. TOM TAYLOR—Poor Law Commissioner, Editor of *Punch*, and so forth—and so forth: "I am an art critic of long standing. I have been engaged in this capacity by the *Times*, and other journals, for the last twenty years. I edited the 'Life of Reynolds,' and 'Haydon.' I have *always* studied art. I have seen these pictures of Mr. Whistler's when they were exhibited at the Dudley and the Grosvenor Galleries. The 'Nocturne' in black and gold I do not think a serious work of art." The witness here took from the pockets of his overcoat copies of the *Times*, and, with the permission of the Court, read again with unction his own criticism, to every word of which he said he still adhered. "All Mr. Whistler's work is unfinished. It is sketchy. He, no doubt, possesses artistic qualities, and he has got appreciation of qualities of tone, but he is not complete, and all his works are in the nature of sketching. I have expressed, and still adhere to the opinion, that these pictures only come 'one step nearer pictures than a delicately tinted wallpaper.' "

[19] "It was just a toss up whether I became an Artist or an Auctioneer."—W. P. FRITH, R.A.

Reflection: He must have tossed up.

[20] *Reflection:* A decidedly honest man—I have not heard of him since.

This ended the case for the defendant.[21]

Verdict for plaintiff. Damages one farthing.

William Morris

"ART AND THE PEOPLE"

MORRIS'S ADDRESS is an eloquent call for Socialist action, made with intelligence and sympathy and possessing the tone and shape of a literary essay. More significantly it reflects the genuine hurt which the separation of the arts from the people occasioned in Morris. It is useful to compare his tone with Ruskin's in "Traffic." Ruskin was also attempting to enlighten an audience, but he lacked Morris's quick natural sympathy and maintained the aloofness of a religious teacher. Morris was more experienced as a craftsman than Ruskin; with his own hands he had shaped wood and paper, iron and stone into furniture, books, ornaments, and dwellings. His criticism of the indifference of manufacturers and designers to the creative-expressive need of the workers is one of his recurrent themes, and the one for which he is best remembered. The address has been slightly shortened as reprinted here.

FELLOW CITIZENS,

I wish to say a few plain words to you on the subject of art; and since I address myself chiefly to those who are called the working-classes, I know well that the plainer those words are the better, since now for many years, for centuries, the working-classes have scarcely been partakers in art of any kind, and the phraseology of

[21] *Reflection:* To perceive in Ruskin's army Tom Taylor, his champion—whose opinion he prizes—Mr. Frith, his ideal—was gratifying. But to sit and look at Mr. Burne-Jones, in common cause with Tom Taylor—whom he esteems, and Mr. Frith—whom he respects—conscientiously appraising the work of a *confrère*—was a privilege! !

"A Socialist's Protest Against Capitalist Brutality: Addressed to the Working Classes" (1883). From May Morris (ed.), *William Morris: Artist, Writer and Socialist* (London, 1936). By permission of Basil Blackwell, publisher.

men learned in the fine arts will be strange to you. For centuries this slavery has been added to the rest of the oppression under which you lie, that you have been forbidden to have any share in the intelligent production of beautiful things.

Indeed, I think it will be news to many of you who toil to live that you may live to toil, that there either is or has been or can be any connexion between Art and the People. It may seem to you, I can well imagine, that art is concerned only in making luxurious toys for rich and idle persons, and that all the working-classes have to do with it, is that some of them can earn their poor wages by working at it as machines work, without knowing or caring what they are doing; while now and then on holidays those of them that chance to think of it and who live in London may stray into the National Gallery or the British Museum, and see the carefully hoarded works of past ages, and get from them such good as men can get who look on a book in an antiquated dialect of their language without an interpreter between them and the past.

And yet there is a phrase which of late has been much in the mouths of those who have been thought to be interested in the welfare of the Fine Arts; they have talked much of Popular Art: what does that mean?

The words Popular Art, or Art of the People, have a meaning you may be sure; the thing which they mean has really existed, or you would have little to look at when you stray into the National Gallery and the British Museum: the Art of the People has in many places and in many times solaced and sustained the people amidst their griefs and troubles.

And a great gift such as art seems to me; an art made intelligently by the whole body of those who live by their labour; instinct with their thoughts and aspirations, moving whither they are moving, changing as they change, the genuine expression of their sense of the beauty and mystery of life: an art born of their joy and outliving their sorrow, though tinged by it: an art leaving to future ages living witness of the existence of deft hands and eager minds not too proud to tell us of their imperfect thoughts and their glimpses of insight into wonders and terrors, as they passed amid the hurry of their daily work through the sunshine and the shadow of their lives.

This, I say, is the Art of the People, and on this is founded all art which is worth anything. I do not believe that Art worthy of the name can long exist, unless it rests on such a foundation: or if it can, if it really be that there can be an art practised by and for a few well-to-do and rich people, and founded on the slavery of the many, I for one will have nought to do with it: to me it will be contemptible and dishonorable, a rag of luxury and folly.

And yet, I must tell you that I am an artist: art is that by which I live; it feeds me body and soul, and without it the world would be empty to me: judge therefore how I must love and long for the Art of the People! For with me it comes to this, that I cannot live with any approach to happiness without art forming part of my life, and I know that my only chance of my having any real share in art, is that it shall be the Art of the People: nay more, I know that what art yet remains to us from the time when man had some pleasure in his labour, is lessening day by day, and that unless some change comes which will give all people a share in art, there will soon be no art at all left in the world. Judge therefore, I say, how I must love the Art of the People!

And one thing I must tell you before I go further, that this art is not a mere dream of something which might have been; as I have said it has in many times and places solaced the lives of toiling men; and this I have noticed of the times and places where it has flourished, that it has always been in advance of the apparent progress of the times that produced it. I have been astonished when I have looked into the popular art of past ages to find work so refined and elegant done in times so rude and rough: work bearing so many tokens of quick wit and invention done in times so ignorant and superstitious: works showing so many signs of freedom of thought and pleasure in life and external nature in days which seem to us to have been so full of oppression, gloom and turmoil; all these, mind you, qualities of hand and soul which could not have been produced to the order of rich men; for such qualities are spontaneous and cannot be bought with money or compelled by power: in short, it is not easy to exaggerate the contrast between the beauty and thoughtfulness of the handicrafts of certain periods, and the folly and disgrace of their history as otherwise told. Can we wonder at this? That written history of 'Kings and Scoundrels' is made up of the deeds of the greedy few ruling arbitrarily; while the history of art is made up of the deeds of the patient many living naturally.

The History of Art! What is that history indeed but the history of the World, since it alone tells us of the deeds of the people, and what they thought of and hoped for? through this and this alone can we look upon times past as they really were and see them alive.

And our own times, the days in which we live, how will those come to know the story of our lives from day to day? Well, when we are gone, and the 19th century has become a mere part of the past history of the world, people will still I suppose study history through the remains and records of popular art, as they do now: but when they come to these days and seek for evidence in their handiwork of the lives of those who lived by their labour, they will be baulked and have to stop short: they will perhaps find evidence of what the upper and middle classes thought working men were like left them in literature, chiefly novels; they will have record more or less trustworthy of their efforts towards political and social advancement; they will know that they made and used certain machines, and that they drew such and such wages: they will in short know something of the people as a political and commercial machine; but of the real story of their lives and the daily labour which was so great a part of them they will know nothing; a blank space will be the history of the popular art of the 19th century.

To make sure that you do not misunderstand me, I will state in the plainest words possible what seems to me to be the condition of Art in civilized countries, and in what proportions such art as there is, is shared amongst the various classes of the community.

Now the fine arts must be divided into two classes or kinds: the first what we may call the intellectual Arts, represented by painting and sculpture, address themselves wholly to the mind of man; they have no necessary connexion with any articles of material use, I mean. It is conceivable that a community might have all bodily necessaries, comforts, luxuries even, and not know what painting and sculpture meant: but besides these strictly intellectual Arts, there is a large body of art (or the pretence of it) which forms part of the matters of our daily life; our houses, our furniture, our utensils for eating and drinking, and our clothes are ornamented by this lesser kind of art, which cannot be dissociated from the things which we use every day; and this is commonly called decorative or ornamental art. I must further explain that while nations and times (though not many) have lacked the purely intellectual art, no nation or time has ever consented to do without the ornamental art; and lastly I must tell you that in all times when the Arts were in a healthy condition there was an intimate connexion between these two kinds of art; nay moreover that in those times when art flourished most, the higher and the lower kinds of art were divided from one another by no hard and fast lines; the highest of the intellectual art had ornamental character in it and appealed to all men, and to all the faculties of a man; while the humblest of the ornamental art shared in the meaning and deep feeling of the intellectual; one melted into the other by scarce perceptible gradations: or to put it into other words, the best artist was a workman, the humblest workman was an artist.

Well, let us see how it fares with art to-day: those who practice the purely intellectual arts, and who are technically called 'artists' are all by virtue of their occupation conventionally of the class of gentlemen, and many of them are men of education from their youth up: it is nowise my business here or elsewhere to criticize the works of these men; but I think I may be allowed to say that they are really subdivided into two classes, the first composed of men who would in any age of the world have held a high place in their art; the second composed of men who hold their present position of gentlemen-artists either by the accident of their birth, or by their possessing industry, business-habits or such-like qualities out of all proportion to their artistic gifts. The work which these latter produce seems to me of little value to the world (though there is a thriving market for it), and their position is neither dignified nor wholesome; yet they are mostly not to be personally blamed for it, since oftenest they have some gifts for art though not great ones, and would probably not have succeeded in any other career; they are in fact good decorative workmen spoiled by a system which urges them to worldly ambition; in times when popular art was flourishing, and when one man was apprenticed to an artist, just as another was to a carpenter, they would have found their level, and in various ways done useful though unambitious work.

Again as to that first class of artists, who worthily fill their place and make the world wealthier by their work, they are very few, and have won their mastery over their craft by dint of incredible toil, painstaking and anxiety: yet in spite of that, or perhaps because of it, they cannot help looking back with longing eyes toward the past times of art when less labour produced greater results: for whatever knowledge they may have of the older art, and its methods of work, they are cut off from *tradition,* that wonderful almost magical accumulation of the skill of ages, which men find themselves sharers in almost without effort on their part, and by which their toil of learning is so very much diminished.

Furthermore these great artists, as they only hold on to the past artificially and by effort, so also, and that is worse, they fail to touch widely those who are living in the present: for as a body the whole public, Upper, Middle and Lower classes, is ignorant of art: apart from the artists themselves and those very few persons who have special gifts of sympathy with them, there is no real knowledge of what art means; nothing at the best save certain vague prepossessions, which are but the phantoms of that Tradition I have spoken of, which once bound artist and public together. Therefore the artists are obliged to express themselves, as it were, in a language 'not understanded of the people': nor is this their fault; if they were to try, as some think they should, to meet the public half-way, and work in such a manner as to satisfy only those prepossessions of men ignorant of art, they would be casting aside their special gifts, and would become traitors to that cause of art which it is their duty and glory to serve: they have no choice save to do their own personal work without any hope of being understood as things now are; to stand apart as possessors of some sacred mystery, which, whatever happens, they must at least do their best to guard: and by this isolation their loss is great; great both to their own minds and to the work they produce; and as to our loss, the loss of the public, it is not easy to measure: for, you see, it comes to this, if we are to consider the distribution of the great and elevating intellectual pleasure of the enjoyment of the higher arts, that only a very few among the most cultivated classes can share in it.

But if it fares thus with that side of the arts which, depending on individual genius, is only acted on indirectly by bad social conditions, what is likely to be the state of that other side of the fine arts which is commonly called decorative art; art which (or the pretence of which) is to be found on nearly every piece of goods which is offered for sale? How is it likely to be with this art which above all other depends on the co-operation of men with each other?

Well I suppose there are many people who have not realized the fact that such an art exists, or who have heard that it ever did exist; and few indeed are those who consider that this great body of art, which has in times past had such a hold on the world, can now be worth the exercise of the thoughts of serious people.

Such as these arts now are, this is the way in which they are carried on; they are made by three sets of people, I won't say working together, but rather jostling along together: the first link in the chain is the capitalist called the manufacturer, a ridiculous misnomer since the word ought to mean a man who makes things with his hands: well he is by virtue of his position conventionally a gentleman, and often enough has received a liberal education; but in spite of any education he may have received it is rarely indeed that he takes any interest in the craft he is supposed to direct, and rarer still that he troubles himself on the quality of any ornament, i.e., art, which may be in it for its own sake: nay, if he be personally inclined to do so his position would soon put a stopper on his wishes: he has been created to 'make a profit' as 'tis called, i.e., to accumulate money which he has not earned, and which most people suppose tumbles mysteriously from the sky as a heaven-sent blessing on capital; but which some of us, who have not been content to accept the miracle, believe really comes of the earnings of those who do labour with their hands, and are called in the jargon of to-day 'operatives' not manufacturers. A good deal more could be said of the manufacturer and his position, but at present I must consider him only as the first link of the chain in the production of popular art (so called) and from that point of view all I need say of him is that he is and is compelled to be quite careless of what art there may profess to be in the wares he gets made. It will illustrate this side of the subject if you think how many rich men there are who profess (no doubt honestly) to be deeply interested in art and literature; who read poems and such-like books, who further the establishment of museums, who buy pictures for great sums of money, and who nevertheless are actually engaged in pushing on the degradation of art, because they are in a position which forces on them the accumulation of money as an imperative duty, not to be set aside by any consideration: which money if they but knew it, is not theirs, but has been forced by the screw of competition out of the earnings of those who are, to speak bluntly, their slaves.

The second link in the chain of the system by which industrial art is produced, as the body of men who go between capital and labour, as managers, foremen, and the like; as far as the ornamenting of wares is concerned they are represented by the designer, who is usually educated technically but seldom liberally: in the few cases in which gentlemen-artists are employed in this intermediate position, they know little or nothing of the way in which the wares are made and have next to no communication with the workman; but whatever the social position of the designer may be as a factor in the production of art, he is bound by the same necessity as the capitalist to consider first of all the 'making a profit,' and is also in most cases only a superior slave to the operative-slave, and competes for a bare existence like the latter.

As for the workman, the third link in the chain, I need not waste many words on his share in the production of art; when he has anything to do save to tend an automatic machine, he has nevertheless no control over the design of the art, or even over the way in which it is to be carried out; he is only responsible for turning out his work rigidly to pattern, is in fact a machine and nothing better.

Now at present I will not ask you workmen whether you are content to spend your working hours fulfilling the office of cog-wheels and cranks, but I will simply assert that under the system I have been speaking of it is impossible to turn out art: you must take an artist's word for that.

Let us look at the system again and summarize its beautiful arrangements: I am supposing it, mind you, to be a system for the production of art as it verily professes to be in some degree in all cases, while sometimes it is supposed to be employed making wares which are pure works of art. This in short is the system: at the head is a man who is absolutely master of the production, who is forced by his position not to heed whether what he produces is good or bad so long as it sells at a profit: his will is carried one step further by subordinates who have to take care that the wares shall sell at a profit and of nothing else; and finally the 'hands' who accomplish the will of the 'captain of labour' have one thing only to do, to make their labour profitable—to their master.

What place can art have in such a system? How much can people care about art who will put up with the products of such a system?

But indeed whatever may be thought of the matter by a public quite ignorant of art, the plain truth is that the system does not intend to produce either art or anything else which might add to the pleasure of life or its dignity: making a profit out of the lives of the great masses of the working-man is its sole aim.

Therefore the sad truth is that there is no popular art to-day, no art which represents the feelings and aspirations of the people at large, as for example the buildings of the Middle Ages represented the feelings and aspirations of the people, gentle and simple, lay and clerk, of that period.

This then is the condition of the fine arts under the rule of Plutocracy: on the one side there remains of the higher intellectual art, the work of poets, painters, and the like, a very small remnant struggling amidst a thicket of pretence and imposture: this remnant is lofty in aim and is not without special skill of its own; but it is quite unregarded by, indeed unknown to the people in general, and is but ill understood even among the cultivated classes by all but a very few.

On the other side of what used to be popular art there remains but a ghastly pretence of ornament which is nothing but a commercial imposture, or at best but a foolish survival of a half-remembered habit. . . .

No; popular art cannot live under the full development of competitive commerce; the revolt against unhuman work which is necessary for its existence would destroy the exploiting system of the capitalists, which appears by this time to be rapidly approaching perfection: nor without popular art can the art of the rich and cultivated long exist; what is now left of it is but a reflex of the days before commercialism began; while it was yet hanging in the balance, whether the days in which a man might be allowed to enjoy the fruits of his own labour were to come without our going through the terrible mill which the gospel of free contract has provided for us.

As fas as the mass of people is concerned, art is gone or all but gone from the daily life of man in civilized countries, and I say that is no mere accident but a necessary consequence of the rule of plutocratic anarchy: some branches of human invention can live under that tyranny: it allows learned men to seek out the secrets of nature and to subdue her forces because these matters can be turned to the advantage of the profit-market. But in art, the romance of each day's life, there is nothing 'practical' that is convertible into money, so long as it is real: all plutocracy can do is to degrade it into an hypocrisy, a sham of real feeling and insight, a set of counters for the picture-dealers; it can do that and in the end kill it, but it cannot use it.

Yes, art is not far from actual death and beauty is fading out of the land before the poison of riches. Green and beautiful places are still left in the countryside of England, but the hand of decay is on them; the life of man is poor and slavish there, and his dwellings, the sure token of the life led in them, which were once sound, trim, and beautiful, are giving place to miserable abortions which it is a pain and grief to look at; mere scrapings from the heaps of filth where you working-men live and which we call great cities.

And those terrible and frightful places; this horror we call London, or those worse because filthier hells the manufacturing districts—if ever the world escapes from the nightmare of riches and poverty which now oppresses us, will people from the midst of order and peace be able to understand what they were like?

And if we choose to consider the matter and face what must be the future unless this living death of Commercialism is swept away, do we not know what it must come to, supposing that national ruin does not overtake us? no rest, no beauty, no leisure anywhere: all England become like the heart of Lancashire is now: a breeding-stye for flesh and blood machines for the production of the profit of capital: machines, yes, but men also who, dimly perhaps, but miserably certainly, will be conscious of their own degradation.

Yes, it may be that Commercialism will find for us plenty of food and clothes and house-room, comforts even or luxuries; for us, I say, for most of us. It may be that, though it must have a body of abject poverty to serve it, it will produce so many rich men, and so many well-to-do men down to the class of the well fed prosperous artizan, that the class of the *poor* slaves will not be very numerous and will be powerless: that I know is the ideal of a large body of so-called advanced thinkers; and they may realize it, though I do not think they will, as I fervently hope they will not: for art, or the beauty of life, would be wholly lacking to all these classes, rich, middle-class, and poor; they would pass a wretched bestial degraded existence, and the hope of the progress of the race would have perished.

What is to save us from this misery, this hell? What but a Social Revolution which shall take away from men at once the power and the temptation of accumulating riches or in other words of keeping a body of slaves to do their dirty work for them: a Revolution which by abolishing men's power of making a profit from their fellows' labour will abolish all classes: not the mere arbitrary distinction between lord and commoner, gentleman and worker, but the real and dreadful distinction between rich man and poor, between the cultivated and the ignorant, between the refined and the brutal, which now exists, and is the foundation of plutocratic society.

I know as surely as I know that I breathe, that this Social Revolution would give to each and all of us a fair share of the good and evil of life: we should have our fair share of troublesome work and no more than our fair share: for we should not then be set to work for the sake of working: there would no longer be any need to cumber the world with mountains of useless wares: no need to weary ourselves with making either the idiotic toys of the rich, or the miserable rags of the poor, which form now by far the greater part of the baggage of commerce.

In all our work would be hope, and the greater part of it would be a labour of love, given freely and happily to the commonweal, as the commonweal would freely and ungrudgingly supply our needs for us: the hours of such work would to most of us be the happiest, but mere rest, time for thought, or dreaming even, would not be lacking to us, nor in any wise be grudged to us.

Then we should have nature beautiful around us again, for surely then no disgrace of foulness in air or water would be suffered, nor would it in anywise need to be, with science set free from the huckster's fetters: and remember once more it is not mere carelessness of beauty as we are now, the serving of our real needs, that has turned half England into a foul and greasy cinder-heap, but the insatiable compulsion of commerce on us to make an extra profit from labour we know not for what or for whom.

Doubt it not that from all this art would spring art in all forms, great and glorious, full of hope with eyes always turned towards perfection....

William Morris

"AT A PICTURE SHOW"

MORRIS's "At A Picture Show" does not introduce workers to specific pictures in the Kingsley fashion, but is rather a polemic intended to agitate its worker audience and to say what the author felt about the cleavage between rich and poor, between the artist and the public, and between beauty and dourness in everyday life. Morris hoped fervently to restore serious art to a deserved central place in the experience of all men, rich and poor alike; and since he believed that beauty should not be diluted for a popular appeal, the task of educating the public was to be a gargantuan one. Morris shows a sensitive understanding of the balance between aesthetics as pleasure and as ethos. The address has been slightly shortened as reprinted here.[1]

NOW IT IS CLEAR TO ME from reading the catalogue of this exhibition that the promoters of it think that the working men, as we call them, of these parts do most seriously need some education in the fine arts, that they need to be told something about them which they do not know, in order that, when they look at pictures or other

A lecture delivered in 1884, from May Morris (ed.), *William Morris: Artist, Writer and Socialist* (London, 1936). By permission of Basil Blackwell, publisher.

[1] The loosely written, somewhat repetitious *Hopes and Fears for Art,* a series of lectures delivered over a period of five years (1877–1882), is another well-known treatment of these favorite themes.

things professing to be works of art in future, they may be impressed by them in a different way from what they have been used to do: in other words, they want to educate people to look at pictures so that the pictures themselves may educate them afterwards. I agree with the promoters of this exhibition that the working men hereabouts do sorely need this double education, nor do I think that the richer classes would be the worse for it either for that matter; and the admission that this education is needed, that it should be necessary to explain to an ordinary intelligent person what the merits and aims of a picture are, just as one has to translate a piece of writing from a foreign tongue into our own: I say the admission that it is necessary to do this, and that it should be justly thought a good work for men to take trouble to do it without any other reward than what their own consciences may give them, shows that there is something amiss in the condition of the population hereabouts, and to cut the matter short, with the population throughout England, and indeed more or less throughout the civilized world.

I don't know if I make my thought clear to you: let me put it in another way: here on the one hand is a mass of work, done with the utmost care, patience and skill by clever and energetic people, who have devoted their lives to doing it; all of them have been men of special gifts and some of them men of the very greatest capacity, who would have succeeded in almost any career that they might have taken to. That is on the one hand I say, and on the other hand is a mass of laborious and intelligent people, who have been brought up in such a way that the mass of work aforesaid is of no value to them, who don't know of its existence, and when by accident they come across any part of it do not understand what it means, till they have been educated into doing so. This is a strange case.

You may say the men who took all this trouble about works of art and gave their lives to making them are dead, they belong to a past state of society, we have our minds fixed on different aims now. Well to a certain extent that is true, and yet there is another wonder: for there are still men alive who understand what these dead artists meant, who chiefly think of them and their works and the times which produced them; and some of these are themselves engaged with no less energy though perhaps with less success than those dead men in producing works of art to-day: they are neither foolish nor ignorant as a rule, and though some of them may be accused of being dreamers without sympathy for the life of men in the present, that is not a necessary characteristic of them, and we should wrong them if we thought it was general with them.

So you see you have on the one side artists and those who sympathize with them, and on the other the great mass of the people, who scarcely know or rather certainly do not know, what the word art means; these two groups of people so far as their ideas go, the thoughts which pass through their minds, might almost be living in two different worlds, although they are of the same country, the same race, speaking the same tongue.

This separation of the lives of two kinds of people seems to me monstrous and strange: and yet in that very fact of this separation lies a stumbling block in my making myself understood by many of you; for to most of you, I imagine it will not seem either strange or monstrous, no more than one man being a carpenter, and another a lawyer's clerk; I can only say that to me it seems much as if the carpenter, he and his, and the lawyer's clerk had got so perversely developed that the carpenter could see nothing in a tree but so many feet of timber and was blind to the leaves and fruit and blossom of it; as if to the lawyer's clerk a sheep was parchment in the rough, and a goose so many bundles of pens. In other words again, it seems to me that the sense of beauty in the external world, of interest in the life of man as a drama, and the desire of communicating this sense of beauty and interest to our fellows is or ought to be an essential part of the humanity of man, and that any man or set of men lacking that sense are less than men, and lack a portion of their birthright just as if they were blind or deaf. This proposition if it be true does certainly impose a duty upon us, the duty of guarding jealously this birthright, this gift of humanity; for those who know anything of the arts know for certain that no other pleasure is so sure and so lasting as that which comes of our exercising this gift, sometimes actively as a worker, sometimes as a looker-on only. Ah friends, seeing how many pains there are which are imposed on men's lives, and are not avoidable, surely we were the worst of fools if we did not treasure up those pleasures which are, if we knew it, a natural part of humanity also; especially when they lie so ready to our hands; for in good truth it is in our daily life and our daily work that the chance lies for us to take hold of the pleasure offered to us by art. Again you are astonished at my saying this: but that is just because of that division between artists and other men, which to me seems monstrous, to you natural: you cannot imagine your daily life, still less your daily work, having anything to do with art: somebody else paints a picture which he hopes a rich man will buy, but scarcely dares to hope anybody but a few artists like himself will understand; you look at it, heed more or less what the newspapers say about it, are sometimes perhaps a little amused by it, oftenest not, and go away quite forgetting what kind of thing it was, and by no means yearning to see another like it. Art, as you understand it, you feel you can do pretty well without: well so could I, though I am an artist. And yet, art as it should be you cannot do without, as I think the coming years will show you; as many men even now are beginning to feel—those who do not understand the why and the wherefore of our lack of art with mere despair, those that do understand it with something like exultation at the signs of the times and the new birth which they promise.

In your daily life and daily work, I have said, your chance alone lies of taking hold of art or the pleasure of life, in your becoming all artists: it is only by our all becoming artists that we shall be able to guard that natural birthright. Again you see because of that fatal schism between art and daily life you are astonished, for you think of an artist as a man working at his picture or image day in day out, disconnected with all other life but the carrying through of his piece of uselessness, as you would, if you said what you thought, most probably think it.

That is not what I mean by an artist at all, when I say we must all be artists: I mean that we should all be able to look with reverence and understanding on the aspect of nature and the deeds of man on the earth, that we should take a deep and thoughtful interest in life in short, and not be merely drifted helplessly hither and thither by the force of circumstances, as we too often are.

And if that were our real feeling, if we were really interested in the life of ourselves and our fellowmen, we should take care first, that our daily work was such as was fit for human beings to do, and secondly, that the time when we were not working included something more than mere animal rest, while it provided all due animal pleasure also: that, it seems to me, would be living due human lives, to have fruitful work-time, pleasant rest-time: I am sure you must agree with me there.

And yet, I must say it, how far we are from that now: how little fruitful work we do, how little pleasant rest we enjoy! Many and many a man goes down to the grave without having done one stroke of useful work, and as a consequence (taking the world all round) without having enjoyed one day of pleasant innocent unanxious rest: we waste our working energies in producing nothing or things harmful; we spoil our capacity for enjoyment in terrible wearing anxieties about how we are to live by working hard in doing nothing or less; and as a sad token of our waste and unrest we are speedily making the world, the face of the earth, once so beautiful, hideous, grievous to look on, unfit for man to dwell on. Nay more, all this might be bearable, if we each and all had taken upon us due share of the torment this state of thing produces; if we had borne one another's burdens and stood together determined to face it out, and mend it if we could, at the worst to live together bold and kind if we could not live happy. But this we have not done but rather the reverse of it; we have divided the world into rich and poor: we have decreed that, as near as could be, there should be two classes of people, one to toil and suffer, one to spend and enjoy; the poor are to be ill-fed, coarsely clad, dirty, wretchedly housed, over-worked, uncertain of their livelihood from day to day, they are to talk coarsely and ungrammatically, to think unconsecutively and illogically, to be uneducated, unrefined, bigoted, ignorant and dishonest; the rich on the other hand are privileged to feed themselves to repletion, to be clad in delicate raiment, to be spotlessly clean at all hours of the day, to live in gorgeous houses, to do no work or little work and to be paid the more the less they do, to talk daintily a tongue of their own, to be carefully and lengthily educated, to think according to the rules of logic, to have a plausible pretence of knowledge at least, to be over refined, as we call it, that is finikin, or may be vulgar only, to be finally, cynical and corrupt and dishonest: all this is their birthright, and hardly can they escape from it however good their dispositions as individuals may be, just as the poor however kindly and valiant they may be can hardly escape from their curse. If this be the case what wonder that there is this severance between artists and non-artists: the artists have been annexed by the rich and are their hangers on, their lackeys, their toy-makers: what wonder that they can no longer talk a language understanded by the people? that is as I have said a token of the severance between rich and poor; it is proper and right according to the system under which we live that the poor should be obliged to do without art and that the rich should be able to have at least a semblance of it, *because,* as the word goes, *money can buy anything,* which fortunately, my friends, is a lying proverb. For if, as is probable, you are inclined to say that all my words about the rich and the poor is but the ordinary frothy talk of the demagogue, I will add this to it, that as far as I can judge—I who belong to the rich classes—they are not happy either. How should they be? how should a cynical man or class feel happy? a corrupt one feel secure, a dishonest man or class feel at rest? Satisfied they cannot be, so soon as any suspicion creeps in on them that they are cynical, corrupt and dishonest: nor will you working-men so soon as you feel that you are ill fed, ill clad, ill housed, overworked, dirty, ignorant, unrefined *because* you belong to a class, cease to feel any content in the wretched scraps of enjoyment of life which are still allowed you; you also will be openly discontented, very openly I hope. No, be sure we are both unhappy, rich and poor, and justly so when we, we children of one mother, have been so led astray, so sported with by circumstance that we can endure the inequalities which underlie those words rich and poor.

And that is why I have been speaking the language of the common demagogue (which is true mind you) in order that I might make you feel, both rich and poor among you, what a gulf gapes between you, and that by some means you might set about trying to bridge it over, to fill it up rather. Indeed both consciously and unconsciously I know you try to do so, and your attempts at it, ineffectual as they are and must be while the present system lasts, do at least testify to your consciousness of there being something wrong: and what I want you to see is that the something wrong is the existence of class distinctions of any kind. I want there to be no more masters and slaves, no more gentlemen and cads (as we used to say at the university), I want us all to be friends, all to be gentlemen, working for the common good, sharing duly the common stock of pleasure and refinement. If this is being a demagogue you must set me down as one: also don't say it is beside the question of an art exhibition; for on this question must depend the answer to the other one whether your art exhibition has any educational value....

George Moore

"RESPECTABILITY," "THE ORGANIZATION OF ART," and "ROYALTY IN ART"

MOORE'S *Confessions* was calculated to shock a "respectable" British public. A curious book, a parade of decadent modes inspired by the author's somewhat limited experience of French Bohemianism and colored by Zola's prose manner, it asserted a premise quite contrary to the public aims of Ruskin and Morris. For Moore, the artist was unique in society, and the inevitable gap between him and the public which Ruskin and Morris had sought to repair was essential to the health of art. "Respectability," the besetting sin of the conformist middle class, was an animality, Moore said, against which true art cries out. Moore was suspicious of the socialist dream, for in a leveled society there would be no role for the individual painter, musician, or writer.

As art critic for *The Speaker*, Moore continued to thrust at Philistinism. Several of the reviews were published in 1893 as *Modern Painting*. One, "The Organization of Art," is an eloquently ironic attack on the Royal Academy; the venerable institution has become hardly more than an extension of the nation's Commerce, and fine art is merchandise. Serious art, and Moore was consistent here, must reflect the spirit of a creator independent of public standards. Moore's final thrust at "Free Trade" recalls Ruskin's jibes at the Goddess-of-Getting-On. A second essay, "Royalty in Art," attacks the stodgy dilettantism of the British Royal family as emphasized by the Diamond Jubilee Exhibition. The Queen's "frauism," her Philistine insensitivity to high talent, and the lack

FROM *The Confessions of A Young Man* (1888) and *Modern Painting* (1893).

of spirit and imagination in the art she and her family produced, were to Moore reflections of her Majesty's failure to lead the nation towards a high cultural fulfillment. Moore's humor and modern tone make him lively reading today.

RESPECTABILITY

NOWADAYS every one is respectable—jockeys, betting-men, actors, and even actresses. Mrs. Kendal takes her children to visit a duchess, and has naughty chorus girls to tea, and tells them of the joy of respectability. There is only one class left that is not respectable, and that will succumb before long; how the transformation will be effected I can't say, but I know an editor or two who would be glad of an article on the subject.

Respectability!—a suburban villa, a piano in the drawing-room, and going home to dinner. Such things are no doubt very excellent, but they do not promote intensity of feeling, fervour of mind; and as art is in itself an outcry against the animality of human existence, it would be well that the life of the artist should be a practical protest against the so-called decencies of life; and he can best protest by frequenting a tavern and cutting his club. In the past the artist has always been an outcast; it is only latterly he has become domesticated, and judging by results, it is clear that if Bohemianism is not a necessity it is at least an adjuvant. For if long locks and general dissoluteness were not an aid and a way to pure thought, why have they been so long his characteristics? If lovers were not necessary for the development of poet, novelist, and actress, why have they always had lovers—Sappho, George Eliot, George Sand, Rachel, Sara? Mrs. Kendal nurses children all day and strives to play Rosalind at night. What infatuation, what ridiculous endeavour! To realise the beautiful woodland passion and the idea of the transformation, a woman must have sinned, for only through sin may we learn the charm of innocence. To play Rosalind a woman must have had more than one lover, and if she has been made to wait in the rain and has been beaten she will have done a great deal to qualify herself for the part. The ecstatic Sara makes no pretence to virtue, she introduces her son to an English duchess, and throws over a nation for the love of Richepein, she can, therefore, say as none other—

Ce n'est plus qu'une ardeur dans mes veines cachée,
C'est Venus toute entière à sa proie attachée.

Swinburne, when he dodged about London, a lively young dog, wrote "Poems and Ballads," and "Chastelard"; since he has gone to live at Putney, he has contributed to the *Nineteenth Century,* and published an interesting little volume entitled, "A Century of Rondels," in which he continues his plaint about his mother the sea.

Respectability is sweeping the picturesque out of life; national costumes are disappearing. The kilt is going or gone in the highlands, and the smock in the southlands, even the Japanese are becoming christian and respectable; in another quarter of a century silk hats and pianos will be found in every house in Jeddo. Too true that universal uniformity is the future of the world; and when Mr. Morris speaks of the democratic art to be when the world is socialistic, I ask, whence will the unfortunates draw their inspiration? To-day our plight is pitiable enough—the duke, the jockey-boy, and the artist are exactly alike; they are dressed by the same tailor, they dine at the same clubs, they swear the same oaths, they speak equally bad English, they love the same women. Such a state of things is dreary enough, but what unimaginable dreariness there will be when there are neither rich nor poor, when all have been educated, when self-education has ceased. A terrible world to dream of, worse, far worse, in darkness and hopelessness than Dante's lowest circle of hell. The spectre of famine, of the plague, of war, etc., are mild and gracious symbols compared with that menacing figure, Universal Education, with which we are threatened, which has already eunuched the genius of the last five-and-twenty years of the nineteenth century, and produced a limitless abortion in that of future time. Education, I tremble before thy dreaded name. The cruelties of Nero, of Caligula, what were they?—a few crunched limbs in the amphitheatre; but thine, O Education, are the yearning of souls sick of life, of maddening discontent, of all the fearsome and fathomless sufferings of the mind. When Goethe said "More light," he said the wickedest and most infamous words that human lips ever spoke. In old days, when a people became too highly civilised the barbarians came down from the north and regenerated that nation with darkness; but now there are no more barbarians, and sooner or later I am convinced that we shall have to end the evil by summary edicts—the obstruction no doubt will be severe, the equivalents of Gladstone and Morley will stop at nothing to defeat the Bill; but it will nevertheless be carried by patriotic Conservative and Unionist majorities, and it will be written in the Statute Book that not more than one child in a hundred shall be taught to read, and no more than one in ten thousand shall learn the piano.

Such will be the end of Respectability, but the end is still far distant. We are now in a period of decadence growing steadily more and more acute. The old gods are falling about us, there is little left to raise our hearts and minds to, and amid the wreck and ruin of things only a snobbery is left to us, thank heaven, deeply graven in the English heart; the snob is now the ark that floats triumphant over the democratic wave; the faith of the old world reposes in his breast, and he shall proclaim it when the waters have subsided.

In the meanwhile Respectability, having destroyed the Tavern, and created the Club, continues to exercise a meretricious and enervating influence on literature. All audacity of thought and expression has been stamped out, and the conventionalities are rigorously respected. It has been said a thousand times that an art is only a reflection of a certain age; quite so, only certain ages are more interesting than others, and consequently produce better art, just as certain seasons produce better crops. We heard in the Nouvelle Athènes how the Democratic movement, in other words, Respectability, in other words, Education, has extinguished the handicrafts; it was admitted that in the more individual arts—painting and poetry—men would be always found to sacrifice their lives for a picture or a poem: but no man is, after all, so immeasurably superior to the age he lives in as to be able to resist it wholly; he must draw sustenance from some quarter, and the contemplation of the past will not suffice. Then the pressure on him from without is as water upon the diver; and sooner or later he grows fatigued and comes to the surface to breathe; he is as a flying-fish pursued by sharks below and cruel birds above; and he neither dives as deeply nor flies as high as his freer and stronger ancestry. A daring spirit in the nineteenth century would have been but a timid nursery soul indeed in the sixteenth. We want tumult and war to give us forgetfulness, sublime moments of peace to enjoy a kiss in; we are expected to be home to dinner at seven, and to say and do nothing that might shock the neighbours. Respectability has wound itself about society, a sort of octopus, and nowhere are you quite free from one of its horrible suckers. The power of the villa residence is supreme: art, science, politics, religion, it has transformed to suit its requirements. The villa goes to the Academy, the villa goes to the theatre, and therefore the art of today is mildly realistic; not the great realism of idea, but the puny reality of materialism; not the deep poetry of a Peter de Hogue, but the meanness of a Frith—not the winged realism of Balzac, but the degrading naturalism of a coloured photograph.

THE ORGANIZATION OF ART

No fact is more painful to the modern mind than that men are not born with equal brains; and every day we grow more and more determined to thwart Nature's desire of inequality by public education. Whether everybody should be taught to read and write I leave to politicians—the matter is not important; but that the nation should not be instructed in drawing, music, painting, and English literature I will never cease to maintain. Everything that has happened in England for the last thirty years goes to prove that systematised education in art means artistic decadence.

To the ordinary mind there is something very reassuring in the words institutions, professors, examinations, medals, and titles of all kinds. All these things have been given of late years to art, and parents and guardians need no longer have any fear for those confided to their charge: the art of painting has been recognized as a profession! The principal institution where this profession is practised is called the Royal Academy. It owes its existence to the taste of a gentleman known as George the Third, and it has been dowered by the State to the extent of at least three hundred thousand pounds. Professors from Oxford, even bishops, dine there. The members of this institution put R.A. after their names; the president has been made a baronet; there was even a rumour that he was going to be made a lord, and that he was not we must consider as another blow dealt against the dignity of art.

Literature does not offer so much scope for organisation as

painting; but strenuous efforts are being made to organize it, and, by the aid of academies, examinations, and crowns, hopes are entertained that, before long, it will be brought into line with the other professions. And the journalists too are anxious to "erect their craft to the dignity of a profession which shall confer upon its members *certain social status* like that of the barrister and lawyer." Entrance is to be strictly conditional; no one is to have a right to practice without a diploma, and members are to be entitled to certain letters after their names. A movement is on foot to Churton-Collinise English literature at the universities, and every month Mr. Walter Besant raises a wail in the *Author* that the peerage is not as open to three-volume novelists as it is to brewers. He bewails the fact that no eminent man of letters, with the exception of Lord Tennyson, has been made the enforced associate of brewers and politicians. Mr. Besant does not think that titles in these democratic days are foolish and absurd, pitiful in the personality of those who own them by inheritance, grotesque in the personality of those on whom they have been conferred. Mr. Besant does not see that the desire of the baker, the brewer, the butcher, and I may add the three-volume novelist, to be addressed by small tradesmen and lackeys as "yer lordship," raises a smile on the lips even of the most *blasé*.

I am advocating an unpopular *régime* I know, for the majority believe that art is in Queer Street if new buildings are not being raised, if official recognition of merits is not proclaimed, and if the newspapers do not teem with paragraphs concerning the homes of the Academicians. The wailing and gnashing of teeth that were heard when an intelligent portion of the Press induced Mr. Tate to withdraw his offer to build a gallery and furnish it with pictures by Messrs. Herkomer, Fildes, Leader, Long, are not forgotten. It was not urged that the pictures were valuable pictures; the merit or demerit of the pictures was not what interested, but the fact that a great deal of money was going to be spent, and that titles, badges, medals, crowns, would be given to those whose pictures were enshrined in the new temple of art. The Tate Gallery touched these folk as would an imposing review of troops, a procession of judges, or a coronation in Westminster Abbey. Their senses were tickled by the prospect of a show, their minds were stirred by some idea of organisation—something was about to be organised, and nothing appeals so much to the vulgar mind as organisation.

An epoch is represented by a word, and to organise represents the dominant idea of our civilisation. To organise is to be respectable, and as every one wants to be respectable, every one dreams of new schemes of organisation. Soldiers, sailors, policemen, members of parliament, independent voters, clerks in the post office, bus drivers, dockers, every imaginable variety of worker, domestic servants—it is difficult to think of any class that has not been organised of late years. There is a gentleman in parliament who is anxious to do something in the way of social organisation for the gipsies. The gipsies have not appealed to him; they have professed no desire to have their social status raised; they have, I believe, disclaimed through their king, whoever he may be, all participation in the scheme of this benevolent gentleman. Nor does any sense of the absurdity of his endeavour blight the worthy gentleman's ardour. How should it? He, like the other organisers, is an unreasoning instrument in a great tendency of things. To organise something—or, put it differently, to educate some one—is to-day every man's ambition. So long as it is not himself, it matters no jot to him whom he educates. The gipsy under the hedge, the artist painting under a hill, it matters not. A technical school of instruction would enable the gipsy to harness his horse better than he does at present; and the artist would paint much better if he were taught to stipple, and examined by salaried professors in stipple, and given prizes for stippling. The general mind of our century is with education and organisation of every kind, and from this terrible general mind art seems unable to escape. Art, that poor little gipsy whose very condition of existence is freedom, who owns no code of laws, who evades all regulations, who groups himself under no standard, who can live only in disastrous times, when the world's attention is drawn to other things, and allows him life in shelter of the hedges, and dreams in sight of the stars, finds himself forced into a uniform—poor little fellow, how melancholy he looks on his high stool in the South Kensington Museum, and notwithstanding the professors his hand drops from the drawing-board, unable to accomplish the admired stipple.

But solemn members of parliament are certain that official recognition must be extended to art. Art is an educational influence, and the Kensington galleries are something more than agreeable places, where sweethearts can murmur soft nothings under divine masterpieces. The utilitarian M. P. must find some justification for art; he is not sensible enough to understand that art justifies its own existence, that it is its own honour and glory; and he nourishes a flimsy lie, and votes that large sums of money shall be spent in endowing schools of art and founding picture galleries. Then there is another class—those who have fish to fry, and to whom art seems a convenient frying-pan. Mr. Tate craves for a museum to be called Tate's; or, if his princely gift gained him a title, which it may, the museum would be called——What would be an appropriate name? There are men too who have trifles to sell, and they talk loudly of the glories of modern art, and the necessity of a British Luxembourg.

That France should have a Luxembourg is natural enough; that we should have one would be anomalous. We are a free-trading country. I pass over the failure of the Luxembourg to recognise genius, to save the artist of genius a struggle with insolent ignorance. What did the Luxembourg do for Corot, Millet, Manet, Degas, Monet, Renoir, Sisley, Pissaro? The Luxembourg chose rather to honour such pretentious mediocrities as Bouguereau, Jules Lefebvre, Jules Breton, and their like. What has our Academy done to rescue struggling genius from poverty and obscurity? Did it save Alfred Stevens, the great sculptor of his generation, from the task of designing fire-irons? How often did the Academy refuse Cecil Lawson's pictures? When they did accept him, was it not because he had become popular in spite of the Academy? Did not the Academy refuse Mr. Whistler's portrait of his mother, and was it not hung at the last moment owing to a threat of one of the Academicians to resign if a place was not found for it? Place was found for it seven feet above the line. Has not the Academy for the last five-and-twenty years lent the whole stress and authority of its name to crush Mr. Whistler? Happily his genius was sufficient for the fight, and it was not until he had conquered past all question that he left this country. The record of the Academy is a significant one. But if it has exercised a vicious influence in art, its history is no worse than that of other academies. Here, as elsewhere, the

Academy has tolerated genius when it was popular, and when it was not popular it has trampled upon it.

We have Free Trade in literature, why should we not have Free Trade in art? Why should not every artist go into the market without title or masquerade that blinds the public to the value of what he has to sell? I would turn art adrift, titleless, R. A.-less, out into the street and field, where, under the light of his original stars, the impassioned vagrant might dream once more, and for the mere sake of his dreams.

ROYALTY IN ART

THE SUBJECT is full of suggestion, and though any adequate examination of it would lead me beyond the limits of this paper, I think I may venture to lift its fringe. To do so, we must glance at its historic side. We know the interest that Julius the Second took in the art of Michael Angelo and Raphael: had it not been for the Popes, St. Peter's would not have been built, nor would "The Last Judgment" have been painted. We know, too, of Philip the Fourth's great love of the art of Velasquez. The Court of Frederick the Great was a republic of art and letters; and is it not indirectly to a Bavarian monarch that we owe Wagner's immortal *chefs-d'œuvre*, and hence the musical evolution of the century? With these facts before us it would be puerile to deny that in the past Royalty has lent invaluable assistance in the protection and development of art. Even if we turn to our own country we find at least one monarch who could distinguish a painter when he met one. Charles the Second [1] did not hesitate in the patronage he extended to Vandyke, and it is—as I have frequently pointed out—to the influence of Vandyke that we owe all that is worthiest and valuable in English art. Bearing these facts in mind—and it is impossible not to bear them in mind—it is difficult to go to the Victorian Exhibition and not ask: Does the present Royal Family exercise any influence on English art? This is the question that the Victorian Exhibition puts to us. After fifty years of reign, the Queen throws down the gauntlet; and speaking through the medium of the Victorian Exhibition, she says: "This is how I have understood art; this is what I have done for art; I countenance, I court, I challenge inquiry."

[1] Moore is in error here; the King was Charles the First.

Yes, truly the Victorian Exhibition is an object-lesson in Royalty. If all other records were destroyed, the historian, five hundred years hence, could reconstitute the psychological characteristics, the mentality, of the present reigning family from the pictures on exhibition there. For in the art that it has chosen to patronise (a more united family on the subject of art it would be hard to imagine—nowhere can we detect the slightest difference of opinion), the Queen, her spouse, and her children appear to be singularly *bourgeois:* a staid German family congenially and stupidly commonplace, accepting a little too seriously its mission of crowns and sceptres, and accomplishing its duties, grown out of date, somewhat witlessly, but with heavy dignity and forbearance. Waiving all racial characteristics, the German *bourgeois* family mind appears plainly enough in all these family groups; no other mind could have permitted the perpetration of so much stolid family placidity, of so much "*frauism.*" "Exhibit us in our family circle, in our coronation robes, in our wedding dresses, let the likeness be correct and the colours bright—we leave the rest to you." Such seems to have been the Royal artistic edict issued in the beginning of the present reign. In no instance has the choice fallen on a painter of talent; but the middling from every country in Europe seems to have found a ready welcome at the Court of Queen Victoria. We find there middling Germans, middling Italians, middling Frenchmen—and all receiving money and honour from our Queen.

The Queen and the Prince Consort do not seem to have been indifferent to art, but to have deliberately, and with rare instinct, always picked out what was most worthless; and regarded in the light of documents, these pictures are valuable; for they tell plainly the real mind of the Royal Family. We see at once that the family mind is wholly devoid of humour; the very faintest sense of humour would have saved them from exhibiting themselves in so ridiculous a light. The large picture of the Queen and the Prince Consort surrounded with their children, the Prince Consort in knee-breeches, showing a finely-turned calf, is sufficient to occasion the overthrow of a dynasty if humour were the prerogative of the many instead of being that of the few. This masterpiece is signed, "By G. Belli, after F. Winterhalter;" and in this picture we get the mediocrity of Italy and Germany in quintessential strength.

These pictures also help us to realise the private life of our Royal Family. It must have spent a great deal of time in being painted. The family pictures are numberless, and the family taste is visible upon them all. And there must be some strange magnetism in the family to be able to transfuse so much of itself into the minds of so many painters. So like is one picture to another, that the Exhibition seems to reveal the secret that for the last fifty years the family has done nothing but paint itself. And in these days, when every one does a little painting, it is easy to imagine the family at work from morn to eve. Immediately after breakfast the easels are set up, the Queen paints the Princess Louise, the Duke of Edinburgh paints Princess Beatrice, the Princess Alice paints the Prince of Wales, etc. The easels are removed for lunch, and the moment the meal is over work is resumed.

After having seen the Victorian Exhibition, I cannot imagine the Royal Family in any other way; I am convinced that is how they must have passed their lives for the last quarter of a century. The names of G. Belli and F. Winterhalter are no more than flimsy make-believes. And are there not excellent reasons for holding to this opinion? Has not the Queen published, or rather surreptitiously issued, certain little collections of drawings? Has not the Princess Louise, the artist of the family, publicly exhibited sculpture? The Princess Beatrice, has she not done something in the way of designing? The Duke of Edinburgh, he is a musician. And it is in these little excursions into art that the family most truly manifests its *bourgeois* nature. The sincerest *bourgeois* are those who scribble little poems and smudge little canvases in the intervals between an afternoon reception and a dinner-party. The amateur artist is always the most inaccessible to ideas; he is always the most fervid admirer of the commonplace. A staid German family dabbling in art in its leisure hours—the most inartistic, the most Philistine of all Royal families—this is the lesson that the Victorian Exhibition impresses upon us.

But why should not the Royal Family decorate its palaces with bad art? Why should it not choose the most worthless portrait-painters of all countries? Dynasties have never been overthrown for failure in artistic taste. I am aware how insignificant the matter must seem to the majority of readers, and should not have raised the question, but since the question has been raised, and by her

Majesty, I am well within my right in attempting a reply. The Victorian Exhibition is a flagrant representation of a *bourgeois,* though a royal, family. From the beginning to the end of the Exhibition is this and nothing but this. In the Entrance Hall, at the doorway, we are confronted with the Queen's chief artistic sin—Sir Edgar Boehm.

Thirty years ago this mediocre German sculptor came to England. The Queen discovered him at once, as if by instinct, and she employed him on work that an artist would have shrunk from—namely, statuettes in Highland costume. The German sculptor turned out this odious and ridiculous costume as fast as any Scotch tailor. He was then employed on busts, and he did the entire Royal Family in marble. Again, it would be hard to give a reason why Royalty should not be allowed to possess bad sculpture. The pity is that the private taste of Royalty creates the public taste of the nation, and the public result of the gracious interest that the Queen was pleased to take in Mr. Edgar Boehm, is the disfigurement of London by several of the worst statues it is possible to conceive. It is bad enough that we should have German princes foisted upon us, but German statues are worse. The ancient site of Temple Bar has been disfigured by Boehm with statues of the Queen and the Prince of Wales, so stupidly conceived and so stupidly modelled that they look like figures out of a Noah's Ark. The finest site in London, Hyde Park Corner, has been disfigured by Boehm with a statue of the Duke of Wellington so bad, so paltry, so characteristically the work of a German mechanic, that it is impossible to drive down the beautiful road without experiencing a sensation of discomfort and annoyance. The original statue that was pulled down in the interests of Boehm was, it is true, bad English, but bad English suits the landscape better than cheap German. And this disgraceful thing will remain, disfiguring the finest site in London, until, perhaps, some dynamiter blows the thing up, ostensibly to serve the cause of Ireland, but really in the interests of art. At the other end of the park we have the Albert Memorial. We sympathise with the Queen in her grief for the Prince Consort, but we cannot help wishing that her grief were expressed more artistically.

A city so naturally beautiful as London can do without statues; the question is not so much how to get good statues, but how to protect London against bad statues. If for the next twenty-five years we might celebrate the memory of each great man by the destruction of a statue we might undo a great part of the mischief for which Royalty is mainly responsible. I do not speak of Boehm's Jubilee coinage—the melting-pot will put that right one of these days—but his statues, beyond some slight hope from the dynamiters, will be always with us. Had he lived, London would have disappeared under his statues; at the time of his death they were popping up by twos and threes all over the town. Our lovely city is our inheritance; London should be to the Londoner what Athens is to the Athenian. What would the Athenians have thought of Pericles if he had proposed the ornamentation of the city with Persian sculpture? Boehm is dead, but another German will be with us before long, and, under Royal patronage, will continue the odious disfigurement of our city. If our Royal Family possessed any slight æsthetic sense its influence might be turned to the service of art; but as it has none, it would be well for Royalty to refrain. Art can take care of itself if left to the genius of the nation, and freed from foreign control. The Prince of Wales has never affected any artistic sympathies. For this we are thankful: we have nothing to reproach him with except the unfortunate "Roll-call" incident. Royalty is to-day but a social figment—it has long ago ceased to control our politics. Would that Royalty would take another step and abandon its influence in art.

Arthur Symons

"AUBREY BEARDSLEY"

Arthur Symons' essay on the *fin de siècle* illustrator Aubrey Beardsley [1] is representative of the many appreciations and analyses of art and artists which Symons wrote during his long lifetime.

(1898: revised, 1905).

[1] Beardsley reflected in his personality and work so many late-century attitudes that the 1890's are sometimes called "the Beardsley Period."

Occasionally he strikes a sentimental note, but for the most part his prose is among the most perceptive and readable of late Victorian "aesthetic" criticism. Symons was clearly a disciple of Pater —his ideas and his style alike bear the imprint; but he was better informed than the master about more of the arts, his style was livelier on the whole since he did not care inordinately for the exact, exquisitely turned phrase, and he was more responsive to modern trends in both British and French art. His *The Symbolist Movement in Literature* (1899) introduced the French writers to Yeats, Eliot, and Pound (Eliot has said that without Symons he would not have discovered Laforgue at the crucial time); and his sensitivity to Whistler, Beardsley, Moreau, and other artists helped fellow aesthetes to appreciate a symbolist design and arrangement, and provided a transition to the twentieth century. The decadent element in "Beardsley" reflects a point of view Symons shared with other *fin de siècle* artists—a view too often taken by literary historians and critics as representative of the closing ten years. The decadent eruption was certainly complex, colorful, and in spite of its many irresponsibilities, often positive in its effect. However, other equally significant writers and painters, among them Kipling, Shaw, Henley, Stevenson, Sickert, and Augustus John, were speaking vigorously for quite different values, and their end-of-the-century role deserves to be held in balance with the better advertised, more bizarre one.

ANIMA NATURALITER PAGANA, Aubrey Beardsley ended a long career, at the age of twenty-six, in the arms of the Church. No artist of our time, none certainly whose work has been in black and white, has reached a more universal, or a more contested fame; none has formed himself, out of such alien elements, a more personal originality of manner; none has had so wide an influence on contemporary art. He had the fatal speed of those who are to die young; that disquieting completeness and extent of knowledge, that absorption of a lifetime in an hour, which we find in those who hasten to have done their work before noon, knowing that they will not see the evening. He had played the piano in drawing-rooms as an infant prodigy, before, I suppose, he had ever drawn a line: famous at twenty as a draughtsman, he found time, in those incredibly busy years which remained to him, to deliberately train himself into a writer of prose which was, in its way, as original as his draughtsmanship, and into a writer of verse which had at least ingenious and original moments. He seems to have read everything, and had his preferences as adroitly in order, as wittily in evidence, as almost any man of letters; indeed, he seemed to know more, and was a sounder critic, of books than of pictures; with perhaps a deeper feeling for music than for either. His conversation had a peculiar kind of brilliance different in order but scarcely inferior in quality to that of any other contemporary master of that art; a salt, whimsical dogmatism, equally full of convinced egoism and of imperturbable keen-sightedness. Generally choosing to be paradoxical; and vehement on behalf of any enthusiasm of the mind, he was the dupe of none of his own statements, or indeed of his own enthusiasms, and, really, very coldly impartial. I scarcely except even his own judgment of himself in spite of his petulant, amusing self-assertion, so full of the childishness of genius. He thought, and was right in thinking, very highly of himself; he admired himself enormously; but his intellect would never allow itself to be deceived even about his own accomplishments.

This clear, unemotional intellect, emotional only in the perhaps highest sense, where emotion almost ceases to be recognizable, in the abstract, for ideas, for lines, left him with all his interests in life, with all his sociability, of a sort essentially very lonely. Many people were devoted to him, but he had, I think, scarcely a friend, in the fullest sense of the word; and I doubt if there were more than one or two people for whom he felt any real affection. In spite of constant ill-health he had an astonishing tranquility of nerves; and it was doubtless that rare quality which kept him, after all, alive so long. How far he had deliberately acquired command over his nerves and his emotions, as he deliberately acquired command over brain and hand, I do not know. But there it certainly was, one of the bewildering characteristics of so contradictory a temperament.

One of his poses, as people say, one of those things, that is, in which he was most sincere, was his care in outwardly conforming to the conventions which make for elegance and restraint; his necessity of dressing well, of showing no sign of the professional artist. He had a great contempt for, what seemed to inferior craftsmen, inspiration, for what I have elsewhere called the plenary inspiration of first thoughts; and he hated the outward and visible signs of an inward yeastiness and incoherency. It amused him to denounce everything, certainly, which Baudelaire would have denounced; and, along with some mere *gaminerie*, there was a very serious and adequate theory of art at the back of all his destructive criticisms. It was a profound thing which he said to a friend of mine who asked him whether he ever saw visions: "No," he replied, "I do not allow myself to see them except on paper." All his art is in that phrase.

And he attained, to the full, one certainly of his many desires, and that one, perhaps, of which he was most keenly or most continuously conscious: contemporary fame of a popular singer or a professional beauty, the fame of Yvette Guilbert or of Cléo de Mérode. And there was logic in his insistence on this point, in his eagerness after immediate and clamorous success. Others might have waited; he knew that he had not the time to wait. After all, posthumous fame is not a very cheering prospect to look forward to, on the part of those who have worked without recompense, if the pleasure or the relief of work is not enough in itself. Every artist has his own secret, beyond the obvious one, of why he works; it is generally some unhappiness, some dissatisfaction with the things about one, some too desperate or too contemptuous sense of the meaning of existence. At one period of his life a man works at his art to please a woman; then he works because he is tired of pleasing her. Work for the work's sake it always must be, in a profound sense; and, with Beardsley, not less certainly than with Blake or with Rossetti. But that other, that accidental, significant motive, was, with Beardsley, the desire to fill his few working years with the immediate echo of a great notoriety.

Like most artists who have thought much of popularity he had an immense contempt for the public; and the desire to kick that public into admiration, and then to kick it for admiring the wrong thing or not knowing why it was admiring, led him into many of his most outrageous practical jokes of the pen. He was partly right and partly wrong, for he was indiscriminate; and to be indiscrimiate is always to be partly right and partly wrong. The wish to *épater le bourgeois* is a natural one, and, though a little beside the question, does not necessarily lead one astray. The general public, of course, does not in the least know why it admires the right thing to-day though it admired the wrong thing yesterday. But there is such a thing as denying your Master while you are rebuking a servant-girl. Beardsley was without the very sense of respect; it was one of his limitations.

And this limitation was an unfortunate one, for it limited his ambition. With the power of creating beauty, which should be pure beauty, he turned aside, only too often, to that lower kind of beauty which is the mere beauty of technique in a composition otherwise meaningless, trivial, or grotesque. Saying to himself, "I can do what I like; there is nothing I could not do if I chose to, if I chose to take the trouble; but why should I offer hard gold when an I.O.U. will be just the same? I can pay up whenever the money is really wanted," he allowed himself to be content with what he knew would startle, doing it with infinite pains, to his own mind conscientiously, but doing it with that lack of reverence for great work which is one of the most sterilizing characteristics of the present day.

The epithet *fin de siècle* has been given, somewhat loosely, to a great deal of modern French art, and to art which, in one way or another, seems to attach itself to contemporary France. Out of the great art of Manet, the serious art of Degas, the exquisite art of Whistler, all, in such different ways, so modern, there has come into existence a new, very modern, very far from great or serious or really exquisite kind of art, which has expressed itself largely in the "Courrier Français," the "Gil Blas Illustré," and the posters. All this art may be said to be what the quite new art of the poster certainly is, art meant for the street, for people who are walking fast. It comes into competition with the newspapers, with the music-halls; half contemptuously, it popularises itself; and, with real qualities and a real measure of good intention, finds itself forced to seek for sharp, sudden, arresting means of expression. Instead of seeking pure beauty, the seriousness and self-absorption of great art, it takes, wilfully and for effect, that beauty which is least evident, indeed least genuine; nearest to ugliness in the grotesque, nearest to triviality in a certain elegant daintiness, nearest also to brutality and the spectacular vices. Art is not sought for its own sake, but the manual craftsman perfects himself to express a fanciful, ingenious, elaborate, somewhat tricky way of seeing things, which he has deliberately adopted. It finds its own in the eighteenth century, so that Willette becomes a kind of petty, witty

Watteau of Montmartre; it parodies the art of stained glass, with Grasset and his followers; it juggles with iron bars and masses of shadow, like Lautrec. And, in its direct assault on the nerves, it pushes naughtiness to obscenity, deforms observation into caricature, dexterity of line and handling being cultivated as one cultivates a particular, deadly *bottle* in fencing.

And this art, this art of the day and hour, competes not merely with the appeal and the popularity of the theatrical spectacle, but directly with theatrical methods, the methods of stage illusion. The art of the ballet counts for much, in the evolution of many favorite effects of contemporary drawing, and not merely because Degas has drawn dancers, with his reserved, essentially classical mastery of form. By its rapidity of flight within bounds, by its bird-like and flower-like caprices of color and motion, by that appeal to the imagination which comes from its silence (to which music is but like an accompanying shadow, so closely, so discreetly, does it follow the feet of the dancers), by its appeal to the eyes and to the senses, its adorable artificiality, the ballet has tempted almost every draughtsman, as the interiors of music-halls have also been singularly tempting, with their extraordinary tricks of light, their suddenness of gesture, their triumphant tinsel, their fantastic humanity. And pantomime, too, in the French and correct, rather than in the English and incorrect, sense of that word, has had its significant influence. In those pathetic gaieties of Willette, in the windy laughter of the frivolities of Chéret, it is the masquerade, the English clown or acrobat seen at the Folies-Bergère, painted people mimicking puppets, who have begotten this masquerading humanity of posters and illustrated papers. And the point of view is the point of view of Pierrot—

> le subtil génie
> De sa malice infinie
> De poète-grimacier—

Verlaine's *Pierrot gamin.*

Pierrot is one of the types we live, or of the moment, perhaps, out of which we are just passing. Pierrot is passionate; but he does not believe in great passions. He feels himself to be sickening with a fever, or else perilously convalescent; for love is a disease, which he is too weak to resist or endure. He has worn his heart on his sleeve so long, that it has hardened in the cold air. He knows that his face is powdered, and, if he sobs, it is without tears; and it is hard to distinguish, under the chalk, if the grimace which twists his mouth awry is more laughter or mockery. He knows that he is condemned to be always in public, that emotion would be supremely out of keeping with his costume, that he must remember to be fantastic if he would not be merely ridiculous. And so he becomes exquisitely false, dreading above all things that "one touch of nature" which would ruffle his disguise, and leave him defenceless. Simplicity, in him, being the most laughable thing in the world, he becomes learned, perverse, intellectualising his pleasures, brutalising his intellect; his mournful contemplation of things becoming a kind of grotesque joy, which he expresses in the only symbols at his command, tracing his Giotto's O with the elegance of his pirouette.

And Beardsley, with almost more than the Parisian's deference to Paris, and to the moment, was, more than any Parisian, this *Pierrot gamin.* He was more than that, but he was that: to be that was part of what he learnt from France. It helped him to the pose which helped him to reveal himself: as Burne-Jones had helped him when he did the illustrations to the "Morte d'Arthur," as Japanese art helped him to free himself from that influence, as Eisen and Saint-Aubin showed him the way to the "Rape of the Lock." He had that originality which surrenders to every influence, yet surrenders to absorb, not to be absorbed; that originality which, constantly shifting, is true always to its centre. Whether he learnt from M. Grasset or from Mr. Ricketts, from an 1830 fashionplate, or from an engraved plate by Hogarth, whether the scenery of Arques-la-Bataille composed itself into a pattern in his hand, or, in the Casino at Dieppe, he made a note of the design of a looped-up window-blind, he was always drawing to himself, out of the order of art or the confusion of natural things, the thing he wanted, the thing he could make his own. And he found, in the French art of the moment, a joyous sadness, the service to God of Mephistopheles, which his own temperament and circumstances were waiting to suggest to him.

"In more ways than one do men sacrifice to the rebellious angels," says St. Augustine; and Beardsley's sacrifice, together with that of all great decadent art, the art of Rops or the art of Baudelaire, is really a sacrifice to the eternal beauty, and only seemingly to the powers of evil. And here let me say that I have no concern with what neither he nor I could have had absolute knowledge of, his own intention in his work. A man's intention, it must be remembered, from the very fact that it is conscious, is much less intimately himself than the sentiment which his work conveys to me. So large is the sub-conscious element in all artistic creation, that I should have doubted whether Beardsley himself knew what he intended to do, in this or that really significant drawing. Admitting that he could tell exactly what he had intended, I should be quite prepared to show that he had really done the very contrary. Thus when I say he was a profoundly spiritual artist, though seeming to care chiefly for the manual part of his work; that he expresses evil with an intensity which lifted it into a region almost of asceticism, though attempting, not seldom, little more than a joke or a caprice in line; and that he was above all, though almost against his own will, a satirist who has seen the ideal; I am putting forward no paradox, nothing really contradictory, but a simple analysis of the work as it exists.

At times he attains pure beauty, has the unimpaired vision; in the best of the "Salome" [1] designs here and there afterwards. From the first it is a diabolic beauty, but it is not yet divided against itself. The consciousness of sin is always there, but it is sin first transfigured by beauty, and then disclosed by beauty; sin, conscious of itself, of its inability to escape itself, and showing in its ugliness the law it has broken. His world is a world of phantoms, in which the desire of the perfecting of mortal sensations, a desire of infinity, has overpassed mortal limits, and poised them, so faint, so quivering, so passionate for flight, in a hopeless and strenuous immobility. They have the sensitiveness of the spirit, and that bodily sensitiveness which wastes their veins and imprisons them in the attitude of their luxurious meditation. They are too thoughtful to be ever really simple, or really absorbed by either flesh or spirit. They have nothing of what is "healthy" or merely "animal" in their downward course towards repentance; no overwhelming passion hurries them beyond themselves; they do not capitulate to an open assault of the enemy of souls. It is the soul in them that sins, sorrowfully, without reluctance, inevitably. Their bodies are faint and

[1] See second group of illustrations.

eager with wantonness; they desire more pleasure than there is in the world, fiercer and more exquisite pains, a more intolerable suspense. They have put off the common burdens of humanity, and put on that loneliness which is the rest of saints and the unrest of those who have sinned with the intellect. They are a little lower than the angels, and they walk between these and the fallen angels, without part or lot in the world.

Here, then, we have a sort of abstract spiritual corruption, revealed in beautiful form; sin transfigured by beauty. And here, even if we go no further, is an art intensely spiritual, an art in which evil purifies itself by its own intensity, and the beauty which transfigures it. The one thing in the world which is without hope is that mediocrity which is the sluggish content of inert matter. Better be vividly awake to evil than, in mere somnolence, close the very issues and approaches of good and evil. For evil itself, carried to the point of a perverse esctasy, becomes a kind of good, by means of that energy which, otherwise directed, is virtue; and which can never, no matter how its course may be changed, fail to retain something of its original efficacy. The devil is nearer to God, by the whole height from which he fell, than the average man who has not recognised his own need to rejoice or to repent. And so a profound spiritual corruption, instead of being a more "immoral" thing than the gross and pestiferous humanity of Hogarth or of Rowlandson, is more nearly, in the final and abstract sense, moral, for it is the triumph of the spirit over the flesh, to no matter what end. It is a form of divine possession, by which the inactive and materialising soul is set in fiery motion, lured from the ground, into at least a certain high liberty. And so we find evil justified of itself, and an art consecrated to the revelation of evil equally justified; its final justification being that declared by Plotinus, in his treatise "On the Nature of Good and Evil:" "But evil is permitted to remain by itself alone on account of the superior power and nature of good; because it appears from necessity everywhere comprehended and bound, in beautiful bands, like men fettered with golden chains, lest it should be produced openly to the views of divinity, or lest mankind should always behold its horrid shape when perfectly naked; and such is the supervening power of good, that whenever a glimpse of perfect evil is obtained we are immediately recalled to the memory of good by the image of the beautiful with which evil is invested."

In those drawings of Beardsley which are grotesque rather than beautiful, in which now all the beauty takes refuge, is itself a moral judgment. Look at that drawing called "The Scarlet Pastorale." In front, a bloated harlequin struts close to the footlights, outside the play, on which he turns his back; beyond, sacramental candles have been lighted, and are guttering down in solitude, under an unseen wind. And between, on the sheer darkness of the stage, a bald and plumed Pierrot, holding in his vast, collapsing paunch with a mere rope of roses, shows the cloven foot, while Pierrette points at him in screaming horror, and the fat dancer turns on her toes indifferently. Need we go further to show how much more than Gautier's meaning lies in the old paradox of "Mademoiselle de Maupin," that "perfection of line is virtue?" That line which rounds the deformity of the cloven-footed sin, the line itself, is at once the revelation and the condemnation of vice, for it is part of that artistic logic which is morality.

Beardsley is the satirist of an age without convictions, and he can but paint hell as Baudelaire did, without pointing for contrast to any contemporary paradise. He employs the same rhetoric as Baudelaire, a method of emphasis which it is uncritical to think insecure. In that terrible annunciation of evil which he called "The Mysterious Rose-Garden," the lantern-bearing angel with winged sandals whispers, from among the falling roses, tidings of more than "pleasant sins." The leering dwarfs, the "monkeys," by which the mystics symbolised the earthlier vices; those immense bodies swollen with the lees of pleasure, and those cloaked and masked desires shuddering in gardens and smiling ambiguously at interminable toilets; are part of a symbolism which loses nothing by lack of emphasis. And the peculiar efficacy of this satire is that it is so much the satire of desire returning upon itself, the mockery of desire enjoyed, the mockery of desire denied. It is because he loves beauty that beauty's degradation obsesses him; it is because he is supremely conscious of virtue that vice has power to lay hold upon him. And, unlike those other acceptable satirists of our day, with whom satire exhausts itself in the rebuke of a drunkard leaning against a lamp-post, or a lady paying the wrong compliment in a drawing-room, he is the satirist of essential things; it is always the soul, and not the body's discontent only, which cries out of these insatiable eyes, that have looked on all their lusts, and out of these bitter mouths, that have eaten the dust of all their sweetness, and out of these hands, that have laboured delicately for nothing, and out of these feet, that have run after vanities. They are so sorrowful because they have seen beauty, and because they have departed from the line of beauty.

And after all, the secret of Beardsley is there; in the line itself rather than in anything, intellectually realised, which the line is intended to express. With Beardsley everything was a question of form: his interest in his work began when the paper was before him and the pen in his hand. And so, in one sense, he may be said never to have known what he wanted to do, while, in another, he knew very precisely indeed. He was ready to do, within certain limits, almost anything you suggested to him; as, when left to himself, he was content to follow the caprice of the moment. What he was sure of was his power of doing exactly what he proposed to himself to do; the thing itself might be "Salome" or "Belinda," "Ali Baba" or "Réjane," the "Morte d'Arthur" or the "Rheingold" or the "Liaisons Dangereuses;" the design might be for an edition of a classic or for the cover of a catalogue of second-hand books. And the design might seem to have no relation with the title of its subject, and, indeed, might have none: its relation was of line to line within the limits of its own border, and to nothing else in the world. Thus he could change his whole manner of working five or six times over in the course of as many years, seem to employ himself much of the time on trivial subjects, and yet retain, almost unimpaired, an originality which consisted in the extreme beauty and the absolute certainty of design.

It was a common error, at one time, to say that Beardsley could not draw. He certainly did not draw the human body with any attempt at rendering its own lines, taken by themselves; indeed, one of his latest drawings, an initial letter to "Volpone," is almost the first in which he has drawn a nude figure realistically. But he could draw, with extraordinary skill, in what is after all the essential way: he could make a line do what he wanted it to do, express the conception of form which it was his intention to express; and this is what the conventional draughtsman, Bouguereau, for instance, cannot do. The conventional draughtsman, any Academy student, will draw a line which shows quite accurately the curve of a human body, but all his science of drawing will not make you feel that line, will not make that line pathetic, as in the little, drooping body which a satyr and a Pierrot are laying in a puffpowder coffin, in the tail-piece to "Salomé."

And then, it must never be forgotten, Beardsley was a decorative artist, and not anything else. From almost the very first he accepted convention; he set himself to see things as pattern. Taking freely all that the Japanese could give him, that release from the bondage of what we call real things, which comes to one man from an intense spirituality, to another from a consciousness of material form so intense that it becomes abstract, he made the world over again in his head, as if it existed only when it was thus re-made, and not even then, until it had been set down in black line on a white surface, in white line on a black surface. Working, as the decorative artist must work, in symbols almost as arbitrary, almost as fixed, as the squares of a chess-board, he swept together into his pattern all the incongruous things in the world, weaving them into congruity by his pattern. Using the puff-box, the toilet-table, the ostrich-feather hat, with a full consciousness of their suggestive quality in a drawing of archaic times, a drawing purposely fantastic, he put these things to beautiful uses, because he liked their forms, and because his space of white or black seemed to require some such arrangement of lines. They were the minims and crotchets by which he wrote down his music; they made the music, but they were not the music.

In the "Salomé" drawings, in most of the "Yellow Book" drawings, we see Beardsley under this mainly Japanese influence; with, now and later, in his less serious work the but half-admitted influence of what was most actual, perhaps most temporary, in the French art of the day. *Pierrot gamin,* in "Salomé" itself, alternates, in such irreverences as the design of "The Black Cape," with the creator of the noble line, in the austere and terrible design of "The Climax," the ornate and vehement design of "The Peacock Skirt." Here we get pure outline, as in the frontispiece; a mysterious intricacy, as in the border of the title-page and of the table of contents; a paradoxical beauty of mere wilfulness, but a wilfulness which has its meaning, its excuse, its pictorial justification, as in "The Toilette." The "Yellow Book" and the first drawings for the

"Savoy," a new influence has come into the work, the influence of the French eighteenth century. This influence, artificial as it is, draws him nearer, though somewhat unquietly nearer, to nature. Drawings like "The Fruit Bearers," in the first number of the "Savoy," with its solid and elaborate richness of ornament, or "The Coiffing," in the third number, with its delicate and elaborate grace, its witty concentration of line; drawings like the illustrations to the "Rape of the Lock," [1] have, with less extravagance, and also a less strenuous intellectual effort, a new mastery of elegant form, not too far removed from nature while still subordinated to the effect of decoration, to the instinct of line. In the illustrations to Ernest Dowson's "Pierrot of the Minute," we have a more deliberate surrender, for the moment, to Eisen and Saint-Aubin, as yet another manner is seen working itself out. The illustrations to "Mademoiselle de Maupin" seemed to me, when I first saw them, with the exception of one extremely beautiful design in colour, to show a certain falling off in power, an actual weakness in the handling of the pen. But, in their not quite successful feeling after natural form, they did but represent, as I afterwards found, the moment of transition to what must now remain for us, and may well remain, Beardsley's latest manner. The four initial letters to "Volpone," the last of which was finished not more than three weeks before his death, have a new quality both of hand and of mind. They are done in pencil, and they lose, as such drawings are bound to lose, very greatly in the reduced reproduction. But in the original, they are certainly, in sheer technical skill, equal to anything he had ever done, and they bring at the last, and with complete success, nature itself into the pattern. And here, under some solemn influence, the broken line of beauty has reunited; "the care is over," and the trouble has gone out of this no less fantastic world, in which Pan still smiles from his terminal column among the trees, but without the old malice. Human and animal form reassert themselves, with a new dignity, under this new respect for their capabilities. Beardsley has accepted the convention of nature itself, turning it to his own uses, extracting from it his own symbols, but no longer rejecting it for a convention entirely of his own making. And thus in his last work, done under the very shadow of death, we find new possibilities for an art, conceived as pure line,

[1] See second group of illustrations.

conducted through mere pattern, which, after many hesitations, has resolved finally upon the great compromise, that compromise which the greatest artists have made between the mind's outline and the outline of visible things.

Arthur Symons

"THE LESSON OF MILLAIS"

FEW PAINTERS have ever achieved anything like the acclaim and wealth of Sir John Everett Millais (1829–1896). After he abandoned his early Pre-Raphaelite principles for the more sentimental values of the middle class, his success was phenomenal. He became, to more dedicated artists, the very archetype of pander; Symon's judgment is in the main fair. Millais is best remembered for "Bubbles," [1] a vapid but technically brilliant oil painting of a glossy curly-haired boy. The picture still enjoys the dubious reputation of being the first work by a supposedly serious painter to be used for mass advertising—it became the trademark for Pears' Soap and was reproduced throughout the world. Millais was elected a full member of the Royal Academy in 1863, was made a baronet in 1885, and in 1896, shortly before his death, was elected president of the Academy.

THE BURIAL OF MILLAIS in St. Paul's should have been an honour done to a great painter, who died at the age of thirty-five, the painter of "The Eve of St. Agnes," of "Ophelia," of "The Vale of Rest;" it was but an honour done to a popular painter, the painter of "Bubbles," and other coloured supplements to Christmas numbers, who died at the age of sixty-seven. In the eulogies that have been justly given to the late President of the Royal Academy, I have looked in vain for this sentence, which should have had its place in them all: he did not make the "great refusal." Instead of this, I have seen only: he was so English, and so fond of salmon-fishing.

FROM *The Savoy* (October, 1896).

[1] See second group of illustrations.

It is not too much to say that Millais began his career with a finer promise than any artist of his time. In sheer mastery of his brush he was greater than Rossetti, greater than Holman Hunt, greater than Watts, greater than anyone but Whistler. He had the prodigal energy of genius, and painted pictures because he was born to paint pictures. It was at his studio that the Pre-Raphaelite Brotherhood took form, and he was the most prominent member of the Pre-Raphaelite Brotherhood. He was elected an Associate of the Royal Academy at the age of twenty-four, a Royal Academician at the age of thirty-four. Up to then he had painted masterpiece after masterpiece, pictures in which there was temperament, intention, a noble interest. From that time to the time of his death he painted continuously, often brilliantly, whatever came before him, Mr. Gladstone or Cinderella, a bishop or a landscape. He painted them all with the same facility and the same lack of conviction; he painted whatever would bring him ready money and immediate fame; and he deliberately abandoned a career which, with labour, might have made him the greatest painter of his age, in order to become, with ease, the richest and the most popular.

Art, let it be remembered, must always be an aristocracy; it has been so, from the days when Michael Angelo dictated terms to Popes, to the days when Rossetti cloistered his canvases in contempt of the multitude and its prying unwisdom. The appeal of every great artist has been to the few; fame, when it has come, has come by a sort of divine accident, in which the mob has done no more than add the plaudits of its irrelevant clamour to the select approval of the judges. Millais alone, since the days of that first enthusiasm in which he was a sort of fiery hand for the more slowly realizing brains of his companions in art, has made the democratic appeal. He chose his subjects in deference to the opinion of the middle classes; he painted the portraits of those who could afford to pay a great price. His pictures of pretty women and pretty children had the success, not of the technical skill which was always at his command, but of the obvious sentiment which makes them pretty. The merit of these interminable pictures varies; he was sometimes more careful, sometimes more careless. Mastery over the technicalities of painting he always possessed; but it had come to be the mastery of a hand which worked without emotion, without imagination, without intellectual passion; and without these qualities there can be no great art.

The newspapers, in their obituary notices, have assured us that in honouring Millais, we are honouring not merely the artist, but the man; "of the Englishmen who have been the sons of Art," said the *Times,* "scarcely one has deserved more honour than Millais." My thoughts have turned, as I read these commendations of the good citizen, so English, so sporting, whose private virtues were so undeniably British, to a painter, also a man of genius, whose virtues were all given up to his art, and who is now living in a destitute and unhonoured obscurity. It has seemed to me that there, in that immaculate devotion to art, I find the true morality of the artist; while in the respectability of Millais I see nothing to honour, for its observance of the letter I take to have been a desecration of the spirit.

Arthur Symons

"THE DEATH OF THE SAVOY"

THE SAVOY was founded in 1896 by avant garde writers disillusioned with the increasing tameness and dullness of *The Yellow Book,* their earlier organ of protest and fresh idea. Arthur Symons was appointed editor, and in his first preface he described the high artistic standard he would pursue, and to which indeed he did adhere during the eight months' life of the magazine. Among the contributors were Bernard Shaw, W. B. Yeats, Havelock Ellis, Ernest Dowson, Edmund Gosse, Joseph Conrad, Aubrey Beardsley, Max Beerbohm, Charles Conder, and Will Rothenstein. But though the journal was priced at half a crown—*The Yellow Book* was twice as costly—and was well within the means of a broad cultured class, the public was not receptive. When the funds were gone, Symons had to write the whole of the last issue himself.

FROM *The Savoy* (December, 1896).

It was in the autumn of last year, that, at the request of Mr. Smithers, I undertook to form and edit a new magazine. As this magazine was to contain not only literature but illustration, I immediately went to Mr. Beardsley, whom I looked upon as the most individual and expressive draughtsman of our time, and secured his cordial co-operation. I then got together some of the writers, especially the younger writers, whose work seemed to me most personal and accomplished; deliberately choosing them from as many "schools" as possible. Out of the immense quantity of unsolicited material which came to me, very little was of any value; a few manuscripts and drawings, however, I was able to make use of. I wish here to return thanks, most gratefully, to all those writers and artists who have helped me, with such invariable kindness, and with such invaluable assistance.

Many things that I had hoped to do I have not done; I have done a few things that I did not intend to do. For these failures I blame partly myself, partly circumstances. It is not given to anyone in this world to achieve anything entirely to his satisfaction; or only to those who aim low. I aimed high.

Yes, I admit it, all those intentions which were expressed in my first editorial note, and which the newspapers made so merry over, were precisely my intentions; and I have come as close to them as I could. It is a little difficult now to remember the horrified outcry—the outcry for no reason in the world but the human necessity of making a noise—with which we were first greeted. I look at those old press notices sometimes, in my publisher's scrap-book, and then at the kindly and temperate notices which the same papers are giving us now; and I find the comparison very amusing. For we have not changed in the least; we have simply gone on our own way; and now that everyone is telling us that we have "come to stay," that we are a "welcome addition," etc., we are obliged to retire from existence, on account of the too meagre support of our friends. Our first mistake was in giving so much for so little money; our second, in abandoning a quarterly for a monthly issue. The action of Messrs. Smith and Son in refusing to place "The Savoy" on their bookstalls, on account of the reproduction of a drawing by Blake, was another misfortune. And then, worst of all, we assumed that there were very many people in the world who really cared for art, and really for art's sake.

The more I consider it, the more I realize that this is not the case. Comparatively very few people care for art at all, and most of these care for it because they mistake it for something else. A street-singer, with the remains of a beautiful voice, has just been assuring me that "if you care for art you don't get rich." No, it is for their faults that any really artistic productions become popular: art cannot appeal to the multitude. It is wise when it does not attempt to; when it goes contentedly along a narrow path, knowing and caring only to know, in what direction it is moving.

Well, we were unwise in hoping, for a moment, that the happy accident of popularity was going to befall us. It was never in my original scheme to allow for such an accident. I return to the discretion of first thoughts; after an experiment, certainly, which has been full of instruction, full also of entertainment, to ourselves. And so, in saying the last words in connection with "The Savoy," which now ends its year's existence, I have the pleasure to announce that in our next venture we are going to make no attempt to be popular. We shall make our appearance twice only in the year; our volumes will be larger in size, better produced, and they will cost more. In this way we shall be able to appeal to that limited public which cares for the things we care for; which cares for art, really for art's sake. We shall hope for no big success; we shall be confident of enough support to enable us to go on doing what seems to us worth doing. And, relieved as we shall be from the hurry of monthly publication, we shall have the leisure to do what seems to us worth doing, more nearly as it seems to us it should be done.

A SELECTED LIST FOR FURTHER READING

THE PUBLICATION DATES listed are for the most part those of the original appearance of the works. In many cases the material has been reprinted by the same or other publishers. The student may consult such lists as *Books in Print, Cumulative Book Index,* or *Paperbound Books in Print* for information about the more current publications.

ARNOLD, Matthew, "Literature and Science," *Discourses in America* (1882; 1885).

ARNOLD, Matthew, *Essays in Criticism: First Series* (1865).

BAGEHOT, Walter, "Wordsworth, Tennyson, and Browning: or, Pure, Ornate, and Grotesque Art in English Poetry" (1864); in *Literary Studies* (1879).

BARNES, William, "Thoughts on Beauty and Art," *Macmillan's Magazine* (May—October, 1861).

BEERBOHM, Max, "A Defense of Cosmetics," *The Yellow Book* (April, 1894).

BEERBOHM, Max, "Whistler's Writing," *Yet Again* (1909).

BROWNING, Robert, "An Essay on Percy Bysshe Shelley," 1852.

CRACKANTHORPE, Hubert, "Reticence in Literature," *The Yellow Book* (July, 1894).

DAVIDSON, John, "Banderole's Aesthetic Bill," *The Man Forbid and Other Essays* (1910).

HALLAM, Arthur Henry, "On Some of the Characteristics of Modern Poetry: and on the Lyrical Poems of Alfred Tennyson," *The Englishman's Magazine* (August, 1831).

HARRISON, Frederic, "The Aesthete," *The Choice of Books and Other Literary Pieces* (1882; 1886).

HENLEY, William E., *Views and Reviews: Essays in Appreciation* (1890).

HUXLEY, T. H., "Science and Culture," *Science and Culture and Other Essays* (1880; 1881).

MACAULAY, Thomas Babington, "Milton," *Edinburgh Review* (August, 1825).

MACAULAY, Thomas Babington, "Moore's Life of Byron," *Edinburgh Review* (June, 1831).

MEREDITH, George, *The Idea of Comedy* (1877).

MORLEY, John, "Mr. Swinburne's New Poems: *Poems and Ballads,*" *Saturday Review* (August 4, 1866).

MORRIS, William, "Address on the Collection of Paintings of the English Pre-Raphaelite School in the City of Birmingham Museum and Art Gallery on Friday, October 24, 1891," *William Morris; Artist, Writer, Socialist, edited by May Morris* (1936).

MORRIS, William, *Gothic Architecture* (1889; 1893).

MORRIS, William, *Hopes and Fears For Art* (1882).

ORCHARD, John, "A Dialogue on Art," *The Germ* (1850).

PATER, Walter, *Appreciations* (1889).

PATER, Walter, *The Renaissance* (1873; 1888).

PATMORE, Coventry, *Principle in Art, etc.* (1898).

PUGIN, Augustus Welby, *An Apology for A Revival of Christian Architecture in England* (1843).

RUSKIN, John, "Ideas of Greatness, Truth, Beauty, and Relation," *Modern Painters,* volume I, Parts 1 and 2 (1843).

RUSKIN, John, "The Lamp of Beauty," *Seven Lamps of Architecture* (1849).

RUSKIN, John, "The Nature of Gothic," *Stones of Venice* (1853).

RUSKIN, John, "Of the Pathetic Fallacy," *Modern Painters,* vol. iii, part 4 (1856).

SAINTSBURY, George, "Modern English Prose: 1876," *Miscellaneous Essays* (1892).

SEWARD, John (F. G. Stephens), "The Purpose and Tendency of Early Italian Art," *The Germ* (February 1850).

SHAW, G. B., "Madox Brown, Watts, and Ibsen," *Dramatic Opinions and Essays* (1897; 1906).

SHAW, G. B., "Meredith on Comedy," *Dramatic Opinions and Essays* (1897; 1906).

SHAW, G. B., "Ruskin on Music," *Shaw on Music* (1894; 1955).

SWINBURNE, A. C., "Notes on Designs of the Old Masters at Florence," *Essays and Studies* (1875).

SWINBURNE, A. C., "The Poems of Dante Gabriel Rossetti," *Essays and Studies* (1875).

SWINBURNE, A. C., "Whistler's Lecture on Art," *The Complete Works of Algernon Charles Swinburne,* ed. by Gosse and Wise, vol. vi (1926).

SYMONDS, John Addington, "Culture: Its Meaning and Its Uses," *In the Key of Blue and Other Prose Essays* (1893).

SYMONDS, John Addington, *Essays Speculative and Suggestive* (1890).

SYMONS, Arthur, "The Decadent Movement in Literature," *London Quarterly Review* (January, 1918).

SYMONS, Arthur, *The Romantic Movement in English Poetry* (1909).

SYMONS, Arthur, *The Symbolist Movement in Literature* (1899).

SYMONS, Arthur, "Whistler," *Studies in Seven Arts* (1903; 1906).

WILDE, Oscar, "The Critic as Artist: with Some Remarks upon the Importance of Discussing Everything," *Intentions* (1891).

WILDE, Oscar, "The Soul of Man Under Socialism," *Fortnightly Review* (February, 1891).

Atalanta in Calydon, 667-672; Laus Veneris
"The Triumph of Time;" "Hymn to Proserpine;"
"Ilicet", "In Memory of Walter Savage Landor"
"Dolores"; "The Garden of Proserpine"; "To Walt Whitman"
"Ave Atque Vale"; "Hymn of Man"